# THE MECHANICAL TRADITION OF HERO
## OF ALEXANDRIA

Hero of Alexandria was a figure of great importance not only for ancient technology but also for the medieval and early modern traditions that drew on his work. In this book Courtney Ann Roby presents Hero's key strategies for developing, solving, and contextualizing technical problems not only in his own lifetime but as an influential tradition of creating accessible technical treatises spanning multiple disciplines. While Hero's historical biography is all but impossible to reconstruct, she examines "Hero" as a corpus, a textual tradition of technical problem-solving capable of incorporating textual transformations like interpolation, epitomization, and translation, as well as intermedial transformation from text to artifact. Key themes include ancient and early modern technical readerships, the relationship between mathematics and mechanics, the materiality of manuscript and printed texts, and the shifting cultural contexts for scientific and technical literature.

**Courtney Ann Roby** is Associate Professor of Classics at Cornell University. She is also the author of *Technical Ekphrasis: The Written Machine between Alexandria and Rome* (Cambridge, 2016). She is the recipient of a fellowship from the Andrew W. Mellon Society of Fellows in Critical Bibliography from the University of Virginia's Rare Book School.

# THE MECHANICAL TRADITION OF HERO OF ALEXANDRIA

*Strategies of Reading from Antiquity to the Early Modern Period*

COURTNEY ANN ROBY

*Cornell University*

CAMBRIDGE
UNIVERSITY PRESS

Shaftesbury Road, Cambridge CB2 8EA, United Kingdom

One Liberty Plaza, 20th Floor, New York, NY 10006, USA

477 Williamstown Road, Port Melbourne, VIC 3207, Australia

314–321, 3rd Floor, Plot 3, Splendor Forum, Jasola District Centre, New Delhi – 110025, India

103 Penang Road, #05-06/07, Visioncrest Commercial, Singapore 238467

Cambridge University Press is part of Cambridge University Press & Assessment, a department of the University of Cambridge.

We share the University's mission to contribute to society through the pursuit of education, learning and research at the highest international levels of excellence.

www.cambridge.org
Information on this title: www.cambridge.org/9781316516232

DOI: 10.1017/9781009029261

First published 2023

*A catalogue record for this publication is available from the British Library.*

Library of Congress Cataloging-in-Publication Data
NAMES: Roby, Courtney, 1978– author.
TITLE: The mechanical tradition of Hero of Alexandria : strategies of reading from antiquity to the early modern period / Courtney Ann Roby.
DESCRIPTION: Cambridge ; New York, NY : Cambridge University Press, 2023. | Includes bibliographical references and index.
IDENTIFIERS: LCCN 2023010586 (print) | LCCN 2023010587 (ebook) | ISBN 9781316516232 (hardback) | ISBN 9781009014052 (paperback) | ISBN 9781009029261 (epub)
SUBJECTS: LCSH: Hero, of Alexandria–Criticism, Textual. | Greek literature–Criticism, Textual. | Technical writing–History–To 1500. | Mechanical engineering–History–To 1500. | Mechanical engineers–Egypt–Biography. | Corpora (Linguistics)
CLASSIFICATION: LCC PA4000 .R63 2023 (print) | LCC PA4000 (ebook) | DDC 888/.0109–DC23/eng/20230510
LC record available at https://lccn.loc.gov/2023010586
LC ebook record available at https://lccn.loc.gov/2023010587

ISBN 978-1-316-51623-2 Hardback

# Contents

# Figures

# Acknowledgments

This book could not have come to life without the network of inter-locutors whose comments and questions shaped it. I am particularly grateful to Cornell's Society for the Humanities, where an idyllic fellow-ship year allowed me to contemplate the "corruption" of the Heronian tradition in a rich discursive environment, as well as to my colleagues in Cornell's Department of Classics for their ongoing support. Special thanks are also given to my friends and teachers at Rare Book School, whose good fellowship and generous knowledge-sharing made the final chapter possi-ble. I likewise offer my gratitude to audiences at the University of Oslo, Harvard University, Pomona College, New York University, the University of King's College, Dalhousie University, the University of Texas at Austin, the Nederlands Interuniversitair Kunsthistorisch Instituut, the Karlsruher Institut für Technologie, the Università degli studi di Bergamo, the University of Exeter, the Getty Research Institute, the University of Florida, and others for their friendly *diorthōsis* as the project evolved. Any remaining errors are of course entirely my own. Finally, for his endless patience and support, my greatest gratitude to Luis, my own technical hero.

Except where noted, citations in Greek and Latin passages refer respec-tively to editions found in the TLG and PHI, for easy reference. Other useful editions are identified in footnotes where relevant. All translations are my own except where noted. Some aspects of the arguments in the final chapter have previously appeared in Roby 2021. My sincere thanks to the editor for his invaluable feedback and to the publisher for permission to further explore and recontextualize these ideas here.

CHAPTER I

# Introduction

This is the story of a mechanical tradition, so let us begin with a machine (Figure 1.1).[1] Take a hollow bronze sphere, drilled at two diametrically opposite points to allow the insertion of two L-shaped tubes, carefully soldered to the outside of the sphere so that it remains completely sealed except for their ends. Add one more tube, in the plane perpendicular to the first two, and a socket for a pivot opposite that. Place the sphere on a covered vat of boiling water so that the third tube conducts steam into the sphere, where it can be ejected from the L-shaped tubes. Once the steam begins to flow, the sphere will rotate on the pivot, propelled by the steam leaving the tubes.

What exactly is this object? Postindustrial readers were often tempted to identify it as a kind of primitive steam engine; for example, Landels reads Hero's device teleologically as a "failure" on the part of an "enthusiastic inventor" to approximate the designs of later engineers.[2] Others read Hero's device more charitably as a single step on the long road to more efficient practical work with steam, as in one of the 19th-century lithographs depicting the history of steam power produced as advertising by the Liebig Meat Extract Company (Figure 1.2). For still others, Hero's "steam engine" was a provocation to dream about a Rome that might have been; Ben Lichius' "Hero of Alexandria" comics suggest a steam-powered Roman world fueled by the technologies that the whirling sphere inspired.[3]

These readings are all flawed in their own ways, beginning from the fact that Hero never refers to this device as a "steam engine" at all, but only describes it as a moving sphere mounted on pivots over a heated cauldron. Unlike the "fire engine" in the same work, he never suggests a practical application for the device, comparing it instead to a ludic device where

---

[1] Hero *Pneumatica* 2.11.   [2] Landels 2000: 28–31.   [3] Lichius 2013.

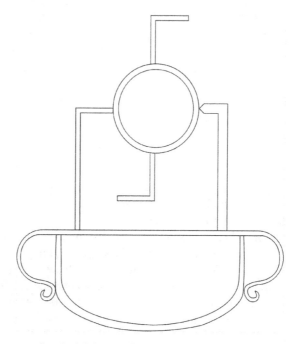

Figure 1.1   "Aeolipile" device, after Cod. Marcianus Gr. Z 516, fol. 187r.

figurines appear to dance beneath a lit fire.[4] The basic principle of ejecting steam through a tube to cause some external effect was likely already present in Philo's *Pneumatica*, as the Arabic tradition includes a device for heating perfume ingredients that incorporates a tube ejecting pressurized steam to fan its own fire.[5] The same self-fanning design is used in other devices in Hero's *Pneumatica*.[6] All this is to say, Hero was well aware that pressurized steam can be used to create practical effects, and he opts not to include any such features in the "steam engine." In Keyser's deft analysis, the device is best viewed as a mechanical contribution to philosophical discourse about the physics of motion rather than an attempt at an industrial engine.[7]

At the same time, these different ways of reading Hero all carry some elements of deeper truth. Hero survives only through works like the *Pneumatica*, since unlike Archimedes' vivid biographical tradition, we have

---

[4] The "pump used to fight fires" is described at *Pneumatica* 1.28; the dancing figurines are at 2.3.
[5] Philo *Pneumatica* 57; Philo 1974: 217.    [6] Hero *Pneumatica* 2.34, 2.35.
[7] In particular, Keyser suggests that the device serves as a counterexample to the Aristotelian idea that a moving object must press against an external resisting object in order to move; see Keyser 1992: 116.

Figure 1.2    Hero's "steam engine" advertising Liebig Meat Extract. Photo by author.

essentially no external biographical information about Hero – we cannot even date him within a century. Reading him through his corpus of texts presents additional challenges since, as we shall see, that corpus is no neatly bounded collection of texts from one man's lifetime, but a sprawling, interpolated collection amassed over centuries. So in some sense Hero can only be understood through the kind of imaginative extrapolations we saw performed on the "steam engine," which (flawed though they may be) each contain a kernel of truth. Landels critiques him for not evolving a single technology to its modern conclusion, and in fact Hero is unapologetic about simply being a part of a long tradition rather than its culmination. The Liebig lithograph puts him in the service of the banal goal of creating a tastier beef extract, and indeed Hero emphasizes utility as the core value of his works and particularly praises the mercantile and manufacturing applications of the five simple machines. Lichius imagines him as the genius of a lost tradition of mechanical wonders, and indeed he is singled out by Pappus as a "wonder-worker (*thaumasiourgos*)" *par excellence.* The historical Hero is a ghostly apparition, but the Hero created through centuries of imaginative recreations and appropriations of his work becomes a vivid and multifaceted figure: inventor and curator, mechanician and mathematician, wonder-worker and cultivator of banal practicalities.

It is that multilayered, centuries-spanning "Hero" that this book seeks to reconstruct. Chapter 2 will explore how he positions himself in existing mathematical and mechanical traditions, both as an author and a technological practitioner. Chapter 3 discusses how his contributions to those traditions seek to teach his reader to analyze objects in the world using experimental and analytical techniques designed to bridge the gap between the mathematical and mechanical, the abstract and the applied. Chapter 4 sets the Hero reconstructed in the previous chapters against the various historical backgrounds he has been assigned to, exploring how his patterns of negotiating with past technical traditions might blend into those different intellectual environments, and then it moves on to consider how Hero himself became a part of later technical traditions. The final chapter focuses on the last of those traditions, the Italian Renaissance, where Hero was a central figure in the humanistic revival of ancient Greek works and in the creation of new technologies.

## The Heronian Corpus

The name "Hero" is threaded through a complex corpus of texts, some of which he surely wrote, some he surely did not, and some whose provenance is not so clear. The corpus includes works on mathematical as well as technical topics; sometimes Hero's approach is precisely geometrical, while elsewhere he engages deeply with the concrete details of material constructions. Indeed, Vitrac comments that a stark division of ancient mathematical and mechanical texts into "pure" or "mathematical" and "applied" or "technical" categories reflects modern disciplinary boundaries more than it does the complex relationship between mathematics and mechanics in antiquity indicated in disciplinary taxonomies like that of Geminus.[8] Giardina likewise points out that taxonomies of the corpus that attempt to draw a hard line between its "theoretical" and "applied" components reflect an anachronistically modern division between "pure" and "applied" work, whereas in antiquity "mathematics" commanded a much broader sphere, incorporating "applied" disciplines like optics alongside geometry and arithmetic.[9] As we will see, Hero's effort to draw connections between the mathematical and the concrete – some of them quite startling – is one of his principal defining features as an author.

The "core" texts that may be reliably attributed to Hero himself survive with relatively stable manuscript traditions; many of them also include intertextual references to other works in the corpus, similarities in technological content or analytical methodology, or other markers that suggest they are the work of a single author. We may begin with the works on pneumatic wonders that served as a signature for Hero throughout the long afterlife of his reception. His *Pneumatica* was heavily influenced by a text on the subject by Philo of Byzantium that now survives only in Arabic and Latin.[10] From the surviving evidence, Hero's version appears to differ from Philo's in beginning with a lengthy preface on the physics of elemental matter and void.[11] In the main body of the text, he proceeds

---

[8] Vitrac 2009: 164–70. Geminus' account is preserved in Proclus, *In primum Euclidis elementorum librum commentarii* 38.1–39.6.

[9] Hero 2003: 31–34. The organizational schemas Giardina is responding to include Gille 1978: 350 and Heath 1921: 308–10. Argoud proposed a three-pronged taxonomy of "mathematical" works (principally the *Metrica*), "scientific applications of theoretical knowledge" (the *Dioptra* and *Catoptrica*), and "technical applications of scientific principles" (exemplified by the *Pneumatica*, *Belopoeica*, *Cheiroballistra*, *Mechanica*, *Baroulkos*, and *Automata*, as well as the lost works on balances and water clocks): Argoud 1994b: 55–58.

[10] Philo was a Hellenistic author who composed a *Mechanikē Syntaxis* that apparently originally comprised nine books: an introduction, μοχλικά (On Levers), λιμενοποιικά (Harbor-Making), βελοποιικά (Artillery-Making), πνευματικά (Pneumatics), αὐτοματοποιητικά (Automaton-Making), παρασκευαστικά (Siege Preparation), πολιορκητικά (Siegecraft), and a ninth volume probably on stratagems. Many of these books are now lost; only the "Artillery-Making," the "Siege Preparation," and the "Siegecraft" are extant in Greek, while the "Pneumatics" survives primarily in Arabic and Latin. On Philo see *RE*, "Ph. von Byzanz," by M. Folkerts; Marsden 1971: 156. The Latin fragments of his *Pneumatica* are available alongside an English translation based on the Arabic manuscript A.S. 3713 in Philo 1974. The Arabic text based on A.S. 2755 and Bodleian Marsh 669 and French translation are found in Philo 1902; also available in Philo 2001.

[11] Several passages of Hero's preface were identified by Wehrli as fragments of Strato (56, 57, 64, 65b, 66, 67, 68): Straton 1944. However, Sharples points out that none of them name Strato, and only one of them (65b) is a close parallel to a reference by Simplicius to Strato, and Sharples has thus

to instruct the reader in building a variety of pneumatic–hydraulic devices for education and entertainment, some with analogs in Philo's text and others apparently newly designed by Hero himself.[12] The complex theatrical devices described in his *Automata* combine mechanisms similar to those in the *Pneumatica* with a host of other mechanical techniques allowing miniature figures to perform plays in multiple acts, all driven autonomously by the falling of a counterweight.[13]

Besides these works on wonders to captivate the spirit and render physical principles visible, a few others catalog more utilitarian devices. The *Belopoeica* provides a brisk evolutionary history of different types of catapults, including some details on how their most distinctive mechanical features are constructed. The fragmentary *Cheiroballistra* balances the breadth of the *Belopoeica* with selective depth, explaining the design and construction of a single type of portable catapult in great detail.[14] The *Dioptra*, named after a surveying device capable of making precisely controlled and measured observations, describes the construction of the eponymous instrument (as well as associated technologies like the targets for sighting and even an odometer), and then walks the reader through a host of surveying problems defined largely in geometrical terms.

The *Metrica* dispenses mathematical techniques for measuring the dimensions and proportions of various geometrical figures; the first book covers plane geometry, the second deals with solid forms, and the third is about dividing figures into certain ratios.[15] While the work draws largely on mathematical material known from other sources including Euclid and Archimedes, most of its chapters have a distinctive structure, presenting the material in the novel form of "doublets" of geometrical analysis and numerical synthesis. The *Definitiones* adopts a comparable strategy of

---

removed all except Wehrli's 65b from his recent edition of the fragments: Desclos and Fortenbaugh 2011: 10–11. On Hero's eclectic influences in his preface, see Berryman 2011. For a brisk summary of Hero's prefaces, see Mansfeld 1998: 49–57.

[12] For the text and translation of the *Pneumatica*, see Hero 1976a; updated in Hero 1997. On the text and its history, see Argoud 1998; Boas 1949; Drachmann 1948.

[13] Text and translation of the *Automata* are found at Hero 1976a; now updated with translation and commentary in Grillo 2019.

[14] For text and translation of these two works, see Marsden 1971. For additional background on the *Belopoeica*, see Cuomo 2002; Schiefsky 2015. Rihll's work on ancient catapults includes discussion of the two works but attributes the work (unconvincingly to my mind) not to Hero but his early predecessor Ctesibius: Rihll 2007: 141–42.

[15] For text, translation, and detailed commentary, along with extensive additional material on the metrological corpus and the text's relationship to other mathematical works, see Hero 2014.

elaborating on Euclid, offering a Euclidean ordering of geometrical forms that allows some extension of Euclid's program to material objects.[16]

Alongside this "core," the Heronian corpus embraces other texts whose authorship cannot be so simply defined. A few texts that are now lost can nevertheless be attributed to Hero with some confidence. In the preface to the *Pneumatica*, Hero himself briefly mentions a lost work on water clocks, which might have shared some technical ground with the hydraulic devices of these two texts.[17] Hero also apparently composed a commentary to Euclid's *Elements*, which is now lost but survives in fragments quoted by Abū al-ʿAbbās al-Faḍl ibn Ḥātim al-Nayrīzī in his own commentary.[18] Hero's affinity for Euclidean subjects is suggested as well by his alleged authorship of a *Catoptrica*, also now mostly lost.[19]

The *Mechanica*, a treatise on the principles of mechanics and their embodiment in the form of machines, survives in Greek only as fragments preserved by Pappus in the eighth book of his *Synagōgē*.[20] Those fragments treat topics including the proportions of mechanical advantage, the five simple machines, and the practical details of handling heavy loads. The text survives more completely in Arabic and Persian translations dating from the 9th or 10th and the 11th or 12th centuries respectively.[21] Both Pappus and the Arabic translator Qusṭā ibn Lūqā al-Baʿlabakkī refer to what appears to be a separate book on the device known as the *baroulkos* or "heavy-lifter," but it is not entirely clear whether this was a work independent of the *Mechanica*.[22] If it were, the two works might have formed a pair comparable to the *Belopoeica* and the more specialized *Cheiroballistra*, or the *Pneumatica* and the lost work on water clocks, or the *Definitiones* and the lost Euclid commentary, but given the poor survival of the texts it is difficult to say for sure whether this was indeed a recurring authorial strategy for Hero.

---

[16] For Giardina's text, translation, and notes, with copious introductory material on the text and Hero's work in general, see Hero 2003.

[17] The work is mentioned as well by Pappus and Proclus: Pappus *Commentaria in Ptolemaei syntaxin mathematicam 5–6* 87–92; Proclus *Hypotyposis astronomicarum positionum* 4.71–79.

[18] On the evidence for the commentary and Hero as its author, as well as the surviving evidence from the Arabic and Arabo-Latin traditions, see Hero 2014: 31–41.

[19] Boutot 2012.

[20] Cuomo argues that the passages in the *Synagōgē* that Pappus identifies with Hero likely reliably transmit Hero's own text of the *Mechanica*: Cuomo 2000: 112 n. 44.

[21] A recent edition of these translations, with English translation, notes, and the Greek fragments, is Hero and Qusṭā ibn Lūqā 2016; the Arabic text is also available with French translation in Hero and Qusṭā ibn Lūqā 1988.

[22] Hero and Qusṭā ibn Lūqā 2016: 281–92.

Other texts are challenging to analyze not because Hero's Greek text has disappeared, but on the contrary because it was enthusiastically supplemented by other authors. While the first hundred or so chapters of the *Definitiones* are Hero's own work, about another thirty were added later on, many of them drawn from Proclus and other Neoplatonist authors. These later chapters, many of them extremely long compared to the earlier ones, deepen the original work's investigation into the relationship between the mathematical and the material and between different subdisciplines of the "pure" and "applied" sciences.

The *Metrica* served as a springboard for additional metrological works that expand on and complement its measurement techniques. Along with the metrological content in the later chapters of the *Definitiones*, Hultsch linked Hero to the *Geometrica, Geodaisia, Stereometrica, De Mensuris*, and *Geoponicus*, as well as some other miscellaneous material.[23] Heiberg subsequently published new editions of these works, which, given their extremely unstable manuscript traditions, required a highly selective reconstruction process. Heiberg argues that the *Geodaisia, De Mensuris*, and *Geoponicus* are Byzantine compilations, their composition perhaps inspired by Hero's work but not actually based on any of his works. The situation is more complicated for the *Geometrica* and the *Stereometrica*, which, as Vitrac noted, sometimes bear a closer resemblance to the problems in the *Metrica*.[24] Vitrac has since carried the study of the complex interrelationships between these texts much further, suggesting that the other texts are not in fact derived from the *Metrica*, even though they incorporate some of the same problems.[25] In contrast to the *Metrica*'s careful blend of rigorous geometric demonstration and numerical synthesis, the other metrological texts are composed almost exclusively of numerical problems solved algorithmically, more closely resembling Greek and Egyptian "practical mathematics" texts.

Hero's corpus is thus a very complex artifact that came into being not over one man's lifetime, but over centuries of recombination, reconfiguration, and elaboration on work in the "Heronian" vein. Those later manipulations were performed on a body of work that was inspired by certain principles and problems presented in the "core" texts, but that took on a life of its own by incorporating new philosophical ideas and problem-solving approaches.

---

[23] Hero 1864.    [24] Vitrac 2008a: 288.    [25] Vitrac 2010.

## Dating Difficulties

The complex and many-handed process of authoring Hero's corpus is inextricably bound up with the unresolved question of when he lived, a problem I make no claim to resolve here. The surest signposts of Hero's date have been his references to Archimedes and Apollonius of Perge, yielding a *terminus post quem* of the 3rd century BCE, and Pappus' reference to Hero, which gives a *terminus ante quem* of the 4th century CE.[26] Vitrac accepts only these as certain, saying that a date in the 1st century CE is likely but unproven.[27] This centuries-long window is rather unsatisfying, and many attempts have been made to narrow it down. Conservative attempts to move the *terminus post quem* forward have largely focused on the relationship between Hero and the Hellenistic engineer Ctesibius, who is named by Vitruvius, Athenaeus, Proclus, and others.

Ctesibius, however, presents dating challenges of his own. Argoud cites evidence from Diodorus Siculus, Vitruvius, and Pliny the Elder that appears to place him securely in the era of Ptolemy II Philadelphus, making him a near-contemporary of Archimedes.[28] Athenaeus mentions an epigram by Hedylus describing a drinking horn in the shape of a dancer, designed by Ctesibius to use pressurized air to emit a blast of sound when its mouthpiece was opened.[29] This horn was supposed to have been left at a temple as a dedication to a certain Arsinoe, whom Tybjerg identifies as the wife of Ptolemy II, dating Ctesibius to the first half of the 3rd century BCE.[30] On the other hand, based on an interpretation of Vitruvius, Martin assigns him to the era of Ptolemy VIII Euergetes II (Ptolemy Physcon).[31] Philo of Byzantium, whom Hero references several times as a source, appears to have been a near-contemporary of Ctesibius, as he reports learning about a catapult from watching workmen who had personally worked alongside him.[32] Philo himself has also been used as a measuring point, though, like Ctesibius, he has not been dated with great security. Drachmann argues that, given Philo's position relative to Ctesibius, he cannot date later than the end of the 3rd century BCE.[33]

---

[26] Hero refers to Apollonius at *Definitiones* 137.4.7; there is also a reference at *Stereometrica* 2.34.1.9, though the ascription of the whole of this work to Hero is questioned at Vitrac 2008a: 288. Pappus refers several times to Hero, placing him among mechanical practitioners known to "οἱ παλαιοί" at *Synagōgē* 8.1024.24–1026.1.

[27] Vitrac 2010: 1.    [28] Argoud 1998: 127.    [29] Athenaeus, *Deipnosophistai* 11 (497d).

[30] Karin Tybjerg, "Ktesibios of Alexandria," in Keyser and Irby-Massie 2008: 496.

[31] Vitruvius, *De architectura* 10.9.13, Athenaeus *Deipnosophistae* 4, 174b–e; Hero 2003: 10; Martin 1854: 22.

[32] Philo, *Belopoeica* 72.36–39.    [33] Drachmann 1948: 1–2, 41.

Hero mentions Philo in his *Automata*, as well as referring to mechanicians divided into "the ancients (οἱ μὲν οὖν ἀρχαῖοι)" and "those among us (οἱ δὲ καθ᾽ἡμᾶς)."[34] Tittel believed Philo belonged to the second group and thus argued that Hero must have been Philo's younger contemporary; however, as Giardina points out, there is no reason to make this assumption.[35]

Hero shares some disciplinary and methodological ground with Ptolemy, and some attempts to date Hero have built on their chronological relationship. Ptolemy can be dated by the *Canobic Inscription*, a list of astronomical parameters dedicated in 146 or 147 CE (some later corrected in the *Almagest*), and by the astronomical observations that the *Almagest* suggests he did between 127 and 141 CE.[36] Hammer-Jensen argues that Hero postdates Ptolemy, on the grounds that their respective solutions to two related geographical problems suggest that a particular technique is a novel invention of Ptolemy's but old hat to Hero, and that Hero describes a more advanced sighting instrument than Ptolemy's.[37]

Briefly, Hammer-Jensen's argument begins with a passage from Ptolemy's *Geography* in which he claims to have developed a method for measuring the length of a strip of ground situated somewhere inaccessible to direct measurement along a great circle that is not a meridian.[38] Hero, on the other hand, is using data from a lunar eclipse (which Neugebauer identifies as the one known to have occurred on March 13, 62 CE) to determine the distance between two sites on different meridians, a method that he does not single out as a novel invention on his part or anyone else's. Hence Hammer-Jensen argues that Hero must have come long enough after Ptolemy that the method had become familiar enough to be not worth mentioning.

As Drachmann shows, however, Hammer-Jensen is conflating two quite different problem-solving methods, and Hero's was formulated at least as early as Hipparchus, so it is small wonder Hero does not draw attention to it as a new technique.[39] Hammer-Jensen next compares Hero's dioptra to

---

[34] *Automata* 20.1.9, 20.3.6; 22.1.1, 22.2.7.     [35] Hero 2003: 12; Tittel 1901: 411–14.
[36] A summary of dated astronomical observations in the *Almagest* can be found at Pedersen 1974: 408–22.
[37] Hammer-Jensen 1913: 228–30.
[38] Ptolemy *Geographia* 1.3. Ptolemy's description of his approach to the problem and the instrument he uses to solve it is not very clear here. Berggren and Jones note that Proclus and Pappus both refer to a lost work where Ptolemy describes this *meteōroskopeion*, and they supply some of the missing details: Ptolemy 2000: 61 n. 12. Drachmann gives a clear summary of the problem-solving methods both authors seem to rely on: Drachmann 1950.
[39] Drachmann 1950: 119–20.

Ptolemy's *meteōroskopeion* instrument, finding the latter an inferior piece of technology.[40] Drachmann, on the other hand, argues that Hammer-Jensen gives insufficient credit to the precision and accuracy of Ptolemy's instrument and overrates the dioptra, which may have been "for its time, quite a remarkable piece of mechanism," but was far from perfect.[41]

Besides deflating the arguments based on the apparent novelty of methodologies and mechanical tools, Drachmann notes (and points out the same argument in Neugebauer) that Hero just wants to show how to find the distance between two places with given latitudes and longitudes; the eclipse is only used to find the time difference and hence the difference in longitude. So, if Hero did in fact postdate Ptolemy, why wouldn't he just have used the tables of latitudes and longitudes in the *Geography* instead, rather than relying on a century-old lunar eclipse?

Hero's reference to the lunar eclipse might itself seem a promising basis for dating him, but this turns out to yield its own set of complications. This eclipse appears in *Dioptra* 35, where Hero sets the problem of determining the distance between two points at different latitudes (he chooses Rome and Alexandria), with the added constraint that some points on the route are unreachable. He proposes: "Let the same eclipse of the moon have been carefully observed in Alexandria and Rome (τετηρήσθω οὖν ἔν τε Ἀλεξανδρείᾳ καὶ Ῥώμῃ <ἡ> αὐτὴ ἔκλειψις τῆς σελήνης)," and he notes the times when an observer in each city saw the eclipse.[42] A concave hemisphere is then employed to help visualize the path of the sun at each place during the night when the eclipse occurred, with a marker of where the sun was at the time of the eclipse. One of the two locations is chosen (Hero proposes an Alexandrian perspective: "ἔστω δὴ ἡμᾶς εἶναι ἐν Ἀλεξανδρείᾳ") and the hemisphere's interior marked with the solstices appropriate to that latitude. The analemma for Rome is then added and the time of the eclipse observation (in local hours) noted. The horizons matching each city are drawn using the observation times of the eclipse and the line segment connecting their poles found. The portion of the horizon's full circle occupied by this segment is the same as the proportion of the great-circle distance between the two cities to the Earth's circumference, which Hero (crediting Eratosthenes) gives as 252,000 stades.[43]

---

[40] Hammer-Jensen 1913: 230–31.
[41] Drachmann 1950: 126. Drachmann's analysis of the two authors' order is affirmed at Asper 2001a: 6.
[42] Hero, *Dioptra* 35.15–16.
[43] Eratosthenes' value for the circumference of the Earth is given by Cleomedes and John Philoponus as 250,000 stades, but by Geminus, Strabo, Theon of Smyrna, Galen, Vitruvius, Pliny, and others

Neugebauer argues that this passage provides a sufficiently detailed description of the eclipse to match it to the lunar eclipse of March 13, 62 CE.[44] This identification has long been a powerful argument for dating Hero alongside the eclipse. Gilbert Argoud takes it more or less as settled, citing Drachmann's study.[45] However, these arguments are not without their flaws. The passage reports that the eclipse occurred at the fifth nocturnal hour in Alexandria and the third in Rome on the ninth or tenth day before the vernal equinox depending on how one interprets the inclusive reckoning of the days. This timing raises some problems. Masià calculates that this timing would mean the eclipse began at 22:09 in Alexandria and 21:09 in Rome (given the different timing of the sunsets in the two cities, which means their nocturnal hours begin at different times).[46] However, as Masià notes, the eclipse of 62 CE in fact began considerably later (22:30 by the NASA tables Masià uses and 22:50 by Neugebauer and Sidoli). Despite the margin for error in knowing just when sunset occurred and hence how the nocturnal hours map onto twenty-four-hour time, the account in the passage is disturbingly imprecise: In fact, Hero does not say that the eclipse began at the times he names, only that it was observed. Moreover, the observation times Hero cites place Rome and Alexandria an even two hours apart rather than one hour and ten minutes, which is troubling if the problem is intended to recount an actual observation made by him and a colleague. On the other hand, as Asper and Netz point out, numerical problems deployed as examples in "algorithmic" mathematical texts are most frequently limited to integer values, so the "error" may in fact be a generically appropriate approximation.[47]

There is of course also a meaningful difference between "contemporary" and "personal observer." As Sidoli points out, from a conservative point of view the eclipse date only gives a likely *terminus post quem* for Hero, who might instead have obtained the eclipse data from a written source.[48] Indeed, the passage follows up the choice of an Alexandria/Rome eclipse sighting by noting that:

εἰ μὲν γὰρ ἐν ταῖς ἀναγραφείσαις εὑρίσκεται, ταύτῃ χρησόμεθα· εἰ δὲ οὔ, δυνατὸν ἔσται ἡμᾶς αὐτοὺς τηρήσαντας εἰπεῖν διὰ τὸ τὰς τῆς σελήνης ἐκλείψεις διὰ πενταμήνων καὶ ἑξαμήνων γίνεσθαι.

---

as 252,000 stades. Acerbi and Vitrac provide a thorough review of the sources for these measurements at Hero 2014: 107–08.

[44] Neugebauer 1938; Rome 1938.     [45] Argoud 1998: 127; Drachmann 1948: 74–77.
[46] Masià 2015: 243.     [47] Asper 2007: 198–99; Netz 2011: 253.     [48] Sidoli 2011: 55.

If it is found in the recorded [eclipses], we will use it. But if not, we can pick one we ourselves have observed, since eclipses of the moon occur every five or six months.[49]

Clearly, this passage of the *Dioptra* does not aim to provide an account of a particular experimental observation; the Rome/Alexandria observational pair is simply an example that the reader can use as a model for their own calculation.

Acerbi and Vitrac offer a new edition of the passage, questioning whether Hero was in fact its author.[50] In their commentary they discuss the probability that such reference texts would have been available in Alexandria or Rome, pointing out in particular the unlikelihood of a text correlating times of eclipse observations in two different locations.[51] Without recourse to such a text, they note, the problem would require access to either two different reference texts or two collaborating observers. Hence they argue that it makes sense to presume that at least part of the information used in the problem came from a reference text, even if one observation was indeed made by the text's author.

The problem then proceeds on the contingency, "let an eclipse be found in said regions (ἔστω οὖν εὑρημένη ἐν τοῖς εἰρημένοις κλίμασιν αὕτη <ἡ> ἔκλειψις), in Alexandria at the fifth nocturnal hour, and the same in Rome at the third." Souffrin points out that the language of the passage could just as well indicate an eclipse with a certain set of hypothetical characteristics as the actual qualities of a particular eclipse event.[52] Masià makes an even stronger argument on the same lines. He suggests that the "hypothetical" grammatical framing of the third-person passive imperative common to mathematical prose ("let an eclipse be found . . .") strongly supports the conjecture that Hero did not even find a recorded eclipse but simply invented one.[53] This might be true, but it is also true that the use of the third-person imperative is a much more common feature of Hero's prose than active imperatives or first-person past tense constructions.[54] So the use of the form here need not be interpreted as an indication that the eclipse is hypothetical any more than the catapults constructed along similar grammatical lines in his *Belopoeica*, the sighting poles placed for surveying elsewhere in the *Dioptra*, and so on. Still, Masià's further arguments about the probability

---

[49] Hero, *Dioptra* 35.17–20.   [50] Hero 2014: 103–15.   [51] Hero 2014: 109–10.
[52] Souffrin 2000: 15.   [53] Masià 2015: 242.
[54] On Hero's choice of verb forms in the *Dioptra*, see Roby 2018.

of an eclipse happening to match the parameters described in the passage, in a timespan likely corresponding to Hero's lifetime, are thought-provoking and well-reasoned additions to the doubts cast on Neugebauer's sure dating.

An addressee of Hero's could surely help to date him, but these are nearly absent from his works, except for the Dionysius addressed as *lamprotate* in the proem to the *Definitiones*.[55] Tannery observes that Diophantus likewise addressed his *Arithmetica* to a Dionysius, and he recounts that at first he attributed the *Definitiones* to Anatolius rather than Hero (who at the time was believed to date to the 2nd century BCE) on the grounds of the likely identification of the two Dionysii. However, he later changed his mind once Hero's date was tentatively moved forward to the 1st century CE, and he was ready to attribute the text to Hero and to believe that the *Definitiones'* Dionysius was another, unknown figure.[56] Tannery's conclusions thus cannot be used to date Hero on the basis of this unknown Dionysius. Hammer-Jensen argues that *lamprotate* was equivalent to *vir clarissimus* and that Dionysius must therefore have lived within or after Diocletian's reign, tentatively identifying him as L. Aelius Helvius Dionysius, the *praefectus urbi* of 301/302 CE.[57] Asper recounts that Stein and Hirschfeld suggest instead that this title was already applied to *praefecti Aegypti* by the 2nd century CE, proposing as Hero's addressee M. Aurelius Papirius Dionysius, who held the post in 187/188 CE.[58]

Asper observes that these identifications are less likely in light of Neugebauer's arguments about the lunar eclipse, and (more damningly)

---

[55] The *Stereometrica* also includes a personal reference (2.54), namely the praetorian prefect Modestus, who is credited with establishing a value of seventy-five *litrae* of bacon to the cubic foot. Corcoran identifies this figure as Domitius Modestus, Valens' praetorian prefect in the east from 369 to 377 CE (Corcoran 1995: 384). However, the text suffers from a chaotic manuscript tradition that makes it impossible to attribute to any single author, so this Modestus should certainly not be used to date the "historical" Hero. The discussion of vaults (*kamarika*) in the text may offer some additional clues. Eutocius credits Hero with having written a whole work on vaults, and Heiberg proposes that the problems on vaults in the *Stereometrica* are likely drawn from that work: Hero 1976e: xxxi. According to Eutocius, Isidore of Miletus (whom he refers to as "my teacher") wrote a commentary on Hero's *Kamarika*, which might thus be used to date the *Stereometrica* compilation more securely: Eutocius, *Commentarii in libros de sphaera et cylindro* 84.8–11. On the controversy over the dating of Eutocius, Isidore, and Ammonius, see Cameron 2005.

[56] Tannery 1883: 536–38.

[57] Hammer-Jensen 1913: 233–34. On the identification of the Latin and Greek terms, see "*vir clarissimus*," in Cancik and Schneider 1996.

[58] Asper 2001a: 135; Hirschfeld 1901; Stein 1912: 167.

that the clear influence of the *Metrica* on the metrological work *Mishnat ha-Middot*, completed by 150 CE by Gandz's reckoning (114 CE by Krafft's), renders them even more implausible.[59] Gandz takes pains to specify that while the *Mishnat ha-Middot* is a work completely independent from the *Metrica* or any other Greek work, it does seem to borrow from a common pool of theorems and calculating algorithms pertaining to the areas of triangles, the value of pi, and the volume of a pyramidal or conic frustum. Ultimately Asper suggests identifying Hero's Dionysius with a student of the famously learned Stoic Chaeremon, the *grammaticus* Dionysius Glaukou, who, during Nero's reign, occupied the offices *a bibliothecis* and *ab epistulis et responsis ad legationes*.[60] The epithet thus bespeaks praise for his brilliant learning rather than his lofty position, an apt addressee for a didactic text like the *Definitiones* that reworks and expands upon Euclid's work.

Finally, a couple of technical arguments may provide some grounds for dating his work. Schmidt accepted the possibility of dating Hero's *Mechanica* by a reference to a style of olive press having its screw in the middle, which is itself used for the pressing.[61] This type of press is mentioned by Pliny as having been invented twenty-two years before the time of writing, which could potentially allow for dating the *Mechanica* very precisely.[62] Of course, this dating only holds secure if Pliny learned of the technique from the *Mechanica* and if Hero was describing a cutting-edge technology (so to speak), neither of which is at all certain. However, Keyser bolsters the evidence from 1st-century Rome by noting that an improvement to the design of a water organ Hero proposes in his *Pneumatica* appears to match an innovative water organ Suetonius and Cassius Dio report Nero as having played.[63] All in all, the range of strategies engaged to solve the thorny problem of Hero's date itself illuminates the breadth of his impact: He is an explorer of past texts, a repository of technical methods, and a name for a type of technical work and text that would long outlast his individual life – whenever it was.

[59] Gandz 1940; Krafft 1973. Acerbi and Vitrac review more recent work calling into question the relationship between Hero and the *Mishnat ha-Middot* and Gandz's dating at Hero 2014: 537.

[60] Asper 2001a: 136–37; Schumacher 2018: 195.

[61] Hero 1976b: xix, xxii–xxiii. The passage on the screw survives only in Quṣṭā ibn Lūqā's Arabic version of Hero's *Mechanica* (3.20); see Hero and Quṣṭā ibn Lūqā 2016: 157–59.

[62] Pliny, *Nat. Hist.* 18.74. For discussion of the different types of presses and the ancient textual evidence, see Drachmann 1932: 56–58, 82–85, 125–28.

[63] Hero, *Pneumatica* 1.42; Suetonius *Nero* 41.2; Cassius Dio 63.26.4; Keyser 1988.

## "Core" and "Cloud"

The multiplicity of cultural, biographical, and bibliographic backdrops against which Hero might have worked thus serves to refract him into multiple possible identities. That already unstable identity ramifies into an even more complex construct in the Heronian texts whose contents are abbreviated, recopied into new locations, contaminated by other texts, and otherwise transformed. From what Cerquiglini describes as the "bourgeois, paternalist, and hygienist" philological standpoint, always seeking to refine the manuscript tradition into a family tree of legitimate heirs, such instability seems intolerable.[64] But as scholars of historical practices of propagating and consuming texts know well, the processes of "contamination" by which one text becomes entwined with others as it is recopied and put to new uses yield a textual artifact that is a complex and interesting object of study in its own right. The manuscript tradition rejoices in variance and recombination at the level not only of the codex, but of the individual work as well.[65] Indeed, "contamination" by multiple authorial and editorial voices was likely common in the ancient world even as texts underwent their initial composition, as Sean Gurd's work on revision and collaboration in authorship has demonstrated.[66]

Even given the unruly practices of ancient text production and the vagaries of propagation over centuries of manuscript transmission, the Heronian corpus as we know it today is especially difficult to set firm boundaries around. An anonymized pool of source material is siphoned into an array of texts (many of them quite frank about their compilatory work), combined in those texts with new material, and then subjected to the usual vagaries of postcompositional time. During this last phase, particularly in the case of the metrological texts, copious additional material might be interpolated into the text, rendering it very dubious indeed to speak of most of these texts as "Hero's." While any ancient author might of course be subject to such interpolations, the practical appeal of the devices and techniques Hero describes, the discrete structure of many of his texts, and Hero's own open hospitality to information from past authors conspire to render his corpus unusually open to later interpolation. The resulting corpus is a multifarious sprawl, exceedingly resistant to attempts to extract a genuine "Hero" without shedding tremendous amounts of useful and interesting text.

---

[64] Cerquiglini 1989: 76.  [65] Cerquiglini 1989: 43–54.  [66] Gurd 2007, 2012.

The unruly Heronian corpus may indeed be viewed as a kernel of authentic works obscured by an inconvenient cloud of interpolations, revisions, and outright fabrications. But it can also be understood, from a perspective less centered on author and authenticity, as a system of interlocking information flows. That is, rather than focusing first and foremost on which components of the surviving corpus are best attributed to the historical Hero, we can instead think about the contents of the corpus as involving the intake of an initial set of textual "inputs," followed by a series of manipulations of those texts that render them into fundamentally different "outputs" for further waves of manipulations. Viewed from this perspective, the corpus need no longer be defined principally by the specific actors who effected these manipulations, leaving us free to contemplate the manipulations themselves, even those carried out by actors definitely different from the historical Hero.

In this vein it may be useful to think in terms of the capacious idea of the "archive" suggested by Paul Needham, who mirrors the more traditional "retained" archive of the papers taken in and stored by a corporate body with the "outward" or "reverse" archive of the papers produced and sent out by that body, which might hypothetically be traced back to their common source. Such papers are "outputs" of their producer, just as they are "inputs" for their receiver:

> These papers, if they survive, become part of the archives of their various recipients. But abstractly, they may equally well be conceived of as an entity, as the "outward archive" or "reverse archive" of the body that created them. The notional reconstruction of outward archives is as fundamental to historical investigation as is that of retained archives.[67]

Needham is, of course, speaking of the peregrination of *papers* in a quite material sense. But it is possible to see a parallel in studying informational outflows as well as inflows and the advantages that this perspective presents, especially for an entity like the Heronian corpus, which so often represents itself as a central locus where texts are taken in, transformed, and exported out. Of course, these informational flows remain bound to the circulation of their physical media; they are not disembodied data circulating via mysterious means. While it will not be possible to speak with any certainty of the early textual history of the Heronian corpus (among other things, just how early it actually was), I will devote attention to the mechanisms and institutions of textual information

---

[67] Needham 2000.

exchange within which manuscripts and printed books of Hero's works moved.

"Hero," construed uncontroversially as the author of the *Dioptra, Automata, Metrica,* and so on, makes frequent references to his having drawn on multiple source texts (usually anonymized) as what we might term "inputs." He describes as well the operations he performs on those texts: he epitomizes, compiles, critiques, corrects, and recontextualizes their contents. The express purpose of those operations is to render the material easier to understand, mathematical results easier to apply, and technologies easier to create. In turn, the Heronian texts themselves become "inputs" for later texts, subjected to the same processes of extraction, recombination, and recontextualization as Hero's own source material.

These complex processes of reintegration and reshaping were intrinsic to the "Heronian" project, both as it seems to have been undertaken by the historical Hero and as it was recapitulated by later authors operating on Hero's own work. I will not be attempting to get back to an "authentic" nucleus – a most difficult task but far from impossible, as Vitrac's exemplary work on the metrological corpus has shown.[68] Instead, while I will predominantly concentrate on the "core" texts here, I will also include connections between the "core" and those texts that an "authenticity"-focused study might throw out, simply because they embody the recombinatory spirit of the "Heronian" project in its greater sense. I will as far as possible adumbrate the historical Hero (or rather "Heros") in all his complexity and controversy, but the "Hero" I speak of will more often be a different sort of creature. This other "Hero" comprises the manipulations he performs on the works of other authors and the ways later authors manipulated his own works: "Hero" embraces the historical Hero along with his reception.

I will speak to a broader scientific and technological tradition, to an evolving cluster of problems and methods for solving them, exemplified by the "Heronian" approach but carried out by multiple authors, commentators, and translators. This tradition was particularly vigorous in the Roman imperial period, flourished anew in late antiquity, enjoyed a resurgence in the medieval Islamic world, and made perhaps its most lasting impact of all in Renaissance and early modern Europe. Alessandro Giorgi, one of the Renaissance translators of Hero's *Pneumatica,* concedes that the precise source of Hero's theory of matter and void was difficult to trace. Rather than representing this difficulty as a flaw or corruption, he eloquently compares the text's trick vessels that produce surprising effects through their

---

[68] Hero 2014: 434–45; Vitrac 2010.

mixtures of water and wine to the "cup of Helen, which as Homer recalls had the power of making people forget all their woes and cares."[69] The Heronian corpus itself, where technological knowledge often sluices between authors and eras in surprising ways, resembles these trick vessels in its own way. While the sources of the flow may be difficult to track down, the whole derives its worth as a spectacle of creative interconnection.

[69] Alessandro Giorgi and Hero, *Spiritali di Herone Alessandrino*, 6v.

# CHAPTER 2

# Systems of Explanation

## Introduction

Strabo portrays the geographer at work, sitting at the nexus of innumerable pathways of information. He collects the data to be inscribed on his *pinax* from an assortment of witnesses, who have seen the far corners of the Earth and bring their information to him for synthesis.[1] Strabo compares these voyagers to sensory organs, each with its own subset of information about an object (he offers an apple by way of example) and each presenting its own part of the story to the understanding (*dianoia*), which then synthesizes them into a single *schēma*.[2] So eyewitnesses transmit their knowledge to those who want to learn it (οἱ φιλομαθεῖς ἄνδρες), who take responsibility for collecting a world's worth of information and synthesizing it into a single synoptic *diagramma*.

They are partners in a trust-based economy of information, like generals who trust messengers to bring them information and disseminate their orders. Jacob compares the geographer's work in the Alexandrian library to Latour's "immutable mobiles": He collates information on various regions' topography, accessibility, and natural and human history, distilling them into a document in which they are juxtaposed with comparable information from other regions.[3] The geographer's sedentary synthesis yields authoritative documentary output, which can then be transmitted outward from his informational headquarters. This work relies on his ability to make careful judgments to resolve conflicts, as the diverse sources that

---

[1] Strabo, *Geographica* 2.5.11.
[2] Compare Ptolemy's *Criterion* 13.3–10, where the sensory faculty of the soul is said to receive impressions from the body's sensory organs, which it then relays to the intellect through *phantasia*; at this point, "like any messenger (καθάπερ ἄγγελός τις)," its work is done, and the task of judgment is left to the intellect. Likewise, Plutarch asserts at *Demetrius* 1 that the sensory organs take in impressions from all kinds of objects and send on all their received input to the understanding (τὸ φρονοῦν).
[3] Jacob 1998: 29; Latour 1986: 7.

come before his eyes may update or contradict existing information. As Jacob observes, when the geographer's own documentary work propagates beyond him, it may become an object of synthesis and correction in its own right. So geographers iteratively correct the work of their predecessors, relying on this gradually refined authority to check new data against as they come in from new travelers.[4]

Hero characterizes the work of constructing his corpus as a comparable project of acquiring and assessing information from a multitude of sources. Its gradual aggregation (first by Hero, then by others in his name) demands that information be received, trusted elements accepted and problematic ones excised, and the remainder synthetically distilled into a systematized form, finally to be transmitted back outward in the form of a text that will be read, judged, corrected, distilled, and transmitted all over again. Hero's "inputs" are not, like Strabo's, portrayed as travelers from around the world; for the most part when he alludes to acquiring information the process is mediated through texts rather than coming from people directly. (Of course, this is not to say that he did not get any information directly from its human carriers, merely that he chooses not to represent that process in his own accounts.) Though texts are the representatives of information transfer in the Heronian corpus, his account of the process reveals the same negotiations of trust in knowledge that Strabo refers to. He positions himself as an arbiter of information flooding in from practitioners, philosophers, and historians of technical disciplines, sifting out what is trustworthy and asking his reader, in turn, to trust his judgment. In exchange for that act of trust, the reader will gain a concise and synoptic view of the topic, which Hero has carefully curated to highlight the most accessible and useful material from his pool of source texts.

## Collecting and Correcting

Much of the information Hero brings together draws on a familiar suite of authorities like Archimedes, Eudoxus, and Euclid. At the same time, Hero often draws attention to the work he does with that textual inheritance; his books do not just anthologize but energetically reshape older material for a new user base.[5] For example, in the preface to his *Pneumatica* Hero spells

---

[4] Jacob 1998: 34–35.
[5] Compare Cuomo on Pappus' *Synagōgē*, where she observes that past mathematical tradition "plays a prominent role" in the collection, but that the reader "is free to use in other ways" the results of that

out the organizational principles that will guide the work to come and emphasizes that his work of ordering is at the core of the contribution he makes to the discipline.[6] Describing the contribution he intends to make, he first announces that he will "bring into order the things handed down from the ancients (τὰ παραδοθέντα ὑπὸ τῶν ἀρχαίων εἰς τάξιν ἀγαγεῖν)." Once he has set the field of information in order, he can then add new discoveries of his own (ἃ ἡμεῖς δὲ προσευρήκαμεν εἰσθέσθαι). The text has been shaped to induct even an inexperienced reader into a system of problems that can be learned and then expanded on once the approved equipment and epistemological infrastructure are in place.

Similarly, at the beginning of the second book of the *Metrica*, Hero describes the work's organizational scheme as having been developed in part in response to readers who had had difficulty reading Archimedes and other authors.[7] He says he will proceed "in sequence (κατὰ τὸ ἀκόλουθον)" from the prior book's guidance on measuring surfaces, both rectilinear and otherwise, to the measurement of solid bodies. He reminds the reader that the surfaces of these bodies have already been covered under the rubric of the first book, referencing their organization there into planar, spherical, conical, cylindrical, and "unclassified (*ataktoi*)" surfaces. The last of these, reports Hero, were labeled "paradoxical" by prior authors attempting to ascribe a chronological sequence to analyses of the different types of surface, who apparently associated them with Archimedes.[8]

Hero, however, is less interested here in rehashing a chronological scheme of authors than in fitting all the information into his own organizational plan. He brushes off the question of authorship here, saying that whether the irregular surfaces are to be attributed to Archimedes or someone else, "it is necessary to sketch them out as well, so that our material will not turn out to be wanting for those who want to deal with them."[9] The *Metrica*'s task is not to produce a history of the discipline's development, but to fit the fruits of that development into a particular logical and textual scheme suitable for lay readers.

Nor is Hero's intervention with the body of past texts limited to rearranging a preexisting body of information; his synthetic distillation often entails strategic reductions and expansions, as well as improvements

---

tradition: Cuomo 1998: 226. While Hero is not writing a single text of the "collection" type Cuomo analyzes, his corpus as a whole exhibits some similarities.
[6] *Pneumatica* 1.pr.5–7.    [7] *Metrica* 2.pr.1–11.
[8] *Metrica* 2.pr.6–7. Acerbi and Vitrac explain the ascription of these forms to Archimedes *because* of their "paradoxical" nature at Hero 2014: 249 n. 1.
[9] *Metrica* 2.pr.8–11.

in method and factual corrections. A particularly common reductive strategy involves selecting and skimming off the material that is deemed most useful. That high-utility core is then often expanded again in turn with a suite of examples, connective and contextual material, or new developments Hero himself claims to have made. For example, the first book of the *Metrica* begins with a claim to collect all that is most useful to know from the substantial body of preexisting literature on its subject and add to them Hero's own new developments.[10]

The concept of utility, which applies variously to the material, mechanical, and informational properties of objects as well as concepts, is admittedly complex and multifaceted in the Heronian corpus. As we will see, Hero uses *chrēsimos* and its cognates (as well as other terms indicating suitability, ease, adaptation, or practicality) to refer to "usefulness" for mechanical applications outside the text, as well as the didactic and other cognitive experiences that occur within it. At the same time, the question "useful to whom?" often lurks behind these assertions, as Hero's peculiar approach is not always shaped to provide the simplest possible introduction to a topic for absolute beginners. For example, the inclusion of "paradoxical," "unclassified" forms in the *Metrica* highlights Hero's aim to blend the material world in all its complexity with the clean clarity of mathematical analysis. As will become apparent, this blending of the mathematical and the material is a common feature of Hero's writing that sometimes conflicts with the notion of "utility" as directed toward the simplest or most immediately practical approach. Doubtless the *Metrica* would be more readily understood by beginners if Hero did not incorporate the references to real-world objects that complicate several of its chapters, yet including them was clearly important to his stated goal of utility.

Other texts depart from the "utility as simple practicality" model by addressing a more generally advanced audience. For example, as we will later see, his *Automata* is explicitly addressed to a relatively advanced readership; Hero notes that it incorporates material from every other subdiscipline of mechanics, so that other books of his ought to be mastered first. This systematization both within and between books is another distinguishing feature of Hero's approach, making works like the *Automata* truly useful only to a reader who follows his system. Some information is thus left out of works like the *Automata* because the reader is meant to acquire it in other books, while other material is not found in

---

[10] *Metrica* 1.pr.22–25.

any of his texts. For example, the figurines that carry out the *Automata*'s spectacles and adorn the devices in the *Pneumatica* are often underspecified; some devices promise a familiar figure like Hercules, but others only specify an "animal figurine (*zōdarion*)." That is, Hero's work often seems to presume a reader with some cultural acquaintance with the types of devices he names, who can fill in the missing decorative details appropriately from their own experience or imagination. Works like the *Automata* are not cookie-cutter guides to be followed exactly, but they aim instead to provide the reader with the tools to imagine their own devices once they have mastered the mechanical principles introduced in the text.

The *Automata* features a more detailed account than the *Metrica* or *Pneumatica* had of the history of the discipline, what his predecessors had accomplished, and what he is going to do with that body of work. He traces the discipline of automaton-making very far back indeed, to theatrical works of much lesser complexity: "[T]he ancients (*archaioi*)" implemented a theatrical device consisting of a painted face, which would appear when the theater (*pinax*) was opened, blink its eyes several times, and then vanish, to be replaced by painted figures indicating the story to be performed, "so that only three different movements happened on the *pinax*: one of the door, another of the eyes, and a third of the [backdrop] coverings."[11] These early theaters' automated movements were apparently limited to their exteriors; Hero is not very clear about the mechanism that changed the painted backdrop within, and indeed this maneuver might even have been performed by hand. By Hero's own time, much has apparently changed since the days of those primitive *pinakes*, as theatrical designers in subsequent generations "adapted stories to elegant *pinakes* and have used many and various movements."[12] The "first-generation" devices were mechanically very different from those Hero describes, yet he presents them as somehow the same kind of thing due to their shared context of use and goal of providing an entertaining spectacle.[13]

He acknowledges his considerable debt to earlier works on the topic but insists that certain corrections must be made. Earlier methods for getting an automaton to travel back and forth along a straight path, for example, were far from foolproof: "[S]eldom came to fruition the things following the methods they had written up, as is clear to those who have tried their

[11] *Automata* 22.1–2.    [12] *Automata* 22.1–2.

[13] For a concise yet detailed review of references to automata (real or imagined) in antiquity, see Grillo 2019: lxxxii–xcvi. Some additional historical material is found in Prou 1884: 117–20. On the possible performance contexts of automata in antiquity, see Bur 2016; Schürmann 1991, 2002: 190–201.

[methods]."[14] Hero, on the other hand, will provide his reader with a reliably field-tested method. He sets up his own work in opposition to this previous work, promising to make improvements both technical and textual:

> Ὅσα μὲν οὖν ἔδει περὶ τῶν ὑπαγόντων αὐτομάτων πραγματευθῆναι, νομίζομεν ἱκανῶς ἀνεστράφθαι ἐν τοῖς προγεγραμμένοις· καὶ γὰρ εὐκόπως καὶ ἀκινδύνως καὶ ξένως παρὰ τὰ πρὸ ἡμῶν ἀναγεγραμμένα κατακεχωρίκαμεν, ὡς ἔστι δῆλον τοῖς πεπειραμένοις τῶν πρότερον ἀναγεγραμμένων. περὶ δὲ τῶν στατῶν αὐτομάτων βουλόμεθα γράφειν καινότερόν τι . . .

> All the things that had to be treated with regard to the moving automata, we consider to have been dwelled upon sufficiently in what has already been written. For we have set down in writing the things that are done easily, reliably, and in an unfamiliar way compared to those written up by those before us, as is clear to those who have tested out the earlier accounts. Now, we wish to write something comparatively novel about stationary automata . . .[15]

He is emphatic about his engagement with past work in this vein, but he is just as emphatic that his mechanical tradition is still very much alive, subject to constant evolution and improvement both in terms of the designs of the artifacts themselves and in the way those designs are propagated in text.

His allusions to the past tradition of texts on automaton design provide almost no details; that tradition is (with one notable exception) presented here as an undifferentiated mass, texts and authors alike unnamed. In presenting that tradition in this way rather than listing his engagements with individual texts, Hero seems to suggest that he has seen it all, cherry-picked the best it had to offer in terms of ease of use, reliability, and novelty, and transmitted the results to his reader. By omitting names of texts and authors, he prevents the reader from going back to perform their own selections and corrections. While he does invite the reader to test his claim to provide a more reliable method than his predecessors did, the invitation is daunting. Go out, he suggests, and try building the automata rejected from his collection because of their complexity and unreliability – if you can even identify them in the first place. Hero does not catalog past actors and authors in his field, leaving them as nameless as the travelers consulted by Strabo's geographer as he weaves their work into his own system, built on its own rules that privilege ease of use and reliability.

---

[14] *Automata* 5.1–2.    [15] *Automata* 20.1.1–7.

The one work he does single out for special attention is Philo's book on automaton-making, which Hero appears to regard as the best of its kind. He reports that "of the texts written before us, we have found none better and more suitable for teaching than those of Philo of Byzantium."[16] That is, to some extent Hero had ideas about what a text on automaton-making should cover, and he finds Philo's text the best match to his ideal from among the mass of other texts he leaves unnamed. His didactic priorities extend to other topics as well; he refers in the preface to his own *Belopoeica* to "mechanical teaching (μηχανικὴ ... διδασκαλία)," deeming it preferable to purely verbal *didaskalia*.

Just because Hero finds Philo's text the best available does not mean it offers no room for improvement. Immediately after giving it his stamp of approval, Hero lists a few problems with Philo's approach. For example, on the mechanical side Philo designed an unnecessarily complex (*ergōdesteron*) crane mechanism that causes a figure of Athena to appear.[17] On the textual side, Hero acknowledges that Philo might have forgotten to include some information, though he will not go so far as to accuse him of failing to complete his project:

> ἔτι δὲ καὶ ὑποσχόμενος πρὸς τούτῳ κεραυνὸν πεσεῖν ἐπὶ τὸ τοῦ Αἴαντος ζῴδιον καὶ βροντῆς ἦχον γενέσθαι οὐ κατεχώρισε· πολλοῖς γὰρ συντάγμασι περιτυχόντες οὐχ εὕρομεν τοῦτο ἀναγεγραμμένον. καὶ ἴσως δόξει τις ἡμᾶς κατατρέχοντας τοῦ Φίλωνος διαβάλλειν αὐτὸν ὡς μὴ δεδυνημένον τὴν ὑπόσχεσιν ἀπαρτίσαι· ἀλλ᾽ οὐχ οὕτως ἔχει. πολλῶν δὲ οὐσῶν τῶν ἐν τῇ διαθέσει ὑποσχέσεων, ἴσως ἔλαθεν αὐτὸν ἀναγράφοντα αὕτη.

> And moreover he promised that besides lightning would fall on the figure of Ajax, and that the sound of thunder would occur, but he did not set it down in writing; for though we have encountered many copies we have not found it written up. And perhaps someone will think we are running Philo down to discredit him as not having been able to fulfill his promise, but that's not the case. Since there are many promises in the arrangement, perhaps this one escaped him as he was writing it up.[18]

Hero concludes these criticisms on a favorable note, saying that he will be satisfied as long as the actions in the play of Nauplius devised by Philo happen "in order and methodically, as written up by him" – plus, of course, the improvements Hero will suggest. This passage suggests the vital role that integrating novel content plays in the Heronian project. Locating

---

[16] *Automata* 20.1–2.     [17] *Automata* 20.2.     [18] *Automata* 20.3.1–4.2.

one's text within a tradition – inscribing oneself among prior authors on the same subject – enhances the text's value rather than detracts from it:

οὕτως γὰρ νομίζομεν τοὺς ἐντυγχάνοντας τῆς μεγίστης ὠφελείας τυγχάνειν, ὅταν τὰ μὲν καλῶς ὑπὸ τῶν ἀρχαίων εἰρημένα παρατιθῆται αὐτοῖς, τὰ δὲ παραθεωρηθέντα ἢ διορθώσεως τυχόντα καταχωρίζηται.

For in this way I consider readers to encounter the greatest benefit, whenever the things said well by the ancients are explained to them, and the things that were overlooked or met with correction are set down in writing.[19]

The evolving technologies embraced by automaton-making, which undergo improving alterations even as they remain recognizably part of the same discipline, are mirrored by the texts that help to propagate them. Hero asserts that his ability to clarify the work done on the same subject by his predecessors will be a major part of his contribution. He calls attention to preexisting works not simply to correct them, but rather to decode and organize them for perplexed readers. He does not position himself on *terra incognita*, solving brand-new problems with brand-new methods, but rather in a prepopulated territory that he will make accessible to a new audience.

Automaton-making is just one of many technical fields where Hero alludes to a crowd of colleagues past and present and then finds room for improvement in their work. The very start of the *Dioptra* identifies several parties the text will draw together: the users whose practical needs will be satisfied thanks to Hero's treatment of the subject matter, the previous authors who have treated the topic, and Hero himself. He celebrates the instrument's broad appeal to many different disciplines but observes as well that its very usefulness has prompted the composition of several other texts on the topic, many of which were somehow lacking. He negotiates a respectful correction of those works:

Τῆς διοπτρικῆς πραγματείας πολλὰς καὶ ἀναγκαίας παρεχομένης χρείας καὶ πολλῶν περὶ αὐτῆς λελεχότων ἀναγκαῖον εἶναι νομίζω τά τε ὑπὸ τῶν πρὸ ἐμοῦ παραλειφθέντα καὶ, ὡς προείρηται, χρείαν παρέχοντα γραφῆς ἀξιῶσαι, τὰ δὲ δυσχερῶς εἰρημένα εἰς εὐχέρειαν μεταγαγεῖν, τὰ δὲ ψευδῶς εἰρημένα εἰς διόρθωσιν προάξαι. οὐχ ἡγοῦμαι δὲ ἀναγκαῖον εἶναι τά τε ἡμαρτημένως καὶ δυσχερῶς ἐκτεθειμένα ἢ καὶ διημαρτημένα ὑπὸ τῶν πρὸ ἡμῶν νῦν εἰς μέσον φέρειν· ἐξέσται γὰρ τοῖς βουλομένοις ἐντυγχάνουσιν κρίνειν τὴν διαφοράν.

---

[19] *Automata* 20.5.5–9.

Since the practice of dioptrics offers many necessary applications and since much has been said about it, I think it necessary to give their due to the matters passed over by those before me that offer utility, to translate what was said with difficulty into ready ease, and to bring what was falsely said to correction. I do not consider it necessary to trot out the things put forth erroneously and with difficulty by my predecessors, or those that were complete failures. For anyone who happens to wish to do so can judge the difference.[20]

Hero will serve as conduit and corrector for the wealth of information about dioptras that he has inherited. He promises his reader a trustworthy compilation, from which he has scoured the inaccuracies and confusion. Yet his correction will not take the form of a point-by-point refutation of each of his predecessors, an in-text demonstration of his own superiority. The correction happens tastefully offstage; Hero's stated goal is to provide his reader with a useful new product, not to embarrass his predecessors even when they proved incompetent. Instead, he will address the problems that plagued previous works one by one, as they become relevant to his own text.

Principal among these problems is the lack of a clear standard for equipment and problem-solving methodology:

ἔτι δὲ καὶ ὅσοι ἀναγραφὴν πεποίηνται περὶ τῆς πραγματείας, οὐ [διὰ] μιᾷ ἢ τῇ αὐτῇ διόπτρᾳ κέχρηνται πρὸς τὴν ἐνέργειαν, πολλαῖς δὲ καὶ διαφόροις, καὶ ὀλίγας δι᾽ αὐτῶν προτάσεις ἐπιτελέσαντες. ἡμεῖς μὲν οὖν καὶ τοῦτο αὐτὸ πεφιλοτιμήμεθα, ὥστε διὰ τῆς αὐτῆς τὰς προκειμένας ἡμῖν προτάσεις ἐνεργεῖσθαι. οὐ μὴν ἀλλὰ καὶ ἂν ἑτέρας τις ἐπινοήσῃ, οὐκ ἀμοιρήσει ἡ κατασκευασθεῖσα ὑφ᾽ ἡμῶν διόπτρα, ὥστε καὶ ταύτας ἐνεργεῖν.

And yet those who have composed writings on the practice do not use one and the same dioptra for the work, but many different ones, solving only a few problems with them. Therefore we pride ourselves on this [design], since it is possible to work through the problems proposed to us using it; but if anyone were to imagine other problems, the dioptra designed by us will not fail to work through them.[21]

The text's included instructions for building the dioptra create an opportunity to popularize a single version of the instrument, which can then be used to solve standard problems in a predictable way, and from there can point the way to an orderly expansion into new problem-solving territory. As it happens, these instructions do not survive very well in the version of the text we have, but of course that does not invalidate the standardizing

[20] *Dioptra* I.1–11.   [21] *Dioptra* I.11–19.

intent behind the recommendation of a "Hero-brand" dioptra and problem-solving approach. That Hero is not content merely to collect past results, but includes his own innovations, is borne out here in the sense of pride he expresses in the design of the dioptra. His evolved design connects the surveying problems proposed in the past and collected in his text with the new problems the reader may encounter and solve in the future. The *Dioptra*, just like the *Automata*, promises a reliable baseline to serve as a springboard for the reader's own elaborations and variations, whether on the mechanism itself or its applications.

While the *Dioptra* illuminates Hero's solicitous attitude toward incorporating his predecessors' work into his own, at the same time it avoids a different possible acknowledgment of the discipline's history, which can be seen by contrasting Hero's work on surveying with that of the Roman *agrimensores*. The Roman authors often refer to an extensive system of archival documents that traced land ownership, taxation, and usage. The *agrimensores* divided the land into square *centuriae* and their "leftovers (*subseciva*)," and they then mapped the terrain on durable materials like bronze and marble at scales ranging from portable bronze sheets to monumental maps like the great cadastral map of Orange and the *Forma Urbis Romae*.[22] Agrimensorial authors like Hyginus Gromaticus indicate that one copy of the local map was to remain in the area it represented, while a second copy was dispatched to the imperial *tabularium* and made available in case of disputes over land ownership. There it was accompanied by the so-called bronze books (*libri aeris, tabulae aeris, aerea tabulae*), which Piganiol suggests might have consisted of a table of ownership for each *centuria*.[23] The surviving works of the *agrimensores* are thus just one piece of a very rich landscape of information, and their practices can hardly be separated from that institutional context of information storage and retrieval.

Hero, by contrast, seems to inhabit a very different informational world. Even in his *Dioptra*, where we might most expect references to a robust information management system accessible to surveying professionals, Hero remains mute. To be sure, that text is where we find Hero's most concrete references detailing how the reader should record their own measurements on tablets or papyrus, as well as a single problem referring

---

[22] On the various types of inscriptions created and used by the surveyors see Ariño Gil and Gurt 2001; Cavalieri-Manasse 2000; Chouquer 2010: 246–61; Dilke 1961; Gorges 1993; Mayer and Olesti Vila 2001; Moatti 1993: 2–3; Nicolet 1991: 95–114, 149–69; Piganiol 1962; Roby 2014a; Sáez Fernández 1990.

[23] Piganiol 1962: 49.

to a "representation (*mimēma*)" of a region of land with no additional context.[24] But there is no reference to compiling the information thus acquired into a larger centralized system, nor to drawing on information already available from previous measurements. He mentions no peculiarities of topography or measurement that pertain to specific localities, both common features in the Roman agrimensorial texts. Moreover, he makes no mention of the pervasive Roman system of topographical markers etched on stones and other elements of the landscape, nor the intricate legal system of land disputes that vexed the Roman surveyors.[25] Perhaps these differences reflect a gulf between Roman surveying practices and their Greek analogs (as we know next to nothing about the latter), perhaps Hero lived at a time or in a place where knowledge of the Roman record-keeping system was unavailable to him, or perhaps he simply saw the discipline as a generalized problem-solving practice rather than one rooted in local variation. Whichever of these was the case, Hero gives us a glimpse of a very different way of establishing a disciplinary tradition for surveying than the Roman *agrimensores* do. His approach is to synthesize information from others into a capacious problem-solving context that eschews the complexity arising from local peculiarities and aims instead at creating a placeless and universalizing tradition.

The *Pneumatica* opens on a note similar to the *Dioptra*: The subject he is about to discuss has prompted a wealth of prior work, which Hero will engage and reshape, intervening with innovations of his own where necessary:

Τῆς πνευματικῆς πραγματείας σπουδῆς ἠξιωμένης πρὸς τῶν παλαιῶν φιλοσόφων τε καὶ μηχανικῶν, τῶν μὲν λογικῶς τὴν δύναμιν αὐτῆς ἀποδεδωκότων, τῶν δὲ καὶ δι' αὐτῆς τῆς τῶν αἰσθητῶν ἐνεργείας, ἀναγκαῖον ὑπάρχειν νομίζομεν καὶ αὐτοὶ τὰ παραδοθέντα ὑπὸ τῶν ἀρχαίων εἰς τάξιν ἀγαγεῖν, καὶ ἃ ἡμεῖς δὲ προσευρήκαμεν εἰσθέσθαι· οὕτως γὰρ τοὺς μετὰ ταῦτα ἐν τοῖς μαθήμασιν ἀναστρέφεσθαι βουλομένους ὠφελεῖσθαι συμβήσεται.

Since the zealous practice of pneumatics was valued by the philosophers and mechanicians of old (the former making demonstrations of its power through logic, the latter through its operation on sensible objects), we consider it necessary ourselves to bring into order the things handed down from the ancients, and to add on what we ourselves have discovered. For in this way it will be possible for those who want to engage in scientific studies afterward to profit from them.[26]

[24] *Dioptra* 6.41–86, 7.22, 25.    [25] On these disputes see Cuomo 2007: 103–30.
[26] *Pneumatica* 1.pr.1–9.

Hero's fluid-driven devices have floated far downstream from Callimachus' pure spring: The ability of pneumatic devices to demonstrate physical principles is a subject that has been tackled repeatedly, using different methodologies, for a very long time.[27] Once again, Hero tasks himself with bringing that superabundance of material into order, transmuting it into whatever will be most useful for his readers.

In the case of the *Pneumatica*, the principal problem facing Hero is the reams of prior philosophical discourse on the question of whether void inheres in matter. After explaining the pneumatic principles behind a few simple physical demonstrations (for example, why sucking the air out of a narrow-necked vessel allows the emptied vessel to dangle from one's lip), Hero establishes his own brand of "perceptible proof (αἰσθητικῇ ἀπόδειξις)" as superior to purely logical discourse:

> τοῖς οὖν φαμένοις τὸ καθόλου μηδὲν εἶναι κενὸν ἐκποιεῖ πρὸς ταῦτα πολλὰ εὑρίσκειν ἐπιχειρήματα καὶ τάχα φαίνεσθαι τῷ λόγῳ πιθανωτέρους μηδεμιᾶς παρακειμένης αἰσθητικῆς ἀποδείξεως· ἐὰν μέντοι δειχθῇ ἐπὶ τῶν φαινομένων καὶ ὑπὸ τὴν αἴσθησιν πιπτόντων, ὅτι κενὸν ἄθρουν ἐστὶν παρὰ φύσιν μέντοι γινόμενον, καὶ κατὰ φύσιν μὲν κενόν, κατὰ λεπτὰ δὲ παρεσπαρμένον, καὶ ὅτι κατὰ πίλησιν τὰ σώματα ἀναπληροῖ τὰ παρεσπαρμένα κενά, οὐδεμίαν οὐκέτι παρείσδυσιν ἕξουσιν οἱ τοὺς πιθανοὺς τῶν λόγων περὶ τούτων προφερόμενοι.

It is possible for those who say that there is no void at all to find many attempts at arguments besides these, and perhaps to appear quite persuasive in words, even though there is no corroborating perceptible proof. However, if it is demonstrated through phenomena and things that occur to the senses that there is continuous void even if it occurs artificially, and that naturally there is void dispersed in small amounts, and that under compression particles fill up the scattered voids, those who present plausible words concerning these things will no longer have any loophole.[28]

Hero will intervene by shifting the terms of this debate away from unsatisfying verbal abstractions and into the world of physical demonstrations. He later goes on to name a few cases for the artificial creation of an extended void using simple means like sucking the air out by the mouth or the egg-shaped cupping vessels used by physicians. The demonstrations (*apodeixeis*) provided by cases like these, he concludes, have yielded enough discourse, "for we made the demonstrations (*apodeixeis*) through the senses themselves."[29]

---

[27] Callimachus, *In Apollinem* (hymn 2) 108–12.  [28] *Pneumatica* 1.pr.190–200.
[29] *Pneumatica* 1.pr.329–32.

The experiments Hero engaged to change the terms of this debate will be explored in more detail in the next chapter. For now, it will suffice to observe that he consistently uses the language of rigorous proof to refer not to the results of verbal philosophical debate but of experimental demonstration. He could have chosen to engage with the past tradition of philosophers debating the nature of matter and void on their own terms by culling the most convincing arguments and relaying them to his reader. Instead, his intervention will be to claim that territory of proof for hands-on work in the technical discipline of pneumatics.

In making this move he is still participating in an existing textual tradition, even though he does not here acknowledge Philo as he did in the *Automata*. Though Philo's *Pneumatica* does not survive in Greek, the preface to the Arabic and Latin versions includes some remarkably similar sentiments. Philo applauds certain unnamed philosophers who, swimming against the tide of false opinion, asserted that empty-seeming vessels are really full of air. However, his text is apparently not the place to revisit their arguments, as he explains in the preface to the Latin version:

> Ego vero, in presenti negotio brevitati cupiens deservire, nec eorum verba in dente nec controversantium objectiones volo pertractare, ne dispensiosam sermo meus prolixitatem incurrat.

> I, however, desiring to serve the interest of brevity in my present concerns, wish neither to protract their words on my tongue nor the opinions of the debaters, lest my discussion incur a weighty wordiness.[30]

Like Hero after him, Philo will intervene in this tradition not through verbal arguments about the principles of physics, but through the mechanical devices he arranges to put those principles into action. His text will not be weighed down by unnecessary words, remaining light as the air in his devices. Indeed, Philo arguably follows through on his promise more sincerely than Hero does, as the various versions of his preface in the Arabic and Latin traditions are indeed brisk and businesslike, proposing quick experimental proofs with short explanations capped off by compact assertions like "this explanation proves that air is a body." Hero, by contrast, ends up expanding the verbal explanation in his preface at great length with examples from everyday life, thought experiments, and (ironically) additional critiques of wordy philosophers that punctuate the text at several intervals. Even as he follows in the footsteps of Philo's "proof by experiment" model, then, Hero effects his own authorial interventions.

---

[30] Latin text at Philo 1974: 80.

## Disciplinary Histories

Hero's practice of situating his works within a tradition (textual, practical, or both) sometimes leads into a fuller disciplinary history. The *Belopoeica* begins with a familiar appeal to the surfeit of existing works on the topic, which nevertheless do not prove useful because they do not make the material accessible to everyone:

> Ἐπεὶ οὖν οἱ πρὸ ἡμῶν πλείστας μὲν ἀναγραφὰς περὶ βελοποιικῶν ἐποιήσαντο μέτρα καὶ διαθέσεις ἀναγραψάμενοι, οὐδὲ εἷς δὲ αὐτῶν οὔτε τὰς κατασκευὰς τῶν ὀργάνων ἐκτίθεται κατὰ τρόπον οὔτε τὰς τούτων χρήσεις, ἀλλ᾽ ὥσπερ γινώσκουσι πᾶσι τὴν ἀναγραφὴν ἐποιήσαντο, καλῶς ἔχειν ὑπολαμβάνομεν ἐξ αὐτῶν τε ἀναλαβεῖν καὶ ἐμφανίσαι περὶ τῶν ὀργάνων τῶν ἐν τῇ βελοποιίᾳ, ὡς μηδὲ ἴσως ὑπαρχόντων, ὅπως πᾶσιν εὐπαρακολούθητος γένηται ἡ παράδοσις.

> Those before us created a great many treatises on catapult construction, writing up their measurements and designs. Yet not a single one of them laid out either the designs of the machines or their uses in a reasonable way, but as though they were creating their treatise entirely for the cognoscenti. So we thought it would be good to extract from them and make clarifications concerning the devices in catapult construction, as though from scratch, so that the tradition would be easy for everyone to follow.[31]

His predecessors' work might have been full of details on the finer points of artillery design, but Hero argues that such a flood of information is useless if it has not been channeled to a readership properly versed in the fundamentals. It is, of course, quite likely that such basic knowledge was transferred tacitly between the kinds of expert practitioners who would likely have been interested in the "measurements and designs" mentioned here.[32] However, that mode of transmission does not count for Hero's rhetorical presentation; only when the foundations of the discipline have been laid out in a textual form suitable for a broad audience does the "tradition (*paradosis*)" really earn its name. The breadth of influence Hero hopes the *Belopoeica* might have is underscored by the promise in its very first words that a sound grasp of catapult technology represents the most reliable road to *ataraxia*, the state of freedom from cares that is the

---

[31] *Belopoeica* 2.1–14.
[32] On mechanisms for transferring tacit knowledge see Collins 2010; Nightingale 2009; Polanyi 2009. For a case study of the tacit knowledge that might be concealed behind Vitruvius' *De architectura* see Cuomo 2016.

principal goal of Epicurean philosophy.[33] While he does not revisit the idea in the main body of the *Belopoeica*, the unexpected – even ludic – blend of the philosophical and the technical at the beginning of the work sets the reader up to appreciate how Hero's technical material might be integrated with other, more familiar knowledge domains.

Hero structures his book in a way that already tells us something about how he imagines that tradition will most accessibly be transmitted. The *Belopoeica* organizes different types of machines into a rough (and specu- lative) chronological order, so that they appear as responses to a series of escalating technical challenges. The resulting order suggests an evolution- ary flow for the rising complexity in ballistic technologies, driven by the borrowing of mechanisms and components from earlier devices into later ones. Hero has challenged himself as an author to make these machines comprehensible to the novice reader despite their growing complexity. An evolutionary history is particularly well suited to achieve this goal, as it imposes a structure of incremental changes from one catapult to the next. After critiquing his predecessors, Hero immediately proceeds to an expla- nation of how his own work will be different:

> Ἐροῦμεν οὖν περὶ κατασκευῆς τῶν ὅλων τε καὶ τῶν ἐν αὐτοῖς κατὰ μέρος τοῖς ὀργάνοις καὶ περὶ τῶν ὀνομάτων, καὶ περὶ τῆς συνθέσεως αὐτῶν καὶ ἐξαρτίσεως, ἔτι δὲ καὶ περὶ τῆς ἑκάστου χρείας καὶ μέτρων, προειπόντες περὶ τῆς τῶν ὀργάνων διαφορᾶς καὶ ὡς τὴν ἀρχὴν ἕκαστον αὐτῶν προεβιβάσθη.

> Therefore we shall speak about the design of the whole devices as well as their parts, one at a time, and about their names, and about their construc- tion and preparation, and moreover about the use of each and its measure- ments, first speaking about the differences between the devices, and how each of them was developed.[34]

Here he makes a promise about what he is going to say (*eroumen*), framed as a sketch of the work's contents. Though light on detail, appropriately enough for a work aimed at relative newcomers to the field, the sketch at the beginning of the work bears some resemblance to the inset "headings (*kephalaia*)" that may have served as a kind of table of contents in certain types of technical text.[35] Part of the *Belopoeica*'s didactic mission involves

---

[33] *Belopoeica* 1.3. On this remark, and the philosophical resonance of the *Belopoeica* more broadly, see Cuomo 2002; Feke 2014: 263–65. Mansfeld calls the reference "a shade bizarre": Mansfeld 1998: 49.

[34] *Belopoeica* 2.14–24.

[35] Such "headings" are one of the defining features of the didactic *Lehrbuch* identified by Fuhrmann 1960: 8. The *Belopoeica*, despite its inclusion of prospective *kephalaia*, does not otherwise conform to the criteria of formulaic language and structure Fuhrmann defines for the *Lehrbuch* form.

letting the reader know in advance what to expect, providing a textual preview as well as an evolutionary framework to organize the varied technologies in the text into a coherent whole. Indeed, that structural promise will be echoed in frequent signposts as the work goes on. For example, Hero signals a transition from design to measurements by noting that he has said enough about building and using the two main types of catapult ("palintone" and "euthytone"), and will now proceed "in order (ἑξῆς)" to write about their measurements.[36]

These sections then cohere internally along the lines of stories about specific technical desiderata and the components developed to satisfy them. Within this structural plan, the local linking structures mirror the temporal development of the devices with the introduction of new information into the text itself. So, for example, the story of the development of the first torsion engines (Figure 2.1) begins with a transition from the "belly-bow (*gastraphetēs*)," which evidently inspired their design. Hero mirrors the process of importing elements of the belly-bow's design into the torsion engine by simply referring back to it as the "aforementioned (*proeirēmenos*)" design and jumping off from there into how its elements were combined into the new engine. The development process required additional revisions over time, which Hero often describes in considerable detail, aided by letter-labeled diagrams:

Ἐπεὶ δὲ συνέβαινεν ἐκ τῆς εἰρημένης κατασκευῆς τὴν ἐπιστροφὴν καὶ τάσιν τῶν νεύρων μὴ ἐπὶ πολὺ γίγνεσθαι διὰ τὰ ΑΔ, ΒΓ διαπήγματα μὴ δυνάμενα δέξασθαι τὸν τόνον· τὰς οὖν ἐπιζυγίδας ἐπιθέντες τοῖς τρυπήμασι τὰ αὐτὰ ἐποίουν τοῖς εἰρημένοις. καὶ οὕτω δὲ πάλιν ἡ ἐπιστροφὴ τῆς ἐπιζυγίδος δυσέργειαν εἶχεν, διὰ τὸ τὴν ἐπιζυγίδα ἐπικαθεζομένην τῷ διαπήγματι μὴ στρέφεσθαι, καὶ κατὰ πᾶν μέρος ψαύειν αὐτοῦ· ὅθεν ἠναγκάσθησαν καὶ τὰς καλουμένας χοινικίδας προσθεῖναι, περὶ ὧν ἑξῆς ἐροῦμεν.

Then from the aforementioned design it happened that the bending and stretching of the sinews most often failed because the cross-beams ΑΔ and ΒΓ were not able to take the spring-cord. Therefore they made them the same as those described, superimposing connecting-pins on the boreholes. And so again the bending of the connecting pins had an ill effect, because the connecting pin set over the cross-beam did not turn, and touched it at every point. Hence they were compelled to add what are called the "washers," about which we will speak in order.[37]

---

[36] *Belopoeica* 30.45–49. On these two forms of catapult see Marsden 1969: 22–23; Rihll 2007: 76–78.
[37] *Belopoeica* 9.1–34.

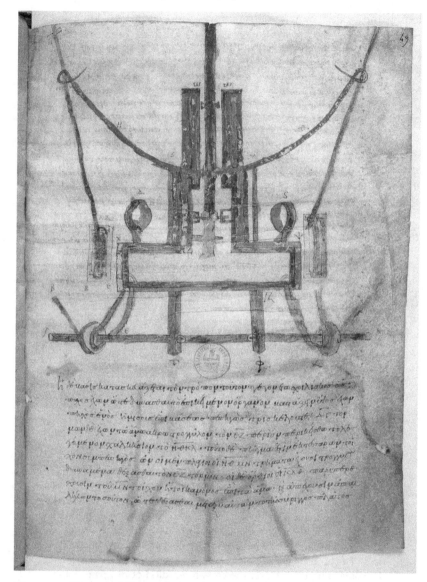

Figure 2.1    Diagram of the torsion catapult. Paris suppl. gr. 607, fol. 49r. Image courtesy of Bibliothèque nationale de France.

Hero paints a picture of a continuous iterative tradition of mechanical tinkering, where each technical solution may create new challenges that must be solved in turn. That continuity is reflected in the text through references that point both backward and forward. The reader, like the catapult designers, has access to information about the catapult frame type previously developed and described. That information is taken for granted as this frame is reconfigured and combined into a new design, which both calls back to elements previously developed and points forward to novel elements that will have to wait their turn to be described. Indeed, the promised description of the washers will have to wait for quite a while; it does not appear until after the firing mechanism, base, and some recent changes to the frame (20.1–21.12). Likewise, the details of the "stretcher (*entonion*)" are hinted at in 22.3 but not fully described until 28.1, after the transition from palintone to euthytone engines has already taken place. Hero makes consistent use of pointers like these, tying together individual passages to create a robustly woven text that emphasizes the mutually supportive, iterative creation of technical and textual traditions alike.

The preface to the first book of the *Metrica* situates that work too within a populated landscape of disciplinary predecessors, beginning with a mythologizing account of the first beginnings of geometry.[38] According to the "old story (παλαιὸς ... λόγος)," geometry was originally "engaged with measurements and divisions on the earth," hence the name. Later, as the demands of "necessary business (χρειώδους ... πράγματος)" became more pressing, the discipline was expanded to account for the measurement and distribution of solid bodies as well. After this glimpse of geometry's prehistory, Hero then transitions to more recent predecessors, distinguished by names and well-defined mathematical achievements. Hero particularly praises Eudoxus and Archimedes for having had such singular impacts on the history of mathematics that some key results were literally inconceivable before their intervention.[39] In the case of Eudoxus, it was "impossible to carry out the proof" that a cylinder has three times the volume of a cone with equal base and height, and that the areas of circles are proportional to the squares on their diameters before Eudoxus' "conception (*epinoia*)" of the problem. In the case of Archimedes, Hero here singles out the "insight (*sunesis*)" that a sphere's volume is two-thirds that of the cylinder that circumscribes it, and its surface area four times the area of its great circle.

---

[38] *Metrica* 1.pr.1–7.    [39] *Metrica* 1.pr.11–22.

The later metrological texts are often quite explicit about the interventions they make in existing problem-solving traditions. So, for example, in the *Geometrica* the reader is advised to "work according to the method previously described (ποίει ὡς κατὰ τὴν προγραφεῖσαν ἔφοδον)" by adding up the lengths of the sides of a triangle, or they are reminded that a process of calculation follows an area-calculating method previously set out (κατὰ τὴν προεκτεθεῖσαν ἔφοδον).[40] Each individual problem may vary in its forms and measurements but will remain situated within a larger textual and disciplinary context through references to overarching commonalities of method. Thanks to the methodological continuity imposed by the text, the problem-solving strategy does not have to be recertified as valid for each individual problem.

Competing strategies can also be compared, as when Hero, in the *Metrica*, compares the results of estimating π as 3 versus 22/7 when calculating the area of a segment of a circle.[41] The first method is ascribed to early mathematicians (οἱ μὲν ἀρχαῖοι) who were rather careless with their measurements (ἀμελέστερον ἐμέτρουν).[42] They solved the problem of finding the area of a segment of a circle (provided it was no greater than a semicircle) by multiplying the arithmetic mean of its base and its perpendicular by the length of the perpendicular. Hero works a sample problem as a demonstration of their method (the circle has radius 6 and the segment is a semicircle) but distances himself from its result through his language. He hints darkly that these mathematicians merely assumed (*hypolambanousin*) their solution corresponded to the area to be measured, and he frames the area of the circle obtained by approximating π as 3 as an interrogative rather than a declarative: "[T]hen wouldn't (*oukoun*) the circumference of the circle be 36 units?" Hence the answer he reaches in his sample problem is only an approximation: "[T]he result is something like (*homoiōs*) 54."

The implicit critique of the method sets up the reader for the next section, which promises a more accurate method:

> Οἱ δὲ ἀκριβέστερον ἐζητηκότες προστιθέασι τῷ εἰρημένῳ ἐμβαδῷ τοῦ τμήματος τὸ ιδ' μέρος τοῦ ἀπὸ τῆς ἡμισείας τῆς βάσεως. οὗτοι δὴ τῇ ἑτέρᾳ φαίνονται ἠκολουθηκότες ἐφόδῳ καθ' ἣν ἡ τοῦ κύκλου περιφέρεια τριπλασία ἐστὶ τῆς διαμέτρου τοῦ κύκλου καὶ τῷ ζ' μέρει μείζων.

---

[40] *Geometrica* 12.32.4, 20.2.7.
[41] On Hero's place in the history of approximations to π see Knorr 1989: 479–83, 497–505.
[42] *Metrica* 1.30.1–2.

Those who have investigated with more precision add to the previously mentioned area of the segment 1/14 of the [square] on half of the base. So they appear to have followed the other method, according to which the circumference of the circle is triple the diameter of the circle plus 1/7 more.[43]

By emphasizing methodological developments like this, the text can also clearly define the limitations of each one. For example, the method referred to in *Metrica* 1.31 is defined as useful only for cases where the segment is less than a semicircle and where the base of the segment is less than three times the length of the perpendicular on it.[44] These very limitations then point the way toward 1.33, which will provide a new method that can be used accurately for cases where the approximation of 1.31 breaks down.[45] Hero's structure subordinates increasingly powerful and precise problem-solving strategies to a narrative of a developing tradition. Rather than a simple "handbook" providing the methods currently in vogue, Hero chooses to induct his reader into the very processes by which those methods developed, highlighting the advantages of more recent solutions precisely by raising the reader's awareness of the past tradition from which they grew.

Hero's emphasis on the continuous development of geometry as a discipline achieves some of its power by making the reader a witness to incremental improvements like these, while explicit disciplinary histories that foreground giants of the field mark some points of special interest along that path of development. Asper differentiates four techniques by which authors of commentaries integrate figures from the past into their own work, whether merely as names or as more fully developed "personae."[46] These techniques include simply putting names of authoritative figures "on parade," putting them in dialogue with one another and with lesser-known figures, developing them into exemplary "normative personae," and framing the commentator's own investigative work as having value comparable to that of the named predecessors.

While Hero's disciplinary histories are not situated in commentaries *per se*, Asper's typology could also be applied to the way Hero treats his

---

[43] *Metrica* 1.31.1–4.

[44] *Metrica* 1.31.15–19. The derivation and motivation behind the factor of three set out here are unclear; see Hero 2014: 225–26 n. 291.

[45] Another promise of an improved approximation, this one not credited to anyone else, appears at 1.18 (on finding the area of a pentagon) in an offhand final note – perhaps too offhand, as Acerbi and Vitrac note some reasons to doubt the improvement (Hero 2014: 195 n. 197).

[46] Asper 2019.

predecessors. The resemblance is closest in the later chapters of the *Definitiones*, many of which are in fact drawn from commentaries like Proclus' commentary to Euclid's *Elements*. Here more than anywhere else in the Heronian corpus, the prior mathematical work upon which the corpus so explicitly relies is often invoked under the names of some foundational figures in mathematics. These figures are sometimes invoked alongside details about their discoveries and contributions to the discipline and at other times simply as a string of famous names. Consider the capsule history of geometry in *Definitiones* 136 (one of the interpolated later chapters of the *Definitiones* that weaves a Neoplatonic intertext into the work). This little guide moves rapidly from the Egyptians to Thales, through a few other Greeks to Pythagoras and Anaxagoras, then to Plato, Eudoxus, and Euclid, with a few other Greek figures along the way.[47] Euclid is the only figure described by more than a name, and barely so: The author stops to establish him as coming not too long after Theaetetus and Eudoxus, who themselves were younger than Eratosthenes and Archimedes. By contrast, Asper notes how Pappus turns Euclid into a "normative persona" by portraying him as a respectful heir to Aristaeus' work on conics, in contrast to Apollonius' boastful manner.[48] Since Euclid's work on conics has vanished and Apollonius does not mention him in the surviving text, this characterization may be an original creation by Pappus. Whatever its foundation, Pappus' choice to present Euclid in these vivid and moralizing terms represents a very different approach to constructing mathematical heritage than the Heronian corpus offers.

The story told in *Definitiones* 136 is in fact an abridgement of the history of geometry Proclus provides in his commentary on the first book of Euclid's *Elements*.[49] Proclus' version, like the one in the *Definitiones*, begins in Egypt; after all, that is where most Greek histories of geometry begin.[50] Proclus fills in more detail about the Egyptians' motivations for developing the discipline, saying that it was a practical necessity for land measurement because the flooding of the Nile routinely obscured property boundaries. He compares it as well to the development of arithmetic among the Phoenicians, who needed it for commercial purposes. And so it goes, up through Euclid: Where Proclus gives some biographical information or professional highlight for most of the figures he names, in the

---

[47] *Definitiones* 136.1.1–16.    [48] Pappus, *Synagōgē* 7.67.25–678.4; Asper 2019: 6.

[49] Proclus, *In primum Euclidis elementorum librum commentarii* 64.16–68.23.

[50] For this trope, see, for example, Herodotus, *Historiae* 2.109; Diodorus Siculus, *Bibliotheca Historica* 1.69.5, 1.81.1–2; Strabo, *Geographica* 17.3.

*Definitiones* they are usually reduced to "names on parade" in Asper's sense. Even this brisk treatment represents a departure from the largely unpopulated landscapes of the "core" texts of the Heronian corpus, including the "authentic" early chapters of the *Definitiones*. Hero appeals to Euclid's name in the preface to the *Definitiones*, and the text is clearly closely modeled on the *Elements* in terms of structure and content. Yet Euclid's name only reappears for the first time in section 104, where Hero distinguishes between the Platonic solids treated by Euclid and the additional "semiregular" polyhedra described by Archimedes. Abridged though it is, the list in *Definitiones* 136 is quite faithful, omitting only Neoclides and his student Leon, younger contemporaries of Leodamas, until the enterprise of listing collapses after Eudoxus. The list in Proclus continues on after this point, adding several more mathematicians associated with the Academy.

*Definitiones* 138.3 offers another history – largely anonymous – of the developing definition of "mathematics (*mathēmatikē*)" as a discipline. The story as told here begins with the competing views of adherents of different philosophical schools, recalling Asper's categorization of certain commentaries as dialogues between multiple predecessors. The passage credits the Peripatetics with naming the discipline, arguing that "mathematics" is distinguished from other activities, such as rhetoric and poetry, by the necessity of the learning process for grasping the *theōria* of the discipline.[51] The Pythagoreans then stipulated that "mathematics" should embrace only geometry and arithmetic:

> ὅτι τὸ ἐπιστημονικὸν καὶ πρὸς μάθησιν ἐπιτηδείως ἔχον εὕρισκον ἐν αὐταῖς· περὶ γὰρ ἀίδια καὶ ἄτρεπτα καὶ εἰλικρινῆ ὄντα ἀναστρεφομένας ἑώρων, ἐν οἷς μόνοις ἐπιστήμην ἐνόμιζον.

> since they found in these something scientific and suitable for learning; for they saw them dwelling on the unseen and unchangeable and pure things, in which alone they considered scientific knowledge [to inhere].[52]

However, in this account the Pythagorean insistence on keeping one's eyes firmly fixed on the unseen and pure does not last long, as some "more recent (*neōteroi*)" people expanded the rubric of "mathematics" to include the study of sensible matter as well. Though the *neōteroi* are unidentified in the *Definitiones*, the shift in the view of mathematics corresponds to the

---

[51] *Definitiones* 138.3.2–8. This passage is credited to an "Anatolius," who, as Vitrac notes, is hard to identify unambiguously; see also "Anatolios of Laodikeia" in Keyser and Irby-Massie 2008: 73; Vitrac 2003: 9 n. 24.

[52] *Definitiones* 138.3.12–16.

history in Proclus that begins with the Pythagorean view of mathematics and the subsequent introduction of Geminus' classification of mathematical sciences embracing applications to sensible as well as intelligible objects.[53] In this view, the sensible world is part of the proper domain of mathematics, which is meant to engage with and describe a host of physical phenomena: Astronomy, optics, harmonics, mechanics, surveying, and logic are all listed here under the rubric of mathematics and the "theoretical (*theōrētikos*)." We will investigate the complexities of the "theoretical" throughout the Heronian corpus later, but for now let us simply note that in this passage of the *Definitiones* the discussion opens and closes with the importance of investigators' experiences of sensible objects. Rather than a list of famous names, in this case the text underlines paradigmatic efforts in the distinctively Heronian practice of connecting the mathematical and the material.

At the end of this same lengthy chapter 138, in a passage drawn from Theon's *De utilitate mathematicae*, the discussion turns from the school-based history to one of who is said to have made which discoveries in mathematics, which naturally invokes more individuals' names than the earlier part of the chapter.[54] Oinopides is credited with discovering how the zodiac encircles the celestial sphere and hence proposing the "great year" cycle; Thales with tracing the circuit of the sun; Anaximander with placing the Earth at the center of the cosmos; and Anaximenes with investigating the moon's reflection of sunlight by studying eclipses. These named discoveries are themselves all referred back to Eudemus' work on astrology at the beginning of the passage. At its end, further discoveries, including the rotation of the fixed stars and the planets, are chalked up to an anonymous "the rest (*loipoi*)."

Though the heavy interpolation of material from Proclus and others in the later chapters of the *Definitiones* is obvious, in an important sense this material is really at home in the Heronian corpus. The *Definitiones*, like many other Heronian texts, seeks to find an ordering scheme capacious enough to handle both geometrical and physical objects and, moreover, an order fashioned like Euclid's *Elements* so it will be accessible to all. None of the *neōteroi* are named here. Yet the expansion of mathematics' disciplinary boundaries attributed to them, whereby mathematical *theōria* becomes

---

[53] Proclus, *In primum Euclidis elementorum librum commentarii* 35.21–39.6. On the philosophical context of Geminus' classification and the taxonomic importance it gives to sensible and intelligible objects see Vitrac 2005: 274–77.

[54] *Definitiones* 138.11; Theon, *De utilitate mathematicae* 198.16–199.

applicable to sensible, material objects, matches up with Hero's own aims in the *Definitiones* and elsewhere. Even if not by name, then, Hero himself is dimly inscribed into the mathematical history in the interpolated chapters of the *Definitiones*. The interpolation itself builds on a strain of Pythagoreanism within the part of the *Definitiones* generally attributed to Hero himself, which Hero has put in dialogue with the more obvious Euclidean model.[55] Later on, as the Neoplatonic texts are entwined into the Heronian corpus, they are transformed in turn, finding a home in a new context where the application of mathematical techniques to material objects represents not merely the "uttermost echoes" of mathematics, but rather its most central concern.[56]

Archimedes stands out against the backdrop of mathematical predecessors who appear on a list of names with only vague links to their achievements, or who are blurred still further as members of an anonymous crowd of forebears. By contrast, Archimedes' name recurs frequently throughout the corpus, where his results are often signaled as foundational to Hero's own work. His *On the Sphere and Cylinder* is especially prominent, particularly the result immortalized as a finial on Archimedes' own tomb: that a cylinder having height equal to a sphere's diameter and a base equal to its great-circle circumference will have volume and surface area equal to 3/2 that of the sphere.[57] Archimedes appears most often in the metrological texts, where the proportional relationships he established between geometrical forms are often invoked to justify Hero's numerical results. Indeed, as Tybjerg notes, Archimedes is almost synonymous with "proof (*apodeixis*)" in the *Metrica*: Fourteen of nineteen mentions of Archimedes involve a form of *apodeiknumi*.[58]

Hero rarely replicates any part of Archimedes' proofs; results drawn from Archimedes are far more often pure inputs used to justify a secondary result. As Netz observes, the same pattern is typical of all surviving mathematical papyri besides the fragments of Euclid: a list of numerical problems in measuring various geometrical objects, providing instructions for how to carry out the calculations but not discussion of the theory

---

[55] On the Pythagorean elements in the *Definitiones* see Hero 2003: 116–22.

[56] Proclus, *In primum Euclidis elementorum librum commentarii* 28.25.

[57] *Metrica* 2.11.2, repeated at *Stereometrica* 1.1.1.2. The inscription was made famous by Cicero's claim to have discovered the tomb neglected and overgrown with bushes while he was serving as quaestor in Sicily (*Tusculan Disputations* 5.64–65; the tomb is also mentioned by Plutarch, *Marcellus* 17). On the rhetoric of the story as told by Cicero, who "usurped Archimedes' role as discoverer," see Jaeger 2002: 56.

[58] Tybjerg 2004: 33 n. 14.

behind the calculation methods.[59] So, for example, what is expressed by Archimedes as a general proportional relationship between the area of a sector of a circle and a rectangle bounded by the sector's arc and the circle's radius is transformed by Hero into a specific numerical relationship:

δέδεικται δὲ Ἀρχιμήδει ἐν τῇ τοῦ κύκλου μετρήσει, ὅτι πᾶς τομεὺς ἥμισύς ἐστι τοῦ περιεχομένου ὑπό τε τῆς τοῦ τομέως περιφερείας καὶ τῆς ἐκ τοῦ κέντρου τοῦ κύκλου, οὗ ἔστιν ὁ τομεύς· τὸ δὲ ὑπὸ τῶν ΑΒ ΒΓ ἐστὶ μονάδων ὑπ· τὸ ἄρα ἐμβαδὸν τοῦ τομέως ἔσται μονάδων σκ.

It has been shown by Archimedes in the *Measurement of the Circle* that every sector is half of [the rectangle] bounded by the arc of the sector and the [line] from the center of the circle of which it is a sector. The [rectangle bounded by] ΑΒ and ΒΓ is 440 units. Then the area of the sector will be 220 units.[60]

Even though the problems of the *Metrica* are not framed as real-world examples using concrete units, the reader is nevertheless invited to play out the proportional relationship on the sample numbers given in the problem statement.[61] The drama of the problems in the *Metrica* thus typically unfolds not through the construction of proofs themselves, but by using results proved in other works (which here are usually treated as givens, albeit not in a formal Euclidean sense) to generate new results and then certify them for specific objects or dimensions.

In the case of 1.37, the numerical example serves as part of a larger argument about the surface area of an isosceles cone. The sector of the circle is relevant because Hero proposes imagining rolling the cone around its center as a way of finding its surface area. In fact, he invites the reader to make the same imaginary maneuver in the *Automata* to prove that the moving automaton can be made to move in a circle on two differently sized wheels that are presented as cross-sections of a cone (see Figures 2.1–Figures 2.3).[62] There, however, the proof is purely geometrical, and the quantitative result drawn from Archimedes is irrelevant and so not present (though, as we will see in the next chapter, a different result from

---

[59] Netz 2011: 252. The various ways numerical calculations, geometrical analysis, and numerical or geometrical synthesis are combined in the *Metrica* can be seen in Acerbi and Vitrac's detailed overview of the work's problems (Hero 2014: 42–53). Particularly interesting are the cases where geometrical analysis and numerical synthesis are combined: 2.6, 2.8–9, 2.13, and 3.4–3.9.

[60] *Metrica* 1.37.20–25. Acerbi and Vitrac note (Hero 2014: 241 n. 318) that the proof does not survive in the *Measurement of the Circle* as we have it but is transmitted by Pappus in his commentary to Ptolemy's *Almagest* (258.20–260.23).

[61] The preface to *Metrica* 1 includes a programmatic statement that no concrete units will be used in the work: *Metrica* 1.pr.51–54.

[62] *Automata* 8.1–3.

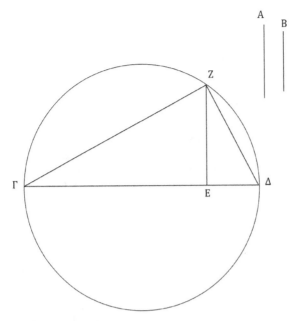

Figure 2.2  *Metrica* 3.17.

Archimedes about mechanical equilibrium is invoked). In the *Metrica*, Hero generally deploys geometrical results from Archimedes and other mathematicians not simply as noteworthy mathematical results, but as "inputs" for numerical calculations. Since numerical methods typically follow the geometrical analysis, the structure suggests a hierarchy in which the deductive proofs in the text serve the broader goal of producing techniques for numerical calculations.[63]

There are, to be sure, some passages in the text where its geometrical inheritance is put more purely on display, like a lengthy stretch of the third book (10–19) where the problems do not include numerical syntheses, though some do feature geometrical syntheses. As an example from this section (Figure 2.2), Hero recounts a method for cutting a sphere with a plane into two segments with any desired proportion between their surface areas not by choosing a proportion and working out a numerical example,

[63] The "synthetic" method in Greek mathematics proceeds formally from given objects and statements about their relationships to a deduced conclusion, whereas the "analytic" method is more or less a heuristic approach moving in the other direction. On the two methods, defined canonically by Pappus, see Pappus 1986: 66–70; Saito and Sidoli 2010. For clear case studies of the methods in action as pairs see Sidoli 2018.

but by providing a geometrical demonstration that follows the typical steps of a deductive proof fairly closely:

Σφαίρας δοθείσης καὶ λόγου τεμεῖν τὴν ἐπιφάνειαν τῆς σφαίρας ἐπιπέδῳ τινὶ, ὥστε τὰς ἐπι<φανείας> τῶν τμημάτων πρὸς ἀλλήλας λόγον ἔχειν τὸν αὐτὸν τῷ δοθέντι. ἔστω γὰρ ὁ δοθεὶς λόγος <ὁ> τῆς Α πρὸς τὴν Β. καὶ ἐκκείσθω ὁ μέγιστος κύκλος τῶν ἐν τῇ σφαίρᾳ, οὗ διάμετρος ἡ ΓΔ. καὶ τετμήσθω ἡ ΓΔ κατὰ τὸ Ε, ὥστε εἶναι ὡς τὴν Α πρὸς τὴν Β, οὕτως τὴν ΓΕ πρὸς τὴν ΕΔ . . .

Given a sphere and a ratio, [the problem is] to cut the surface of the sphere at some place, so that the surfaces of the segments have the same ratio to one another as the given one. Let the given ratio be that of A to B. And let a great circle on the sphere be laid out, whose diameter is ΓΔ. And let ΓΔ be cut at E, so that as A is to B, so ΓΕ is to ΕΔ . . .[64]

The proof proceeds through results drawn from Euclid and Archimedes, though it is only at the end that Archimedes receives credit for proving the result in the second book of his *Sphere and Cylinder*.[65] A few passages later, at *Metrica* 3.23, Hero will again adopt a geometrical approach for a closely related construction, again involving cutting a sphere with a plane, this time to generate segments whose volume (rather than surface area) has a given ratio. Once again Archimedes receives credit at the end of the passage for proving a result the proof draws on (indeed, in the *Sphere and Cylinder* the result directly follows the one used in *Metrica* 3.17).

The same result may of course be reused at multiple points in the same Heronian work. Sometimes Hero explicitly points out such repetitions, as in the case of a result derived from Archimedes' *Method* that a figure bounded by a straight line and a parabolic section of a right cone occupies an area 4/3 the size of the triangle with the same base and height as the section of the parabola. He delivers this result at *Metrica* 1.32 and then repeats it at *Metrica* 1.35, with a reminder that the reader has seen this result recently (ὡς προείρηται).[66] Results from Euclid are often used repeatedly in adjacent or nearby problems, as in 1.12 and 1.13, which refer to several of the same Euclidean propositions as well as explicitly referring to earlier proofs from the *Metrica*.[67] Such reminders are not only a convenience for the reader, but also a marker of the text's own internal

---

[64] *Metrica* 3.17.1–8.     [65] Hero 2014: 345.
[66] However, Acerbi and Vitrac suggest the repetition might be a reason to doubt the authenticity of this passage (Hero 2014: 231 n. 302).
[67] Acerbi and Vitrac catalog these internal references at Hero 2014: 42–54.

coherence.[68] The connection between two different results from the same work of Archimedes may likewise build continuity between the otherwise discrete chapters of the *Metrica*. So, in the second book of the *Metrica*, Hero refers in two adjacent passages to two different results from the *Method*:

ἀποδέδειχεν Ἀρχιμήδης ἐν τῷ ἐφοδικῷ, ὅτι τὸ τοιοῦτον τμῆμα ἕκτον μέρος ἐστὶ τοῦ στερεοῦ παραλληλεπιπέδου τοῦ βάσιν μὲν ἔχοντος τὸ περιγραφόμενον περὶ τὴν βάσιν τοῦ κυλίνδρου τετράγωνον, ὕψος δὲ τὸ αὐτὸ τῷ τμήματι.

Archimedes has shown in the *Method* that such a segment is a sixth part of the solid parallelepiped having as base the rectangle drawn around the base of the cylinder, and height equal to the segment.[69]

Ὁ δ’ αὐτὸς Ἀρχιμήδης ἐν τῷ αὐτῷ βιβλίῳ δείκνυσιν, ὅτι ἐὰν εἰς κύβον δύο κύλινδροι διωσθῶσιν τὰς βάσεις ἔχοντες ἐφαπτομένας τῶν πλευρῶν τοῦ κύβου, τὸ κοινὸν τμῆμα τῶν κυλίνδρων δίμοιρον ἔσται τοῦ κύβου.

The same Archimedes in the same book shows that if two cylinders with bases touching the edges of a cube intersect, the common segment of the cylinders will be 2/3 of the cube.[70]

In the second passage the *Method* is not identified explicitly as the work in question; that information must be gained from the previous passage, encouraging the reader to read the text continuously even though its discrete problem-based structure might otherwise suggest the text could be dipped into at will.

The *Metrica* is structured as a series of problems threaded together with microhistories of their refinement at the hands of past mathematicians both named and unnamed, all in the service of developing increasingly accurate methods for measuring objects of all shapes. It thus naturally lends itself to the same kind of evolutionary history of the discipline as we find in the *Belopoeica*, albeit a more diffuse narrative than that text's focused framework of responses to emergent battlefield needs. The discipline gradually unfolds to reveal what was previously dark and even undreamt-of, which itself makes aggregative, systematizing work like Hero's vitally necessary. As we saw earlier, the preface to the first book of the *Metrica* valorizes the ongoing work of collection and correction that

---

[68] Such a deliberate structuring move within a single text is, of course, quite different from the repeated instances of a given result that emerge from compilation and interpolation, as happens in this case when this result is repeated at *Stereometrica* 1.93.

[69] *Metrica* 2.14.4–8.    [70] *Metrica* 2.15.1–5.

constantly recreates geometry and other disciplines, in which Hero himself takes part.[71] Nor is this evolutionary process subject to any natural end. Archimedes and Eudoxus did not exhaust the supply of results, as some problems remained to plague even more recent mathematicians:

καὶ ἐπειδὴ οὐκ ἐξήρκει τὰ πρῶτα ἐπινοηθέντα θεωρήματα, προσεδεήθησαν ἔτι περισσοτέρας ἐπισκέψεως, ὥστε καὶ μέχρι νῦν τινὰ αὐτῶν ἀπορεῖσθαι, καίτοι Ἀρχιμήδους τε καὶ Εὐδόξου γενναίως ἐπιβεβληκότων τῇ πραγματείᾳ.

And since the theorems that were initially conceived of did not suffice, they demanded yet further investigation, so that some of them had no answer even until now, even though Archimedes and Eudoxus applied outstanding effort to the discipline.[72]

The continuity between the interventions of figures like Archimedes and Eudoxus and the moment of their inclusion in the Heronian corpus is enhanced not only by references to specific texts and theorems, but by the very fact that those ancestral figures left certain problems unsolved.

A characteristic of the Heronian corpus: The boundary between past traditions and present developments remains somewhat fluid, the author a porous gatekeeper between the two. A long and living history of metrical problems stretches from a deep and murkily understood Egyptian prehistory, to the giants like Archimedes who contributed results that continue to bear fruit, to the mathematicians who will follow in their footsteps and solve the problems that still remain. Within this history, Hero does not cast himself as a savior who will step in and solve the stubborn problems, but as a collector, cataloger, and systematizer of the discipline as it stands. He thus situates himself in a kind of textual "imaginary community," in dialogue with past and future author–practitioners, where a well-cultivated trove of past knowledge updated with his own more recent findings is the ideal bequest to those who will come after him.

## Elements of Euclid

Euclid seems to have special significance as a predecessor for Hero, who makes liberal use of results from Euclid in texts like the *Metrica*, derives much of the material in his *Definitiones* from Euclid's *Elements*, and is credited with writing a commentary to the *Elements* itself. In keeping with his typical impersonality, in the "core" texts Hero seldom references Euclid by name, though his debts are clear; we have already seen that the later

---

[71] *Metrica* 1.pr.21–25.     [72] *Metrica* 1.pr.7–11.

contributions to the Heronian corpus much more often name Euclid's contributions explicitly. Some of these references are generic, situating Euclid as one of the cornerstones of the mathematical edifice that has been constructed by Hero's own time. The brief history of geometry drawn from Proclus in *Definitiones* 136 places Euclid among the defining figures of mathematics, featured alongside Plato and Archimedes as in Proclus, with the novel additions of Aristotle, Zeno, Apollonius, and Eudoxus.[73]

Euclid does not simply play the role of a generic mathematical "founding father" in the Heronian corpus; he has a special identity as the composer of the *Elements*. The *Definitiones* in particular will rely on the *Elements* as a model, as Hero indicates in the preface:

Καὶ τὰ μὲν πρὸ τῆς γεωμετρικῆς στοιχειώσεως τεχνολογούμενα ὑπογράφων σοι καὶ ὑποτυπούμενος, ὡς ἔχει μάλιστα συντόμως, Διονύσιε λαμπρότατε, τήν τε ἀρχὴν καὶ τὴν ὅλην σύνταξιν ποιήσομαι κατὰ τὴν τοῦ Εὐκλείδου τοῦ στοιχειωτοῦ τῆς ἐν γεωμετρίᾳ θεωρίας διδασκαλίαν· οἶμαι γὰρ οὕτως οὐ μόνον τὰς ἐκείνου πραγματείας εὐσυνόπτους ἔσεσθαί σοι, ἀλλὰ καὶ πλείστας ἄλλας τῶν εἰς γεωμετρίαν ἀνηκόντων. ἄρξομαι τοίνυν ἀπὸ σημείου.

Writing out and outlining for you as concisely as possible the rules prescribed for the elementalization of geometry, most illustrious Dionysius, I will set out the principle and the whole organization according to Euclid the elementalizer's teaching of the *theōria* in geometry. For I think that in this way not only will his material be easy for you to see at a glance, but also most of the rest of what pertains to geometry. I shall begin now from the point.[74]

Hero's aim for this text will be to fit geometrical objects of all kinds into a Euclidean format, which he views as the optimal textual structure for facilitating the reader's understanding of how individual components make up a connected whole.

Several Heronian texts refer to a "Euclidean" organizational scheme, and the term appears to have a spectrum of meanings as it is deployed throughout the corpus. The principal associations with Euclid's name have to do with the "elemental" construction of a substance, a text, a device, or a methodological toolbox from increasingly complex combinations of relatively simple building blocks.[75] What it meant in antiquity to be

---

[73] *Definitiones* 136.1; Proclus, *In primum Euclidis elementorum librum commentarii* 68.4–10.

[74] *Definitiones* pr.1.1–9.

[75] On the significance of works with the *Elements* label and other invocations of *stoicheiōsis* see Asper 2001b. See also Netz 2017: 386–88. On the broader usage history of the term *stoicheion* see Crowley 2005.

"systematic" in the same way as Euclid of course depends on the textual form in which readers would have encountered him. Netz observes that the surviving population of papyri and ostraka suggests the *Elements* was in fact usually not owned as a "collected works" or even as "collected Elements," but as individual books.[76] The Euclidean system praised by Hero and others might thus have been encountered principally as an ordering of propositions at the level of the book, rather than the higher-level ordering of books into the *Elements* as a whole. In return for Hero's enthusiastic perpetuation of the Euclidean "elemental" tradition within his own works, it seems he enjoyed some success in inscribing himself into that tradition: Pappus describes the account of centers of mass given in his *Mechanica* as "element-like (*stoicheiōdēs*)," and he promises to follow this order in his own introductory account.[77]

Euclid is often given the epithet "elementalizer (*stoicheiōtēs*)," in the Heronian corpus and elsewhere. So, for example, in the later part of the *Definitiones* the definitions of commensurable and incommensurable magnitudes are credited to Euclid, and the author presents himself as "following Euclid the elementalizer (Εὐκλείδη τῷ στοιχειωτῇ ἑπόμενοι)."[78] Pappus distinguishes him thus alongside Apollonius and Aristaeus as the three mathematicians whom he credits with having developed the "analytic" and "synthetic" methods.[79] In his commentary to Euclid's *Data*, Marinus praises the broad applicability of the theory of givens, and in particular its development by Euclid, "whom they also properly denote 'Elementalizer.'"[80] The name is so deserved, says Marinus, because Euclid extracted the "elements" not only of geometry, but also astronomy, music, and optics, and he arranged them all in eisagogic form in their proper volumes.[81] The association between Euclid's harmonic work and his "Elementalizer" nickname is raised later on in Porphyry's commentary to Ptolemy's *Harmonics*, where "Euclid, the elementalizer himself (αὐτὸς ὁ στοιχειωτὴς Εὐκλείδης)" is invoked alongside Dionysius of Halicarnassus and Archytas as having written in terms of harmonic intervals rather than ratios.[82]

These are, of course, just a few of a vast number of references to Euclid and his "elemental" work, and even in this small sample it is apparent that

---

[76] Netz 2011: 248.   [77] Pappus, *Synagōgē* 8.1034.1–6.   [78] *Definitiones* 128.4.
[79] Pappus, *Synagōgē* 7.634.7–10.   [80] Marinus, *Commentarium in Euclidis Data* 254.5–19.
[81] Marinus, *Commentarium in Euclidis Data* 254.13–20. On the "givens" see Acerbi 2011; Sidoli 2018.
[82] Porphyry, Εἰς τὰ ἁρμονικὰ Πτολεμαίου ὑπόμνημα 92.19–93.4.

"elementalizing" is not at all limited to geometry.[83] Asper analyzes the broader literary tradition in which Euclid's *Elements* participates, arguing that texts marked by unity on the level of the problem or theorem, highly standardized vocabulary and syntax, and impersonal forms of address serve to present the material in a space without place, time, author, or other historical context – all indeed very Heronian attributes.[84]

The significance and capacities of the "elemental" text are more explicitly defined by Proclus in his commentary to the first book of Euclid's *Elements*. He introduces Euclid as having come after a host of geometrical forebears, who left a legacy of work that Euclid subjects to manipulations comparable to those we have seen performed and claimed by Hero. Euclid is shown compiling (*synagagōn*) his *Elements* as the end product of a process of having arranged (*syntaxas*) material from Eudoxus, perfecting (*teleōsamenos*) Theaetetus' work, and subjecting to more rigorous demonstration material that had been treated haphazardly by other predecessors.[85]

While Proclus acknowledges the wide range of Euclid's writings, he singles out the *Elements* for special admiration because of its systematic organization (*taxis*) and selectivity (*eklogē*). He praises Euclid on the grounds that although he had access to much more material than appears in the final work, he picked out only the suitably "elementary" material.[86] Proclus later clarifies that the material for inclusion in a text like the *Elements* should be aimed at a comprehensive general understanding of the subject rather than an exploration of its details, as such "overly-minute slicing and dicing (τὰ γὰρ εἰς τὰ μερικώτερα τεμαχίζοντα)" is not conducive to learning.[87] Moreover, the *Elements* represents not just a subset of geometrical material suitable for beginners, but a maximally economical coherent system; if any part of it is removed, says Proclus, the reader would be subject to falling into error.[88] Careful arrangement, painstaking selectivity, a synoptic perspective, and completeness without excess: These qualities made Euclid's *Elements* the perfect text for newcomers to

---

[83] A few Byzantine references that are of particular interest in this context include George Pachymeres' commentary to Aristotle's *Metaphysics* 3.1.25–27; the emperor Theodorus' *Sermones VIII de theologia christiana* 7.128–33; and Demetrius Chomatenus' Ποιήματα διάφορα 109.28–32. While all these instances use Euclid in a similar way, the chronological and disciplinary range over which he is invoked with this epithet is remarkable.

[84] Asper 2001b: 74–79.   [85] Proclus, *In primum Euclidis elementorum librum commentarii* 68.4–10.

[86] Proclus, *In primum Euclidis elementorum librum commentarii* 69.5–9.

[87] Proclus, *In primum Euclidis elementorum librum commentarii* 73.25–74.9.

[88] Proclus, *In primum Euclidis elementorum librum commentarii* 69.24–70.1.

geometry, and Hero too will single these out as principles for constructing his own "elementary" texts.

The brief preface of the *Definitiones* starts by establishing the work's Euclidean *bona fides* in the dedication to Dionysius.[89] Though named dedicatees are not uncommon in prefaces to Greek and Roman technical works, they are almost unheard of in the Heronian corpus, as Hero generally limits personal references to himself and the unnamed readers whose interests he promises to serve through his writing.[90] Dionysius is the sole exception, as Hero makes him a personal promise to present surveying problems as efficiently as possible, conveniently organized according to the principles of Euclid's *Elements*.[91] However, this attractively organized and concise work is not meant for Dionysius' sole benefit; Hero immediately clarifies that he hopes that it will turn out to be an easy way to get a grip on geometry not for him alone, but also many other newcomers to the discipline.[92] By following Euclid's organizational scheme Hero hopes his own text will achieve the same didactic utility, making his material as "readily grasped (*eusynoptos*)" as Euclid's own. He begins making good on this promise right away, saying that "I will begin, then, from the point (ἄρξομαι τοίνυν ἀπὸ σημείου)" – perhaps the most Euclidean possible start to a text.[93]

## *Manipulating the* Elements

Euclid's is clearly a name to conjure with, and Hero has no qualms about invoking the Euclidean "brand" to motivate his own projects. This does not mean simply rehashing work already done by Euclid, however. Like other past authors, Euclid is subject to correction and expansion. For example, Hero incorporates an update to Euclid's list of solids in his own homage to Euclid, the *Definitiones*: Whereas Euclid only thought to discuss inscribing the five Platonic solids into the sphere, Hero says Archimedes had added eight more.[94] Hero makes a more significant adjustment to Euclid's approach early in the *Definitiones*. This work expands on the typical set of Euclidean objects, mapping them onto objects in the material world. In moving the objects of his analysis out

---

[89] *Definitiones* pr.1.1–9.

[90] For a quantitative study of features like addressees in mathematical prefaces from Autolycos to Damien, accompanied by extensive qualitative discussion of their historical and literary context, see Vitrac 2008b.

[91] *Definitiones* pr.1–6.     [92] On Dionysus see Asper 2001a; see also Corcoran 1995: 378.

[93] *Definitiones* 1.9.

[94] *Definitiones* 104. In fact, Archimedes had proposed thirteen semiregular polyhedra, not eight. On Hero's claims here and the polyhedra themselves see Hero 2003: 332–33.

of the purely geometrical domain and into the real world, Hero makes a remarkable alteration to the Euclidean definition of a solid:

Στερεόν ἐστι σῶμα τὸ μῆκος καὶ πλάτος καὶ βάθος ἔχον ἢ τὸ ταῖς τρισὶ διαστάσεσι κεχρημένον. καλοῦνται δὲ στερεὰ σώματα καὶ οἱ τόποι. σῶμα μὲν οὖν μαθηματικόν ἐστι τὸ τριχῆ διαστατόν, σῶμα δὲ ἁπλῶς τὸ τριχῆ διαστατὸν μετὰ ἀντιτυπίας.

A solid is a body having length, width, and depth, or one making use of three dimensions. Spaces are also called solid bodies. A mathematical body is three-dimensional, while body plain and simple is three-dimensional with an *antitypia*.[95]

What is the *antitypia* that distinguishes mathematical bodies from "body" in the more general sense? It is obviously something different from a "surface" in the sense of an *epiphaneia*, and the context here suggests a material rather than a mathematical object. Aristotle uses the verb *antitypein* in the *Meteorologica* to refer to the resistance wind encounters as it tries to flow through a narrow passage.[96] Thwarted, it causes shocks Aristotle compares to a throbbing sensation in the body (a similar effect occurs when winds run into one another). *Antitypos* appears twice in the Peripatetic *Problems*, once referring to the resistance of hard ground that fatigues those who walk upon it, and once to the resistance encountered by gourds grown in a confining receptacle in order to give them a desirable shape.[97] Galen often refers to *antitypia* as a symptom of inflammations like redness and swelling, recalling Aristotle's comparison of the trapped wind to a throbbing in the body.[98] He often pairs it with the pulse, suggesting that *antitypia* is a quality the physician must judge by touch. These cases suggest that *antitypia* is the resistance something living, moving, or growing encounters when it runs up against something unyielding.

Sextus Empiricus, who, like Galen, was a physician but is best known as a member of the Pyrrhonist Skeptical school, similarly relates *antitypia* to touch. Like Hero, he places *antitypia* in the broader context of the quality of "resistance" any body may possess in addition to length, breadth, and depth. After introducing *antitypia* as a quality "some" use (along with length, breadth, and depth) to define body, he then argues that "if

[95] *Definitiones* 11.   [96] Aristotle, *Meteor.* 368a1–7, 370b17–19.
[97] *Problemata* 885a36, 932b27. Theophrastus mentions the practice of shaping gourds in containers at *Hist. Plant.* 7.3.5, and the constrained gourd's growth is compared to that of the fetus in the womb in the Hippocratic *De natura pueri*, section 9.
[98] See, for example, *De methodo medendi*, Kühn, *Claudii Galeni Opera Omnia* v. 10 pp. 948, 973–75; *De differentia pulsuum*, Kühn v. 8 p. 689.

*antitypia* is grasped, it must be grasped through touch (αὕτη γὰρ εἴπερ καταλαμβάνεται, ἁφῇ καταλαμβάνοιτο ἄν)."[99] While he unsurprisingly goes on to argue that touch is ungraspable and therefore *antitypia* is too, for non-Skeptical readers *antitypia* resonates with less specialized definitions like Galen's as the quality of embodied objects that engages the sense of touch by resisting against it. *Antitypia* recurs in the *Adversus mathematicos* as a quality inseparable from body, just as yielding is inseparable from void or accidents are inseparable from the things to which they occur.[100]

*Antitypia* thus appears in these texts as an addition to the geometrical attributes of length, breadth, and width, which renders bodies in the world sensible through touch (except from a Skeptical viewpoint where nothing is really sensible). Yet when the Euclidean project is examined in the first book of the *Geometrica*, the relationship of the *antitypia* to the Euclidean world is subverted:

> ἐπιγέγραπται δὲ στοιχεῖα, διότι ὁ μὴ διὰ τούτων πρότερον ἀχθεὶς οὐχ οἷός τέ ἐστι συνιέναι τι τῶν γεωμετρικῶν θεωρημάτων. ἡ δὲ γεωμετρία ἐξ ἀφαιρέσεως τὴν διδασκαλίαν ἐποιήσατο· λαβοῦσα γὰρ φυσικὸν σῶμα, ὅ ἐστι τριχῇ διαστατὸν μετὰ ἀντιτυπίας, καὶ χωρίσασα τούτου τὴν ἀντιτυπίαν ἐποιήσατο τὸ μαθηματικὸν σῶμα, ὅ ἐστι στερεόν, καὶ ἀφαιροῦσα κατήντησεν ἐπὶ τὸ σημεῖον.

> The *Elements* were written because anyone who has not first been led through these is not suited to grasp any of the geometrical theorems. Geometry created its teaching from abstraction: taking a physical body, which is a three-dimensional extension with an *antitypia*, and separating off this *antitypia*, it created the mathematical body, which is a solid, and continuing to abstract it arrived at the point.[101]

This version of geometry's conceptual development is still situated in a world where the *Elements* takes pride of place as a didactic tool. However, here the "elemental" orthodoxy of constructing objects from less to more complex (point, line, surface) is turned on its head. Following a conventional construction that moves from point to solid via line and surface, geometry is here portrayed as beginning with the "physical" body and creating the "mathematical" ones through a process of *subtraction*: Here we move from the solid, firm body to the mathematical "solid," and thence

---

[99] *Antitypia* is introduced at Sextus Empiricus, *Pyrrhonae hypotyposes* 3.39.1–2; its relationship to touch is found at *PH* 3.45.1–2. The term is later used by Iamblichus (*De communi mathematica scientia* 34.14–20), where it refers to the quality of sensible things (as opposed to mathematical objects) that allows them to cast a shadow. On this passage and its commentary by Philoponus see Hero 2003: 283.

[100] Sextus Empiricus, *Adversus mathematicos* 10.221.4–222.4.　　　[101] *Geometrica* 1.1.34–41.

eventually to the point. The *Geometrica* is one of the more philologically troubled texts of the Heronian corpus, so tracing the conceptual shifts that shaped the remarkable reversal expressed here is impossible. We can at least say that maneuvers like this in the Heronian corpus bring philosophical work like Sextus Empiricus' on bodies and surfaces into a new context. The very variety and multivocality of the Heronian corpus creates a conceptual space where the geometrical and material worlds intersect complexly, neither ceding definitively to the other even when Euclid is invoked or material objects are in play.

## Elemental Bodies, Elemental Texts

The *Elements* is a particularly important reference for the *Pneumatica*, where Hero adopts the structural principles of Euclid's work even when it is not identified by name. The "elements" in the *Pneumatica* are sometimes the microscopic building blocks of physical substances, sometimes the individual subassemblies of complex devices, sometimes explanatory passages in texts or even whole books. The text begins with a very lengthy preface, which indeed accounts for more than a tenth of its total length. It covers, among other topics, how matter is constituted from particles and void, how to construct a device to demonstrate the existence of void experimentally, and why this experimental approach is superior to the endless ongoing philosophical debates over the existence of void.

Diels speculated that the theory of matter advanced in Hero's preface originated with Strato of Lampsacus (who succeeded Theophrastus as head of the Lyceum) and was likely adopted by Hero from Philo.[102] This view remained more or less standard for over a century, but more recently Berryman has called some of Diels' assumptions into question. First, she observes that its very characterization as a "theory" seems misplaced, since Hero himself says he has drawn from multiple sources, and he gives a number of explanations for the effects described in the preface, not all of which seem to emerge from a unified theory of matter and void.[103] Second, she argues that Hero's explanations for rarefaction effects are known from authors who predate Strato (including Democritus and Plato), whereas his explanation of how air particles can be packed closely together and then spring forcefully back to their original volume seems to be a "new view of matter."[104] Hero packs this new approach in among his eclectic gathering of older ideas – as we have seen, a typical authorial move for Hero.

---

[102] Diels 1893.    [103] Berryman 2009: 165–70.    [104] Berryman 2011.

Whatever its sources, Hero's preface argues that substances that comprise bodies in the world generally consist of mixtures of particles of the four elements arranged in different ways and threaded through with small interstitial voids. These complexes of elemental particles and void may be altered by the application or removal of heat. For example, he explains that applying heat to a cupping glass causes the matter contained in it to rarefy, since fire tends to reduce particles of matter down to their elemental water, air, and earth.[105] Burning coals can show more clearly what exactly happens in this process, for the fire again separates out the elements, allowing the subtler components to rise up toward the domain of fire, the moderate ones to hover in air, and the densest to sift toward the earth.[106] Within the Earth, too, the purer water rises up as dew at night, because the sun is then heating up the opposite side of the world, driving the dew up to the surface where it evaporates into the air through the application of the sun to the near surface during the day.[107] Natural and artificial systems alike operate through the same kind of elemental interplay.

At the end of the lengthy preface, Hero summarizes how the existence of interstitial voids may be proven by readily observable examples, from rays of light passing through one another to wine mixing with water. He then makes some promises about the form and content of the work to come:

> τούτων δὴ διασεσαφηνισμένων ἑξῆς τὰ διὰ τῆς συμπλοκῆς τῶν εἰρημένων στοιχείων ἐπιτελούμενα θεωρήματα γράψομεν. ἔστι γὰρ δι' αὐτῶν εὑρίσκειν πάνυ ποικίλας καὶ θαυμασίας κινήσεις.

> With these things having been clarified in order, we will write down the completed *theōrēmata* about the interweaving of the elements mentioned. For it is possible through them to discover many varied and marvelous motions.[108]

The word "*epiteloumena*" seems to suggest that he will aim at a kind of combinatorial completeness in his observations of how the elements combine, matching the variety of natural phenomena to the cavalcade of devices to come. What are the *theōrēmata* here? They are something subject to inscription (*graphein*), pertaining to how elemental particles move and interact, through which it will be possible to discover a full spectrum of elemental-level physical principles. We will see in more detail in the next chapter how Hero uses *theōria* and its cognates to denote a set

---

[105] *Pneumatica* 1.pr.98–108.     [106] *Pneumatica* 1.pr.108–24.     [107] *Pneumatica* 1.pr.124–34.
[108] *Pneumatica* 1.pr.343–47.

of strategies for exploring the natural world using artificial tools. For now, let us focus on how the elements structure not only the natural and artificial objects he describes, but the text in which he situates them.

Far from abandoning his "elemental" promise as a conceit of the premise, Hero treats it seriously as a building block of the treatise proper, as the main text begins by immediately invoking the "elements" again:

> Τούτων δὴ προτεθεωρημένων στοιχείου ἕνεκα γράφομεν καὶ περὶ τῶν καμπύλων σιφώνων· εἰς πολλὰ γὰρ τῶν πνευματικῶν εὔχρηστοι τυγχάνουσιν.

> These things having been theorized in advance, in the interest of the elemental we write also about bent siphons. For they turn out to be most useful for many of the pneumatic devices.[109]

The siphon is a neat device to carry the preface's "elements" theme into the main text's program of exploration. The first few sections of the text each describe a different type of siphon, allowing the reader to see how a simple principle can be expanded and varied to produce a suite of different effects. Hero introduces the simplest form at the beginning and, having delivered his lesson on how it works, proceeds to introduce some more complicated variations: The standard bent siphon is first, followed by the concentric siphon, then a siphon that keeps the flow of liquid at a steady rate, then one that combines uniform and nonuniform flows.

Hero then transitions from siphons to devices that use siphons as components, marking another stage in his expansion of "elements" from microscopic to macroscopic. He uses the word a little later on to refer to the components of a device:

> Τῶν δὲ εἰς ἐνέργειαν κατασκευαζομένων νῦν ἀρξώμεθα κατασκευὰς ποιεῖσθαι ἀπὸ τῶν μικροτέρων ἀρξάμενοι στοιχείου χάριν.

> Now let us begin to construct the designs for the things designed to achieve effects, beginning from the lesser, for the sake of the elemental.[110]

Having impressed upon the reader that "elements" are to be regarded not only as units of bulk matter but an order also reflected on the macroscopic scale of the devices themselves, he does not continue to repeat the term explicitly throughout the treatise.[111] Meißner argues that the "elemental" structure of the text represents the reader's induction into the practice of pneumatics, beginning with the first components one would engage with as a practitioner.[112] Tybjerg reads Hero's explanation of his text as

---

[109] *Pneumatica* 1.1.1–3.    [110] *Pneumatica* 1.7.1–3.
[111] I discuss this structure briefly at Roby 2016b: 290–93.    [112] Meißner 1999: 60.

structured "στοιχείου χάριν" as a strategy for building a "geometry of machines."[113]

The links between the simpler "elements" of the preface and the more complex assemblies in the text are sometimes indicated less formally, through echoes of form or operating principle. Several of the simple, commonplace examples used in the preface to illustrate the microscopic interactions of the elements also serve as bridges to the devices Hero will describe in the main body of the text. So, for example, he describes how when a lamp runs out of oil, its flame can no longer rise up steadily but is increasingly mixed up with thicker air until it "becomes air itself."[114] The main text then features a lampstand designed so that whenever the lamp's oil supply dwindles, it is replenished from a reservoir below the lamp by turning a tap on the other end of the lampstand. Two subsequent variants make the new oil flow in by blowing on an external tube or by allowing water to flow into the stand's base so as to raise the level of the oil.[115] The reader is thus encouraged to reflect back on the example in the preface and consider how these more complex new designs address the physical process described there. Likewise, the preface uses a steaming cauldron and coals that burn down to embers to help the reader understand the separation of heated matter into denser and rarer components; images that are recalled in a water boiler (*miliarion*) in the second book. This device features a figure that blows on coals placed over the boiler, their heat communicated as steam by internal pipes "just as we see steam carried up from the water in heated kettles."[116]

Even Hero's arguments about how the physics of elemental interaction operate on the scale of the Earth as a whole are echoed in miniature in two devices juxtaposed in the main text. The first is a "model cosmos (ὑπόδειγμα τοῦ κόσμου)" in which a small sphere rests between two larger hemispheres of water and air.[117] The second, called the "spring," more directly illustrates the solar-powered hydrological cycle of the preface.[118] A sphere and a funnel mounted on a hollow base are connected by a siphon. Water is introduced into the sphere, enough that when the air inside is heated by the sun it compresses the water, which percolates out via the siphon, much as Hero argued the dew emerges from the Earth as the sun shines on its other side. When the device is placed in the shade to cool down, the condensing air in the sphere causes the siphon to draw the water back up. While the "spring" is not explicitly described as a model of the Earth, the

---

[113] Tybjerg 2004: 50.     [114] *Pneumatica* 1.pr.168–76.     [115] *Pneumatica* 2.22–24.
[116] *Pneumatica* 2.34.     [117] *Pneumatica* 2.7.     [118] *Pneumatica* 2.8.

reader has been primed to think in these terms both by the discussion in the preface and by the "model cosmos" that immediately precedes it.

As the more complex devices of the main text resonate with the reader's memories of the simpler devices and explanations of elemental behavior (first pure, then mixed) in the preface, they are thus encouraged to contemplate the twin Euclidean expansions of text and matter from simple to complex. Indeed, the connection between the building blocks of text and of matter extends not only to the *Pneumatica*'s internal interconnections, but also to the way the text as a whole will fit in with other parts of his own corpus:

ἀκόλουθον δὲ εἶναι νομίσαντες τῇ τῶν ὑδρίων ὡροσκοπείων ἕξει, ἥτις ἡμῖν ἐν τέσσαρσι βιβλίοις προαναγέγραπται, ταύτην συνεχῆ ὑπάρχειν γράφομεν καὶ περὶ αὐτῆς, ὡς προείρηται· διὰ γὰρ συμπλοκῆς ἀέρος καὶ πυρὸς καὶ ὕδατος καὶ γῆς καὶ τῶν τριῶν στοιχείων ἢ καὶ τῶν τεσσάρων συμπλεκομένων ποικίλαι διαθέσεις ἐνεργοῦνται, αἱ μὲν ἀναγκαιοτάτας τῷ βίῳ τούτῳ χρείας παρέχουσαι, αἱ δὲ ἐκπληκτικόν τινα θαυμασμὸν ἐπιδεικνύμεναι.

Considering it to follow upon the structure of the work *On water-clocks* which was previously written up by us in four books, we write about this as well, to fit contiguously with it, as said earlier. For through the interweaving of air and fire and water and earth, and the three or four interwoven elements, manifold designs are put into action, some providing the most necessary utilities for this life, and others demonstrating a surprising wonder.[119]

While Hero does not here make completely explicit the pivot he will eventually effect on the word *stoicheia*, the parallel between physical and textual "elements" is already clear. The physical elements are simple building blocks that are "interwoven" into more complex and varied configurations, some useful and others wondrous. Individual books of texts are here likewise presented as building blocks that can be assembled according to a structural logic of their own into more complex configurations: first as whole texts and then as components of a coherent corpus that fits together in a particular way. Hero's prior work on water clocks has its own "structure (*hexis*)," a term normally applied to external or internal structures of living things: the postures and positions of human or plant bodies or the skills and habits imprinted on the mind or body. The organic logic of Hero's corpus then demands that the work on water clocks be interwoven with a new aggregation of books: The *Pneumatica* will grow "contiguously" with it.

---

[119] *Pneumatica* I.pr.9–17.

The parallel between the elements of matter and verbal or textual elements is, of course, not unique to Hero. Indeed, as Crowley observes, the use of *stoicheion* for a unit of matter is likely to have been adapted metaphorically from its use as terminology for a letter of the alphabet, probably by Plato or a close contemporary.[120] Crowley argues that both the "alphabet" and "matter" domains are invoked by Plato casually enough to indicate that the metaphorical transfer had already been normalized by that time, binding the two uses closely together.[121] When Aristotle defines *stoicheion* in the *Metaphysics* as a primary and indivisible component of anything, he begins from the "elements" of a sound or a syllable, before moving on to "elements of bodies" as an extension of that basic idea, and "elements of diagrams" as a further step still.[122] Geometrical diagrams lead naturally to proofs (*apodeixeis*), whose *stoicheia* can be viewed as "primary syllogisms (συλλογισμοὶ οἱ πρῶτοι)" that may be built up into new, more complex proofs. Other uses of the term, for Aristotle, require a metaphorical leap.

Proclus likewise begins by noting that letters can be considered "elements" of words and sentences, before going on to apply this term specifically to texts consisting of propositions (especially mathematical propositions), where it has special significance.[123] Among theorems (*theōrēmata*), he says, there is a subset called "elements (*stoicheia*)" and another called "elementary (*stoicheiōdē*)," plus of course many that do not meet the criteria for either category. "Element" theorems are those whose contemplation (*theōria*) leads to knowledge of the rest and through which it is possible to resolve difficulties.[124] "Elementary" theorems are defined by their outstanding simplicity and grace, as well as their applicability to a multitude of tasks, but they are distinguished from "element" theorems because they contribute knowledge that does not extend to every part of geometry.[125] Proclus later goes on to reconcile the physicist's "elements" of air, fire, water, and earth with the geometer's "elements" of point and line, which in Proclus' view are simpler than the physical elements.[126]

---

[120] Crowley 2005: 368.       [121] Crowley 2005: 378.       [122] Aristotle, *Met.* 1014a26–b15.

[123] Proclus, *In primum Euclidis elementorum librum commentarii* 72.23–73.14. Proclus observes, citing Menaechmus, that "element" in a propositional text can mean two different things: either a simpler component into which a compound can be broken down (so a postulate is an element of a theorem) or a component of a proof used in the proving process, which may itself be a theorem (so, says Proclus, Euclid's first theorem may be called an "element" of his second). Proclus says that it is the first sense that is meant in the case of Euclid and of the other mathematical and astronomical texts that are called *Elements*.

[124] Proclus, *In primum Euclidis elementorum librum commentarii* 72.3–6.

[125] Proclus, *In primum Euclidis elementorum librum commentarii* 72.13–19.

[126] Proclus, *In primum Euclidis elementorum librum commentarii* 93.6–94.7.

The latter are not thereby disqualified as elements, however; they simply exist in different domains. It is up to practitioners in each discipline to see their way down to the basic elements most appropriate for their domain.

The *Pneumatica*'s account of the relationship between textual and material elements does not merely draw a structural parallel between the two, but blends them so closely that they become inseparable. Hero's pneumatic *theōrēmata* and the promise of "perceptible proof (*aisthētikē apodeixis*) they offer merge Aristotle's "elements of bodies" and "elements of proofs" (and indeed the "elements of diagrams") into a unified whole. The different layers of elements he builds up into his *Pneumatica* are reminiscent of Proclus' distinction between "element" and "elementary" *theōrēmata*: Some are essential threads strung throughout the whole as explanatory and structural elements, while other building blocks may not extend throughout the entire work but are called on repeatedly for their simplicity and broad applicability.

## *Taxis*

In the face of his commitment to Euclidean principles of didactic textual ordering, Hero finds the extensive textual tradition upon which the *Pneumatica* draws less than commendably organized, and he promises to "bring it into order (εἰς τάξιν ἀγαγεῖν)" himself.[127] The state of disorder perhaps owes something to the fierce debate over matter and void, which created divisions between philosophical schools as well as between philosophers and practitioners. We have already seen how Hero commences the preface by distinguishing between philosophical and mechanical approaches to pneumatics, the one relying on logic and the other on sensible information.[128] Hero naturally emphasizes the value of using the devices described in the work to make practical demonstrations of physical principles. At the same time, the Euclidean order with which he structures those demonstrations testifies to his intention to bind up prior contributions from the philosophers with the new methods of the "mechanicians" in his novel organizational scheme. His *taxis* will be capable of accommodating the practical alongside the theoretical, the new alongside the old, organized so as to make navigating all that information feasible for those just embarking on a study of the sciences (τοὺς μετὰ ταῦτα ἐν τοῖς μαθήμασιν ἀναστρέφεσθαι βουλομένους).

---

[127] *Pneumatica* 1.pr.6.     [128] *Pneumatica* pr.1–9.

Describing how elements are organized into substances, Hero argues that the particles that make up material objects are interlaced with tiny voids, all with their own proper structure and spacing. An artificial force might distort that order – a sponge may be squeezed small by a compressing hand, for example – but once it is removed everything will reclaim its natural arrangement:

> διὸ καὶ πιλεῖσθαι τὸν ἀέρα συμβαίνει ἐκ βίας τινὸς προσελθούσης καὶ συνιζάνειν εἰς τὰς τῶν κενῶν χώρας, παρὰ φύσιν τῶν σωμάτων πρὸς ἄλληλα θλιβομένων· ἀνέσεως δὲ γενομένης πάλιν εἰς τὴν αὐτὴν τάξιν ἀποκαθίσταται τῇ τῶν σωμάτων εὐτονίᾳ, καθάπερ καὶ τοῖς τῶν κεράτων συμβαίνει ξέσμασι καὶ τοῖς ξηροῖς σπόγγοις, ὅταν συμπιληθέντα ἀνεθῇ, πάλιν ἐπὶ τὴν αὐτὴν χώραν ἀποκαθίστασθαι καὶ τὸν αὐτὸν ὄγκον ἀποδιδόναι.

Hence it happens that air is compressed by some applied force and collapses to the spaces of the voids, against the nature of the particles squeezed against one another. Upon relaxation, the air is restored to its original arrangement by the tension of its particles, just as happens to shavings of horn and dried sponges: when compressed and released, they are restored to the same space and return to their same bulk.[129]

The physical idea that certain substances have a springiness (*eutonia*) that manifests in their forcefully pushing back against compression was already cited by Philo, who credits Ctesibius with realizing that air is *eutonos* and turning that realization into a novel compressed-air catapult.[130] At the same time, Berryman cautions that Philo does not, as Hero does, track this phenomenon down to the level of particles, and that Hero's explanation thus appears to represent the novel idea that in addition to being subject to bulk compression into their void spaces, the particles of matter themselves have a compressible elasticity.[131]

Hero's emphasis on the *taxis* of a material as a natural property of its arrangement of particles also appears to be original. Philo does once use *taxis* in a comparable sense, speaking of the tendency of a skein of spring cord for a catapult to lose its elasticity if stretched too tightly, as it is pulled askew and reverts to a less springy *taxis*.[132] There, however, the use is subtly different, as this *taxis* is an attribute of the arrangement of cords, not the sinew material from which they are braided. In this sense Philo's use is closer to the more common use of the word to denote a macroscopic arrangement of components (including humans arranged in a military formation).

---

[129] *Pneumatica* 1.pr.72–79.     [130] Philo, *Belopoeica* 77.16–40.     [131] Berryman 2011: 285–88.
[132] Philo, *Belopoeica* 58.22–26.

Hero explains the principles of pneumatics to his reader in terms of these general principles observed "in the wild" before teaching them how to capitalize on those same principles in pneumatic–hydraulic machinery. Compressed air inside a mechanical device wants to return to its natural arrangement of particles in a larger volume, just like the handful of squeezed horn shavings, and just like air everywhere. So Hero describes the operation of a figurine that expels liquid from one opening when air is blown in at another as the result of the air seeking to regain its natural *taxis*:

ἀνοιχθέντος οὖν τοῦ σμηρίσματος, μετ᾽ ὀλίγον χρόνον ὁ πιληθεὶς ἀὴρ ἐκθλίψει τὸ ἐν τῇ βάσει ὑγρὸν διὰ τοῦ Κ στομίου μετὰ πολλῆς βίας, ἄχρις ἂν ἤτοι πᾶν ἐκπυτισθῇ τὸ ὑγρὸν καὶ ὁ ἀὴρ εἰς τὴν κατὰ φύσιν τάξιν κατασταθῇ, τουτέστιν ὅταν πίλησιν ἐν ἑαυτῷ μηκέτι ἔχῃ.

When the double-sleeved tube has been opened, after a little time the compressed air will squeeze the liquid in the base through the mouth K with great force, until all the liquid has been spat out and the air settles back to its natural order – that is, when it no longer has compression in it.[133]

The organizing principles of the text itself, as it builds from general principles in the preface to more varied devices in the main text, help the reader acquire some new information about compression. The image of decompressing air expanding to occupy its natural *taxis* and the "compression (*pilēsis*)" that disrupts that *taxis* are already familiar from the preface. Now the reader is invited to consider compression not only as an externally applied force, but as an attribute that the air possesses while it is compressed into its artificial *taxis*.

Nor is it only simple materials that have their proper *taxis*; every type of system has its own spatial arrangement to which it will naturally return if allowed, even if it has been integrated into an artificial apparatus. The water organ, perhaps the most spectacular device in the text, uses pressurized air to draw sound from pipes of different sizes. The right pipe to play a given note is selected by pressing on a key, which in turn pulls a cord that draws on a small curved piece of horn (which Hero calls a "little blade [*spathion*]"). This action straightens out the curved piece of horn, which in turn draws open the pipe's aperture to allow the air to flow from the reservoir into the pipe through a perforation (Figure 2.3):

ἐὰν οὖν κατάξαντες τὸ Μᴮ ἄκρον τοῦ ἀγκωνίσκου παρώσωμεν τὸ πῶμα εἰς τὸ ἔσω μέρος, ἡ νευρὰ ἐπισπάσεται τὸ σπαθίον, ὥστε ἀνορθῶσαι τὴν καμπὴν αὐτοῦ βίᾳ· ὅταν δὲ ἀφῶμεν, πάλιν τὸ σπαθίον εἰς τὴν ἐξ ἀρχῆς

---

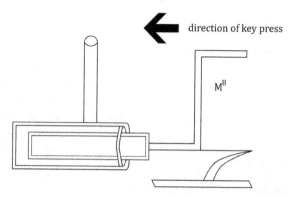

Figure 2.3    Water organ key, after Cod. Marcianus Gr. Z 516, fol. 184v.

τάξιν καμπτόμενον ἐξελκύσει τὸ πῶμα τοῦ στόματος, ὥστε παραλλάξαι
τὸ τρῆμα.

Then if we push down the end of the little arm $M^B$ and drive the cover
inside, the cord will pull on the little blade, so that its curved part will be
straightened by force. Then when we let go, the blade, bent back to its
original arrangement, will drag out the lid of the mouth, so that the
perforation changes place.[134]

Just like the small shavings of horn that appeared in the preface, when the
cord's force is no longer being exerted the *spathion* snaps back to its
original *taxis*, which here indicates an object deployed in a specific
arrangement of space and force. *Taxis* may also of course be used in its
more common sense to indicate a macroscopic spatial arrangement, as
when it refers to a siphon held perpendicular by rods so it will flow
properly.[135] Even in these cases, however, Hero's *taxis* is about more than
simple shape: It is the material properties of a structure – natural or
contrived – that allow a certain physical effect to manifest.

*Taxis* may also indicate objects arranged so as to enable a whole series of
actions, as in the *Automata*, where those actions add up to a narrative
effect. Hero describes the construction of the stationary type of automaton
in terms of the *taxis* and *diathesis* of the figurines that act out its story:

ἔστι δὲ καὶ τούτου ἡ ὑπόσχεσις τοιαύτη· ἐπί τινος κιονίσκου πίναξ ἐφέστηκε
θύρας ἔχων ἀνοιγομένας, καὶ ἐν αὐτῷ ... διάθεσις ζῳδίων πρός τινα μῦθον
διεσκευασμένων. κεκλεισμένου οὖν τοῦ πίνακος αἱ θύραι αὐτόματοι
ἀνοίγονται, καὶ φαίνεται ἡ τῶν ζῳδίων τάξις γεγραμμένη· καὶ μετ' οὐ
πολὺν χρόνον κλεισθεισῶν τῶν θυρῶν πάλιν αὐτομάτως καὶ ἀνοιχθεισῶν,

---

[134] *Pneumatica* 1.42.67–73.    [135] *Pneumatica* 1.6.19.

ἑτέρα φαίνεται διάθεσις ζῳδίων ἁρμόζουσα τῇ πρότερον φανείσῃ· καὶ πάλιν κλεισθεισῶν καὶ ἀνοιχθεισῶν τῶν θυρῶν ἑτέρα διάθεσις πάλιν φαίνεται ζῳδίων ἁρμόζουσα τῇ πρότερον κειμένῃ, καὶ ἤτοι ἀπαρτίζει τὸν προκείμενον μῦθον ἢ πάλιν μετὰ ταύτην ἑτέρα φαίνεται, ἄχρις ἂν ἀπαρτισθῇ ὁ μῦθος.

The design of this kind is as follows: upon a little column stands a miniature theater, which has open doors, and within it is an arrangement of figurines designed to suit a story. Then, after the theater has been closed, the doors open of their own accord, and the painted arrangement of figurines appears. When the doors have been closed for a short while, they open up automatically once again and a different arrangement of figures appears, connected to the one that appeared first, and either it completes the act previously set in motion or yet another one appears after this, until the tale is complete.[136]

The puppet-like figurines are installed within the automaton, carefully contrived to carry out the spatial instructions programmed into them by the complexly wound cord. Anachronistic though it may seem, "programmed" is precisely the right term for the cord's arrangement: The automaton's actions and pauses are encoded in tight coils and looser loops of cord. Information – on several levels, from the motions of individual components to the complete story the figurines act out – is organized and translated into a physical form through the medium of the cord.

The automaton embodies the crossroads *taxis* marks between physical and informational organization in the Heronian corpus. The information to be organized, of course, includes not only the *Automata* itself, but also the texts on which it draws. Hero's assessment of Philo's prior work on automaton design is largely complimentary, though he does say he has devised ways to achieve some of the effects more simply. Hero's esteem for Philo's work extends not just to the good design of his technology, but of his text as well:

περὶ δὲ τῶν λοιπῶν τῶν ἐν τῇ διαθέσει τοῦ Ναυπλίου κατὰ μέρος γινομένων εὐαρεστούμεθα ὡς ἐν τάξει καὶ εὐμεθόδως ὑπ᾽ αὐτοῦ ἀναγεγραμμένων.

About the remaining things in the representation of Nauplius that happen one by one, we are satisfied that they have been written up in order and methodically.[137]

The methodical description of mechanical events in Philo's text is inseparable here from their orderly material unfolding through the automaton. The dramatic narrative of Nauplius' story is bound up with the mechanical

---

[136] *Automata* 1.3–5. Grillo, following Schmidt, suggests *phainetai* for the lacuna (Grillo 2019: 2).
[137] *Automata* 20.5.1–3.

narrative the cord encodes. The *Automata* binds its parts together in a winding organizational scheme as complex as the structure of the machines themselves.[138] Rather than consisting of carefully graded incremental steps of difficulty or stages in the historical development of a particular mechanical tradition, this work is explicitly divided up only coarsely, into a first section on mobile automata and a second section on stationary devices. Within each of the two main sections, Hero makes a number of different demands on the reader, from following a mathematical proof to testing out the material properties of grease-soaked lengths of cord.

Hero also on a few occasions describes a mechanism in considerable detail before informing the reader that he has devised an easier way to achieve the same effect, for which he then provides an equally detailed description. These include the instructions for getting the moving automaton to travel on a rectangular path (sections 9–10 and 11, respectively, provide the harder and easier methods) and for scaling the travel distance at will either by creating space for an arbitrarily tall and wide counterweight tube or, more simply, by adding a drum to one of the axles (sections 17 and 18, respectively). The latter scheme is followed by a third that involves adding a second counterweight tube; one handles the external movements of the theater itself, while the other creates the motion of the components within the theater.

This third method is simpler in some ways and more complex in others, so it might be debated whether this sequence constitutes progress from more complicated to less. However, in any case the basic significance is the same: Hero chooses to show the reader both more and less complicated versions of the same mechanism rather than merely introducing the reader to the simplest or most reliable method he knows. The latter approach would be appropriate for an introductory text, whereas this structure is designed to show how Hero improves on the state of the art; in order to appreciate the argument, the reader must be able to follow the more difficult version as well as the easy way. Whereas the structure imposed on the *Pneumatica* is largely a matter of progressing from simpler to more complex mechanical principles, the *Automata* follows a path that repeatedly loops back on itself. Its iterative structure emphasizes the discipline's constant creative development, and its complexity highlights its place as the culmination of the mechanical arts.

Even objects much simpler than the automata can sport material irregularities sufficient to throw purely textual analysis into disarray. In

---

[138] On the organization of the text see Grillo 2019: lxxiii–lxxxii.

some cases, new measuring techniques will need to be developed to meet the challenge of measuring irregular forms, and those methods may press the boundaries of textual order or even require the reader to step outside the text entirely. The *Metrica* takes on the challenge of prescribing methods for measuring all kinds of different shapes, including irregular forms as well as the regular polygons, spheres, and pyramids that make up the bulk of the text. Through each of the three books, Hero follows an organizational strategy that can be quite readily understood. The first book accounts for how to measure surfaces, beginning with problems of measuring rectilinear planar figures, with frequent references to Euclid's work, particularly the *Data*. Hero moves on to curvilinear planar surfaces in the second half of the book; as Acerbi and Vitrac observe, this transition marks a shift in reference material as well as subject matter, as this half contains all the references to Archimedes in the first book.[139] The second book covers measurements of volumes, beginning with the basic foundations of the cone, cylinder, parallelepiped, prism, and pyramid, and moving on to their more complex variants. The third book treats methods for dividing the figures explored in the previous books into components having desired proportional or numerical relationships.

Yet when Hero tries to map his mathematical techniques onto objects in the real world, occasional notes of disorder creep into this orderly scheme. For example, *Metrica* 2.12 begins with a method, drawn from Archimedes, for measuring a segment of a sphere (whose diameter is here specified as 12). Hero proceeds, as he often does, through a geometrical demonstration followed by an algorithmically structured numerical synthesis.[140] In a typical passage from the *Metrica*, this would conclude the problem. In this case, however, after he has finished treating the measurement of these ideal geometrical objects, Hero concludes the section with remarks on how the method could be applied to objects in the real world that *almost* have the shape of segments of spheres:

καὶ λουτῆρα δὲ ἀκολούθως μετρήσομεν τῇ τοῦ τμήματος μετρήσει· ἔστι γὰρ δύο τμημάτων ὑπεροχή. ἀπὸ τοῦ μείζονος οὖν ἀφελόντες τὸ ἔλασσον ἀποφα[ι]νούμεθα τὸ τοῦ λουτῆρος στερεόν. καὶ κόγχην δὲ ὁμοίως μετρήσομεν ὡς ἡμισφαιρίου ἢ τμήματος ἥμισυ ὑπάρχουσαν. αἱ γὰρ ἐν αὐτῇ ξύσται ἐν ἀδιαφόρῳ παραλαμβάνονται εἰς τὰς μετρήσεις.

---

[139] Hero 2014: 43.

[140] On the appearance of the same algorithm elsewhere in the metrological corpus as well as in Diophantus see Hero 2014: 283 n. 122.

We will also measure washtubs in accordance with the measurement of the
segment, for it is the remainder between two segments. Then taking away
the lesser from the greater, we will reveal the volume of the washtub. And
similarly we will measure a shell as consisting of a hemisphere or half of a
segment. For the ripples in it are taken as not making a difference to the
measurements.[141]

The case of the seashell puts the need to approximate irregular natural
forms front and center, suggesting (without proof) that a scallop shell can
be analyzed as a segment of a sphere, since the convex and concave ripples
cancel out. The washtub described here is modeled as a spherical cap with
an additional parallel segment removed to create a flat bottom, so the
volume of the tub is the spherical segment between the two parallel cuts. If
the washtub's cross-sections are in fact circular, the model is precise;
otherwise it is just an approximation.

The washtub recurs as a model for the next problem, where Hero
proposes to extend the previous techniques for measuring conical, cylindrical, or spherical forms to measure vaults (*kamarai*) or rotundas (*tholoi*)
with those shapes.[142] These structures, he says, will be equal to the
difference between spherical segments, similar to the washtub. However,
he follows this assertion not with a progression through techniques for
measuring different shapes of vaults, but with a shift to the architecturally
related context of measuring the toric forms that appear on columns.
Vaults reappear only briefly a few problems later, where Hero recalls a
result mentioned in the preface to Archimedes' *Method* about the relationship between the volume of a cube and the space where two cylinders
inscribed perpendicularly inside it intersect.[143] This result, he says, is very
useful for constructing the vaults of baths with entrances or windows on all
four sides, as well as "places difficult to roof over with wood." The mystery
of the application is matched by the opacity of the problem as given here;
as Acerbi and Vitrac note, the problem is set out quite differently from its
expression in the *Method*'s preface, and the problem does not survive in the
main text as we possess it.[144] Once again, rather than offering further
discussion of this shape or a systematic extension of the vault-building
problem into other shapes, Hero opts in the second half of the problem to
move on to more orderly forms, announcing that "it follows" at this point
to discuss the five Platonic solids, abruptly transferring the reader from the

---

[141] *Metrica* 2.12.30–36.    [142] *Metrica* 2.13.1–6.    [143] *Metrica* 2.15.1–9.
[144] Hero 2014: 293 n. 145.

world of shells, baths, and roofing materials to the more tractable one of tetrahedra and icosahedra.

The first two books close with methods that surpass the individual approximations of seashells or vaulted roofs by proposing ways of measuring any object at all, no matter how irregular. In the case of the first book's surfaces, Hero can appeal to methods developed earlier in the book to help him with this task. In problems 18–23 of the book, he works through methods for finding the areas of polygons with successively greater numbers of sides, using the Euclidean strategy of circumscribing a circle around them to establish proportional relationships between their angles and sides. In the last chapter of the book, he then extends this method to a surface bounded by an irregular (*ataktos*) line. Any arbitrary rectilinear plane figure, he says, can be measured to a close approximation by first using a strategy like the one from problem 23 to connect an arbitrary number of points around the perimeter with line segments and then dissecting the resulting area into triangles.[145]

What about an irregular object bounded by nonplanar surfaces? Hero chooses a statue as an example, and he cautions that measuring its surface area will require a very different method. Instead of approximating the surface mathematically by dividing it into triangles, one has to move the whole operation into the material world. The approximation no longer occurs within a diagram, but is instead carried out by physically wrapping the object in thin paper or linen. The wrapper is stretched carefully around each part of the irregular surface and can then be trimmed or marked along its edges and unfurled again to yield a measurement of surface area.[146] The reader is thus empowered to measure the surface area of any kind of object, no matter how unusual its shape, but in these "disorderly" cases the text can only take him so far. The actual work of measurement will have to happen on the body of the object itself, until the three-dimensional body has been reduced to a complicated polygon drawn on linen or paper; only then can the reader return to the text for instructions in measuring that polygon.

Hero returns to this problem in the second book of the *Metrica*, where he is now concerned with measuring volumes rather than surface areas.[147] As in the first book, Hero formally concludes that since the "orderly (ἐν τάξει)" volumes have been adequately discussed, the logical next step is to

[145] *Metrica* 1.39.20–26.
[146] *Metrica* 1.39.26–36. The passage recurs with some variations at *De mensuris* 46.1.
[147] *Metrica* 2.20.

inquire into their "irregular (*atakta*)" cousins, the "rootlike or rocklike (ῥιζώδη ἢ πετρώδη)" solids. For this task, he recommends a "method some say Archimedes invented." Since Hero had recently appealed to Archimedes' *Method* in 2.14 and 2.15, a reader might expect him here to offer a version of the *Method*'s powerful and rigorous technique of reducing complex volumes to slices that can then be measured using a conceptual balance. But they are in for a surprise – instead, Hero recommends a more rough-and-ready experimental approach based on a very different Archimedean achievement. Assuming the object can be readily moved and is dense enough to sink in water, a tub in the shape of a rectangular prism is constructed and filled with water, and the object is tossed in. The water displaced from the tub will be equal in volume to the object and can easily be measured since it is a slice of the prism. A messy approach, but it certainly makes the math easier. If the object cannot be dunked into a tub for some reason, Hero offers an alternative:

> ἢ καὶ ἄλλως δυνατόν ἐστι τὸ αὐτὸ μετρῆσαι· ἐὰν γὰρ προσπλασθῇ τὸ ἄτακτον σῶμα κηρῷ ἢ πηλῷ, ὥστε γενέσθαι ἀποκρυβὲν πάντη ὀρθογώνιον, καὶ τοῦτο μετρήσαντες ἀφέλωμεν τὸν πηλὸν καὶ ὀρθογώνιον πλάσαντες ἐκμετρήσωμεν καὶ ἀφέλωμεν ἀπὸ τοῦ πρότερον μετρηθέντος τὸ καταλειπόμενον, ἀποφανούμεθα τὸ τοῦ σώματος στερεόν· τῇ δὲ τοῦ περιπλάσματος μεθόδῳ χρῆσθαι δεῖ ἐπὶ τῶν μὴ δυναμένων μετατίθεσθαι σωμάτων.

> It is also possible to measure the same thing in a different way. For if the irregular body is cladded in wax or clay, so that it is completely disguised as a rectangular [prism], we measure this, then take away the clay and make a rectangular [prism], and we measure it and subtract this remainder from the previous measurement, we will reveal the volume of the body. It is necessary to use the method of molding on bodies that cannot be moved.[148]

Both methods take advantage of the *Metrica*'s agenda of moving mathematical objects into the real world: No need for the fancy mathematics of the *Method*, or indeed the other methods Hero has painstakingly gone through in the book so far, when the problem can be sidestepped with concrete measurement techniques like these. On the other hand, both solutions are inelegant and inconvenient in different ways. The first requires that the object be movable, waterproof, and dense enough to displace its true volume of water (which then sluices messily onto the floor), while the second is more flexible but might require a great deal of clay or wax. The clash between precise, elegant, yet limited mathematical

---

[148] *Metrica* 2.20.14–22.

methods and experimental methods that, despite their crudeness, offer solutions in domains where mathematical tools are unavailable turns out to be a central concern in the Heronian corpus, as we will see in the next chapter.

## Conclusion

The texts of the Heronian corpus struggle to organize their subject matter using strategies as varied as the disciplines they cover. Hero seeks to create guides to each subdiscipline that are appropriate for previously under-served readerships, who range from novice aficionados of catapults to mechanical experts ready to try their hand at the complexities of theatrical automata. Each requires an organizational scheme specifically shaped to the task at hand; for example, progressions of mathematical problems or pneumatic components from simple to complex, technical developments in catapult technology folded into a historical sketch, or cross-referenced webs of mechanical specifications for the two types of theatrical automata, which share some crucial features even as they offer distinctive technical challenges.

In many cases, these schemes owe much (explicitly or implicitly) to the textual features Proclus cites as characteristic of Euclid's *Elements*. As we have seen, Proclus particularly praises the organization (*taxis*) and selectiv-ity (*eklogē*) of the *Elements*, a text designed for didactic purposes with no extraneous information. To be sure, Hero does not always meet those strict Euclidean standards of economy and simplicity. His decision to include "irregular" forms in the *Metrica* certainly opens the door to greater com-plexities, while the explanatory path he takes in the *Automata* meanders more than one might expect. Yet we have noted as well his intense interest in creating didactic routes through those complexities, his application of the concepts of *taxis* and *stoicheia* to material as well as textual objects, and his careful deployment of combinatorial structures that entice the reader with the rich possibilities offered by combining simple elements. All these features suggest that Hero has Euclid in mind as a model, but a model to be transformed rather than simply imitated. From the introduction of the *antitypia* near the beginning of the *Definitiones* to the elemental combina-tions of air, water, and fire in the *Pneumatica*, Hero indicates that he imagines himself as transferring Euclidean concepts from the purely geo-metrical domain to new objects with their own material and technical complications. Just how this transfer works will be the subject of the next chapter.

In many cases, Hero inherited those objects from his predecessors in mechanics. As we have seen, he makes no effort to disguise the fact that he is working with material originated by others, and indeed it is a point of pride in his works that he is able to transform the older material precisely by virtue of the innovative organizational schemes he devises to shape it. Often his innovations take the form of opening up lines of communication between disciplines, so that the significance of "elements" can phase back and forth between domains or geometrical methods can be carried into the real world. As we saw above, the *Pneumatica* is explicitly intended to draw on the elemental theory already explored in his work on water clocks, and the *Automata* (which he stipulates should be considered the culmination of mechanical know-how) presupposes that the reader is familiar with the kinds of hydraulic devices introduced in the *Pneumatica*. The *Definitiones* introduce the basic varieties of geometrical forms that supply the problems of the *Metrica*, while the *Metrica*'s final book on dividing up areas aims to provide a basic foundation in the surveying problems that will be encountered in more complex forms in the *Dioptra*.

The Heronian corpus is thus characterized in large part by the effort to systematize multiple disciplines into a corpus of texts shaped to facilitate a reader's journey from one discipline to the next. This is not to say Hero produces an internally unbounded network of homogenizing connections: Heronian disciplinary organization is as much about carefully delimited boundaries as it is about connectivity. Disciplines and subdisciplines are distinguished from one another by acting on different objects, using different methodologies, preceding or succeeding other disciplines in order of study. At the same time, Hero's multidisciplinary didactic plan emphasizes the continuity of objects of study even as it advises temporal and methodological separation. Even when objects and methods are differentiated from one another, they are still often connected analogically. The cells of the Heronian corpus emerge from many disciplines, individually bounded and methodologically heterogeneous but linked into a complex whole. That whole cannot be seen in its entirety from anywhere in the corpus; there is no "master text" that shows how all the rest are organized. Instead, the connections are local, particular, and organic.

The fuzzy boundaries between Heronian disciplines recall the limits Strabo sets on the geographer's work. Though he argues that geography is universally useful for rulership, he acknowledges that each geographer should not pretend to encompass the whole *oikoumenē*. As we saw earlier, Strabo conceptualizes the geographer as the center of a network of flowing information, but he also says that each geographer makes his own center wherever he is. So one geographer might properly take as his remit India, another Ethiopia, still another the Mediterranean; the latter certainly ought to include in his work details from Homer about Boeotia, but the former would have no reason to render Boeotia in such depth, as that would not serve Strabo's central aims of utility and accessibility.[149] From each center, territory spreads outward, at the boundaries growing fuzzier, containing more of what Strabo describes as "the more or less (τὸ μᾶλλον καὶ ἧττον)" and less of what is peculiarly proper to the central territory. The delimiting lines of the territories themselves may likewise be hard to discern, and Strabo advises that the geographer must develop a surgeon's eye for the right place to cut off his discussion of a region, lest his divisions resemble limbs accidentally hacked off rather than clean amputations.[150] Like Hero, Strabo assembles his own work from such pieces, gathered from many different sources and carefully arranged.[151] Crucially, Strabo emphasizes that the geographer should be prepared not only to draw upon other geographers, but also to integrate material from a host of interconnected disciplines: Geographers rely on the geometers who calculate the Earth's latitudes and longitudes, who themselves require guidance from astronomers, who in turn need physicists.[152]

Likewise, the texts of the Heronian corpus are not hermetically sealed by discipline; each object of study is presented at the center of its own gradually diffusing pool of explanatory material, which may include theories or methods useful to other disciplines. Hero's systematic explanations of individual subdisciplines share a compulsion to put things in order, even though the order itself may vary to include introductory guides as well as detailed works for specialists, strings of discrete problems as well as holistic histories, and clear progressions from simple to complex as well as looping iterations of more complexly layered material. As we will see in the next chapter, Hero's panoply of strategies for ordering these topics into books corresponds to an equally broad range of ways to explore the world his books open up for the reader.

---

[149] Strabo, *Geographica* 1.1.16. On these goals see Dueck 2000: 161–62.
[150] Strabo, *Geographica* 2.1.30.   [151] Dueck 2000: 165.   [152] Strabo, *Geographica* 2.5.2.

# CHAPTER 3

# *Theorizing the World*

## Introduction

Hero's concern for systematization within and between the texts of his corpus, his emphasis on organizing his works to facilitate their legibility and utility, and his respect for the differences between the parts of his complex disciplinary superstructure reflect a belief that the reader should be able to take his works into the world and *do things with them*. These "things" include building new (and possibly improved) artifacts, measuring or otherwise defining natural and artificial objects, and finding appropriate analytical regimes (mathematical, physical, mechanical, etc.) for further analyzing and describing those objects. It would not be going too far to say that Hero intends that the textual and disciplinary structures discussed in the previous chapter should help his reader learn to see the world in a new way. Just how that process is meant to work is the question that drives this chapter.

"Learning to see the world" here means developing an educated eye for the physical properties of materials, learning techniques for analyzing objects mathematically, and setting them within a broader context of natural phenomena and artificial interventions. These activities are frequently seen as the province of what are often called "scientific" texts, which emphasize theory over practice and discovery over application, rather than a "technical" author like Hero. But in the absence of strict disciplinary or professional boundaries there was of course no one to police this notional border in antiquity. Although Hero's works usually tend more toward the "technical" than the "scientific" side of this blurry boundary, the interweaving of disciplines and techniques that characterizes the texts of the Heronian corpus allows them to participate alongside more clearly "scientific" works in a shared discourse about exploring the world. The treatment of theoretical mechanics in the *Mechanica*, for example, is clearly in dialogue with the problems and theories of the Peripatetic

*Mechanical Problems*, as well as Archimedes' mechanical approaches to mathematical problems. The detailed discussion of the dioptra's use for conducting terrestrial and celestial observations recalls Ptolemy's close attention to protocols of observation in the *Almagest* and *Harmonica*. The difference is a matter of balance rather than kind; rather than focusing centrally on the natural phenomena to be observed, the Heronian texts' contributions to this discourse often center on techniques and technologies for making observations and recording their results in a systematic and readily useful way. Hand in hand with these concerns comes a recurrent interest in how the texts themselves can mediate that observational work.

Instruments used to make observations in the world frequently take center stage in the "technical" context of the Heronian corpus, establishing the conditions that ratify observations as reliable and developing appropriate analytical methods for each discipline. The preface to the *Dioptra*, for example, asserts that the eponymous instrument will prove useful for both practical and scientific applications: Not only does it facilitate the building of homes and aqueducts, but it can also be used to make astronomical and geographical observations, offering precision views of everything from the moon and stars to islands and seas.[1] The dioptra is quite a complicated device by the standards of surveying instruments, and it is understandable that Hero prefaces his guide to its construction and problem-solving applications with an assurance that its relative complexity will pay off in breadth of application. The dioptra can solve surveying problems that might also be amenable to solution using simpler instruments like the *chorobates* or *groma*.[2] However, its ability to precisely measure angles and heights from a distance provides advantages unique to the dioptra, whether it is called upon to make astronomical observations or measure the height of a besieged city's wall.

The surveyor's gaze, instrumentally mediated by the dioptra, is very often labeled by Hero as *theōria*. Indeed, this term and its cognates are used throughout the Heronian corpus to encompass a variety of acts of observation disciplined by tools ranging from external instruments to the text itself. The objects observed include natural phenomena and artificial devices, as well as the spatial and logical structures that underlie the systematic textual structures explored in the previous chapter. The term seems in the Heronian corpus to reflect a set of disciplined observational activities that interrogate the links between disciplines and their methodologies, the boundaries between nature and the artificial structures

---

[1] *Dioptra* 2.1–10.    [2] On the *chorobates* and *groma* see Lewis 2001: 30–35, 125–33, 2012: 142–44.

(including texts) that mediate our experience of it, concrete and abstract objects, and the limits of our abilities to observe and describe the world around us. In what follows we will explore how these acts of disciplined observation provide a toolbox of methodologies used to unfold natural and artificial phenomena through both textual and experimental exploration, but first let us see a few examples of Hero's *theōria* in action.

At the very outset of the *Definitiones*, Hero appears to identify the *theōria* of geometry with its underlying conceptual structures and rule set, as outlined by Euclid and further transmitted by Hero himself. We have already seen how he promises to set out his text "according to Euclid the elementalizer's teaching of the *theōria* in geometry."[3] The *Definitiones* are structured along Euclidean lines, to be sure, but the Euclidean armature of mathematical structures is broadened by occasional ventures into the relationships between geometrical objects and their real-world analogs. As early as the second chapter, a discussion of the line that begins with the usual "length without breadth" definition quickly leads on to a proposal that

λέγοιτο δὲ ἂν εἶναι γραμμὴ τὸ διαιροῦν ἀπὸ τῆς σκιᾶς τὴν ἡλιακὴν ἀκτῖνα ἢ ἀπὸ τοῦ πεφωτισμένου μέρους τὴν σκιὰν καὶ ἐν ἱματίῳ ὡς ἐν συνεχεῖ νοουμένῳ τὸ χωρίζον τὴν πορφύραν ἀπὸ τοῦ ἐρίου ἢ τὸ ἔριον ἀπὸ τῆς πορφύρας.

A line might be said to be what divides the sun's ray from the shadow or the shadow from the lit-up part, and in a cloak (insofar as it is apprehended as continuous) what divides the purple from the wool or the wool from the purple.[4]

In short order Hero introduces the surface, beginning with a stark definition of the surface as length and breadth without depth, as in the passage on the line. Here, too, Hero moves on first to give an alternative definition of the surface as "what is apparent (*epiphainomenon*) in two dimensions (length and breadth) as the boundary of every planar solid form." He then proposes that "every shadow and every skin could be considered to be a surface," citing a Pythagorean locution calling surfaces "skins" and pointing the way forward to the *antitypia* discussion in the eleventh chapter.[5] These passages are programmatic for the *Definitiones* in linking the abstract to the concrete and that which is comprehended by intellect to that which we experience directly. As Giardina argues, the seamless balance Hero

---

[3] *Definitiones* pr.1.1–7.
[4] *Definitiones* 2.1–11. On this passage, with particular emphasis on its relevance to later texts in the Pythagorean and Neoplatonic traditions, see Hero 2003: 265–70.
[5] *Definitiones* 8.1–9.

strikes between the theoretical and the practical is the feature that distinguishes him from, for example, Archimedes, the theoretical and applied components of whose work are more sharply distinguished.[6]

The part of the *Definitiones* likely to have been authored by Hero himself concludes with a lengthy list of units of measurement including not only palms and feet but more peculiar units like the "vine (*ampelos*)," suggesting the practical utility of those numerical conversions.[7] The final chapters of the book, which represent a later interpolation, focus even more intensely on the connections between the mathematical and material domains. The history of mathematics in *Definitiones* 138.3 seen in the previous chapter deepens the negotiation that *theōria* effects between abstract and concrete domains. The passage begins with an appeal to the Aristotelian division of intellectual activity into practical and theoretical domains, where the former is subdivided into ethics and politics and the latter into theology, physics, and mathematics.[8] However, the "theoretical" in the late *Definitiones* is indeed considerably more complex than that introductory mention alone suggests. At the stage of disciplinary development associated in the *Definitiones* with "more recent (*neōteroi*)" thinkers (specifically with Geminus in Proclus' close analog), mathematics is knitted together with representatives of the "mixed" sciences, all under the rubric of the "theoretical (*theōrētikos*)."[9] Here "mathematics" and the "theoretical" are not only meant to embrace geometry and arithmetic, but to define and describe phenomena that can be observed in the world:

οἱ δὲ νεώτεροι περιέσπασαν ἐπὶ πλεῖον τὴν προσηγορίαν οὐ μόνον περὶ τὴν ἀσώματον καὶ νοητὴν ὕλην ἀξιοῦντες πραγματεύεσθαι τὸν μαθηματικόν, ἀλλὰ καὶ περὶ τὴν ἐφαπτομένην τῆς σωματικῆς καὶ αἰσθητῆς οὐσίας . . .

Then in turn more recent people for the most part diverted and expanded the name, considering it worthwhile for mathematics not only to engage with bodiless and intellectual matter, but also with the tangible matter of embodied and sensible being.[10]

The expansion of mathematics and the "theoretical" to include sensible as well as intellective objects requires not just adjustments to metamathematical

---

[6] Hero 2003: 125–29.    [7] *Definitiones* 131.

[8] *Definitiones* 138.1.1–7. Aristotle's third division, the "productive," is not mentioned here. On the Aristotelian categories see especially *Met.* 1025b25–28, 1026a18–19, 1064a16–19, 1064b1–3; *Top.* 145a13–18. For their impact on defining mathematics (including in the texts that influenced the *Definitiones*) see Vitrac 2005: 272–73.

[9] Proclus, *In primum Euclidis elementorum librum commentarii* 35.21–39.6.

[10] *Definitiones* 138.3.16–20.

rhetoric, but also profound changes in how the objects of study are apprehended. "Theorization" becomes a matter of observation as well as contemplation.

Indeed, practices of observation are crucial to this evolved concept of the "theoretical," which ought, in the "more recent" view, to embrace the movements and velocities of celestial bodies, their sizes, and their relative positions, as well as to subjects nearer to hand like harmonics, mechanics, and surveying. It ought to extend as well to the sensory tools we use to apprehend those worldly phenomena, notably the complexities of optics, catoptrics, and optical illusions. It should provide a causal and mathematically descriptive account of perceived images in the celestial realm, in air, in mirrors, and in transparent materials.[11] The "mixed" approach to *theōria* here is indeed rooted in observations of sensible things, including the mechanisms of sensory observation themselves. The later *Definitiones'* "theoretical" can embrace topics traditionally admitted to the territory of mathematics, like reflections in mirrors and refractions in transparent substances, but it is first specifically tasked with investigations into "the experiences of vision" and their causes, and finally with thinking about the nature of body and sensible matter.[12] *Theōria* here, as usual in the Heronian corpus, is not set in opposition to a domain of praxis. Hero does not conceive of geometry as unsuitable for practical operations in the world, nor is *theōria* itself somehow limited to a separate domain from that of praxis or *phantasia*; indeed, it serves as a guide to help navigate these disparate domains.

Consider, for example, a passage from the preface to the third book of the *Metrica* on the problem of dividing up land fairly, where Hero identifies *theōria* as the act that certifies the value and justice of proportionally divided land, "for the geometrically proportional apportionment of an equal area to equals, and more to those who are worthy, is observed (*theōreitai*) to be very useful and necessary."[13] While the term he uses here for "area (*chōrion*)" presents some initial ambiguity between geometrical areas and areas of land, Hero's reference to just apportionment immediately makes clear that he has the latter in mind. Indeed, Hero identifies Nature herself as the author of the "geometrical" division of land that is allegedly the most just form of distribution.[14]

---

[11] *Definitiones* 138.3.20–30.      [12] *Definitiones* 138.3.34–35.
[13] *Metrica* 3.pr.3–5. Hero is here indebted to earlier discussions of just distribution in Plato (*Laws* 757a–e) and Aristotle (*Nicomachean Ethics* 1131a10–1132b20). Guillaumin 1997 discusses the connections between these passages and Hero's preface and introduces the further possibility of a Stoic connection.
[14] *Metrica* 3.pr.5–9.

Feke traces another thread of Hero's argument in this passage: the claim that geometry alone generates indisputable (*anamphisbētētos*) truth.[15] Feke emphasizes the common ground Hero's argument shares with one made by Plutarch in the *Quaestiones conviviales*: that the "geometrical" division was preferred over the "arithmetical" type by the Spartans as well.[16] Feke argues that Hero picks up this well-used trail of reasoning to make a brand new methodological claim: This is the "first extant occurrence" of the claim that mathematical reasoning is uniquely indisputable (*anamphisbētētos*) when compared to philosophical argument.[17] But the rhetorical connection in the *Metrica* between geometrically proportional (κατὰ τὴν ἀναλογίαν) land division and a methodological approach that privileges mathematical rigor is not limited to the context of pure mathematical demonstration. In this passage Hero shifts a well-known philosophical trope with mathematical trappings into more firmly mathematical territory, using the versatile term *theōria* to shift the problem again into the context of observations made in the real world.

As we shall see, *theōria* and its cognates are often associated in the Heronian corpus with the work of marshaling observable phenomena into arguments that may be quite rigorous. It is not only the logic of *apodeixis* that strengthens the claim of justice, but the fact that the demonstration is rooted in a phenomenon that can be directly observed (*theōreitai*) to be both useful and necessary. Land division is identified here with land measurement, a rhetorical move framed as taking sides in a debate, which serves the additional purpose of relocating the debate over justice from the philosophical realm onto *terra firma*. Direct and scrupulous observation of the admirable philosophical ramifications of such a system of division is connected to the direct and scrupulous observation performed in the field by the surveyor as he makes the actual measurements.[18]

Those observations are quite visible in the *Dioptra*, where they continue to occupy the semantic territory of *theōria*. The dioptra disciplines the surveyor's sightings of terrestrial objects as well as the astronomer's observations of celestial ones:

---

[15] *Metrica* 3.pr.19–22.

[16] Plutarch, *Quaestiones conviviales* 719a11–b5; Feke 2014: 267. The sentiment repeats the idea associated earlier in the *Quaestiones conviviales* with a Homerically aristocratic division of food at a feast: Plutarch, *Quaestiones conviviales* 643b9–d5.

[17] Feke 2014: 271. It is not, of course, the last; the trope appears in Sextus Empiricus, Nicomachus of Gerasa, Galen, and others. See for example Feke 2014: 267–72; Netz 2017. Cuomo discusses Pappus' conviction that philosophical reasoning in the style of Plato in particular is less rigorous than mathematical reasoning at Cuomo 1998: 228.

[18] On the ethical responsibilities of the surveyor in the Roman world, see Cuomo 2007: 103–30.

Ὅτι δὲ πολλὰς παρέχεται τῷ βίῳ χρείας ἡ πραγματεία, δι᾽ ὀλίγων ἐστὶν
ἐμφανίσαι. πρός τε γὰρ ὑδάτων ἀγωγὰς καὶ τειχῶν κατασκευὰς καὶ
λιμένων καὶ παντὸς οἰκοδομήματος εὔχρηστος τυγχάνει, πολλὰ δὲ
ὤνησεν καὶ τὴν περὶ τὰ οὐράνια θεωρίαν, ἀναμετροῦσα τά [τε] μεταξὺ
τῶν ἀστέρων διαστήματα, καὶ τὰ περὶ μεγεθῶν καὶ ἀποστημάτων καὶ
ἐκλείψεων ἡλίου καὶ σελήνης.

It will be possible quickly to make clear that the practice [of dioptrics]
presents great utility for life. For in addition to paths for water and designs
of walls and harbors and what is most useful for every home construction, it
greatly benefits the observation of celestial objects, measuring the intervals
between the stars, as well as those concerning the sizes and distances and
eclipses of the sun and moon.[19]

*Theōria* through the dioptra links together earth, sky, and sea in service of
human needs; even astronomical observations that could be called "scientific" fall under the rubric of activities valued for their utility. Clearly,
*theōria* here is in no way defined by opposition to the practical; instead, it
is defined by certain acts of instrumentally and textually disciplined seeing,
which will be spelled out in more detail as the *Dioptra* goes on.

The process of "learning to see the world" on which Hero's reader
embarks involves, first of all, learning to negotiate the fuzzy boundary
between the mathematical and material domains. Hero will provide useful
mathematical techniques as well as guidance in coping with the approximations and material complications that haunt the verge between these
domains. The challenge of trying to approximate material objects and
phenomena using mathematical techniques is a common refrain throughout the Heronian corpus, and indeed it lies at the heart of many of the
techniques of disciplined seeing Hero sets out for his reader. The geometrical framework that demonstrates the efficacy of the simple machines
must be studied alongside the epiphenomena that emerge when those
machines are put to work in a quarry or a building site, the theoretical
promise of an automaton's smooth motion around a circular path can only
come to fruition if all its components are carefully crafted, and so on.
Hero, true to the careful interdisciplinarity of his corpus, will not attempt
to impose a "one-size-fits-all" method for coping with the irregularities of a
material world that sometimes behaves in very unmathematical ways.

Once the reader has acquired the tools to negotiate the boundary
between the mathematical and the material, they need a mechanism that
allows results from one domain to be applied in the other. Such

---

[19] *Dioptra* 2.1–10.

mechanisms emerge from practices of disciplined observation like the varieties of *theōria* discussed above, often taking the form of "experimental" engagements with objects in the world. These experiments may be simple or complex, formal *apodeixeis* or informal tinkering, and they might involve textually mediated "thought experiments" as well as hands-on work. The ordering schemes discussed in the previous chapter play a particularly important role here, as Hero organizes his texts to carefully induct his reader in exploratory techniques appropriate to the level of the text and serving the work's particular overall goals. These goals are diverse: They include developing the ability to perform geometrically precise and pragmatically adaptable surveying maneuvers with the dioptra, learning to see into the mysteries of elemental physics using the amplifying devices of the *Pneumatica*, and confronting the material quirks of an automaton's unwinding cord. The exploratory techniques Hero teaches share some conceptual foundations but are ultimately as varied as his texts. In this chapter, we will consider how Hero helps his reader develop a wide range of strategies for observing and analyzing objects in the world.

## Mathematics and Materials

The complexities of observation are particularly apparent in the optical sciences, since phenomena in the world are naturally subject to optical illusions that must be artificially corrected. The artificial and the natural come into dialogue in the later interpolated chapters of the *Definitiones* that touch on optics. The author considers not only questions about how transmission, reflection, and refraction affect the rays of the sun and the shadows they cast, but also how to apply that understanding of the sun's rays to the construction of a burning mirror.[20] The author's physiological remarks are limited to taking an emissionist stance on the mechanics of vision, asserting that visual rays emanate from the eyes, allowing the eye to perceive whatever the rays encounter.[21] Left to their own devices, those rays will behave like geometrical lines, but like the sun's rays they are reflected or refracted upon encounters with glass, membranes, or water at angles that depend on the angle of incidence and the material encountered.

The changing behavior of light rays as they interact with different kinds of materials complicates visual perception, leading not only to reflections and refractions, but also to optical illusions: Square towers look round from far away, cylindrical columns seem to shrink in the middle, ceiling

---

[20] *Definitiones* 135.12.8–17.     [21] *Definitiones* 135.10.2–5.

coffers appear as different sizes depending on whether the viewer is near or far, and so on.[22] These discussions of optics expand on Proclus' commentary to Euclid, which puts the challenges of optical illusions in the foreground for the different branches of optical study.[23] The optical sciences interrogate the boundaries between the mathematical and the material: Rays of light and the boundaries of shadows can be modeled as geometrical rays only under certain conditions lest they be diffracted into a blur, while architects or painters may need to violate the truths of geometrical proportion in order to create buildings and images that can be experienced by viewers as proportional.

Elsewhere in the Heronian corpus, mathematics is celebrated as an "eye" in its own right. The preface of the *Geometrica* opens with a gambit in which the utility of both mathematics and engineering is first doubted, then (unsurprisingly) reaffirmed, *on condition* that the two be used together:

> Ἡ γεωμετρία αὐτὴ καθ᾽ ἑαυτὴν εἰ κρίνοιτο, εἰς οὐδὲν ἂν νομισθείη συντελεῖν τῷ βίῳ. ὃν τρόπον καὶ τὰ τεκτονικά [καὶ], εἰ τύχοι, ὄργανα αὐτὰ καθ᾽ ἑαυτὰ σκοπούμενα ἄχρηστ᾽ ἂν δόξειεν εἶναι, τὴν δὲ δι᾽ αὐτῶν γινομένην σκοπῶν χρῆσιν οὐ μικρὰν οὐδὲ τὴν τυχοῦσαν εὑρήσεις, τὸν αὐτὸν τρόπον καὶ γεωμετρία τῶν μὲν δι᾽ αὐτῆς περαιουμένων γυμνωθεῖσα μάταιος εὑρίσκεται, εἰς δὲ τὴν πρὸς ἀστρονομίαν εὐεργεσίαν αὐτῆς ἀφορῶντες ὑπερθαυμάζομεν τὸ πρᾶγμα· οἷον γὰρ ὄμμα τῆς ἀστρονομίας τυγχάνει.

If geometry were judged only on its own, it would seem to contribute to life not at all. Both engineered products and instruments themselves viewed in and of themselves in this way would seem to be totally useless, but in looking at the utility that arises through them you will find that this ends up not being small. In the same way geometry, stripped of the things that come about through it, appears pointless, but when we focus on its useful astronomical work we marvel greatly at the effect, for it is as it were the eye of astronomy.[24]

Geometry on its own seems not to serve the daily needs of life, but on the other hand engineered instruments are likewise inert and useless until they are put into practical action. Astronomy might be crippled without its "eye," but geometry on its own is as useless as a lone eye, stripped of its organic functionality in the context of the body. While the authorship of the *Geometrica* is doubtful, this passage echoes ideas that recur throughout the Heronian corpus: Disciplines are judged according to their utility,

---

[22] *Definitiones* 135.9.1–5, 135.11.1–15, 135.13.11–18.
[23] Proclus, *In primum Euclidis elementorum librum commentarii* 40.8–22.      [24] *Geometrica* 1.1–10.

mathematics is contextualized through its applications, and observational instruments are the keystone linking geometry and scientific work.[25]

Similarly, an attempt to define mathematics in the later chapters of the *Definitiones* invokes its problem-solving applications as key to the discipline's very identity:

Τί ἐστι μαθηματική; Μαθηματική ἐστιν ἐπιστήμη θεωρητικὴ τῶν νοήσει τε καὶ αἰσθήσει καταλαμβανομένων πρὸς τὴν τῶν ὑποπιπτόντων δέσιν. ἤδη δὲ χαριεντιζόμενός τις ἅμα καὶ τοῦ σκοποῦ τυγχάνων μαθηματικὴν ἔφη ταύτην εἶναι,

ἥτ᾽ ὀλίγη μὲν πρῶτα κορύσσεται, αὐτὰρ ἔπειτα

οὐρανῷ ἐστήριξε κάρη καὶ ἐπὶ χθονὶ βαίνει·

ἄρχεται μὲν γὰρ ἀπὸ σημείου καὶ γραμμῆς, εἰς δὲ τὴν οὐρανοῦ καὶ γῆς καὶ συμπάντων ἀσχολεῖται πραγματείαν.

What is mathematics? Mathematics is a theoretical science of the things grasped both by intellect and sense, aiming at binding together the things that fall under this rubric. Indeed, someone aiming at this goal jokingly said that mathematics was that "which is equipped in few things at first, but then bumps its head on heaven and walks upon the earth." For it begins from the point and line, but then engages all the practices of heaven and earth and everything.[26]

The Homeric tag refers in its original context to Discord. Here the joke turns out to be that rather than spreading rage and chaos as it stretches out to encompass heaven and earth, mathematics has the capacity to bind together the abstract and applied into a harmonious whole. Of course, this is easier said than done. Objects in the real world must be treated differently from geometrical objects until methods are in place to reconcile them, and a wide-ranging array of disciplines like those represented in the Heronian corpus will require an equally wide range of strategies for making observations, crafting machinery, and applying mathematical tools to material things. The disciplines of surveying, mechanics, and automaton-making provide particular insight into how the Heronian corpus soothes the potential discord between the mathematical and the material.

### Surveying

The tension between the irregularities of the material world and the orderly system of the Heronian texts reaches a particular urgency in texts

---

[25] On the various versions of the *Geometrica* see Hero 2014: 474–81.
[26] *Definitiones* 138.4; Homer *Iliad* 4.442–443.

where measurement is central to their program. These texts include the *Dioptra*, which tasks its reader with envisioning irregular landscapes as forms that can be analyzed geometrically, as well as the abstract *Metrica* and its contaminated practical siblings the *Geometrica, Stereometrica*, and *De mensuris*. Like the *Definitiones*, these texts mean to impose mathematical order on a wide array of objects encountered in the world, some of which lend themselves more readily than others to mathematical expression and standardization.

In the later sections of the *Definitiones*, surveying emerges as a practice that will move the geometer's objects to a new, material operational space. An introductory query about the nature of surveying first acknowledges that, from a mathematician's perspective, its objects leave something to be desired:

> Λαμβάνει τὰ σχήματα οὐ τέλεια οὐδ' ἀπηκριβωμένα τῷ σωματικὴν ὕλην ὑποβεβλῆσθαι, καθώσπερ καὶ ἡ λογιστική· μετρεῖ γοῦν καὶ σωρὸν ὡς κῶνον καὶ φρέατα περιφερῆ ὡς κυλινδρικὰ σχήματα καὶ τὰ μείουρα ὡς κώνους κολούρους.

> It includes forms which are neither complete nor quite perfected for appropriating bodily matter, just as is the case for calculation. So it measures a heap like a cone, and the peripheries of wells as cylindrical shapes, and tapered shapes like truncated cones.[27]

At first glance this might seem like a slightly odd collection of sample objects for a surveyor to handle. In fact, the first two are drawn not from a surveying text at all, but from Proclus' commentary to the first book of Euclid's *Elements*, which this part of the chapter follows closely.[28] The mathematical structures embedded within these unruly real-world objects echo the proem of the second book of the *Metrica*, where Hero acknowledges that his project will have to include techniques for measuring irregular or arbitrary surfaces as well as those of spheres, cones, and cylinders.[29] They also recall the list of objects Eratosthenes says the calculating device called the "mesolabe" can measure; in an epigram on the device he describes it as being useful for doubling the volume of

---

[27] *Definitiones* 135.8.2–6.

[28] Proclus, *In primum Euclidis elementorum librum commentarii* 39.19–40.2: "γεωδεσία δὲ καὶ λογιστικὴ ταύταις ἀνάλογον, οὐ περὶ νοητῶν ἀριθμῶν ἢ σχημάτων, ἀλλὰ περὶ αἰσθητῶν ποιούμεναι τοὺς λόγους. οὐ γὰρ κύλινδρον ἢ κῶνον ἔργον τῆς γεωδεσίας μετρεῖν, ἀλλὰ σωροὺς ὡς κώνους καὶ φρέατα ὡς κυλίνδρους, οὐδὲ δι' εὐθειῶν νοητῶν, ἀλλὰ δι' αἰσθητῶν, τότε μὲν ἀκριβεστέρων, ὡς διὰ τῶν ἀκτίνων τῶν ἡλιακῶν, τότε δὲ παχυτέρων, οἷον διὰ σπάρτων καὶ στάθμης."

[29] *Metrica* 2.pr.5.

everyday objects like grain pits and cisterns.[30] As we will see in the next chapter, Berrey has observed that the objects Eratosthenes mentions are staples of the Egyptian village economy, lending a specifically Alexandrian flair to the poem.[31] Unlikely as it is that Proclus or any other contributor to this text had Eratosthenes' text in mind, it nevertheless reflects a common thread of local lived experience that binds together these different Alexandrian approaches to "mixed" mathematics.

The author of the *Definitiones* passage, again drawing on the passage of Proclus cited above, compares the surveyor's reliance on techniques of calculation to the geometer's use of arithmetical methods. Calculation has just been introduced in the previous section of the chapter as the application of number to things; so the arithmetical monad becomes an individual man where men are being numbered and a drachma where drachmai are being numbered (even though, as the author notes, unlike the man, the drachma can be further divided into small change).[32] The list of "imperfect" objects the surveyor will operate on is followed by a more detailed study of the tools he has available to him:

χρῆται ὀργάνοις εἰς μὲν τὰς διοπτείας χωρίων διόπτραις, κανόσι, στάθμαις, γνώμοσι καὶ τοῖς ὁμοίοις πρὸς διαστημάτων καὶ ὑψῶν ἀναμετρήσεις, τοῦτο μὲν σκιᾷ, τοῦτο δὲ αὖ διοπτείαις, ἔστι δὲ ὅτε καὶ δι' ἀνακλάσεως θηρᾶται τὸ προβληθέν.

Surveying uses instruments for sighting areas: dioptras, measuring rods, plumb-lines, gnomons, and the like for measurements of distances and heights; one by a shadow [plot], another by sightings with the dioptra, and another when the thing proposed is tracked down through back-sightings.[33]

The Roman treatises that provide us with most of our information on the surveyor's arsenal of tools can fill in some of the details that are only hinted at here, though the dioptra is treated only by Hero. Gnomons, observed over the course of a day or a year, provide shadow plots that can be used to orient a settlement along the cardinal directions or to construct a sundial tuned to the appropriate latitude. Measuring rods and sighting poles are used along with the relatively simple *groma* (also known as a *ferramentum* or *asteriskos*), a simple cross mounted on a staff, from whose ends plumblines depend. Sighting across opposing plumblines, together with the error correction provided by a combination of forward and reverse

---

[30] The "mesolabe" is a tool for calculating mean proportionals, a technique useful for the task of "doubling the cube" (finding the side length of a cube whose volume is twice that of a given cube).
[31] Berrey 2017: 166–67.  [32] *Definitiones* 135.7.5–8.  [33] *Definitiones* 135.8.7–12.

sightings, can produce a reliable grid of orthogonal lines across a large expanse of space, even up and down hills.[34] The precise yet complex dioptra can be used, in concert with its own more complex sighting poles, to solve problems that require more advanced measurement techniques. Hence it lends itself well to solving surveying problems through techniques analogous to those used by geometers. The surveyor's instruments may be simple or complex, precise or crude, creating a shifting boundary between the work's material and mathematical elements.

The *Definitiones* passage expands on Proclus in some important ways. Proclus merely differentiates between the geometer's "more precise/intelligible (*akribesterai/noētai*)" lines and the "thicker/perceptible (*pachyterai/aisthētai*)" lines the surveyor works with, and names the sun's rays, cords, and rulers as the latter's tools. The author of the *Definitiones* passage similarly assigns "logical (*logikai*)" lines to the geometer and "perceptible" ones to the surveyor:

ὥσπερ καὶ ὁ γεωμέτρης τὰς λογικὰς εὐθείας μεταχειρίζεται πολλαχοῦ, οὕτως ὁ γεωδαίτης ταῖς αἰσθηταῖς προσχρῆται· τούτων δ' αἱ μὲν ἀκριβέστεραι διὰ τῶν ἀκτίνων τοῦ ἡλίου λαμβάνονται ἢ δι' ὀπτήρων ἢ τῶν ἐπιπροσθετήσεων ἐκλαμβανόμεναι, αἱ δὲ σωματικώτεραι διὰ τάσεως καὶ ἕλξεως μηρίνθων ἢ στάθμης· τούτοις γὰρ χρώμενος ὁ γεωδαίτης μετρεῖ πόρρωθεν ἀφεστῶτα χωρία, ὁρῶν ἀναστήματα, τειχῶν ὕψη, ποταμῶν πλάτη καὶ βάθη, καὶ ὅσα τοιαῦτα.

And just as the geometer takes in hand logical straight lines everywhere, in the same way the surveyor avails himself of perceptible [straight lines]. And the most precise of these are from the rays of the sun, either taken by eye-witnesses or derived from objects casting a shadow. On the other hand, the more corporeal ones [are taken] through arranging and dragging cords and plumblines. Using these the surveyor measures from far away the most remote places, seeing the distances, the heights of walls, the width and depth of rivers, and everything like that.[35]

The geometer operates on "logical" straight lines, which is to say lines belonging to an abstract domain, opposed quite explicitly to the physical domain in the Peripatetic and Stoic traditions. The surveyor, on the other hand, operates within that physical space on lines that make themselves available to the senses in two different ways. Gnomons and other shadow-casting tools give him access to lines as precise as sunrays; these are made perceptible and useful to the senses through the intervention of properly deployed tools, while minimizing the compromises material things impose on accuracy or precision. These processes depend, further, on reliable

---

[34] On this process see Lewis 2012: 134–39.    [35] *Definitiones* 135.8.12–21.

eyewitness observers. The formulation here echoes Hero's own definition of the line at the beginning of the *Definitiones*, where he suggested a line might be understood as the boundary between sunlight and shadow, or the natural and purple-dyed sections of a cloak.

The author goes on to specify that precise measurements like shadow plots only work for a certain subset of the surveyor's problems, and he must often resort to "more corporeal (*sōmatikōterai*)" kinds of lines, such as the plumblines over which trajectories and angles are sighted and the stretched cords that mark those trajectories out on the ground. The very physicality of these lines is strongly emphasized here, not just through the choices of words for the cords themselves (*mērinthos* and *stathmē* both retain unmistakable connotations of handwork operations ranging from fishing to carpentry), but also through the act of "dragging" the marking cords, which conjures up the hard physical work of pulling the cords taut to ensure their most accurate placement.

The resemblance between the passage from the *Definitiones* and its original in Proclus is obvious, but the differences are as important as the similarities. Proclus' outline of the surveyor's work, part of an overview of applications of mathematics to the sensible world he traces back to Geminus, elides the details of how the work in that world actually takes place. The passage in the *Definitiones*, even though it is still a topical overview rather than a dedicated guide to the surveyor's craft, offers a much more concrete perspective on how that work actually takes place: the eyewitnesses and instruments used for observations, the hard work of dragging the surveyor's cord to make measurements, and the vistas the surveyor takes in as he makes his measurements. The crucial importance of eyewitness measurements conjures up a context of active experimentation that is of no concern to Proclus. All in all, the contrast between the intelligible and perceptible worlds takes on deeper shading in the *Definitiones* than Proclus gave it.

The distinction between "logical" and "corporeal" straight lines also recalls the distinction between lines in the mathematical, material, and legal domains made by the Roman surveyor Balbus, who likely dates to the late 1st or early 2nd century CE.[36] His *Expositio et ratio omnium formarum* offers its own kind of Euclidean approach to Roman surveying practice, building up a collection of shapes and measurement techniques from the familiar geometrical primitives of point, line, and plane. The Euclidean and Heronian parallels are clear from the very beginning, where he defines line, plane, and solid alongside analogs like racetracks, lengths of rivers, and so on. Throughout his treatise Balbus maintains the impersonal verb

---

[36] On Balbus' dates see Chouquer and Favory 2001: 27; Dilke 1971: 42; Toneatto 1994.

forms and preference for generalized geometrical forms over numerical examples characteristic of Euclidean geometry. At the same time, his presentation and definition of the geometrical forms appears to be an end in itself rather than a tool for proofs, so that much of his material might seem at home in a work like the *Definitiones*.

Indeed, so close is the resemblance that Guillaumin argues that Hero himself likely influenced Balbus' text, although he singles out the *Geometrica* and the later chapters of the *Definitiones* as the probable sources based on some remarkable lexical parallels between Balbus' Latin and Hero's Greek.[37] Acerbi and Vitrac, in rejecting the possibility that Hero wrote the *Geometrica*, maintain that this line of influence is unlikely, noting further that Balbus explicitly mentions Euclid's name but not Hero's.[38] Still, it seems clear from Balbus' vocabulary and mathematical approach to surveying that he was drawing on a Greek technical tradition that is largely invisible in the other Latin agrimensorial texts.

Balbus distinguishes between a legal boundary (*extremitas*) and the line (*rigor*) by means of which it can be observed (*observatur*).[39] The *rigor* thus seems to play the role of the "perceptible" lines in the *Definitiones*, and indeed Balbus goes on to define it as "whatever is seen (*perspicitur*) to stretch straight between two points in the form of a line."[40] Moreover, this act of perception takes place specifically in the field, as Balbus proposes that the *rigor*'s representation on a map transforms it further into a *linea*.[41] Balbus thus clearly demarcates the legal, observational, and diagrammatic domains from one another; while the object under consideration might appear to the untrained eye to be simply a line in all cases, there is no mistaking the surveyor's work for the geometer's in Balbus' text, any more than in the *Definitiones*.

The *Dioptra* yields a more sustained consideration of the relationship between the surveyor's work and the geometer's than the scattered passages of the *Definitiones*. The work of seeing according to the *Dioptra*'s prescriptions requires a careful sequence of physical activities grounded in the landscape like setting up the sighting rod, adjusting the height of the dioptra's stand, and then adjusting the orientation of the dioptra itself in each dimension (Figure 3.1).[42] The operation could be further refined using

---

[37] Guillaumin 1992.    [38] Hero 2014: 522–23.
[39] Balbus, *Expositio et ratio omnium formarum* 98.3–6. For more context on this problem in Balbus see Roby 2014a: 34–50; Roby 2016a: 227–29.
[40] Balbus, *Expositio et ratio omnium formarum* 98.6–8.
[41] Balbus, *Expositio et ratio omnium formarum* 98.12–14.
[42] For more details on the structure of the dioptra as indicated by Hero and reconstructed variously by Schöne, Drachmann, and others see Feyel 2000; Hairie 2000.

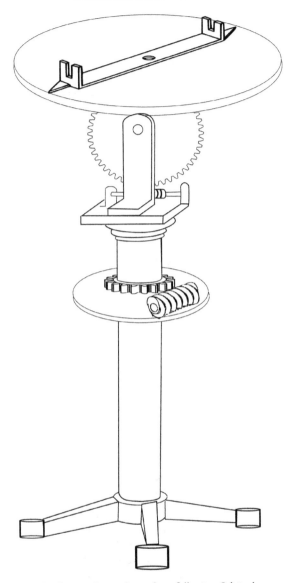

Figure 3.1 The dioptra. Image by author, following Schöne's reconstruction.

Hero's model of the dioptra by aligning the height of the sighting targets with the water level that could be mounted on the dioptra's stand. Only at this point is the surveyor ready to engage in the linked acts of "sighting (*diopteuein*)" and "viewing (*theōrein*)" that will yield his measurements:

καὶ κατασταθέντων οὕτως τῶν λεπιδίων διὰ τῶν ἐν αὐτοῖς ἀνατομῶν διοπτεύω θεωρῶν τὸν ΑΓ κανόνα, τῆς ἀσπιδίσκης μετεωριζομένης ἢ ταπεινουμένης, ἄχρις ἂν φανῇ ἡ μέση τοῦ λευκοῦ καὶ μέλανος χρώματος γραμμή. καὶ μενούσης τῆς διόπτρας ἀκινήτου μεταβὰς ἐκ τοῦ ἑτέρου μέρους διοπτεύω διὰ τῶν ἀνατομῶν, ἀποστήσας ἀπὸ τῆς διόπτρας τὸν ἕτερον κανόνα τοσοῦτον ὥστε βλέπεσθαι· καὶ πάλιν χαλωμένης τῆς ἑτέρας ἀσπιδίσκης θεωρῶ τὴν ἐν αὐτῇ μέσην τῶν χρωμάτων γραμμήν.

And when the plates are placed thus, I sight through the slits, viewing the rod ΑΓ, with the aforementioned small disk elevated to the point where the middle of the line of the white and black color appears. And with the dioptra remaining unmoved, having shifted from the other part I view through the slits, standing the other rod apart from the dioptra far enough so as to see it. And once again, with the other disk having been slackened, I view the middle line of the colors on it.[43]

The text of the *Dioptra* guides the reader through the highly disciplined actions that certify acts of viewing as acts of measurement: making careful sequences of forward and reverse sightings, calculating distances and recording the results, and situating those precise local observations within the larger canvas of the landscape. The surveyor's ability to "theorize" relies on imposing geometrical precision on the terrestrial features being viewed, insofar as it is possible.[44] Diagrams are crucial to this process, serving in the *Dioptra* as a kind of idealized gloss over the unpredictable details of the terrain in which the surveyor works. They allow him a kind of "double vision," maintaining the diagram's synoptic bird's-eye view as he navigates the ground-level view afforded through the dioptra's sights.

The precision of the dioptra facilitates the surveyor's attempt to straddle the material and mathematical domains. Hero continually argues, implicitly or explicitly, for the use of the dioptra as a surveying instrument, despite its considerable structural and technical complexity compared to other available instruments.[45] Most of the advantages he cites for the dioptra have to do with the broader range of problems it can solve with greater precision compared to competing technologies; that is, his emphasis is more often on the problems than the instrument itself. However, he does rather late in the work break away to describe in detail the problems that plague the so-called *asteriskos* (similar to the Roman *groma* or *ferramentum*), whose simplicity might make it appealing at first glance but which turns out to be quite difficult to manipulate precisely. The *asteriskos*,

---

[43] *Dioptra* 6.21–30.    [44] I discuss some of the complications of this process in Roby 2018.
[45] Lewis 2001, 2012.

he warns, is only useful for a relatively narrow range of dioptrics applications (πρὸς ὀλίγας παντελῶς διοπτρικὰς χρείας), but some people unadvisedly attempt to use it for more than it is good for. The principal problem they will face is due to the flimsy construction of the *asteriskos*; the dioptra is positioned for sighting using a stable mechanism of screws and toothed drums, but the *asteriskos* relies instead on weighted cords, which refuse to keep still:

τοὺς μὲν οὖν κεχρημένους οἶμαι <πε>πειρᾶσθαι τῆς δυσχρηστίας αὐτοῦ, ὅτι αἱ σπάρται, ἐξ ὧν τὰ βάρη κρέμανται, οὐ ταχέως ἠρεμοῦσιν, ἀλλὰ χρόνον τινὰ διαμένουσι κινούμεναι, καὶ μάλιστα ὅταν σφοδρὸς ἄνεμος πνέῃ. διὸ πειρῶνταί τινες, παραβοηθεῖν βουλόμενοι ταύτῃ τῇ δυσχρηστίᾳ, ξυλίνας σύριγγας κοίλας ποιοῦντες, ἐμβαλεῖν τὰ βάρη εἰς ταύτας, ὥστε μὴ ὑπὸ τοῦ ἀνέμου τύπτεσθαι. παρατρίψεως οὖν γινομένης τῶν βαρῶν πρὸς τὰς σύριγγας οὐκ ἀκριβῶς αἱ σπάρτοι ὀρθαὶ διαμένουσιν πρὸς τὸν ὁρίζοντα· . . .

I think some who have used it have tried things ill-suited to it, because the cords, from which weights are suspended, do not quickly come to rest, but remain in motion for some time, especially whenever a strong wind blows. Hence some, wishing to ameliorate this inconvenience, try making hollow wooden tubes, and enclose the weights in these so that they will not be blown by the wind. But then, when the weights experience friction against the tubes, the ropes do not remain precisely vertical.[46]

The material shortcomings of the structurally simple *asteriskos* render it useless for the kind of geometrically precise work Hero claims the dioptra can do. Introducing structural complications like the wooden wind-shield tubes interferes with the simplicity that constitutes the major advantage of the *asteriskos* and does not fix its disadvantages.

Hero then argues that even if it were the case that the ropes could be held still and perpendicular to the horizon, the planes through them would not be aligned with one another. Rather than allowing this explanation to stand on its own, however, Hero offers to prove it geometrically. He structures his proof in such a way that it is very difficult at first to understand the analogy between the geometrical objects and their analogs on the surveyor's field: That is, the reader must consciously move into a purely geometrical analytical space for the proof before beginning to contemplate what any of it has to do with the *asteriskos*. He begins by asking the reader to construct a plane through two nonperpendicular lines AB and ΓΔ, the perpendicular EZ drawn from their intersection, and two

---

[46] *Dioptra* 33.1–15.

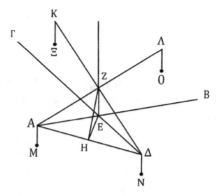

Figure 3.2   The *asteriskos*. Image by author, after Schöne.

additional planes EAZ and ΓEZ, which are proved not to be perpendicular
to one another (but are rather angled at the acute angle AEΓ). Hero then
introduces some new line segments to the picture, as shown in
Figure 3.2.[47] It is not necessary here to follow through every step of this
section, but in broad strokes it serves to construct four line segments AM,
ΔN, KΞ, and ΛO all perpendicular to the plane through AB and ΓΔ, and
two further line segments AΛ and ΔK perpendicular to one another.

His geometrical proof completed, Hero proceeds to map the mathematical objects back onto their real-world analogs. Only at this point do
we learn (or rather "suppose (ὑποστησώμεθα)") that our initial plane
through AB and ΓΔ was the plane through the horizon, that the lines
AΛ and ΔK were the rods of the *asteriskos*, and the cords hanging from the
*asteriskos* were AM, ΔN, KΞ, and ΛO. He concludes by arguing that the
planes through the opposite pairs of cords slant toward one another at the
acute angle defined by AEΓ rather than being perpendicular to one
another. Hero thus chooses to shift what could have remained a purely
material, practical critique of the *asteriskos'* lack of stability and precision
into the geometrical arena where he has labored to situate so much of the
*Dioptra's* problem-solving, and where the instrument's metrical capabili-
ties really shine.

The dioptra will often be called upon to solve problems involving
measuring irregular territory. Hero offers a quite general case in problem

---

[47] *Dioptra* 33.28–41. Image here based on Schöne's diagram; compare Cod. Par. suppl. gr. 607,
fol. 77v.

23; here the problem is to measure a given space enclosed by an irregular line. The surveyor is required to draw perpendicular lines crossing the space and intersecting at the dioptra, and then further to dissect the space, as far as possible, into a rectangle surrounded by right triangles and trapezoids. In order for these shapes to make the best approximation of the irregular outer area, says Hero, they should be bounded by a rope or chain stretched as tightly as possible between points along the perimeter, so that its measurement will not be compromised by additional stretching or contraction. Thus we are reminded that it is not only the territory to be measured that presents material inconveniences, but even the tools of measurement themselves. Hero, as usual, suggests how best to minimize these inaccuracies, without abstracting them out of the picture entirely. The reference here to the material properties of the rope that must be pulled tight recalls the emphasis on the physical work of hauling ropes introduced into the passage altered from Proclus in *Definitiones* 135.

The surveyor's world comes more vividly to life in problem 25, where Hero posits an irregular parcel of land, most of whose borders are no longer visible but a "model (*mimēma*)" of which, presumably like a map or plan, survives (Figure 3.3).[48] He proposes a method to use the few remaining boundary points (in this case B and Θ) and the map to restore the missing borders by subdividing the shape described by the map into parallelograms and triangles, approximating the irregular borders of the actual region. He remarks that he aims to make this method "quite general (*katholikōteros*)," but that as a result it is also "quite indirect (*skoliōteros*)." He also acknowledges here that the resulting solution will be only an approximation consisting of lines "nearby (σύνεγγυς)" the actual boundary. Much as he did for the description of the *asteriskos*, Hero defines the subregions geometrically, using the third-person imperatives characteristic of geometric prose. He stipulates a certain arrangement of intersecting lines bounding those subregions, perhaps the "indirect" or "winding" route he warned of at the beginning of the passage. He then moves on to explain

---

[48] On this problem, including a possible parallel in the Roman agrimensorial texts, see Vincent 1858: 268–77. The text in question is from the *Limitis repositio* attributed to Marcus Junius Nipsus and may be found as well at Lachmann 1848: 286–89. There are certainly some similarities between the problem described there and *Dioptra* 25; both concern the reconstitution of boundaries from a few points and proceed by using an instrument (in the case of Nipsus, the *ferramentum*) to establish a set of intersecting lines perpendicular to one another to cover the territory. Still, there are at least as many differences; Hero frames his solution initially as a somewhat abstract geometrical problem, whereas the Latin author instead uses the infrastructure of boundary lines (*limites*) and inscribed marker stones, for which there is no equivalent in Hero's text, and he does not refer to any kind of map, although as we have seen many other agrimensorial texts refer to them.

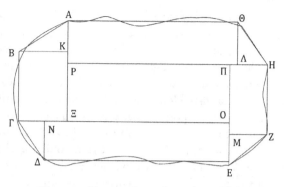

Figure 3.3   *Dioptra* problem 25. Image by author, after Vincent 1858.

how each of these regular subregions can be measured in the real world
with the help of the dioptra and measuring cord. This part of the text is
framed in first-person plural futures, which, as we shall see, is characteristic
of Hero's transitions between the mathematical and material domains.[49]

When he applies geometrical or numerical methods from a purely
mathematical domain to a more complex real-world context, Hero sometimes seems to adopt marked mathematical terminology as a rhetorical
strategy to preempt objections about the validity of that domain transition.
For example, he will often formulaically "reveal (*apophainomai*)" an answer
obtained through an algorithmic calculation that can be verified by any
reader who learns to follow through the algorithm. However, Hero sometimes uses the same term to "reveal the answer" to problems that cannot be
so straightforwardly verified. For example, problem 9 of the *Dioptra* poses
the problem of finding the shortest distance across a river by sighting from
one bank. The solution involves finding a line across the river perpendicular to a line along the bank that is assumed to be roughly parallel to a line
along the opposite bank. This maneuver obviously calls for some approximations, which he attempts to smooth over by deploying a form of
*apophainomai* in the conclusion:

τὸ ἐλάχιστον πλάτος τοῦ ποταμοῦ τὸ ΕΖ· ἡ γὰρ ΕΖ ὡσανεὶ κάθετός ἐστιν
ἐπ' ἀμφοτέρας τὰς ὄχθας, εἴπερ παραλλήλους αὐτὰς ἐννοοίμεθα. ὡς οὖν
ἐμάθομεν ἐπάνω, εἰλήφθω τὸ ἀπὸ τοῦ Ε διάστημα ἐπὶ τὸ Ζ τὸ πρὸς
διαβήτην, ὃ καὶ ἀποφανούμεθα ἐλάχιστον εἶναι τοῦ ποταμοῦ πλάτος.

---

[49] On this pattern see also Roby 2018.

The least width of the river will be EZ, for it is as though perpendicular to both banks, if we imagine them to be parallel. Let the crossing distance from E to Z be defined as we learned above, which we will reveal to be the least width of the river.[50]

The problem ends here. Hero does indeed continue on to another problem involving distances over perpendicular lines, whose answer is also promised to be "revealed," but that one is framed as a geometrical problem without the complicating factor of the riverbank approximation. The use in problem 9 of the same verb, with its strong mathematical associations, represents a kind of rhetorical prestidigitation, in which the possibly problematic approximation of the river's banks as parallel lines is glossed over by relocating that problem to a geometrical milieu in which such assumptions are warranted as part of the problem statement.

In problem 31 of the *Dioptra*, Hero shines a brighter light on the complications real-world problems introduce into arithmetical or geometrical problems that look relatively simple on the surface. Here the problem is to determine the amount of output (*anablusis*) a spring produces. As Hero immediately points out, this parameter is highly variable depending on the amount of local rainfall, though he designates certain springs as "high quality (*gennaiai*)" based on their relatively stable flow. Measuring the output is challenging, because the problem is not to measure the spring's total output for a season or a year, but to get an idea of the average rate of flow (though Hero of course does not use that term). Modern solutions to this problem require a whole toolbox of differential equations and fluid dynamics models that Hero does not possess. Instead, he proposes an experimental method:

δεῖ οὖν περιλαβόντα τὸ πᾶν τῆς πηγῆς ὕδωρ, ὥστε μηδαμόθεν ἀπορρεῖν, σωλῆνα τετράγωνον μολιβοῦν ποιῆσαι, στοχασάμενον μᾶλλον μείζονα πολλῷ τῆς ἀποθύσεως· εἶτα δι᾽ ἑνὸς τόπου ἐναρμόσαι αὐτὸν ὥστε δι᾽ αὐτοῦ τὸ ἐν τῇ πηγῇ ὕδωρ ἀπορρεῖν.

It is necessary to account for all the water of the spring; so that none flows away, make a square channel out of lead, aiming for something much larger than the output, and then insert it at some point so that the water in the spring runs off through it.[51]

The square channel is to meet the spring at its lowest point (the reason why this is a job for the dioptra) in order to divert the water from the spring so it can be measured. The channel is specified as square because

[50] *Dioptra* 9.13–20.    [51] *Dioptra* 31.8–14.

Hero is trying to devise a way of accounting for flow over time; hence the outflow of water from the spring is specified as "2 dactyls" in the numerical example he provides. How does a measure of length become a measure of volume? Hero's mathematical method here is murky at best, but it appears his strategy is to ignore the depth of the water running out through the channel and treat it as an area: A shallow stream of water runs over the given length of 2 dactyls through a channel of a known width (6 dactyls in the example) to produce a total of 12 "square" dactyls. This maneuver may be compared to a passage from the *De mensuris* on converting from linear to square or solid units (e.g. dactyls, feet, or unciae) by squaring or cubing them.[52] The author remarks in particular that these conversions are used "according to the outline and tradition of the mechanical authors (κατὰ τὴν τῶν μηχανικῶν διατύπωσιν καὶ παράδοσιν)" to answer questions about the capacities of water channels. The numerical example provided converts the capacity of a channel of 12 dactyls to square dactyls, and then to feet, unciae, and modii. However, despite the context it shares with the *De mensuris* passage, *Dioptra* 31 is notable for not mentioning the conversion of units.

The next complication is more serious, as Hero acknowledges that (even if one accepts the concession that the water's depth as it flows through the channel is negligible) so far all he has done is provide a way to measure a "snapshot" of the water flowing over an arbitrary distance. He has yet to account for the rate of flow:

> εἰδέναι δὲ χρὴ ὅτι οὐκ ἔστιν αὔταρκες πρὸς τὸ ἐπιγνῶναι, πόσον χορηγεῖ ὕδωρ ἡ πηγή, [ἢ] τὸ εὑρεῖν τὸν ὄγκον τοῦ ῥεύματος, ὃν λέγομεν εἶναι δακτύλων ιβ, ἀλλὰ καὶ τὸ τάχος αὐτοῦ· ταχυτέρας μὲν γὰρ οὔσης τῆς ῥύσεως πλέον ἐπιχορηγεῖ τὸ ὕδωρ, βραδυτέρας δὲ μεῖον. διὸ δεῖ ὑπὸ τὴν τῆς πηγῆς ῥύσιν ὀρύξαντα τάφρον τηρῆσαι ἐξ ἡλιακοῦ ὡροσκοπίου, ἐν τινι ὥρᾳ πόσον ἀπορρεῖ ὕδωρ ἐν τῇ τάφρῳ, καὶ οὕτως στοχάσασθαι τὸ ἐπιχορηγούμενον ὕδωρ ἐν τῇ ἡμέρᾳ πόσον ἐστίν, ὥστ' οὐδὲ ἀναγκαῖόν ἐστι τὸν ὄγκον τῆς ῥύσεως τηρεῖν· διὰ γὰρ τοῦ χρόνου δήλη ἐστὶν ἡ χορηγία.

It must be known that to discover how much water the spring emits it is not sufficient to find the [cross-sectional] size of the flow (which we say to be 12 dactyls), but also its speed. For when the flow is faster more water runs in, and less when it is slower. Therefore it is necessary to dig a ditch under the flow of the spring and to observe, using a sundial, in what time a given amount of water flows in the ditch, and thus to estimate how much water is

---

[52] *De mensuris* 23.1.

output over a day. Thus it is not necessary to observe the extent of the flow, for the supply is clear from the time.[53]

The approach here might be seen as a kind of reverse water clock (clepsydra): Whereas a clepsydra allows elapsed time to be told using the flow of water from a standardized vessel whose shape is taken to regulate the outflow of water at a steady rate, Hero's method here uses a sundial to measure the quantity of elapsed time, which can then be compared with the amount of water flowing from the spring to allow the previously unknown rate to be found. In both cases there is a strong empirical element; many smaller clepsydrae from both Egypt and Greece are crafted with tapering forms that aim to keep the flow rate steady, and they seem likely to be the result of trial and error rather than mathematical calculation.[54] Argoud notes as well the connection between this problem and the more sophisticated water clocks (associated with Ctesibius) that integrated additional components like floats with meters mounted on them to indicate the time.[55]

Hero's method might also be compared to the Roman designation of the *quinaria* as a measure of how much water would flow through a circular pipe with a standard diameter of one and a quarter *digiti* in a period of twenty-four hours. Frontinus says that the measure is credited alternately to Agrippa or to plumbers working under the advice of Vitruvius.[56] By his own time, Frontinus says, the capacity of a pipe could be expressed in inches of diameter, in square *digiti* of cross-section, in multiples of *quinariae* or approximations thereof, or some combination of these factors. Frontinus here claims that all of the major aqueducts yield the correct amount of water as indicated both by calculation and in the records (*rationi et commentariis*), except for the few that have been deliberately tampered with.[57] So far so good, but later he says that in fact he has measured and found a much larger quantity of water than the *commentarii* would indicate, blaming the discrepancy on others' sloppy calculation, as well as the use of inconsistent measures either from incompetence or dishonesty.[58] Clearly, the problem of measuring water flow remains a challenge, even in the controlled and standardized environment of the Roman aqueduct system – to say nothing of Hero's arbitrary, irregular natural spring.

[53] *Dioptra* 31.21–32.
[54] On the history of the clepsydra (including other shapes and sizes) see Hannah 2009: 98–110.
[55] Argoud 2000: 243–56.
[56] Frontinus, *De aquaeductu Urbis Romae* 1.25. On Frontinus' struggles see Peachin 2004: 62–67.
[57] Frontinus, *De aquaeductu Urbis Romae* 1.34.    [58] Frontinus, *De aquaeductu Urbis Romae* 2.74.

Hero thus marshals a host of different techniques for managing the domain transition between the (largely static) world of geometrical constructions and arithmetical calculations and the dynamic real world. The shifts he effects between the mathematical and material aspects of surveying can sometimes be a trickier matter than he explicitly acknowledges, particularly when he moves from well-established mathematical methods like dissecting a surface into triangles to new methods like the scheme in problem 31 for measuring the flow of a spring. When purely mathematical methods prove insufficient, the narrative of mathematical persuasion may need support from an additional narrative of experimental observation, in this case digging a ditch and using a sundial to time the flow of water.

## Mechanics

A comparable negotiation between mathematical rigor and experimental observation characterizes Hero's treatment of theoretical mechanics in the remnants of the *Mechanica*. The Greek text of this work survives only in fragments preserved in the eighth book of Pappus' *Synagōgē*, but Cuomo argues persuasively that the passages relevant here can be taken more or less as verbatim quotations from Hero.[59] Fleury comments that Hero's general approach differs from that of the Peripatetic *Mechanical Problems*: Whereas the Peripatetic text reduced mechanical problems of various kinds to the principles of the lever and the circle, Hero instead focuses on the relative difficulty of moving heavy and light objects with a given force, or conversely on the relative difficulty of moving a given weight with a greater or lesser force.[60] Fleury points out as well that the apparent argumentative rigor of Hero's text is less than that of the Peripatetic work, since he does not begin his discussions by enunciating principles whose resolution he notes at the end.

In fact, Hero seems to make a virtue of differentiating his presentations of the simple machines from pseudo-mathematical proof structures like those found in the Peripatetic text. For the most part, he depicts the simple machines not as abstractions like inclined planes, but as creations made in the real world from tangible materials with properties of their own. The presence of the material world in Hero's treatment of the simple machines does not, of course, render the "theoretical" component inert. Schiefsky observes that a common device, the balance, is present as a unifying model throughout Hero's descriptions of the simple machines: "[T]he intellectual

[59] Cuomo 2000: 112 n. 144.      [60] Fleury 1993: 56.

operation is that of 'seeing' how each of the powers really is a kind of balance."[61] Indeed, the function of the balance in Hero's *Mechanica* recalls the dynamics of water flow discussed in *Dioptra* 31. Whereas Krafft had categorized Hero's mechanics as "static" in contrast to the "dynamic" approach of the Peripatetic *Mechanical Problems*, Schiefsky argues that in fact Hero's account is "dynamic" in its own right by virtue of using an analogy to the balance to analyze the relationship between time, distance, and force enacted by the wedge and screw.[62] Cuomo comments as well on the different balance between the theoretical and the material that Hero strikes compared to Pappus. For example, she notes that in their respective presentations of the problem of a body moving up an inclined plane, Pappus' version of the demonstration and its associated propositions is purely mathematical, whereas Hero is preoccupied by the effects of material friction and how they might be addressed by attaching smoothly planed boards to the sliding bodies or coating them with grease.[63]

The wheel and axle is first on Hero's list of simple machines, sending a strong signal that these devices are meant to be conceptualized as material entities:

Ὁ μὲν οὖν ἄξων ὁ ἐν τῷ περιτροχίῳ κατασκευάζεται οὕτως. ξύλον δεῖ λαβεῖν εὔτονον τετράγωνον καθάπερ δοκίδα καὶ τούτου τὰ ἄκρα σιμώσαντα στρογγύλα ποιῆσαι καὶ χοινικίδας περιθεῖναι χαλκᾶς συναραρυίας τῷ ἄξονι, ὥστε ἐμβληθείσας αὐτὰς εἰς τρήματα στρογγύλα ἐν ἀκινήτῳ τινὶ πήγματι εὐλύτως στρέφεσθαι, τῶν τρημάτων τριβεῖς χαλκοῦς ἐχόντων ὑποκειμένους ταῖς χοινικίσι. καλεῖται δὲ τὸ εἰρημένον ξύλον ἄξων. περὶ δὲ μέσον τὸν ἄξονα περιτίθεται τύμπανον ἔχον τρῆμα τετράγωνον ἁρμοστὸν τῷ ἄξονι, ὥστε ἅμα στρέφεσθαι τόν τε ἄξονα καὶ τὸ περιτρόχιον.

The axle in the wheel and axle is constructed thus. It is necessary to take springy wood, rectangular like a plank, and tool its edges to make them round, and to place around it bronze washers closely joined to the axle, so that when they have been placed into round boreholes in a stationary frame they will turn easily, since the boreholes have bronze flanges underlying the washers. That wood is called the axle. Around its middle the axle is encased by a wheel having a square borehole joined to the axle, so that both the axle and the wheel turn together.[64]

---

[61] Schiefsky 2008: 17. On Hero's strategies to reduce every simple machine to the balance see Schiefsky 2008: 22–32.

[62] Krafft 1970; Schiefsky 2008: 28–31.

[63] Cuomo 2000: 115. Pappus *Synagōgē* 1054.4–1058.26; Hero *Mechanica* prop. 1.21 in Qusṭā ibn Lūqā's translation, with text and translation at Hero and Qusṭā ibn Lūqā 1988: 89–90, 2016: 72–73.

[64] *Mechanicorum fragmenta* 2.1.19–30.

We do not even begin here with a finished product, but rather with a lump
of wood that has to be shaped into its final form in the passage itself, losing
its rough edges and being bound up in the bronze fittings that will enable
the system to rotate. Its other half is likewise "constructed" in the text:
beginning life as a board that is then drilled through, and the borehole
then fitted with a bronze sleeve, all done before our eyes rather than
appearing readymade. Bronze is better suited than wood for sustaining
the friction of rotational motion; were this a purely notional system
perhaps the whole mechanism could just have been introduced as being
made of bronze, but of course that is not how devices using the wheel and
axle are actually made, given its much greater weight and cost. The version
of the wheel and axle we encounter here in the text is basically the same as
the one we encounter in the world. The resemblance is highlighted by the
way it comes into being in the text, through a layering of materials so
awkward that the reader has to be reminded that the so-called axle is, in
fact, the wood rather than its practical bronze fittings.

The descriptions of the other simple machines are likewise embedded in
a world of material objects – and, moreover, material objects being
manipulated by embodied actors. Just as the physical affordances of the
human eye made themselves felt in the optical domain, demanding solutions to correct optical illusions, so the physical affordances of the human
body, even down to the hand, motivate the development of the lever in the
*Mechanica*'s account:

> προελόμενοι γάρ τινες μεγάλα βάρη κινεῖν, ἐπειδὴ ἀπὸ τῆς γῆς ἔδει πρῶτον
> μετεωρίσαι, λαβὰς δὲ οὐκ εἶχον διὰ τὸ πάντα τὰ μέρη τῆς ἕδρας τοῦ φορτίου
> ἐπικεῖσθαι τῷ ἐδάφει, ὑπορύξαντες βραχὺ καὶ ξύλου μακροῦ τὸ ἄκρον
> ὑποβαλόντες ὑπὸ τὸ φορτίον κατῆγον ἐκ τοῦ ἑτέρου ἄκρου, ὑποθέντες
> τῷ ξύλῳ παρ' αὐτὸ τὸ φορτίον λίθον, ὃ δὴ καλεῖται ὑπομόχλιον.

> Some who decided to move great weights, since it is first necessary to lift
> them from the earth, and they did not have a grip because of the whole of
> the base of the weight resting on the ground, dug out a little underneath
> and placed the tip of a large piece of wood under the weight, and raised it to
> another height, then placed under the wood and near the weight a stone,
> which is called the fulcrum.[65]

Here we get a close, embodied look at what it means to lift something; it is
not just a matter of mass but of getting a grip on the thing and raising it
incrementally off the ground. In this version of the story, the epiphany of

---

[65] *Mechanicorum fragmenta* 2.2.3–9.

the lever only becomes available by scrabbling in the dirt to get under the weight.

Hero's account is not like the bare-bones description other authors give of the lever, which (if they reference human operators at all) at most feature an abstract man who wants to raise a certain weight and work their way to the leverage he will need to do so.[66] The Peripatetic *Mechanical Problems* begins with the lever, first observing the apparent strangeness of its ability to raise heavy weights with relatively little effort, and then tracing the cause to the natural physics of the circle.[67] The author then argues that propositions about the balance reduce to propositions about the circle, propositions about the lever reduce to the balance, and that indeed most other problems in mechanics are reducible to the lever.[68] On this basis Sophie Roux describes the lever as the "privileged object of mechanics," both as an exemplary case of using the principles of nature to achieve effects that may appear to flout those principles themselves and as a common element in most mechanical problems.[69]

Roux notes that while Archimedes is often referred to by his commentators (including Hero) as having developed the theory of the lever, the first book of his *Planes in Equilibrium* (which appears to be the text referred to by several slightly different names across the Heronian corpus) does not in fact deal with concrete levers at all, but rather develops the notion of equilibrium in a way that harmonizes mathematics and physics.[70] Likewise, in the Peripatetic text the lever's action is introduced through a geometrical diagram located in a world of physics (in the sense of analyzing the motion of weights at different distances), but not a physical world (in the sense of Hero's men struggling to get a grip on a concrete object).[71] To be sure, De Groot is correct in arguing that textual treatments (in Aristotle, the Peripatetic *Mechanical Problems*, and elsewhere) of the "moving radius principle" by which the lever and other objects in rotational motion operate are read against a deep background of physical experience. As she argues, Aristotle and the other authors she discusses are able to exploit the reader's past physical experiences of sailing, swinging objects, and other common activities to build up "kinesthetic awareness," a kind of physical intuition into proportional forces.[72] But for

---

[66] Even elsewhere in the Heronian corpus manpower is abstracted in this way: *Dioptra* 37 defines a man as being able to lift five talents without mechanical assistance. On this passage (and a parallel in *Mechanicorum fragmenta* 1.1) see Schiefsky 2008: 21.

[67] *Mechanical Problems* 847b1–20.    [68] *Mechanical Problems* 848a11–15.    [69] Roux 1992: 104.

[70] Fleury 1993: 63–64; Roux 1992: 142.    [71] *Mechanical Problems* 850a30–850b2.

[72] De Groot 2014: 51–63.

all that the *Mechanical Problems* and Aristotle's own examples of mechanics in action draw on a wide variety of lived experiences, that background is left tacit when the lever is introduced.

Vitruvius treats the lever in his tenth book as an example of how mechanical effects must be produced through the cooperation of rectilinear and rotational motion.[73] His lever is introduced simply as a thing made of iron (*ferreus*) applied to a weight that cannot be lifted by a crowd of people (*manuum multitudo*), which once a fulcrum is placed below it allows the weight to be lifted by the power of a single man (*unius hominis viribus*). Vitruvius then goes into more detail about how the lever's mechanical advantage depends on the placement of the fulcrum. However, even though the lever remains made of metal throughout this discussion, and though it is placed on the ground (*in areae solo*), its materiality remains sketchy, and the "hands" of the would-be lifters are simply a metonym for "people." As Fleury observes, Vitruvius does not strongly suggest a conceptual separation between the theoretical lever and its material instantiation.[74] So Hero's decision to treat the lever in his *Mechanica* as a concrete object, grounded in earth and grasped by human hands, represents a conscious decision to move his treatment of mechanics into much more material territory than his predecessors had afforded it.[75]

Indeed, the world of Hero's *Mechanica* is not only material but also mercantile. The wedge is commended for its "great utility for squeezing perfumes and sticking stacked carpentry joins, and most of all, whenever it is necessary to drag apart rocks from the quarries which are stuck on the bottom."[76] Like the wedge itself, the scale of its work expands from the tiny to the huge. The perfumer's extraction of precious aromatics from natural materials and the shims that compress the carpenter's joins conjure up a world of small-scale, skilled manufacturing work. By contrast, the hauling at the quarry is heavy, stressful work – not just for the quarrymen but for the wedge itself, which produces "shrieks and fractures (ψόφους καὶ ῥήγματα)" as it works, even sometimes when it is not actively being struck. The quarry work also puts the wedge in context with the other

---

[73] Vitruvius, *De architectura* 10.3.1–3.

[74] Fleury 1993: 67. For a comparison of Vitruvius' treatment and that in the Peripatetic *Mechanical Problems* see Fleury 1993: 58–61, 63–64.

[75] None of this is to say, of course, that other authors on mechanics do not treat material instantiations of the lever. The Peripatetic *Mechanical Problems* builds a whole world of levers: Balances (849b22–30), ship rudders (850b28–851a35), oars (850b10–17), and more are modeled as levers, while De Groot argues persuasively that Aristotle himself models the motions of animal limbs around their joints as levers (De Groot 2014: 31–38).

[76] *Mechanicorum fragmenta* 2.4.1–12.

machines, a reminder that the lifting work of the lever and *polyspaston* is performed not on rocks that lie conveniently strewn around the landscape, but on natural accretions of raw stone that must be chiseled out before they can be used. Hero notes here that none of the other simple machines can perform this work, "not even if they are all combined," emphasizing the wedge's great power when deployed in the proper context, even compared to the complex *polyspaston*'s theoretically unlimited capacity for raising dead weight.

The *Mechanica* survives much more completely in the 9th-century Arabic translation by Quṣṭā ibn Lūqā, a Christian author and translator of Greek and Syriac texts who worked in Armenia as well as in Baghdad. The striking allusions to the practical and mercantile applications of the simple machines are considerably amplified in his version of the text. For example, most treatments of the *polyspaston* give little to no attention to how weighty objects are actually attached to the pulley system, focusing instead on the proportional relationship between the effort expended and the weight lifted depending on the number of pulleys. This is even true of the surviving Greek fragment from Hero describing a hauling machine based on differential gears, where some attention is indeed paid to the material constitution of the gears and their hauling power but none to how the weight is attached.[77] By contrast, in Quṣṭā ibn Lūqā's text, the attachments that hook onto the stone to be lifted are described in some detail, even down to the appropriate material.[78] The iron must not be too hard, lest it be brittle, nor too soft, lest it bend under the weight. A similar concern for materials pervades other devices in the text, like an olive press that needs to be made of strong wood that is neither too pliable nor too stiff.

Quṣṭā ibn Lūqā's text strongly emphasizes the experience of using the devices described in the text. The passage on a contraption for letting a large stone down a slope at a gentle pace includes an explanation of how the transporters use two roads and two wagons with different loads, each with its team of oxen, to create an enormous counterweight for the stone.[79] The process of efficiently extracting olive oil with a press is described in extraordinary detail: A screw is turned with handspakes, a

---

[77] *Mechanicorum fragmenta* 1.1, Pappus *Synagōgē* 8.1060.4–1068.23. On the question of whether this passage derives from a separate text called the *Baroulkos* rather than from the *Mechanica* see Drachmann's notes to Carra de Vaux's edition of the Arabic text at Hero and Quṣṭā ibn Lūqā 1988: 217–26, as well as Gatto, Gatto, and Ferriello's arguments at Hero and Quṣṭā ibn Lūqā 2016: 281–92.

[78] Quṣṭā ibn Lūqā *Baroulkos* 3.8; Hero and Quṣṭā ibn Lūqā 1988: 192–95, 2016: 143–44.

[79] Quṣṭā ibn Lūqā *Baroulkos* 3.9; Hero and Quṣṭā ibn Lūqā 1988: 195–96, 2016: 145.

beam moves down to press on another piece of wood, which in turn presses another, which in turn presses the olives, which yield some juice, and then the whole process is reversed and repeated until every last bit of juice has been extracted.[80] The mechanical ease or difficulty of using the different machines is a prominent feature. He even mentions the risk that a bend in the stone-lifting hook could endanger the workmen if a stone falls out of the apparatus, and he warns as well that workmen are vulnerable to broken supports in a grape-pressing system using a counterweight.[81]

We should, of course, be cautious about ascribing any of these passages to the lost *Mechanica*. To be sure, certain elements resemble the few surviving Greek passages, as well as elements of Hero's style from other texts, like the insistent focus on material properties and construction techniques (especially for screws), the blend of geometrical and craft terminology, and the emphasis on the practical applications of the devices he describes. Other features, however, seem unique to Qusṭā ibn Lūqā's text, like the references to workmen who might get injured on the job, who are not a concern in Hero's largely unpopulated texts. These workmen are also absent from the Persian version of the text, which hews much more closely to the Heronian norms of an unpopulated text that nevertheless devotes considerable attention to the material details of the machines it describes. The stylistic resemblance is particularly close in the section on the so-called Balance of Wisdom, which describes the structure and operation of a precision balance for weighing gold and silver in terms reminiscent of Hero's *Dioptra*.[82] While this section is almost certainly an interpolation since it has no equivalent in the Arabic text, like the passages on workmen from Qusṭā's text it is easy to see why Hero's text provided an attractive home for discourse on mechanics firmly rooted in the practical aspects of building and operating the machines themselves.

Of course Hero's vignettes of the work of quarrymen, perfumers, carpenters, and other workmen are not genuine accounts of life on the job, much as we might wish that any such evidence survived from antiquity. For the most part, except in the passages from Qusṭā's text mentioned above, the workmen themselves are sketched very thinly or not at all. Then what are they? The descriptions of the simple machines at work in the *Mechanica* are perhaps best conceived of as thought

---

[80] Qusṭā ibn Lūqā *Baroulkos* 3.19; Hero and Qusṭā ibn Lūqā 1988: 207–10, 2016: 155–56. On these devices see Drachmann 1932: 60–77.

[81] Qusṭā ibn Lūqā *Baroulkos* 3.15; Hero and Qusṭā ibn Lūqā 1988: 200–204, 2016: 150.

[82] Hero and Qusṭā ibn Lūqā 2016: 234–35.

experiments situated within simple yet concrete narratives such as that of being in a quarry. In this sense they are similar to the scene-setting sketches that introduce some passages of the Peripatetic *Mechanical Problems*. There, for example, the balance is first introduced abstractly as a compound of circle and lever, but it is later integrated into a more complex mercantile environment where unscrupulous merchants will exploit different densities of wood to make small amounts of precious purple dye look weightier.[83] And while the lever is first analyzed as a geometrical–physical abstraction, the author later uses the principle thus derived to explain why, for example, the rowers near the middle of a ship add the most power to its movement, or why two men carrying something heavy suspended from a beam do not feel its weight equally unless it is placed exactly in the center, or why dentists yank teeth using forceps.[84]

These "thought experiments" are framed quite differently in the context of their works than, for example, the surveying instructions provided in the *Dioptra*. Those problems make use of the same blended language of mathematics and physics, but they are also prefaced with elaborate instructions for setting up and using the observational instrument. Those instructions strongly suggest the reader is meant to act on them in performing the work of surveying, whereas the reader of Hero's *Mechanica* is probably not meant to take on work in a quarry, nor the reader of the Peripatetic *Mechanical Problems* to become a rower or practice heaving weights around with a beam to test the merits of their mechanical explanations. Instead, the robustly narrated thought experiments in both these texts provide the reader with De Groot's "kinesthetic awareness," an intuition of how the simple machines work. They do not simply acquaint the reader with their basic operating principles, but also give a quasi-quantitative sense of their motive power to propel a ship, heave a quarry stone, or extract a tooth. I discuss the various levels of formality and narrative techniques Hero uses for these "thought experiments" in more detail below.

Other passages of the *Mechanica* foreground the ability of mechanics to blend concrete components with more explicitly mathematical elements. Hero presents the construction of the screw through the geometrical method of inscribing a helix on a cylinder.[85] But whereas the initial construction of the helix was framed as a precise geometrical operation of drawing a line on a "cylinder" of indeterminate materiality, converting

---

[83] *Mechanical Problems* 849b20–850a2.
[84] *Mechanical Problems* 850b10–29; 857b9–20; 854a16–31.
[85] *Mechanicorum fragmenta* 2.5.1–4.

that line into the threads of a screw requires a definite step into the material domain.[86] Those who aim to construct a screw do so by "cutting in a channel along this line to the depth of the cylinder and chopping it out, so as to join up a solid threading-knob in the channel." They must then round off the ends, attach crossbars to them in smoothly turning bearings, and then fit those crossbars to a bar that runs the length of the screw, with a lengthwise channel attached to the threading knob. By the end of the passage, the geometrical construction has been fully realized in a concretely material form.

The final fragment of the second book of Hero's *Mechanica* invokes even more visibly the mathematical–physical principles that underlie Greek theoretical mechanics.[87] The passage is preserved in Pappus, who begins it with a promise that the reader will discover centers of mass to be "elementary (*stoicheiōdē*)" through studying the analyses available in a text on equilibrium by Archimedes (which Roux argues is likely the first book of *Planes in Equilibrium*, though Fleury disagrees) and in Hero's *Mechanica*.[88] Given that these texts are unknown to most (μὴ γνώριμα τοῖς πολλοῖς), Pappus will offer a brief summary for the problem of finding the center of mass of a triangle.[89]

It is difficult to distinguish Hero's views in this passage from Pappus' own, since the Greek text is, as usual, only preserved through Pappus, the proof is not complete, and the Arabic text has been subjected to more alterations than many other passages.[90] Still, it is instructive to follow through the steps that the passage prescribes, as they can be usefully compared both to Archimedes' approach and to strategies Hero employs elsewhere in the corpus. He first establishes a triangle ΑΒΓ, then bisects legs ΒΓ and ΓΑ at Δ and Ε, connects the midpoints to their opposite vertices, and establishes their point of intersection Ζ as the center of mass (Figure 3.4).[91] Just what does this mean? He argues that were the triangle to be stood upon a perpendicular plane along either ΑΔ or ΒΕ, it would not tilt to one side or the other, since triangles ΑΒΔ and ΑΓΔ are equal. Since

[86] *Mechanicorum fragmenta* 2.5.35–42.     [87] *Mechanicorum fragmenta* 2.35.

[88] Pappus *Synagōgē* 8.1034.1–6; Roux 1992: 142. Fleury suggests the analysis Pappus gives is too different from that of *Planes in Equilibrium* for that to be the book he is referencing and suggests instead a lost Archimedean text on levers to which Pappus refers elsewhere: Fleury 1993: 58.

[89] On the differences between Hero's treatment of this problem and Pappus' see Cuomo 2000: 111–12.

[90] Hero and Qusṭā ibn Lūqā 2016: 344–56.

[91] Although there is a textual problem at the point in Pappus' text where Ζ is identified as the center of mass, the identification and nomenclature are confirmed by the remainder of the passage. For the Arabic version, see Hero and Qusṭā ibn Lūqā 1988: 172–74, 2016: 131.

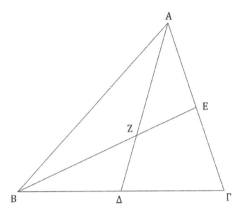

Figure 3.4    Finding the center of mass of a triangle.

the triangle is thus in equilibrium (*isorrhopei*) upon AΔ and BE, their intersection point Z must then be the center of mass.

Roux characterizes Hero's and Pappus' analyses of the center of mass as similarly "inexact," since they are not based on Archimedes' rigorously derived mathematical analysis.[92] Instead, they rely on intuitive physical concepts of what "center of mass" means, like drawing an equivalence between bodies suspended at their center of mass and bodies at rest or parallel to the horizon while suspended. Indeed, Hero uses the term *isorrhopein* in the *Pneumatica* to refer to a quite different phenomenon. In the very first chapter of the main text, he explains that the curved siphon is able to cause water to move upwards because it tends to maintain equilibrium between the portions of water in its two legs.[93] He continues the discussion into the next chapter, where he raises the markedly Archimedean point that the surface of the liquid at rest in either leg of the siphon will, like all liquids at rest, conform to a sphere with its center at the Earth's center.[94]

Roux's characterization of this approach to the center of mass as "inexact" and "intuitive" compared to Archimedes' rigorous geometrical derivations is thus quite fair. But at the same time, the approach here is being applied to an ostentatiously different type of object: Whereas Archimedes glossed over the question of thickness in *Planes in Equilibrium*, here a triangle is explicitly granted material properties of thickness and density (uniform, for convenience).[95] The triangle's

[92] Roux 1992: 147.    [93] *Pneumatica* 1.1.1–21.    [94] *Pneumatica* 1.2.19–22.
[95] Roux carefully considers the question of what it meant for Archimedes, Hero, or Pappus to speak of the "center of mass" of a geometrical object: Roux 1992: 115–16, 142–47.

thickness is a prominent feature of the Arabic version of the text as well; it is introduced as an "evenly thick and heavy triangle," and point Z is specified as being "in the middle of the thickness of triangle ΑΒΓ."[96] It thus seems likely that the heftiness of the triangle, which distinguishes the treatment here from purely geometrical objects and Archimedes' own theoretical mechanical analysis, originated with Hero. The Heronian approach represents not so much a failure to meet what Roux calls Archimedes' "ascetic" standard as an intentional domain shift from the mathematical to the material. As elsewhere in the corpus, Hero recognizes that material objects may call for different analytical methods and standards than purely mathematical objects do. At some times the two may converge more closely, at others they may necessarily veer away from one another, but the mechanician's responsibility at all times is to remain sensitive to the analytical regime suitable for the problem at hand.

## Automata

The materially embodied approach Hero's *Mechanica* takes to problems of equilibrium recurs in the *Automata*, a work that renders the interchange between mathematical and material elements even more prominent in a variety of ways. When he is able to draw on the conventions of mathematical prose to describe certain components or functions of the automaton, Hero gains access to a useful set of textual tools, including geometrical diagrams and accompanying styles of proof that implicitly claim the rigor of pure geometrical proofs. This mathematical style is most readily available to Hero when he describes how to achieve the different patterns of motion a designer might desire the mobile automata to perform, as the linear paths of locomotion naturally map onto geometrical forms. Hero introduces his strategy for producing circular motion through an extravaganza of mathematical notation and geometrical models of the automaton's wheeled framework (Figure 3.5):

Ἔστω γὰρ κύκλος, καθ' οὗ φέρεσθαι δεῖ τὸ πλινθίον, τὸ ΑΒΓ, οὗ κέντρον τὸ Δ. καὶ διήχθω τις ἡ ΑΔ, καὶ ταύτῃ ὀρθὴ ἀπὸ τοῦ Α ἡ ΕΑΖ· ἡ δὲ ΕΖ διάμετρος ἔστω ἑνὸς τῶν τριῶν τροχῶν, ἡλίκου ἂν προαιρώμεθα. διχοτομία δὲ αὐτῆς ἔστω τὸ Α. καὶ ἐπεζεύχθωσαν αἱ ΔΕ, ΔΖ. τῷ δὲ μεγέθει τοῦ ἄξονος τῶν τροχῶν ἴση ἔστω ἡ ΑΗ, καὶ τῇ ΕΖ παράλληλος ἡ ΗΘΚ. τὸ δὲ πλινθίον ἔστω τὸ ΜΛΝΞ παράλληλον ἔχον τὴν ΝΞ τῇ ΑΔ. καὶ ἤχθω τις ἑτέρα ἡ ΔΟ, καὶ ταύτῃ πρὸς ὀρθὰς ἡ ΠΡ δίχα τεμνομένη ὑπὸ

---

[96] Qusṭā ibn Lūqā *Baroulkos* 2.35; Hero and Qusṭā ibn Lūqā 1988: 172–74, 2016: 131–32.

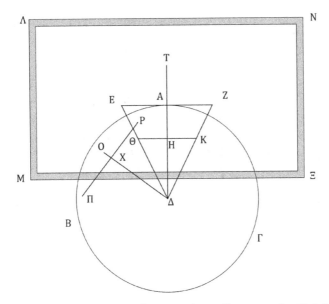

Figure 3.5   Diagram illustrating circular motion by a rolling cone, after Cod. Marcianus
Gr. Z 516, fol. 199r.

τοῦ Ο· ἔσονται δὴ αἱ τῶν τροχῶν θέσεις κατὰ διαμέτρους τὰς ΕΖ, ΘΚ, ΠΡ, ἄξονες δὲ αὐτῶν οἱ ΤΥ, ΟΧ. οὕτως οὖν τετάχθωσαν οἱ τροχοὶ τῇ θέσει, ὥστε ἑστὸς ἐπ' αὐτῶν τὸ πλινθίον ἰσορροπεῖν.

Let the circle along which the frame is supposed to be carried be ΑΒΓ, its center Δ. And let some line ΑΔ be drawn across it, and perpendicular to it, from Α, ΕΑΖ. And let ΕΖ be the diameter of one of the three wheels, of whatever size we choose, and Α its bisector. And let ΔΕ and ΔΖ be joined. Let ΑΗ be equal to the length of the axis of the wheels, and ΗΘΚ parallel to ΕΖ. Then let the frame be ΜΛΝΞ, with ΝΞ parallel to ΑΔ. And let some other [line] ΔΟ be drawn, and ΠΡ perpendicular to this, bisected by Ο. Then the positions of the wheels will be along their diameters ΕΖ, ΘΚ, and ΠΡ, and their axes ΤΥ and ΟΧ. Then let the wheels have been arranged in this way as to position, so that the frame, having been stood on them, will be in balance.[97]

This passage draws very heavily on the conventions of geometrical prose, like the use of third-person imperatives and letter-labeled diagrams. The assimilation of components of the device to their geometrical analogs is quite clear here: Radii, diameters, midpoints, parallels, and perpendiculars

---

[97] *Automata* 7.1.2–3.2.

all figure very prominently in the description of the wheel assembly, and the mathematical perfection such descriptors assume is necessary if the promised circular motion is going to result. Such perfection is probably in fact unattainable, but what is important here is that Hero exploits the well-defined conventions of mathematical prose to assimilate this subassembly of the automaton to mathematical objects. He follows up this construction by insisting that the frame be situated on the wheels in such a way as to "be in equilibrium (*isorrhopein*)." As we saw in the discussion of centers of mass above, this term is characteristic of the fusion of mathematics and theoretical mechanics developed by Archimedes and adapted by Hero in his *Mechanica*.[98]

By the end of this passage the reader has been given an idealized model of a rectangular frame arranged precisely on three wheels, with geometrical points defining every feature from the corners of the frame to the points where the axles meet the wheels. Yet, elaborate as it is, this geometrical setup arguably does not clearly explain why the automaton is now set to move in a circle; instead, its markedly mathematical prose and rhetoric of precision and symmetry serve to draw the reader into a geometrical domain where new kinds of work can be done. That work will require the diagram set up in this passage, so even though the proof itself has yet to appear, its construction has already been "prefabricated" by this point.[99]

In the next section Hero puts his elaborate setup to work. First, he stipulates that the wheels (labeled EZ, ΘK, and ΠP) can be imagined as circular cross-sections of a right cone. Modeling the wheels as frusta of a cone gives Hero access to a geometrical proof that they will then roll in concentric circles around the cone's stationary vertex (labeled Δ). Hero's proof that a right cone's vertex remains stable as it rolls draws on a theoretical mechanical approach of the type favored by Archimedes in *Planes in Equilibrium*.[100] The proof itself combines the kind of geometrical vocabulary we saw in the previous passage (perpendiculars, bisections, and so forth) with the term *isorrhopein*, which, as we have seen, is strongly associated with the blend of mathematics and theoretical mechanics

[98] Roux 1992: 110.

[99] For the analogous case of the crucial proof-work done by harmonic diagrams see Creese 2010: 71.

[100] *Automata* 8.2.1–3.7. Compare Aristotle, *De motu animalium* 701b2–7, which compares the movements of animals to a child riding a toy carriage who pushes himself along with a straight impulse but ends up moving in a circle when the wheels are of unequal size. Aristotle assigns the role of center to the smaller wheel, an error corrected by Hero through the introduction of the imaginary cone's vertex. On the differential wheels in Aristotle and Hero as exemplars of a broader "moving radius principle" that includes the lever and circle see De Groot 2014: 113–24.

Archimedes uses. The cone is "in equilibrium with itself (ἰσόρροπός ἐστιν ἑαυτῷ)" because in Hero's model its rolling motion comes from all the semicircles formed by slicing the cone perpendicular to its axis and bisecting it along its axis.

De Groot notes that the cone's equilibrium means that it can be moved in either direction by even a very small force.[101] Once a force is applied to get it rolling in the first place, from that point "each of the semicircles on its surface will overwhelm (*katakratēsei*) the other semicircle of this circle with the same force, and thus it is moved." This language of "overwhelming" appears twice in the Greek fragments of the *Mechanica*, and it is used as well by Pappus, who connects it to a theory ascribed to Archimedes (though it is not found in the surviving works of Archimedes himself) that balances rely on the principle that larger circles "overwhelm" smaller ones.[102] Comparing the extended proof about the frame's equilibrium on the wheels and the cone's equilibrium across its diameter to the proof from the *Mechanica* about the triangle's center of mass, we find that in this case the components are treated even more strictly as mathematical objects than the triangle was. Here no thickness or density of material is prescribed; the solid objects are treated purely as geometrical solids, subjected to external and internal forces subject to theoretical mechanical analysis along Archimedean lines.

Hero is able to analyze some other components of the automaton using comparable strategies. For example, when Hero describes the relationship between the size of the moving automaton's axle and the speed of the counterweight's emptying, and hence between the size of the counterweight and the range of motion of the automaton, he invokes some additional mechanical properties of rolling circles.[103] He first introduces the relevant structures of the automaton: the base where the wheels and axles are mounted, the cords that extend from axles to the counterweight that produces the automaton's action, and the counterweight itself in its tube of draining millet. The height of the tube must be scaled to accommodate the distance of desired motion and the length of cord required for the automaton's other motions.[104] Then the wheels around the axle should be sized according to the desired distance for the automaton to travel, since for every rotation of the axle the automaton will travel a distance equal to the wheel's circumference.

[101] De Groot 2014: 121.
[102] *Mechanicorum fragmenta* 1.1.61, 1.1.81; Pappus *Synagōgē* 8.1068.19–23. The same concept appears in the Arabic version of the text; see for example Qusṭā ibn Lūqā *Baroulkos* 2.12.
[103] *Automata* 18.1–3.     [104] *Automata* 17.1–3.

In the next section Hero looks more closely at the mechanics behind the motion. The automaton has two axles, one connected to the wheel and another to a drum (larger than either axle) and the counterweight. Since components attached to one another will rotate together, one rotation of the (larger) drum will rotate the (smaller) axle and attached wheel more than once. Hero explains this phenomenon by saying "larger circles are being moved by smaller ones, and this is because of levers."[105] The connection drawn between the motions of differently sized circles and the lever is reminiscent of the Peripatetic *Mechanical Problems*, where "what happens for the balance is referred to the circle, and what happens for the lever to the balance, and just about everything else concerning mechanical motion to the lever."[106] The practical question of why larger pulleys and rollers are more efficient at moving weighty loads is answered in the Peripatetic text in a way that recalls Hero's claims for his differentially sized axles and drums: A point on the circumference of a larger circle moves further in a given time than that of a smaller one attached to it.[107]

However, despite the similarities, Hero's connection between levers and differently sized circles in the *Automata* seems to be more closely related to the "overwhelming" of smaller circles by larger ones connected by Pappus to Archimedes than to the Peripatetic analysis of time and distance of circumferential points. The dynamics of rotating tangent circles are addressed elsewhere, in Qusṭā ibn Lūqā's Arabic translation of Hero's *Baroulkos*: Points on the circumferences of two unequal tangent circles will travel an unequal distance in a given time.[108] The text there feints at a quantitative example, supposing one circle has a diameter twice that of the other, and referring to Archimedes for a claim that the arc swept by the larger circle will thus be twice that of the smaller. So Hero's work in theoretical mechanics – and the echoes of that theory in applications like automata – seems to have a complex genealogy that draws upon a "static" approach associated with Archimedes as well as the "dynamic" Peripatetic one.[109] At the same time, in all these cases Hero's analysis is considerably less rigorous than that used by Archimedes in *Planes in Equilibrium*, once

---

[105] *Automata* 18.3.2–3.    [106] Peripatetic *Mechanical Problems*, 848a11–15.
[107] Peripatetic *Mechanical Problems*, 852a14–20. The puzzling question of how a composite of a larger and smaller circle joined at the center can apparently engage in two motions at once is addressed later in the work at considerable length: Peripatetic *Mechanical Problems*, 855a28–856a40. In brief, the author says the motions are not really two, but only the motion of the circle that moves the other should be counted.
[108] *Baroulkos* 1.4; Hero and Qusṭā ibn Lūqā 1988: 64–65, 2016: 55–56.
[109] Hero and Qusṭā ibn Lūqā 2016: 317–26.

again relying on intuitive ideas about balance and disequilibrium rather than on a locally articulated, rigorous proof.

Indeed, the degree of rigor Hero can apply to his geometrical treatment of the problems of circular motion is not available for most of the other kinds of motion (internal or external) the automaton might be expected to carry out. Much of the text concerns "hybrid" objects, whose textual representation makes use of some aspects of the "mathematical" discourse described above, alongside some very different types of explanation. For example, if the automaton is to move along a rectilinear rather than a circular path, the designer will need to construct a subassembly consisting of a screw with cord wound around it, so that upon turning the screw a frame will be raised and lowered by means of a projecting knob. Hero proposes a way to get this to happen by itself, involving a system of three screws with cord wound around them in a certain way. The initial introduction of the screw looks something like the introduction of the wheels in the passage above: It is defined by letter labels and "created" in the text by an impersonal third-person imperative like those used so commonly in mathematical prose.[110] Hero likewise suggests the need for a degree of precision comparable to that of the wheels: The three screws are to be of exactly equal thickness, and the windings and slack parts of the cord around them exactly equal as well.

But this goal is in fact considerably harder to achieve than the bisections, parallels, and perpendiculars that characterized Hero's design for the automaton's circular locomotion. The demand for standardization here conceals a great deal of complex manual work that must be done even to approximate the goal: planning and refining the windings and slackenings of the cord, the quixotic goal of creating exactly equal screws, and the aim of combining these individually unpredictable elements into three standardized assemblies.[111] This work is underspecified in the text and diagram because of its very unpredictability: Hero cannot tell the reader exactly how many windings there will be because each cord is different (and, to only a slightly lesser extent, so is each screw), nor what sort of pattern might govern the tight and slack parts of the winding (as this depends not only on material peculiarities but also on the exact actions the automaton is meant to perform). Trial-and-error testing is the only way to resolve a host of uncertainties about the automaton, from the assurance

[110] *Automata* 10.3–4.
[111] On the serious challenges presented by screws see Hero, *Dioptra* 34.68–73. For discussion of just how recently those challenges were overcome see also Baird 2004: 152.

that the material for the cord has been sufficiently prestretched that it will not present any troublesome elasticity to the arrangement of windings and kinks that allow the cord to control the automaton's timing.[112]

The whole automaton, being a composite of such "material" and "mathematical" elements, does not overall admit of the kind of rigorous proof of concept that we saw in the case of the wheel subassembly for circular motion. When he focuses on the mathematical aspects of a component, Hero uses one set of textual tools and a rigorous standard of proof that approximates that found in geometrical texts. When he focuses on their material aspects, he uses a different set of tools and techniques to convince the reader of his claims, and that set necessarily includes extra-textual activities if the reader wants to judge the device fully. In this sense, the unpredictable material elements, which resist complete textualization, overwhelm the mathematical ones, so that "proofs" of the overall func-tioning of the automaton have to be done by trial and observation in the world rather than on the page. Hero indicates as much when he invites any reader who doubts that his own designs are simpler and more controllable than those of his predecessors to try the earlier plans out for themselves (though of course without providing any access to the earlier designs that might help the reader take up his invitation).[113] In this sense the claims made in the *Automata* that a given component will function in a certain way are quite different from the rigorous proofs made in mathematical texts, which can be completely contained within the text itself. In order to judge Hero's claims about his automata, the reader must step outside the text to put his designs to the test through their own manual work, or at least observe those created by others.

## Experiments

The mutual influence of the mathematical and the material in the *Automata* suggests that informal experiments can help to define the prop-erties of objects and devices that cannot be convincingly modeled using mathematical techniques alone. These experiments are part of a larger array of techniques in the Heronian corpus, ranging from informal trial-and-error tinkering to more formal procedures of making and recording observations with specialized instruments, which might be given the name "experiments." Although Hero follows no standardized operations or proof procedures throughout the different texts of the corpus, we can

[112] *Automata* 2.5, 11.6.    [113] *Automata* 5.1, 20.1.

nevertheless identify some recurring patterns in the ways he negotiates between the discovery of generalizable physical principles and the peculiarities of a given instantiation of an artifact. These "experimental" engagements are part of the much larger picture of how Hero conceives of his texts as tools to mediate between domains: the material and the mathematical, the physical and the textual. More important still for the Heronian project of ordering technical knowledge are the narrative structures in which he embeds these processes of discovery. These narratives enable the text itself to transform the way the reader will experience the objects of investigation (both natural and artificial) when they encounter them in the real world.

## *Degrees of Formality*

With his characteristic respect for the peculiarities of material things, Hero calls attention to the informal "experimental" processes that must be performed anew each time an artifact is made. He cannot communicate to the reader the tacit knowledge that must be engaged in that process, but he can at least point it out. Material irregularities can creep in at any phase of the design or construction process for many of the artifacts Hero describes. The remedy Hero prescribes is usually a manual test of the individual construction, like the windings of the automaton's temperamental cord or the rate of liquid flow through a clepsydra. Even components that look simple may need to be manually tested so the device of which they are a part will work properly. For example, the worm gear that drives the odometer he describes in the *Dioptra* – a screw, itself one of the simple machines – still has to be manually tested to check how many times it turns in a single rotation of the toothed drum attached to it.[114] All these little experiments teach the reader not just about how to build an individual device, but about how important scrupulous manual testing is for creating precise, predictable mechanisms.

Other Heronian "experiments" more readily yield rigorous or generalizable results. Unsurprisingly, such results are usually the product of specialized observational equipment like the dioptra. Hero even goes so far as to apply the term *apodeixis*, with all its connotations of demonstrative rigor, to the measurements the dioptra makes on earth and in the heavens:

---

[114] *Dioptra* 34.68–73.

Ἐπεὶ οὖν διὰ τῆς κατασκευασθείσης ἡμῖν διόπτρας τὰς ἐπὶ γῆς χρείας πρὸς τὰς διοπτρικὰς ἐπαγγελίας ἀπεδείξαμεν, εὔχρηστον δέ ἐστιν εἰς πολλὰ καὶ πρὸς τὰ οὐράνια πρὸς τὸ τὰς τῶν ἀπλανῶν ἀστέρων ἢ καὶ τῶν πλανητῶν ἀποστάσεις εἰδέναι, ἀποδείξομεν διὰ τῆς διόπτρας ὡς δεῖ καὶ τὰ <τούτων> ἀποστήματα λαμβάνειν.

Now that we have demonstrated, through the dioptra designed by us, its terrestrial uses for the profession of dioptrics, knowing the distances of the fixed stars and of the planets is also quite useful for studying the heavens. We will demonstrate how one must obtain their distances through the dioptra.[115]

The first appearance of *apodeiknumi* in the passage might appear to be relatively unmarked, indicating only that certain applications of the dioptra have been included in the text. But *apodeixis* and its cognates are not used elsewhere in the Heronian corpus in such a casual way, so it seems reasonable to suppose that here too the word is meant to carry the force of rigorous proof. The dioptra's level of utility for the surveyor is of course not the kind of thing that can be directly demonstrated rigorously, but the aggregation of relatively rigorous individual proofs perhaps licenses Hero to use the term here for a kind of "meta-proof."

Regardless of how we interpret the term's first appearance in the passage, by the second Hero clearly intends to indicate a more rigorous demonstration of how to use the dioptra for astronomical observations, which first requires an assurance that the dioptra's measurements correspond proportionally to the far-off celestial bodies. Making these measurements requires precision and accuracy, and Hero walks the reader through the steps of setting up the apparatus (see Figure 3.1). First, a circle is to be drawn on the drum of the dioptra, concentric with the drum, divided into 360 degrees and of a radius equal to the dial that measures the degrees (*moirognōmonion*). Whenever the user wants to measure the angular distance between two celestial bodies (stars or planets), the drum is to be tilted until its plane intersects both bodies:

ἀφελόντες τὸν κανόνα, δι᾽ οὗ διοπτεύομεν, ἀπὸ τοῦ τυμπάνου ἐγκλίνομεν αὐτὸ τὸ τύμπανον, ἄχρις ἂν διὰ τοῦ ἐπιπέδου αὐτοῦ φανῶσιν οἱ εἰρημένοι ἀστέρες ἅμα ἀμφότεροι. εἶτ᾽ ἐντιθεὶς τὸν κανόνα ὡς εἴθισται, τῶν ἄλλων ἀκινήτων, ἐπιστρέψω αὐτὸν, ἄχρις ἂν εἰς τῶν ἀστέρων φανῇ· καὶ παρασημηνάμενος τὴν μοῖραν, καθ᾽ ἣν ἐν τῶν μοιρογνωμονίων ὑπάρχει [τὸ μέρος αὐτῆς], ἐπιστρέφω τὸν κανόνα, ἄχρις οὗ καὶ ὁ ἕτερος ἀστὴρ δι᾽ αὐτοῦ φανῇ. εἶτα ὁμοίως παρασημηνάμενος τὴν μοῖραν, καθ᾽ ἣν τὸ αὐτὸ

---

[115] *Dioptra* 32.1–7.

μοιρογνωμόνιον ὑπάρχει, ἐπιγνώσομαι τὸ πλῆθος τῶν μοιρῶν τὸ μεταξὺ τῶν ληφθέντων δύο σημείων· καὶ τοσαύτας ἀποφανοῦμαι τοὺς ἀστέρας ἀπέχειν ἀπ᾽ ἀλλήλων μοίρας.

Moving the bar across which we sight away from the drum, we tilt the drum until the stars in question both appear at once through its plane. Then, positioning the bar as usual, I will turn it until one of the stars appears, leaving everything else alone. I will mark down the degree where the pointer on the dial is, and then turn the bar to the point where the other star appears by it. Then likewise marking down the degree marker where one of the pointers is, I will know the number of degrees between the two points taken. And I will reveal that the stars are separated from one another by this many degrees.[116]

The experimental procedure here is, first of all, performed by actors in the first person, similar to the transition from the mathematical to the material domain we saw in problem 25, where a map of erased boundaries was to be reconstructed on the ground. "We" made the previous demonstrations about terrestrial surveying using the dioptra, and "we" will carry out the following astronomical demonstrations as well.[117] "We" first tilt the dioptra into the plane that connects our observational standpoint with the bodies under investigation, and thereafter "I" take over the experiment. This "I" will handle not only the physical manipulation of the dioptra itself, but also the information it reveals: marking down the raw data, reckoning (*epignōsomai*) the angular distance the experiment was intended to determine, and ratifying (*apophanoumai*) that number as the correct answer. Creese observes a comparable pattern in Ptolemy's *Harmonica*, where the account of tinkering with the harmonic *kanōn* until its strings are more or less uniform is likewise delivered through future first-person indicatives, with the addition of imperatives and hortatory subjunctives.[118]

The dioptra's ability to mediate between the material and the mathematical owes much to its careful design as a measuring instrument. Hero begins the treatise by specifying the features that enhance the precision of its measurements, like the markings that accompany the measuring rods and the frame containing water levels in glass cylinders that could be mounted on the dioptra's own stand. The glass cylinders appear early in the text, just after Hero has described the installation of the drum assembly (Figure 3.6).[119] A bronze pipe of a certain length is to be fitted into a

[116] *Dioptra* 32.15–26.
[117] On the persons of verbs used for different ways of conceptualizing the work of the dioptra see Roby 2018.
[118] Ptolemy *Harmonica* 1.8; Creese 2010: 69.    [119] *Dioptra* 4.1–17.

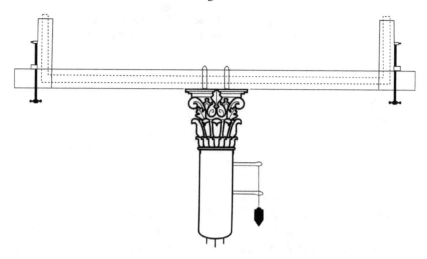

Figure 3.6    Water level instrument for dioptra, following Drachmann's reconstruction
and Paris suppl. gr. 607.

channel excised for it in the upper surface of the rod on top of the dioptra,
and two short perpendicular pipes are attached perpendicularly to its ends.
The glass cylinders are attached to the upturned ends of the pipe and
capped off with wax so that the water will not leak out of them. The water
levels are an important part of the dioptra's precision and its ability to
reduce many three-dimensional surveying problems, viewed across the
instrument parallel to the ground, to two-dimensional geometry problems,
described by Hero as if they were viewed from above or in a cutaway side
view. The glass cylinders provide a more compact and stable way of
ensuring that the instrument is evenly positioned compared to the plumb
bobs on the *asteriskos*, which, as Hero complains, have an annoying
tendency to blow around in the wind.

The cylinders' position at roughly the same height as the sighting tube
of the dioptra also allows the surveyor to transfer seamlessly to using the
next precision-enhancing feature of the dioptra, which lies not on the
instrument itself but on the sighting rods. Right after describing the glass
cylinders, Hero moves on to describe the sighting rods and the painted
disks used with them.[120] Whereas the Roman *agrimensores* simply describe
their rods as poles, without mentioning any inscriptions, Hero's are more
complex. Each rod is incised with the socket of a dovetail running along its

[120] *Dioptra* 5.1–50.

length, into which a tailpiece is fitted so that it can run up and down the length of the rod without falling out. Onto this tailpiece a circular disk painted half white and half black is mounted, with the division line perpendicular to the length of the rod. Then the rod is inscribed with markings dividing it into cubits, palms, and dactyls, and a pointer is mounted on the disk pointing to the markings. The surveyor holding the rod moves the disk up and down on the rod until the operator of the dioptra sees the division between white and black through the sighting tube, and he then records the measurement off the rod.

The dioptra's precision as an instrument is matched by precise instructions for the inscriptions that commemorate the surveyor's observations. Hero specifies the columnar format appropriate for the measurements of the surveyor's forward and reverse sightings, and in the next chapter he instructs that the measurements should be recorded on papyrus or a tablet (ἐν χάρτῃ ἢ δέλτῳ).[121] Hero gives these instructions for recording the results of the measurement in the first two surveying problems of the text. Despite being situated in the context of a specific surveying problem, the instructions represent a general protocol the reader will be expected to follow throughout the text, except for the unusual passages on the odometer and the eclipse near the end of the surviving text.[122] Thanks to the precision of the dioptra as an observational instrument, the techniques that allow Hero to reduce many surveying problems to geometry problems, and the normalized protocols for recording the observations, the *Dioptra* offers a highly disciplined method for turning the undulating landscape into neat columns of data.

Of course, the kind of precise measurement the dioptra enables and the features of surveying problems that lend themselves to geometrical analysis are not common to all technical activities. Hero's theatrical automata may possess a few features – like the cone-like wheel arrangement that allows for circular motion – that can be trusted to work as predictably as the dioptra. However, for the most part the automata require considerable experimentation on the machines themselves, as opposed to the external observational experiments the dioptra eased. These devices are complex and unpredictable, and their successful deployment demands that the program should proceed smoothly from beginning to end.

Even where mathematical (or "hybrid") assurances of the mechanism's viability are impossible to include in the text, Hero sometimes proposes tests that can be run in advance to verify that the subassembly will function

[121] *Dioptra* 6.41-86, 7.22.     [122] *Dioptra* 35, 37.

as planned. The stationary automata have to open up and close their doors at certain points in the performance, so the doors are mounted on pivots. During the actual performance, the pivots will be turned by means of cords fixed on one end to the pivot and then wound around an axle; the axle is then attached to the counterweight mechanism so that the doors open as those cords are unwound and close as they are wound up again. But before the automatic mechanism is introduced, Hero opens up a brief window for manual testing of the pivot mechanism: "[I]f someone (*tis*) turns the sockets with their hands on each side, he will open up and close the doors."[123] Introducing the pivot mechanism in isolation from the rest of the assembly and using the indefinite pronoun, Hero frames its action as a kind of thought experiment any reader can run in their own mind, or as a practical experiment anyone actually in the process of building an automaton can run *in vivo*.

Hero repeats this strategy a few chapters later when he is describing how to create a scene where ships appear to sail across the sea flanked by diving dolphins. The dolphins are drawn on a piece of wood, cut out, and mounted on little rods around a peg, so that they revolve in a circle as the peg is rotated. The peg is attached to a pulley and situated so that the dolphins extend above into the stage area, and below into the hidden space below the stage. This mechanism will of course eventually be connected to the counterweight cord, but Hero once again first extends an invitation to test it out in isolation:

> οὐκοῦν ἐάν τις περιάγῃ τὸν τρόχιλον τῇ χειρί, ὁτὲ μὲν καταδύσεται ὁ δελφινίσκος κάτω διὰ τῆς ἐκκοπῆς εἰς τὸ θωράκιον, ὁτὲ δὲ ἀναδύσεται ἐν τῷ πίνακι.

> If someone rotates the pulley-sheave by hand, the little dolphin will sometimes dive down below through the notch into the breastwork, and sometimes rise up into the stage area.[124]

Here, as in the case of the pivoting doors, the hypothesis of turning by hand is set up with an "*oukoun*" that seeks assent – not a proof *more geometrico*, to be sure, but an invitation to informal experiment.

Elsewhere in the text, the indefinite figure who tests the individual components like the doors' pivots or the dolphin rotation device gives way to a more personalized embodiment of the experimenting craftsman. Already in the section on opening and closing the doors, when Hero transitions from testing the mechanism by hand to the scheme for getting

---

[123] *Automata* 23.3.3–5.    [124] *Automata* 27.3.2–4.1.

it to function automatically with the counterweight, he moves to a first-person account. "Anyone (*tis*)" can test the pivot in isolation, but it was "I" who looped cords carefully around the axles, sticking extra loops on with wax and resin so that the doors will open and close at the right intervals. As in the case of the dioptra, these delicate manipulations are carried out by a first-person figure who takes on the challenge of craftsmanship and certifies the results. The presence of this more concrete figure in the text helps add to the sense of the automaton-in-progress as a laboratory where an expert and a student examine its systems together. Hero's use of the first person in this context is reminiscent of Ptolemy's use of the form to describe the construction of astronomical instruments in the *Almagest*. As Creese notes, in that text (in contrast to the *Harmonica*) Ptolemy usually describes his constructions of instruments with first-person verbs in the past tense, suggesting they are prior achievements of his own.[125]

The following chapter introduces the mechanisms that move the arms of the carpenter puppets, and the creation of those miniature hands invokes the hands of the creators in even more concrete detail:

ἐτρύπησα οὖν αὐτὴν κατὰ τὸν ὦμον καὶ ἐποίησα τὸ τρύπημα τετράγωνον, ὡς γέγραπται, καὶ λαβὼν κεράτινον ἐπίουρον ἐνήρμοσα εἰς μὲν τὸν ὦμον τετράγωνον ποιήσας καὶ ἐνεκόλλησα, τὸ δὲ λοιπὸν τοῦ ἐπιούρου στρογγύλον καὶ λεῖον καλῶς. τρυπήσας δὲ κατὰ τοῦ δεξιοῦ ὤμου ἐδίωσα τὸν ἐπίουρον καλῶς, ἕως οὗ προσκαθίσῃ τὸ χερίον εἰς τὸ ζῴδιον. ἐὰν οὖν καταλάβωμεν τοῖς δακτύλοις ἐκ τῶν ὄπισθεν μερῶν τοῦ πίνακος τὸ ὑπερέχον τοῦ ἐπιούρου στρέφοντες, κινηθήσεται τὸ χερίον.

I drilled it at the shoulder and made the borehole square, as pictured. I took a peg of horn, made it square, joined it to the shoulder by gluing it on, and made the rest of the peg round and nicely smooth. Then I drilled into the right shoulder and pushed the peg well in, until the hand was mounted upon the figurine. Then if we grab the extending part of the peg with our fingers from the side behind the stage and turn it, the miniature hand will be moved.[126]

The first-person singular here indicates the construction work done ahead of time, while the first-person plural invites the reader into the testing process, the subjunctive in the conditional softening it into a sense of possibility rather than necessity. Hero repeats this pattern a few lines later, where he is describing the mechanism to connect the arm assembly to the counterweight for automatic operation. As the counterweight falls, it rotates a star-shaped group of pegs, which repeatedly strike a sinew spring

---

[125] Creese 2010: 56–57, 63–68.    [126] *Automata* 24.2–3.

(*hysplēnx*) that is drawn down by the peg and then allowed to snap back up. As in the first assembly, Hero relates the initial construction of this assembly in the first-person singular aorist and then shifts to the first-person plural for a manual test, as "we" press down on the spring and then release it with a noise (*psophos*).

Although the Greek first-person plural is not necessarily strongly marked as literally including the reader, nevertheless its use here in combination with the details of a hands-on craft process strongly resembles what Rodie Risselada refers to as the "commissive" aspect of its Latin analog, where first-person plural subjunctives and future indicatives implicate both speaker and reader in the action of a verb.[127] In particular, by shifting into the plural form to provide guidance on the experimental testing process, Hero seems to approach what Roy Gibson describes as the "exemplary" use of the Latin version of the form, which gently encourages the reader to follow in the author's footsteps rather than giving a direct order.[128] Hero's use of the first-person plural creates a notional space for tinkering in which the reader is invited to imagine being guided by the author himself.

The cords whose windings determine the actions of the automaton present a special material challenge; their speed of unwinding must be as predictable as possible in order for these complex devices to achieve the right timing, but at the same time the materials of which they are constructed (usually gut) are very hard to standardize. In order to prevent the cords from stretching or shrinking once they are part of the automaton, Hero recommends stretching the cords tight and leaving them that way for a period, then repeating the process, after which they are coated with resin and wax.[129] Sinew, he stresses, is not to be used, because it is susceptible to size changes depending on the weather; the only exception to this is when one wants to make a spring (*hysplēnx* or *hysplēngion*), where sinew's natural elasticity is an asset rather than a liability.[130] This type of object does not lend itself to the letter-labeled diagram: Whereas the important features of the overall structure or the mechanical subassemblies can be usefully portrayed in such visualizations, there is no way of effectively representing visually the ungeneralizable complexities of such material preparations, which vary from one instantiation of the automaton to another.

Indeed, it appears to be very difficult to represent them even verbally; as in the case of the screw assembly referred to above, the preparation and

---

[127] Risselada 1993: 6, 158; Roby 2016a: 225–26, 2016b: 203–07.      [128] Gibson 1998: 71.
[129] *Automata* 2.4.      [130] *Automata* 2.6.

winding of the cord involves manual activities whose specifics cannot be fully predicted. Their representation in the text is thus sometimes incomplete. For example, when a rest lasting "for some time (ἐπί τινα χρόνον)" is desired, Hero directs the reader to time its delay using "a little strand" (*mērymation*) of extra cord stuck on and wound around the cylinder and then connected to the counterweight.[131] The uncertainties here are legion, from the time of the delay to the length of the extra bit of cord. There can be no generalized quantification of either the length of time or the length of cord, since these depend absolutely on the peculiar characteristics of the materials involved and must be discovered by trial and error. The user has to stand at the endpoint of the automaton's path and run it backwards, so that the cords will wind up to a certain point, which is then set as the starting point of the windings.[132] Again, Hero cannot prescribe the lengths of cord that must be wound: That will vary greatly not just with the overall design of the theater (which he has emphasized can be altered at will), but also with subtler variations like the weight of the components and the behavior of the cord.

As Cuomo points out for the case of Vitruvius, very often "gaps" in a textual account like this should lead us to contemplate the tacit knowledge that lurks behind the text rather than to accuse its author of "incompetence or poor literary skills."[133] Hero's unabashed acknowledgment of the parts of the automaton's run that cannot be precisely described or quantified sets up his appeal to the reader to do some hands-on testing. The reader will have to work through all the steps of trial and error Hero describes here in order to make their own working version of the device. In this sense the "utility" of the text is necessarily limited; no matter how sincere Hero's intentions are to create a text that will be useful to his reader, at some point the text is not enough. "Utility" in cases that demand supplementary tacit knowledge might consist in encouraging the reader to step outside the boundaries of the text as Hero does here rather than pretending that the text itself can encompass every aspect of the machine.

The *Pneumatica*'s dazzling array of trick vessels for dispensing wine and water demand the same kind of predictable performance as the theatrical automata and so must likewise be tested in advance. One of these uses the motion of a counterweight to dispense a preset quantity of wine into a cup at each turn.[134] The vessel is equipped with two parallel lever systems, one at the top (attached to the vessel's handle) and one at the bottom

---

[131] *Automata* 6.2.3–3.1.     [132] *Automata* 11.6.1–7.1.     [133] Cuomo 2016: 139.
[134] *Pneumatica* 2.30.

(where the cup rests, awaiting its measure of wine). These levers are linked externally by a perpendicular rod attached on pivots and within the vessel by a valve system that starts and stops the flow of liquid. The device is calibrated by measuring in advance how far a descending counterweight that opens the valve will travel before dispensing a *kotylē* of wine. This is done by placing a premeasured *kotylē* of liquid into the cup and marking the place on the rod where the counterweight has descended far enough to stop the flow when counterbalanced by the *kotylē* of liquid. The process is then repeated, so the rod can be inscribed with the measures that will correspond to dispensing a *hemikotylē*, two *kotylai*, or any other desired amount. Hero here emphasizes even more strongly than he did for the automata that testing by hand is the only way to verify that the dispenser will work precisely and predictably.

Another device uses a clepsydra to dispense variable quantities of wine; in this case the amount dispensed is determined by a weight that can be manually moved along a rod protruding from the vessel.[135] The device will allow wine to flow out as long as the clepsydra is releasing water; the rod controls how far the clepsydra is raised in an internal water reservoir and hence how long it will flow. Like the dispenser with the counterweight, the clepsydra device must be tuned by hand. The designer finds "by trial (*peira*)" the correlation between the weight's position on the rod and the measure of liquid dispensed and then makes incisions on the measuring rod and keeps a record of the measures. The user can then use these inscriptions as place markers for where to set the weight on the rod.

A pneumatic device featuring figurines of a trumpeting Triton and a bird alongside another figurine (*zōdarion*) mounted on top of the device's built-in boiler demands a comparable process of tuning by hand. When the device is heated, water and air circulate through its interior pipes; the figurine on top appears to blow steam on the fire, the hollow bird (partially filled with water) is made to "sing" when steam is allowed to pass through the pipe on which it perches, while Triton plays his instrument when the steam enters the pipe that leads to it. All of these effects depend on lining up the small holes drilled in each of the pipes to allow the steam to travel to whichever part of the device is meant to operate, and that can only be achieved by trial and error:

πείρᾳ οὖν σκεψώμεθα, πότε μὲν κατάλληλον τὸ τρῆμα τῷ ΜΟ σωλῆνι, πότε δὲ τῷ ΝΠ, πότε δὲ τῷ Ξ ἐπὶ Ζ τῷ ἐπικειμένῳ ζῳδαρίῳ. καὶ ταῦτα

---

[135] *Pneumatica* 2.27.

γνόντες σημεῖά τινα ἐν αὐτοῖς παρασημειωσόμεθα παρὰ τὴν ΚΛ περόνην πρὸς τὸ ὁπόταν μὲν προαιρώμεθα σαλπίζειν, ὅταν δὲ πάλιν βουλώμεθα φυσᾶν, αὐτὸ φυσᾶν, ὁπόταν δὲ βουλώμεθα, κοσσυφίζειν.

We must observe by experiment when the borehole faces the pipe MO, and when it faces ΝΠ, and when it faces Ξ on which the figurine Z is placed. And when we know these things, we will mark some points on them along the peg ΚΛ so that the trumpet will play whenever we choose, or when we wish [the figurine] to blow, that it will blow, and likewise that there will be birdsong whenever we wish.[136]

As in the case of the wine cup, the trial proceeds by testing where the device gives the required results and inscribing the device itself with a marker to show the operator how to use it.

These "experiments" focus relentlessly on the individual artifact; the goal is never to devise a generalized formula for standardizing the measurements of a device that will, for example, always dispense a *kotylē* of wine. Hero does refer in the *Belopoeica* to the formula that correlates the dimensions of a catapult (reckoned in proportion to the size of the hole for the spring cord) with its ballistic power, a result previously celebrated by Philo as a triumph of generalizable formula over trial and error.[137] Yet that is already a different matter from cases where he directs the reader to test something out for themselves; the catapult formula was discovered in the Hellenistic period, the "experiment" long being over by the time even Philo's text was written.

The variety of testing procedures alluded to in the *Pneumatica*, *Automata*, and *Dioptra* suggests that, for Hero, the "experimental" is not a rigorous, one-size-fits-all protocol, but a flexible system for inculcating in his reader certain methods of observation that will help them see the world more clearly, whatever that means in any given text. Sometimes learning to "see" experimentally is more a matter of feel for an individual artifact, as with the manual "experiments" of the *Pneumatica*. Sometimes it is about learning a measurement technique that brings something close to geometrical generalizability and precision to work in the real world, like the diagrammed *apodeixeis* of the *Dioptra*. While many of these texts explicitly or implicitly invite the reader to try things out for themselves, others induct the reader into new habits of seeing by making the text itself a kind of teaching laboratory.

---

[136] *Pneumatica* 2.35.     [137] Hero *Belopoeica* 31.1–8; Philo *Belopoeica* 50.8.

*Narrating Experiments*

Parts of the *Automata*, fittingly enough, are indeed set up as a kind of "experimental theater" where the reader gradually learns to see more and more deeply into the complicated workings of these wonder-making devices. The reader starts out very much on the automaton's exterior, highlighting what Tybjerg calls the "epistemic superiority" of mechanician over spectator.[138] Indeed, we begin not even outside one of Hero's own automata but with the eye-blinking masks Hero identifies as simple ancestors of his own devices, as we saw in the previous chapter.[139] The automata of Hero's own time, and those devised by his more recent predecessors like Philo, were of course much more mechanically and dramatically sophisticated; indeed, he describes them as "urbane (*asteioi*)" in their elegance. They feature a wide variety of mechanisms for motion and special effects, but the reader begins their journey on the other side of the theatrical veil, seeing the play unfold, for the most part, as a naive viewer would. When Hero first introduces the reader to the stationary automaton's play, he takes the reader through it scene by scene, each formulaically bounded by "and when [the doors] were again closed and re-opened (κλεισθεισῶν δὲ καὶ πάλιν ἀνοιχθεισῶν)."[140] The play begins with the appearance of twelve figures of shipbuilders; the ships they build then sail the seas; Nauplius then lights a signal fire; the ships are wrecked and Athena strikes Ajax with lightning; *fin*.

All of this is presented as a viewer would see it, from the outside, with no mention of the mechanisms that make it work. There is, however, one important difference: While the viewer of the play would see it enacted in real time before their eyes, Hero describes the action to his reader in imperfects and aorists. This past tense structure is quite uncommon for Hero and for technical authors in general. On the comparatively rare occasions when it is used, it often seems to indicate specific historical instantiations of a construction. Philo reports on Dionysius' repeating catapult (which he remarks never made it into general use), while Biton (another Hellenistic author on catapult construction) introduces several different kinds of catapults through historical exemplars.[141] In other cases it correlates with an author's assertion that he actually constructed or

---

[138] Tybjerg 2003: 451. On Hero's playfully gradual revelation of the workings of the automaton see also Roby 2017: 529–32.

[139] *Automata* 22.1–2.      [140] *Automata* 22.3–6.

[141] Philo *Belopoeica* 73.32–76.34; Biton *Kataskeuai polemikōn organōn kai katapaltikōn*, e.g. 2.3–4, 3.3–4.

manipulated something, as we have seen Creese argues for Ptolemy's astronomical instruments. Hero's use of the past tense here to narrate the action of the play reads like an argument for its feasibility: All this actually happened, he suggests, and can happen for you as well once you learn my techniques.

Hero also appears to certify the play's engaging realism from the viewer's perspective. At the appearance of the shipbuilders:

> ἐκινεῖτο δὲ ταῦτα τὰ ζῴδια τὰ μὲν πρίζοντα, τὰ δὲ πελέκεσιν ἐργαζόμενα, τὰ δὲ σφύραις, τὰ δὲ ἀρίσι καὶ τρυπάνοις χρώμενα <καὶ> ψόφον ἐποίουν πολύν, καθάπερ <ἂν> ἐπὶ τῆς ἀληθείας γίνοιτο.

> These figures moved, some sawing, others working with axes, others with mallets, others using bow-drills and borers, and making a great racket, just as would happen in reality.[142]

Likewise, the dolphins in the sailing scene "repeatedly dove past, sometimes diving into the sea, sometimes reappearing, just as in reality."[143] This claim, of course, only works from the viewer's perspective; once Hero reveals the mechanism that creates the dolphins' motion, it will be clear that it is completely different from the way dolphins actually move. It only *looks* like the real thing from outside.

The viewer's experience of the play's drama would be enhanced by shifts in its pacing, like pauses in the action and suspensefully slow movements, and Hero likewise controls the reader's experience of the play's pace. After the scene where the ships are constructed and another where they are dragged down to the sea, they go suddenly missing at the beginning of the next:

> κλεισθέντος δὲ πάλιν καὶ ἀνοιχθέντος, τῶν μὲν πλεόντων οὐδὲν ἐφαίνετο, ὁ δὲ Ναύπλιος τὸν πυρσὸν ἐξηρκὼς καὶ ἡ Ἀθηνᾶ παρεστῶσα, καὶ πῦρ ὑπὲρ τὸν πίνακα ἀνεκαύθη, ὡς ὑπὸ τοῦ πυρσοῦ φαινομένης ἄνω φλογός. κλεισθέντος δὲ καὶ πάλιν ἀνοιχθέντος, ἡ τῶν νεῶν ἔκπτωσις ἐφαίνετο καὶ ὁ Αἴας νηχόμενος. ... μηχανῆς τε καὶ ἄνωθεν τοῦ πίνακος ἐξήρθη, καὶ βροντῆς γενομένης ἐν αὐτῷ τῷ πίνακι κεραυνὸς ἔπεσεν ἐπὶ τὸν Αἴαντα, καὶ ἠφανίσθη αὐτοῦ τὸ ζῴδιον. καὶ οὕτως κλεισθέντος καταστροφὴν εἶχεν ὁ μῦθος.

> When [the *pinax*] again closed and re-opened, nothing appeared of the sailing party, but there was Nauplius raising a signal-fire and Athena standing by, and a fire was kindled above the stage, as though a flame above had appeared from the signal-fire. And when it again closed and re-opened, the wreck of the ships appeared and Ajax swimming ... and a mechanism was raised above the stage, and as thunder was produced, in the

---

[142] *Automata* 22.4.  [143] *Automata* 22.5.

*pinax* itself lightning fell upon Ajax, and his figurine was made to vanish. And thus, with another closure, the story had its conclusion.[144]

The reader experiences the suspense of the empty sea before the ships reappear, the slow gathering of the storm and their wreck, and the sudden stillness of Nauplius and Athena at their first appearance. These dramatic touches harmonize with the sophistication of the device's mechanical movements to create what Hero praises as "the most polished design (γλαφυρωτάτην διάθεσιν)."[145]

Having presented the play as a viewer would experience it, Hero then proceeds to walk the reader in deeper by explaining how the theater itself is constructed, from its doors to the breastwork that conceals most of the mechanisms within, before moving deeper still to describe those mechanisms. As we saw above, many of these mechanisms have to be verified by manual testing, and Hero introduces those informal experiments into the text only where the reader has already made progress on his journey inside the automaton. The typical sequence of progress is to introduce how a viewer sees a particular mechanism, then to tell the reader how it works as a standalone unit and suggest manual tests for the system in isolation, and then to describe how it is integrated into the larger automated system run by the counterweight. As Tybjerg observes, Hero appropriates *apodeixis* for mechanics and relegates philosophers to the realm of the merely plausible (*pithanos*).[146] There are thus serious epistemic stakes as Hero guides the reader into the automaton: Not only should they come to understand the mechanisms that drive it, but they should come to *believe* in their efficacy. The "polished" automaton the viewer encounters is of course the end result of many iterations of trial-and-error experiment, which will confront the reader once they peer inside the stage. It is a risky gambit on Hero's part to reveal the delicacy and material peculiarity of the inner workings of the machine – the manual testing that itself cannot be described as *apodeixis* and yet contributes crucially to Hero's proof of the machine's viability.

Hero's search to establish a mechanical, material *apodeixis* is even more central to the *Pneumatica*, a particularly complex nexus of thought experiments, physical experiments, and *theōria* of different kinds. As we saw earlier, he promises in the preface that generating demonstrations of the requisite precision and reliability will be possible thanks to some kind of *theōrēmata* about the recombination of elements.[147] It might be

---

[144] *Automata* 22.5–6.   [145] *Automata* 21.2.   [146] Tybjerg 2003: 452–53.
[147] *Pneumatica* 1.pr.343–47.

tempting to assume that Hero here refers simply to a set of philosophical arguments about physical principles, but this cannot be the case, given his strong objections to purely verbal debate about these matters.[148] In fact, the *theōrēmata* of the *Pneumatica* appear to be complex overlays of design, diagram, and constructed artifact, which collectively create opportunities to "see" physical phenomena that are not perceptible under natural circumstances.

Where the *Automata* inducts its reader into the man-made mysteries of a complex artifice designed to conceal its workings from a naive spectator, the reader of the *Pneumatica* is granted a gradual revelation of the hidden forces of nature. Hero's pneumatic devices offer the viewer a kind of *theōria* very different from the spectacles of the *Automata*, but the way he walks the reader into progressively deeper understanding of their physics is reminiscent of the *Automata*'s unfolding drama of mechanical insight. The *Pneumatica*'s artifacts range from building blocks like various kinds of siphons to complex performance installations that certainly qualify as *theōrēmata* in the sense of "spectacle," like those he describes in his later work on automaton-making. But those installations, taken along with the rest of the devices in the book, simultaneously create the opportunity for another kind of *theōria* entirely. By reading the text as an ordered whole, the reader is enabled to participate in a special kind of observation that might well be likened to experiment: a disciplined way of seeing physical principles in action through material artifacts.

One must begin, Hero says, by taking a stand on the controversy over whether there is any such thing as a naturally occurring void. Hero will stand with those who argue that void is "scattered (*paresparmenon*)" throughout all kinds of bulk matter, drawing his argument not from philosophical rhetoric but from the evidence of the senses.[149] Hero places philosophical arguments under suspicion by identifying them with rhetoric, suggesting that their authors will seek any "loophole (*pareisdusis*)" in their desperation to convince a listener.[150] He instead identifies "perceptible proof (αἰσθητικῆς ἀπόδειξις)" as the gold standard for making convincing arguments about the physics of matter: If the structure and behavior of matter can be made accessible to the senses, there will be no more need for slippery philosophical arguments. But of course evidence for the invisible "microvoid" is not immediately available, or there would not be a controversy; instead, it has to be carefully created – out of thin air.

---

[148] *Pneumatica* 1.pr.190–03.  [149] *Pneumatica* 1.pr.18–25.
[150] *Pneumatica* 1.pr.197; Tybjerg 2003: 453.

There is a marked theatricality to Hero's argumentation in the proem of the *Pneumatica*: As he reveals his physics he creates moments of suspense, revelation, and sudden reversal that remind one of the spectacles executed by Hero's own automatic theaters.

After setting the scene of the ongoing battle over the microvoid, he presents bulk matter as it appears to common folk, but he immediately, conspiratorially draws the reader over to his side: Vessels that look empty to *hoi polloi* are of course nothing of the kind – they are full of air.[151] *They* assumed the vessels were empty, but not you, reader. You are ready to begin to see air as it looks to "those practiced in physics (τοῖς περὶ φύσεως πραγματευσαμένοις)": a substance made up of "small and tiny-particled bodies, for the most part invisible to us." Hero's task is to create the special circumstances that will enable his reader to see through their cloak of invisibility.

He begins with something to prove: "[S]o indeed if someone pours water into a vessel that appeared empty, to the degree that the mass of water is poured into the vessel, to that degree the mass of air is displaced." The initial hypothetical, in its arm's-length conditionality (ἐὰν ... ἐγχέη τις ὕδωρ), might suggest an impending thought experiment based on the hypothesis, but instead Hero introduces another layer of dramatic action:

> κατανοήσειε δ' ἄν τις τὸ λεγόμενον ἐκ τοῦ τοιούτου· ἐὰν γὰρ εἰς ὕδωρ
> καταστρέψας ἀγγεῖον τὸ δοκοῦν εἶναι κενὸν πιέζῃς εἰς τὸ κάτω ἀκλινὲς
> διαφυλάσσων, οὐκ εἰσελεύσεται τὸ ὕδωρ εἰς αὐτό, κἂν ὅλον αὐτὸ κρύψῃς·

> Someone might grasp what was said from something like this: for if you upturn a vessel that seemed empty into water, and press on its underside, making sure it remains straight, the water will not be permitted into it, even if you submerge the whole thing.[152]

Another observing everyman (*tis*) can be enlightened about air's true nature if *you* flip the original setup on its head. While both a vessel being filled up with water as the air inside escapes and a vessel refusing to fill with water while the air is trapped inside are cases of air behaving according to its nature, only the latter case *shows* you that nature, since the air escapes invisibly in the former. Hero's project in the *Pneumatica* is to create this kind of spectacle: The text and instrument are both privileged, specialized spaces where a viewer can see physics in action.

The instructive spectacle of the vessel has further acts to unfold after Hero reviews the lesson of the second act. In the third, *tis* produces a drill

---

[151] *Pneumatica* 1.pr.25–27.    [152] *Pneumatica* 1.pr.32–37.

and makes a hole in the inverted bottom of the vessel, at which point the water rushes in as the air rushes out. But now Hero creates a narrative surprise by rewinding the third act so that the reader can appreciate a bit of evidence from the second they might not have noted at the time:

πάλιν δὲ πρὸ τοῦ τρυπῆσαι τὸν πυθμένα ἐάν τις ὀρθὸν ἐκ τοῦ ὕδατος τὸ ἀγγεῖον ἐπάρῃ, ἀνατρέψας ὄψεται πᾶσαν τὴν ἐντὸς τοῦ ἀγγείου ἐπιφάνειαν καθαρὰν ἀπὸ τοῦ ὑγροῦ, καθάπερ ἦν καὶ πρὸ τοῦ τεθῆναι.

Then again, if someone raises the vessel straight up out of the water before the drilling, when once it has been overturned it will be observed that all the internal surface of the vessel is free from water, just as it was before it was placed.[153]

The quick *palin* undoes the drill's destructive work and draws the reader's viewpoint inside the vessel to survey its dryness. The surviving Arabic version of Philo's *Pneumatica* indicates that Hero largely draws the simple experiments in the preface from his predecessor, while expanding considerably on the discussion of their significance. The move he makes here, however, is entirely new. Philo does mention a perforated vessel that is submerged upside down in water. However, his starts out with a hole, which is plugged with wax; after the submersion, the wax is simply removed.[154] Where Philo suggested a physical tool to effect the transformation of the vessel, Hero offers a narrative dramatization.

Is Hero's account here a thought experiment? Nothing prevents the reader from executing the steps described, turning the vessel's inversion, perforation, and immersion from a hypothesis to a reality. At the same time, the process of discovery cannot proceed in the real world in the same way that it does in the narrative, punctuated by the surprise of the "rewind." So Hero's text offers the reader a kind of heightened drama, not just for its own sake but because the interruption in the experiment's flow creates a strong focus for the moment when the mind's eye enters the unperforated vessel to find the interior bone-dry.

Hero then fast-forwards back to the point where the vessel has been drilled and invites the hand into the drama:

ἐὰν γοῦν τετρυπημένου τοῦ ἀγγείου κατὰ τὸν πυθμένα καὶ εἰσπίπτοντος τοῦ ὕδατος παραθῇ τις τῷ τρυπήματι τὴν χεῖρα, αἰσθήσεται τὸ πνεῦμα ἐκπῖπτον ἐκ τοῦ ἀγγείου· τοῦτο δὲ οὐκ ἄλλο τί ἐστιν ἢ ὁ ἐκκρουόμενος ὑπὸ τοῦ ὕδατος ἀήρ.

[153] *Pneumatica* 1.pr.43–46.  [154] Philo *Pneumatica* section 3; Philo 1974: 128–29, 2001: 98–99.

So indeed, when the vessel has been drilled and dunked into the water, if someone places their hand over the borehole, the wind will be felt escaping from the vessel. This is nothing other than the air being forced out by the water.[155]

Hero's description of the sensory experience of feeling the escaping air rush over the hand is a slight expansion on the version in the Arabic text of Philo. The sensory detail recalls Tamar Gendler's appeal to the important role imagined sensory experiences play in thought experiments:

> [I]n the case of imaginary scenarios that evoke certain sorts of quasi-sensory intuitions, their contemplation may bring us to new beliefs about contingent features of the natural world that are produced not inferentially, but quasi-observationally; the presence of a mental image may play a crucial cognitive role in the formation of the belief in question.[156]

This experiment could easily be carried out in the real world, but at the same time the focalizing features of the account in the text give the reader a carefully directed spectacle that transcends the purely visual to include a proprioceptive imaginary as well: better, perhaps, than the real thing. By inviting the reader to imagine an amplified version of the experience of holding their hand over the vessel, Hero focuses the imagination on the feeling of the air rushing out through the hole. In combination with the previous imagined experience of looking into the vessel and finding its interior is dry, this stage of the process enhances the reader's belief that the vessel indeed contains air that, though invisible, can still be experienced through other senses.

Now the curtains close on the inverted vessel, as Hero provides two brief case studies on the properties of materials with different densities. Adamant consists of bodies too closely packed to admit even the tiny particles of fire, and so this substance would drive itself into the anvil rather than be smelted. By contrast, sponge and shavings of horn can easily be compressed in the hand and return to their former bulk upon release. From these materials one can apprehend through analogy even the invisible behavior of air particles, as Hero argues that the body of those materials is like the particles of air, and the air in them like the void in it (an analogy he previously constructed using grains of beach sand as a stand-in for air particles). After this brief excursion to the invisible physics of particles, the reader is returned to experiments that can be performed with ordinary vessels. This time, the vessel's form is important:

---

[155] *Pneumatica* 1.pr.49–53.    [156] Gendler 2004: 1154.

ἐὰν οὖν ἀγγεῖον λαβών τις κουφότατον καὶ σύστομον, προσθεὶς τῷ
στόματι ἐκμυζήσῃ τὸν ἀέρα καὶ ἀφῇ, ἐκκρεμασθήσεται ἐκ τῶν χειλέων τὸ
ἀγγεῖον, ἐπισπωμένου τοῦ κενοῦ τὴν σάρκα πρὸς τὸ ἀναπληρωθῆναι τὸν
κενωθέντα τόπον· ὥστε ἐκ τούτου φανερὸν γενέσθαι, ὅτι ἄθρους κενὸς
ὑπῆρξεν ἐν τῷ ἀγγείῳ τόπος.

Then if someone takes a vessel, as light as possible and with a narrow neck,
and holding it by the mouth he sucks out the air and gets rid of it, he hangs
the vessel from his lips, with the void attracting the flesh to refill the
emptied-out space. Thus it becomes clear from this that a continuous void
is present in the vessel.[157]

But Hero is not insisting that only this single type of apparatus can make
this experiment work; he immediately opens up alternative theaters for
seeing the continuous void in action. The cupping glasses commonly used
in medical practice for drawing blood and other humors to a particular
place on the skin will work as well, both the narrow-necked "egg (ᾠόν)"
vessels and the ones called "gourd-shaped (σικύα)." The former work by
having the air sucked out of them, the physician preserving the semi-
vacuum thus created by placing a finger over it before applying it to the
skin, where they attract the humor through an artificial (παρὰ φύσιν)
upward force. The latter are heated, reducing the density of the air within
and so drawing the humor upward as the air cools by a mechanism Hero
identifies as "no different (οὐκ ἀλλότριον)" from the one operating in the
"egg" vessel.[158]

But even if the mechanism is similar, Hero's account of the "gourd-
shaped" vessel serves his narrative quite differently from the "egg" vessel,
for he immediately proceeds to analyze the physics of their operation in
very different terms from the familiar bodily experiences that illustrated the
"egg." He delves immediately down to the level of the behavior of the
particles within, and his language is quite technical, as when he says that
the vessels draw nearby matter toward them as their internal heat dies
down "because of the interstices (*araiōmata*) of the particles." This, he says,
is a specific case of the more general process whereby fire destroys macroscopic objects and reduces them down to their components of water, air,
and earth.[159] Hero returns to the macro-world to shift his analogy to the
familiar sight of burning coals, which keep much of their structure but are
reduced in weight. He then once again dives back down into the micro-
world to explain that this phenomenon occurs because the coals' lighter
elemental components moved upward in the smoke, while their denser

---

[157] *Pneumatica* I.pr.86–91.    [158] *Pneumatica* I.pr.98–100.    [159] *Pneumatica* I.pr.100–08.

components sank down.[160] He argues that this process is just like what you see when water vapor in a heated vessel is refined into air as steam and just like the process by which the sun's heat on the other side of the world extrudes dewdrops of refined water which leave the earthy matter behind.[161] In every case the basic mechanism is the same: Fire dissolves bulk matter, allowing the more refined elements to float up, while the denser ones sink down.

Hero thus propels this section of the narrative away from the human scale: downward into the microcosm of the individual particles, upward in a discussion of rising plumes of steam, and outward to an explanation of the Earth itself as a body exhaling moisture whose denser components sink while the rarer rise under the sun's heat. Ultimately, Hero follows the condensing, cooling moisture back down to earth as it falls into a puddle and sinks into the ground: an elegant narrative mirror of the hydrological cycle. But that cycle, of course, happens on a very large scale indeed; while Hero includes vignettes of locally observable phenomena that support his meteorological claims, like the mud puddle and morning dew, the whole remains out of reach for a human observer. So Hero scales back down to human size, suggesting how one can observe the same phenomena by placing a vessel (glass, bronze, or something else) of water in the sun and watching how just a small part of it evaporates, leaving earthy impurities behind.

As the steaming vessel becomes a theater for observing what happens to air and water, so Hero turns a lamp into a parallel theater for air and fire. As the lamp runs low on oil, you can watch the fire go from a steady rising flame to an admixture with air, eventually becoming air alone. Hero then concludes with the final combination of elements that can be readily observed: If a small air-filled vessel is dunked (mouth upright this time) into a vessel of water, you can watch the water displacing the air, mixing with it until only water remains. This elegant elemental triptych uses the mixture of water and earth to teach the reader about water, the mixture of fire and air to teach them about fire, and the mixture of air and water to teach them about air. Hero then returns to the "gourd-shaped" vessel; having observed the "theaters" of elemental admixture (in person or in the mind's eye), the reader is now ready to appreciate the microscopic dynamics of what is really happening in there.

It is at this point that Hero makes the claim we encountered earlier: Even though it is possible for philosophers to make any number of purely verbal arguments against the void's existence, a demonstration before the

[160] *Pneumatica* 1.pr.108–19.    [161] *Pneumatica* 1.pr.119–54.

senses will leave them no loophole. He springs his trap by introducing a new apparatus, more elaborate than the everyday vessels used previously:

κατασκευάζεται γὰρ σφαῖρα πάχος ἔχουσα τοῦ ἐλάσματος, ὥστε μὴ εὔθλαστος εἶναι, χωροῦσα ὅσον κοτύλας ἤ. στεγνῆς δὲ οὔσης αὐτῆς πάντοθεν τρυπήσαντα δεῖ σίφωνα καθεῖναι χαλκοῦν, τουτέστι σωλῆνα λεπτόν, μὴ ψαύοντα τοῦ κατὰ διάμετρον τόπου τοῦ τετρυπτημένου σημείου, ὅπως ὕδατι διάρρυσις ὑπάρχῃ, τὸ δὲ ἄλλο μέρος αὐτοῦ ἐκτὸς ὑπερέχειν τῆς σφαίρας ὅσον δακτύλους τρεῖς· τὴν δὲ τοῦ τρυπήματος περιοχήν, δι᾽ οὗ καθίεται ὁ σίφων, στεγνοῦν δεῖ κασσιτέρῳ προσλαμβάνοντα πρός τε τὸν σίφωνα καὶ τὴν ἐκτὸς τῆς σφαίρας ἐπιφάνειαν, ὥστε ὅταν βουλώμεθα τῷ στόματι διὰ τοῦ σίφωνος ἐμφυσᾶν, κατὰ μηδένα τρόπον τὸ πνεῦμα τῆς σφαίρας διεκπίπτειν. σκοπῶμεν δὴ τὰ συμβαίνοντα . . .

For a sphere is constructed having some thickness of beaten metal, so that it will not be easily collapsed, having a capacity around eight *kotylae*. When it has been sealed up everywhere, it is necessary to drill into it and insert a bronze siphon, that is a narrow tube, not touching the part diametrically opposite the drilled point, so that there is a channel for water; its other end must extend outside the sphere, about three dactyls. Then it is necessary to seal up with tin the circumference of the drilled part where the siphon enters, integrating the siphon and the surface outside the sphere, so that whenever we wish to blow through the siphon with the mouth, the breath will not at all escape the sphere. Let us watch what happens . . . [162]

The solidly built and tightly sealed sphere allows one to create internal air pressure that compresses the air within "artificially (*para physin*)"; that is, this apparatus is marked as an environment where one can see things happen that go beyond what one witnesses in nature.[163] By specifying the terms of its materials and construction even down to the approximate size of the components, Hero can make a stronger argument about the existence of the void than he could based on the uncontrolled apparatus of the previous experiments. Those vessels were contingent on what the reader had to hand, whereas here the apparatus is specified as uncollapsible and soldered against leaks, permitting fluids to flow only through its siphon.

Hero offers a gentle reminder that just like all other vessels called "empty," this one is filled with air, and tightly sealed so that even if one were by brute force to introduce more air into the vessel, it would break under the pressure – unless, that is, there were a way for the air to yield

---

[162] *Pneumatica* pr.200–13.
[163] *Pneumatica*, pr.241. Note that *para physin* should not be taken as meaning "against nature" in the strong sense of being "unnatural," as Berryman has shown: Berryman 2009: 44–46.

(*hypochōrein*). They – the opponents of the theory that there is void in matter – think it is now impossible to introduce more air into the vessel. Time to prove them wrong:

καὶ μὴν ἐάν τις ἐθέλῃ τὸν σίφωνα βαλὼν εἰς τὸ στόμα ἐμφυσᾶν εἰς τὴν σφαῖραν, πολὺ προσεισκρινεῖ πνεῦμα, μὴ ὑποχωρήσαν τος τοῦ προϋπάρχοντος ἐν αὐτῇ ἀέρος· τούτου δὲ ἀεὶ συμβαίνοντος, σαφῶς δείκνυται συστολὴ γινομένη τῶν ὑπαρχόντων ἐν τῇ σφαίρᾳ σωμάτων εἰς τὰ παρεμπεπλεγμένα κενά.

Yet if someone wishes to put the siphon to his mouth and blow into the sphere, he will introduce a lot of extra air, without the air that was already in there making its way out. Since this always happens, it is clearly demonstrated that there is some compression of the particles already present in the sphere into the interstitial void.[164]

"This always happens" is a strong experimental claim. On the other hand, it is not yet quite clear from the text how to verify this claim through observation. In order to help the reader understand what the observable effects of the compression might be, Hero then "replays" the experiment, with a little poetic license:

ἐάν τις οὖν ἐμφυσήσας καὶ παρ' αὐτὸ τὸ στόμα προσαγαγὼν τὴν χεῖρα συντόμως ἐπιπωμάσῃ τῷ δακτύλῳ τὸν σίφωνα, μενεῖ πάντα τὸν χρόνον συνεσφιγμένος ὁ ἀὴρ ἐν τῇ σφαίρᾳ· ἐὰν δέ τις ἀναπωμάσῃ, πάλιν ἐκτὸς ὁρμήσει μετά τε ψόφου καὶ βοῆς πολλῆς ὁ προσεισκριθεὶς ἀὴρ διὰ τὸ ἐκκρούεσθαι, καθάπερ προεθέμεθα, κατὰ τὴν τοῦ προϋπάρχοντος ἀέρος διαστολὴν τὴν κατὰ τὴν εὐτονίαν γινομένην.

Then if someone blows in, places his hand at the mouth, and immediately covers the siphon with a finger, the air will remain trapped in the sphere. If anyone uncovers it, the aggregated air will rush outside again with a blast and a roar in the expulsion, as we established before, because of the expansion of the air that was previously there, and this happens on account of its tension.[165]

Of course the air probably does not produce "a blast and a roar" on its escape if it was only compressed as much as a normal set of lungs can manage, but Hero is here prefiguring the sound effects produced by some of the devices described later in the text. In fact, those sound effects lie at the very foundation of the practice of pneumatics by Hero's predecessor Ctesibius, at least in Vitruvius' account. In that story, typical of Vitruvius'

---

[164] *Pneumatica* pr.235–42.    [165] *Pneumatica* pr.242–49.

tales of discovery, Ctesibius fortuitously learned that compressed air makes a sound as it escapes from a tube while he was inventing a counterweight for a mirror used in his father's barbershop.[166] Though Vitruvius' invention-tale is surely a fable, it speaks to the central role of sound in pneumatic wonders, and Hero is perhaps satisfying the reader's expectations by providing in the preface a glimpse of what is to come.

The preface to the *Pneumatica* thus tempts any reader to press further into the text and see these physical effects unfold in many different ways. The conscientious reader will be spurred to solve a mystery not yet addressed: How *do* we know that "this always happens," and thus that compression occurs inside the vessel, given that Hero's report on the results of the experiment are so clearly narratively amplified beyond what can actually be observed? The devices in the main text will amplify those effects mechanically instead, forcing air into greater degrees of compression and using it to create highly visible (or audible) effects like ejecting pressurized air or steam. The casual "experiments" of the preface, with their dramatic presentation of elementally simple processes, create a hunger in the reader to see how they might play out on the more advanced stage of Hero's siphons, fire-powered steam systems, and singing figurines. These experimental narratives induct the reader into a new regime of seeing, where natural phenomena like steam and dew are reflected and amplified by artificial devices; the reader learns to see the artificial processes through the natural ones, and the natural through the artificial.

The physical arguments made in the *Pneumatica* are predicated, for the most part, on operations carried out on well-defined material instruments, yielding results perceptible to the senses. Textual and experimental investigation are tightly linked here: Not only does Hero's text host the instructions and diagrams that make it possible to construct the artifacts, but the text itself is structured to help discipline the reader's deepening understanding of the physical principles on display. Indeed, the very simplicity of the pneumatic devices Hero first introduces to the reader – the perforated vessel, the cupping glass, even the siphon soldered into the hollow sphere – invites them to try the experiments out for themselves. Even if the reader does not take Hero up on the invitation, the way he dramatizes quasi-experimental processes lets the text play a crucial role as a site of experimental learning in its own right. Through his vivid accounts of creating "perceptible proof" through artificial instruments, Hero

---

[166] Vitruvius, *De architectura* 9.8.3–4.

disciplines the reader's eye for the natural world, teaching them to see through the instruments to otherwise invisible phenomena.[167]

## Conclusion

Hero offers an array of strategies to enable his reader to see the world in new ways: revealing the mathematical "skeletons" that underlie certain material phenomena, creating experimental regimes to discover the details of those phenomena, and using his carefully organized textual structures to foster those processes of discovery right in the text. The new ways of seeing that Hero's reader comes to experience are often labeled by *theōria* and its cognates. The Heronian "theoretical" is not defined in opposition to perception and experience, but rather indicates ways of deriving knowledge *from* lived experience and disciplined through a range of analytical regimes.

The geometrical structures that Hero reveals lurking within the *Dioptra*'s exercises in precise surveying represent a bridge from the careful ordering of geometrical structures and measurement problems in the *Definitiones* and *Metrica* to their more complicated material analogs in the real world. In the later chapters of the *Definitiones*, the lines of the mathematician and the surveyor are given additional material heft, equipping the reader with a kind of "double vision" not unlike the varied perspectives Hero prescribes for the surveyor in the *Dioptra*. The theoretical mechanics of the simple machines takes on a materiality of its own, embedded in a material, mercantile world, which in the Arabic version of the text is populated as well with figures of workmen carrying out tricky manual tasks. Even the more unpredictable aspects of material objects find a home in the Heronian corpus, from the *Metrica*'s somewhat comical advice to measure intractable shapes by coating them in clay or tossing them in a bathtub to the *Automata*'s taming of stretchy sinew and quirky screws.

In the Heronian corpus, instruments play a crucial part in mediating an observer's experiences of the world. These instruments include specialized devices like the dioptra, of course, but even simple, everyday objects like the vessels in the preface to the *Pneumatica* can serve this purpose if they are embedded in a properly structured narrative. Hero presents the devices at the beginning of the *Pneumatica* as highly accessible building blocks,

---

[167] On the power of the text to communicate a sense of experimental learning in its own right, albeit in a very different cultural setting, one might compare the idea of "virtual witnessing" developed by Shapin and Schaffer in their study of Robert Boyle's pneumatic instruments in the 17th century: Shapin and Schaffer 1985: 60–61.

which the reader can use as an entry point into the more complex devices that feature in the rest of the work. Together with his universalizing references to the everyman (*tis*) who can carry out his experiments, Hero's simple devices offer an inviting inroad to the study of pneumatics. The main text is then organized so as to usher the reader further along that road to more complex devices, and then, if the reader takes seriously Hero's organizing principles at the level of the whole corpus, on to even more advanced constructions like the automata.

Over the last two chapters, a clearer picture of the shape and aims of the Heronian corpus has emerged. A broadly accessible starting point, leading to a carefully structured induction into a technical discipline: Hero's principles of organization are not meant to be confined to the text, but to play out through the reader's engagement with objects in the real world. Although he aims for order in his texts, he allows the textual boundary to break where necessary to accommodate more chaotic and irregular objects, inviting the reader to extend their investigation from the text into the world. The next chapter will explore how the "Hero" sketched in these chapters fits into the broader cultures of scientific and technical writing into which Hero has been hypothetically inscribed, from the Hellenistic world to late antiquity, and then will examine how the figure of Hero himself is instrumentalized by later authors.

# CHAPTER 4

# Hero in Context

## Hero(s) of Alexandria

The previous chapters unfolded how Hero inscribed himself into an evolving textual tradition and the strategies he devised to turn books into sites for exploratory engagements (real or imagined) with the world. Hero's most distinctive features as an author are his systematic reorganization of a body of past technical knowledge into an accessible and orderly group of new texts and his deployment of that systematic knowledge to restructure how his reader negotiates between the textual and material worlds. He exhibits a deep concern that his reader be able to understand everything in his texts, and he often seeks to augment that understanding with vivid accounts of embodied engagements with the technologies he describes. His texts are often quite simple in their rhetoric and structure, but they open a window onto a world of material complexities.

Here we can reconsider those features in light of the difficulties of establishing a time frame for the historical Hero. That is, we can ask: Given what we know about Hero's authorial program, how would he have fit into each of the different cultural contexts of scientific and authorial practice into which he has been refracted? What features might the Hero sketched in the previous chapters have drawn from each of the cultural environments in which the historical Hero has been conjectured to have lived? And what elements of his authorial style and problem-solving approaches did he transmit to the later authors, known or anonymous, who transformed his works in later centuries?

We might draw on Needham's work on the flow of paper in and out of archives (discussed in Chapter 1) to think of this Hero as an "archive" of a different sort. In this sense he is a fluid repository of the texts and techniques he finds already in place and a rich vein of new texts and techniques for those who followed him. The unstable evidence for Hero's flesh-and-blood lifetime creates an opportunity to rebuild the Hero who survives in text in a new way, as a collection of information flows that intersect in different ways with their possible "inputs" and "outputs." In constructing this new portrait of Hero, I draw on König and Woolf's evocative idea of the "bookworld." The "bookworld" is shared cultural territory, representing "an imaginary community of sorts."[1] These communities are their own domain, constructed out of the relatively durable raw material of text-borne knowledge; as such, a single shared "bookworld" might last over decades or even centuries as part of an ongoing long-wavelength dialogue. Although the historical Hero remains elusive, we can still project some glimpses of possible bookworlds out from his surviving texts. Inevitably, this will also be a story about what the world does to books, as the vagaries of material preservation see them altered, interpolated, and transfigured in new cultural environs.

The "bookworlds" Hero inherited, inhabited, or inspired can be fleshed out by examining the patterns of traffic in technical knowledge that characterized them. The "traffic" under examination here is predominantly textual. However, this is not meant to suggest that technical work in any of these periods was entirely or even mostly carried out in textual form. Tacit knowledge and craft practice, not polished texts like those that make up the Heronian corpus, were the backbone of ancient technical work, albeit one that is almost entirely out of reach for us given the poor survival of evidence for those practices.[2] Instead, the focus on texts here is meant to reflect the fact that Hero survives for us as a swarm of texts and textual references, rather than as a fully rendered participant in an economy of *technē* that was built on manual labor and tacit knowledge at least as much as it was on textual knowledge.

As we saw earlier, Hero has been dated alternatively to the Hellenistic period, the 1st century CE, and the later empire. Let us briefly try on for size a few scenarios for Hero's background as an author and technical practitioner in the various intellectual milieux these time frames represent.[3] For each possible "bookworld," I will sketch out a few possible contexts of knowledge transmission, look at the textual forms such knowledge seems to have taken, and consider how they might be reflected in the surviving Heronian corpus.

---

[1] König and Woolf 2013: 33.
[2] For an exemplary study of how we might go about restoring the background of tacit knowledge that the surviving ancient texts tend to elide see Cuomo 2016.
[3] This collection of imaginary versions of Hero is of course quite different from conjectures of literal multiples of Hero, like Corcoran's set of three: "the pupil of Ctesibius (c. 250 BC), the teacher of Proclus (c. AD 400) and 'Hero the Younger' (c. AD 950)": Corcoran 1995: 377.

## Hellenistic Alexandria

Our first Hero is anchored most tightly by several references to Archimedes, who fixes a *terminus post quem* at 212 BCE, when Syracuse was sacked by invading Romans. His closest disciplinary colleagues in this period would have been the Hellenistic engineers Ctesibius, Philo of Byzantium, and Biton (Hero mentions the first two in his own work, but not Biton).[4] All three were known for their work on catapult design, and Ctesibius and Philo also for work on pneumatic wonders. How closely Hero's works resemble theirs is difficult to answer with certainty for Philo or Biton and impossible for Ctesibius, given that no text from him survives. Meanwhile, only a single text survives in Greek from Biton, and just two texts from Philo's nine-book *Mechanikē Syntaxis*, along with Arabic and Latin versions of his *Pneumatica*. However, we can at least compare their surviving works with Hero's to reach some tentative conclusions. Sparse though Hero's surviving work on theoretical mechanics is, the Peripatetic *Mechanical Problems* is another important comparandum from this period, and Archimedes' work also offers a few possible comparisons.[5]

Let us say, then, that this Hero's tenure in Alexandria would have occurred sometime between the late 3rd century BCE and the early 1st century BCE. The remarkable intellectual culture that flourished in Hellenistic Alexandria, especially strategies for collecting, organizing, critiquing, and reusing information, might have left some traces on the way Hero himself absorbed and transformed his predecessors' technical works.[6] This culture is most often discussed in the context of the Library–Museum complex, though not much is known for certain about the details of working life there.[7] Positions at the Museum may have carried prestige, but their intellectual culture was not without its critics. Most famous is the

---

[4] The challenges of dating Ctesibius and Philo were mentioned in Chapter 1. Biton presents difficulties of his own, as all attempts to date him rely on his dedication to a king Attalus, but which one? On the various responses to this question, see Roby 2016b: 19 n. 1. Biton's single surviving work, on catapult designs, is translated alongside Philo's and Hero's texts on the subject in Marsden 1971.

[5] An excellent edition of the text with a discussion of its history through the early modern period is Aristotle 2000; however, see also cautionary notes in van Leeuwen 2013. The text's authorship is uncertain, though as Berryman notes, differences from Aristotle in terminology and basic physical principles (e.g. the distinction between natural and nonnatural motion) seem to make Aristotle himself an unlikely prospect: 2009: 106–14. On the authorship of the text see also Lloyd 1971: 135.

[6] On Alexandrian scientific culture see for example Argoud 1994a; Argoud and Guillaumin 1998; Berrey 2017; Netz 2009; von Staden 1996.

[7] Fraser 1972: I p. 315; Hardiman 2013: 211–12; Méasson 1994: 31–32.

poet Timon's satirical portrait of the Museum and its *sussition* as a fattening-coop for "the fanciest birds (πολυτιμότατοι ὄρνιθες)," a menagerie of scholars quarreling ceaselessly in the "birdcage of the Muses."[8] The vast amount that has been written about the Library of Alexandria from antiquity to today overshadows the little that is known for certain about its genesis, structure, size, and destruction.[9]

Of course, the Library was not a unique project; Varro remarks on the fierce bibliophilic competition between the Ptolemies and the Attalids of Pergamum.[10] And for technical practitioners, more modest and specialized book collections might have been at least as important as those monumental civic collections. Pliny observes a long Greek tradition of stockpiling records of patients' experiences at the temple of Asclepius at Kos so that they could be referenced later by physicians, while Strabo seems to suggest that the votive tablets left at Epidaurus may have been used the same way.[11] Martínez and Senseney suggest that these archives could have been part of a broader system of specialized technical libraries in the Greek and later the Roman worlds, used by medical, legal, and other professionals, though little can be said for sure.[12]

Alexandrian scholarship is associated particularly with the minutely detailed literary work of the *philologoi* or *grammatikoi*, many of the official librarians among them. The library acquired a wealth of resources to aid in the scholiasts' explication of Homer, from the early days of Philitas of Cos, through Zenodotus of Ephesus, Aristophanes of Byzantium, and Aristarchus of Samothrace. Philological projects included compiling lists of archaic terminology known as *glōssai*, standardizing editions of Homer's

---

[8] Athenaeus *Deipnosophistae* 1, 41.1–8, citing Timon of Phlius. Another memorable portrait of squabbling Alexandrian scholars is Callimachus *Iambus* 1, where a time-traveling Hipponax contrasts Callimachus' petty-minded colleagues with the Seven Sages.

[9] On the Library see for example Blum 1991; Canfora 1990; El-Abbadi 2004; Harder 2013; Hatzimichali 2013a, 2013b; Pfeiffer 1968: 95–151. Too cautions that the Alexandrian Library is often chosen uncritically as a representative exemplar of ancient libraries, but it is equally compelling because of its idiosyncrasy: Too 2010: 1.

[10] Varro's story is recounted by Pliny at *Nat. Hist.* 13.70. On the Pergamene library see also Vitruvius, *De architectura* 7.pr.4; Coqueugniot 2013; Hardiman 2013: 213–14. While the story itself is likely just another of Pliny's provocative fictions, Takács points out that it is nevertheless an important reminder of the intellectual competition between the two kingdoms: Takács 1995: 266.

[11] Pliny, *Nat. Hist.* 29.2.4; Strabo, *Geographica* 8.6.15. It is of course true that Pliny references this practice en route to his notorious claim that Hippocrates burned the temple to the ground so that he could corner the market in medicine, but skepticism about that particular claim need not call the whole into question. On the literary and material evidence for the sanctuaries of Asclepius as hubs of information storage and exchange see Perilli 2006.

[12] Martínez and Senseney 2013.

poetry, and transmuting work done in the intervening centuries in biology, geography, and other subjects into explicatory context for Homer.

Ordering this wealth of knowledge was an important intellectual contribution in its own right. The most famous organizational tool associated with the Alexandrian library was Callimachus' *Pinakes*. Though Callimachus was never the official librarian, both his own extraordinarily erudite poetry and his association in the Suda Lexicon with the *Pinakes* suggest an intimate knowledge of the institution's holdings.[13] The *Pinakes* represented far more than a list of the library's holdings at a given moment; the surviving fragments indicate that the work arranged the authors alphabetically, categorized them, classified the works of each author to some extent, indicated their approximate length, and included biographical information about the author.[14] Hatzimichali characterizes the critical work of the *Pinakes* not only as an inventory of a static store of carefully arranged knowledge, but also as "inviting reassessment and revision."[15] The *Pinakes* thus encourage the user to consider the cataloging of book-knowledge as a living, dynamic activity.

Once integrated into this mediating superstructure, that knowledge can be critiqued, repurposed, rearranged: As Jacob puts it, the objects of knowledge become "transitive."[16] Harder finds traces of this searchably organized library in the poetry of Callimachus and Apollonius, noting their marked use of unusual vocabulary and abundant references to mythical, antiquarian, and geographical knowledge that seems likely to have been excavated from the library.[17] Like Hatzimichali and Jacob, she emphasizes that their use of this older knowledge was transformative, and it "showed the vitality of the tradition and the importance of preserving it in an institution such as the Alexandrian library."[18] The library itself was not just a "birdcage" of scholars, but a carefully structured repository of elaborately organized knowledge made available for living traditions of scholarship and poetry.

The philologists' love of recherché terminology inflected not only scholarship on poetic authors like Homer, but mathematical and technical work as well. Vallance and Handis comment on the philological interest in terms from the Hippocratic corpus exhibited by Alexandrian medical practitioners.[19] Netz explores the transition in this period away from purely literal names for objects of scientific and mathematical interest

---

[13] Adler 1971: Kappa, entry 227.   [14] Blum 1991: 153.   [15] Hatzimichali 2013b: 70.
[16] Jacob 1998: 26.   [17] Harder 2013: 97, 100.   [18] Harder 2013: 107.
[19] Handis 2013: 369; Vallance 2000: 100–04.

(for example, "dodecahedron") to imaginative metaphorical terminology (for example, "conchoid").[20] As Netz observes, some of these metaphorical terms invited comparisons to familiar objects like shells (for all that the metaphor itself was often complex), while other terms and book titles required more strenuous excursions into unusual vocabulary (like Apollonius' lost *Okutokion*). Unearthing the roots of rare terminology like this would have been as demanding for a mathematical reader as Callimachus' use of exotic poetic vocabulary and suggests a comparable case for the availability of book collections where authors and readers alike might discover them.

Hero, for his part, does not seem to delight in lexical gymnastics. While ancient book titles are of course subject to slippage, there is no indication that Hero's works ever bore any but the most straightforward names. *Pneumatica, Belopoeica, Dioptra*: exactly what it says on the tin. Nor are the texts themselves adorned with rare vocabulary; of course Hero's terminology is often technical by necessity, but his terms are generally attested in other mechanical or mathematical authors. The most systematic study of Hero's terminology is on the *Metrica*, included in Acerbi and Vitrac's edition as a project in collaboration with Masiá.[21] Indeed, the most exotic terms in the text are borrowed from other authors (for example, "*mikropsychoterois*" appears in the proem to the third book, where Hero draws on Plato and Aristotle's arguments on just distribution of resources). And indeed, Hero's frequent celebrations of his work's ready accessibility seem at odds with many Alexandrian authors' excursions into the more exotic corners of the lexical world.

Like the philological culture of the *grammatikoi* and the poets, much Alexandrian scientific and technical work reflected the institutional environment that fostered it. Technical experts in this cultural environment could win Ptolemaic patronage in exchange for shaping their work into aesthetically pleasing, entertaining packages. At the same time, the tools for information storage and retrieval fostered by the Library enabled and incentivized Alexandrian authors in various disciplines to tie their scholarly work back to the culture that made it possible. Eratosthenes of Cyrene stands out as a "scientific" author associated with the library of Alexandria, chosen by Ptolemy III Euergetes to replace Apollonius of Rhodes as head of the Library. He composed philological, historical, and poetic works, as well as technical works in mathematics and geography (where he remains best known for calculating the circumference of the Earth). The very

---

[20] Netz 2009: 149–60.    [21] Hero 2014: 59–74.

breadth of his work earned him the nickname "Beta," at best a rather backhanded compliment. In another backhanded move, Strabo calls him a "mathematician among geographers, a geographer among mathematicians," and elsewhere he straightforwardly criticizes him as a dilettante philosopher and desultory fun-seeker.[22]

Eratosthenes' mathematical contributions included a text on the duplication of the cube (that is, how to find the edge length of a cube with double the volume of a given cube), preserved in Eutocius' commentary to Archimedes' *Sphere and Cylinder* alongside solutions to the problem from other authors, including Hero.[23] This treatise takes a courtly form: a letter to Ptolemy III Euergetes, heralding a text of ornately varied design, which Taub characterizes as a "mosaic" and Leventhal as a "textual machine."[24] Eratosthenes sets a fable-like history of the problem alongside a geometrical solution, gives an account of the "mesolabe" (an instrument for solving the problem mechanically), describes a monumental stele surmounted by a real mesolabe, and even closes with an epigram celebrating the mesolabe's many practical applications.

The text is a remarkable display of the author's command of multiple disciplines including mathematics, mechanics, and poetic composition, as well as of the device's utility for solving practical problems including the construction of wells, grain pits, and cattle enclosures. In fact, as Berrey points out, the practical applications laid out in the epigram that closes the work precisely reflect the mainstays of the Egyptian village economy, advertising his mechanical calculator's utility for Ptolemaic rule.[25] Netz proposes that Eratosthenes chooses these objects to conjure the context of bucolic poetry, since a mere list of measures would be too "dry" for poetry.[26] Leventhal emphasizes the tragic character of the epigram's reference to the death of Minos' son, Glaucus, arguing that the emotional note is calculated to appeal to the Ptolemaic image of royal fathers and sons.[27] From his Ptolemaic addressee to his adoption of a characteristically Hellenistic mode of poetry crossbred with the humble furnishings of local Egyptian village life, Eratosthenes repeatedly stamps his work with signs of its cultural context.

---

[22] Strabo, *Geographica* 2.1.41, 1.2.2.
[23] Berrey 2017: 147, 164–78; Taub 2008. Eutocius preserves several solutions (including Eratosthenes') at *Commentarii in libros de sphaera et cylindro* 56.14–106.25, translated with notes in Archimedes and Eutocius 2004: 273–306.
[24] Leventhal 2017: 45; Taub 2008: 289.    [25] Berrey 2017: 166–67.    [26] Netz 2009: 150–51.
[27] Leventhal 2017: 51–53.

Eratosthenes is far from the only Alexandrian author to weave the Alexandrian intellectual context of patronage and competition tightly into his works. The astronomer and mathematician Conon of Samos is known to us in part from Archimedes, who repeatedly mourns Conon's death in his own work.[28] Conon's Alexandrian associations were cemented by his having identified a group of stars as the catasterism of a lock of the Ptolemaic Berenice II's hair.[29] Conon's mathematical work on conics was taken up and expanded on by Apollonius of Perge, whose own association with Alexandria is clear from the preface of his own text.[30] Apollonius treats Conon's prior work in a somewhat polemical fashion; indeed, as Berrey remarks, "Hellenistic science is imbued with agonism."[31] Though we know comparatively little about Conon's work and less still about his life, the courtly aura built up around him and Callimachus and Catullus' poetic representations of the "*coma Berenices*" suggest he occupied a key role in what Berrey calls the "court science" of the Hellenistic period.[32]

The practical role of Ptolemaic patronage is particularly visible in the context of medical theory and practice in and around Alexandria. Marasco details Cleopatra's role as a patron of the scientific developments that occurred under her rule, but there were also rumors that she herself experimented with poisons and claims that she authored a treatise on cosmetics.[33] Herophilus of Chalcedon and Erasistratus of Ceos achieved remarkable new insights into human anatomy at Alexandria, though there is no evidence that links them with certainty to the Library or Museum, nor any other system of formal royal patronage.[34] Still, the legal framework that made it possible to dissect human specimens there created

---

[28] Netz 2009: 101.

[29] Callimachus *Aetia* fr. 110, Catullus 66; on the lock see Netz 2009: 151–52. On Berenice more generally see Clayman 2014. Conon's biographical details are somewhat sketchy, and the star chart Ptolemy attributes to him is based on observations from Sicily, but the lock of Berenice links him tightly to Alexandria in the eyes of other ancient authors: see Berrey 2017: 1–5.

[30] Apollonius *Conica* 1.pr.8–16, where he describes his embarking on the project as a favor for Naucrates, another geometer who was staying with Apollonius at Alexandria at the time.

[31] Berrey 2017: 28. [32] Berrey defines "court science" at Berrey 2017: 1–27.

[33] Marasco 1998: 48.

[34] On their dissection work see for example Lloyd 1975; von Staden 1989: 138–39. Von Staden points out that Herophilus' own students were sometimes referred to as the "house (*oikia*) of Herophilus"; while the term is hardly straightforward, it might suggest an operation independent from outside patronage: von Staden 1989: 27–28. If a much-discussed story from Celsus is to be believed (*De medicina* 1.pr.23–26), the kings made convicted criminals available to them for vivisection. But however attractive this narrative of extreme political patronage of scientific investigation may be, Celsus' claims should be taken with a grain of salt: von Staden 1989: 139–52.

opportunities for anatomical discoveries that would have been impossible elsewhere in the Greek world. Lang enumerates the tax advantages and subsidies available to physicians in Egypt who propagated "Greek" medical practices.[35] A wide range of administrative, institutional, and legal factors thus underscored the peculiarly Alexandrian nature of much of this scientific work.

By contrast, rather than representing himself in his *Belopoeica* as a source of expertise on the latest developments in catapult technology that might serve a ruler or other patron at a particular place and time, Hero instead presents an evolutionary history of catapult designs from the very beginning, unmoored from any particular historical ground. There is indeed some reason to believe that Alexandrian craftsmen were key contributors to the development of catapults. In his own earlier work on the subject, Philo of Byzantium credited "fame-loving and technophiliac kings" in Alexandria with having sufficiently subsidized the work of craftsmen developing catapults there that they were able to discover the formula connecting the size of the hole into which the spring cord was packed with the size of the missile it could fire.[36] But despite Alexandria's exceptional status as a hotbed of research in this area, Hero elides all geographical specifics from his own account. Likewise, his *Dioptra* describes solutions to surveying problems carried out on a landscape endowed with topographical features like hills and rivers but not located in any particular place with distinctive property laws. The elaborate pneumatic and hydraulic wonders of the *Pneumatica* and *Automata* might indeed have been at home in a courtly environment, but Hero gives no indication that they were deployed for the enjoyment of any particular elites.

The absence of a sense of place in Hero's texts is rendered even starker by an absence of people like addressees, users, or designers. Philo and Biton, Hero's closest disciplinary analogs from the Hellenistic period, both frame their texts as missives to specific recipients, who yield within the body of the text to a generic figure often addressed as "you," a space for the reader to imagine themselves.[37] Biton addresses his book on catapults to the king Attalus (though, as noted earlier, just which Attalus is the subject of debate). Each entry in Philo's nine-book collection is destined for an "Ariston" who, although unknown, nevertheless gains a kind of shadowy identity from the repeated references to his learning process. Philo also peppers his work with references to inventors like Ctesibius and Dionysius

---

[35] Lang 2011: 122–25.     [36] Philo, *Belopoeica* 50.20–45.
[37] For more detail on authorial voice in Philo and Biton see Roby 2016a: 209–21.

of Alexandria, their work situated in Alexandria and Rhodes, which he populates as well with engineers and swordsmiths. Archimedes not only addresses many of his texts to named recipients, but brings other people (like the dead Conon) into his introductions as well; as Netz notes, a very personal approach to writing mathematics.[38] Hero, by contrast, typically issues his instructions using impersonal constructions like the Greek *dei* +infinitive, "it is necessary," or the passive imperative characteristic of mathematical prose. As noted above, on only one occasion does he include an addressee, and this single reference to an obscure "Dionysius" suggests a very different aim for his body of work compared to Eratosthenes' and Biton's royal addressees.

The developing Alexandrian practices of knowledge formation demanded a delicate balance between old and new knowledge, as the antiquarian adventures of the philologists yielded nuggets of archaic terminology that adorned new poetic forms, physicians informed by new anatomical discoveries made their way into the hinterlands to integrate their new knowledge with older Egyptian practices, and so on.[39] The (admittedly distorting) lens of the intellectual and technical work performed at the Alexandrian Library shows us something about how the scholars and scientists there used its resources to help interpret, critique, correct, and broaden the knowledge streams in which they swam. As Jacob observes, "rectification (*diorthōsis*)" was the watchword for much of this work, as the library provided a philological theater where different versions of a text could be compared and an authoritative version produced.[40] Perfection, not conservation, was the aim. The library was itself crucial for the "rectifying" work of the Alexandrian scholars, which depended heavily on access to unusual texts and multiple variants of more common ones. Their knowledge was refined from the accumulated weight of pre-existing textual authorities into new ones and transmuted into new textual products.

Yet this yearning for the new was not necessarily framed as a disruption of past knowledge. Herophilus and Erasistratus did not aim to explode the Hippocratic tradition, though Erasistratus' theory of *pneuma* represented something of a break. John Vallance points to the philological side of the study of medicine at Alexandria, where medical authors delved into the

---

[38] Netz 2009: 67.
[39] On the ways in which Alexandria's "frontier qualities" may have incentivized intellectuals there to innovate see Flemming 2007: 455. On the connections between that "frontier environment" and the breaking of traditional Greek taboos on dissection see von Staden 1989: 29.
[40] Jacob 1998: 30.

Hippocratic treatises to "re-invent Hippocrates in their own image" through debates over lexicography and commentaries and notes to Hippocratic case studies.[41] Unlike the Hellenistic physicians, Hero did not inherit a textual canon like the Hippocratic corpus, but he does nevertheless inscribe himself in several longer traditions (mechanical, mathematical, and even philosophical). As we have seen, the technical innovations that he makes are often incremental, and where he emphasizes his own contributions they are often focused on the form of the text. Even though he does not portray himself as a philologist, his emphasis on improving the textual form of his technical work might suggest some common ground with Hellenistic medical commentators.

Apollonius of Citium developed additional techniques for mediating the Hippocratic past through text in his commentary to the Hippocratic treatise *On Joints*, which he dedicated to a Ptolemaic king, most likely Ptolemy Auletes.[42] His book, which, as Asper points, out is the earliest surviving medical commentary, is devoted more to highlighting and explicating what Apollonius deems the most important passages of the Hippocratic work than to critical engagement with its ideas.[43] Apollonius' innovation comes rather from blending his textual explanations with images (*hypodeigmata*), versions of which still survive in a 10th-century manuscript copy.[44] Apollonius frequently refers to his images as explanatory tools that will help the reader understand just how a certain arrangement of limbs and traction systems works, which ought to be particularly useful when the method is unfamiliar.[45] He promises his reader,

> τοὺς δὲ ἑξῆς τρόπους τῶν ἐμβολέων δι' ὑπομνημάτων, ζωγραφικῆς δὲ σκιαγραφίας τῶν κατὰ μέρος ἐξαρθρήσεων παραγωγῆς τε τῶν ἄρθρων ὀφθαλμοφανῶς τὴν θέαν αὐτῶν παρασχησόμεθά σοι.

> I will provide to you the following methods of bone-setting through commentaries, with naturalistic scene-paintings furnishing an image of each part of the dislocation and the limbs in a way clear to the eye.[46]

Berrey contextualizes Apollonius' choice of "naturalistic" images rather than sparse diagrams as part of an effort to appeal to his royal patron

---

[41] Vallance 2000: 101.    [42] Flemming 2007: 456.    [43] Asper 2013: 44.

[44] These images are discussed in depth, along with their textual references and consideration of their appeal to a lay patron, at Berrey 2017: 140–45.

[45] See for example Apollonius, *In Hippocratis de articulis commentarius* 10.4, 20.10, 20.38, 31.2; 18.12–17. Indeed, on the strength of these references, Asper describes Apollonius' images as "the visual equivalent of paraphrase": Asper 2013: 44.

[46] Apollonius, *In Hippocratis de articulis commentarius* 2.30–33.

through a contribution (*eranos*) that a relative layman will not find intimidating.[47]

The verbal and visual harmonize in Apollonius; he makes certain to match the Hippocratic lexicon he uses to the features displayed in the image (18.17–19), and the reader is sometimes referred back to previous illustrations (e.g. 30.46), so that they help bind the text together into a continuous whole. Indeed, in the passage where he describes his images as "scene-painting (*skiagraphia*)," he labels their work of bringing the scene of limb-setting to the reader's eye as a *paragōgē*, which, besides its general sense of "leading" or "furnishing," can also refer to joining together tissue in the work of repairing a dislocation. This pointed pun on the drawing together of bookish and bodily experience signals the "naturalistic" image as a site where text, image, and body are tightly bound together.

Textual technologies like the images used by Apollonius created new opportunities to convey "experiential" ways of knowing not only from directly witnessing experimental engagements, but even through text. Apollonius' naturalistic medical images aim to provide the reader with a visual experience that somehow approximates what an in-person observer would see. Given the static nature of the images and the textual explications that accompany them, the images might indeed provide a layperson with a better knowledge base than a live demonstration would.

Hero's narratives of experimental processes both real and imagined and his own use of extensively letter-labeled diagrams might be seen as building on Apollonius' efforts to create innovative experiential affordances in text. On the other hand, while the poor survival of the mechanical texts and their diagrams makes assessment difficult, it does seem that the Hellenistic mechanical authors drew on different image-making principles than Apollonius' crowd-pleasing "naturalistic" images of the human body. All the surviving Hellenistic authors on mechanics identify parts of the structures and devices they describe using letter labels, a strategy adapted from geometrical works, and, as in geometry, the letter labels correspond to elements of diagrams. (Philo's diagrams have unfortunately all been lost from the manuscript tradition, but extensive lettered references to diagrams in the text survive, as do spaces left for the diagrams in two manuscripts.[48]) The Peripatetic *Mechanical Problems* seems to follow the same basic principles: sparse diagrams consisting of lines and arcs, with letter labels defining important points of flexion, leverage, and so on.[49]

---

[47] Berrey 2017: 127, 142.     [48] Roby 2016b: 167–70.

[49] On this text's diagrams and their variations in the manuscript tradition, see van Leeuwen 2014.

Philo, like Hero, also provides detailed instructions to the reader to picture, construct, and manipulate the devices they describe. To a lesser extent so does Biton, though his descriptions are much briefer, the bulk of the detail apparently having been outsourced to an account of parts and measures (*logothesia*), which is briefly mentioned in the text but does not survive.

While Biton shares the mechanical tradition of letter-labeled diagrams with his disciplinary colleagues, in providing an abbreviated verbal and visual presentation of his material for a royal addressee he perhaps comes closest to matching Apollonius' example (Figure 4.1). Certainly he makes no claims for the insights his diagrams will provide, and the letter labels impose some labor on the reader to look back and forth between text and diagram, but there might be more than one way to please a king with pictures. While it is dangerous to conjecture about Hellenistic images on the basis of medieval manuscripts, the surviving images of catapults from Biton and Hero are often elaborately colored and delightful to look at in their own right. On the other hand, their mechanical complexities have to be puzzled out a bit by the reader rather than offering the kind of immediate intelligibility Apollonius claims for his own images.

Beyond his use of diagrams, to what extent did Hero's work resemble the other kinds of engagements with past bodies of knowledge that characterized Alexandrian literary and technical work? As we have seen, Hero often contemplates the tradition he inherited, representing himself as intervening in various mechanical subdisciplines principally by making past work more accessible.[50] In this sense, Hero certainly participates in a project of "rectification" comparable to those Jacob identifies as characteristically Alexandrian. Yet he presents his project as a kind and gentle form of correction, as when he says in the *Dioptra* that it is not his intention to publicize the errors of his predecessors by name, but only to make corrections where necessary so his readers will not be led astray.[51] In the preface to the *Pneumatica*, though he insists that purely verbal philosophical debate over matter and void has run its course and the time for empirical demonstrations has arrived, he does not name any particular philosophers with whom he disagrees.[52]

---

[50] See for example Hero, *Pneumatica* 1.pr.5–7, *Metrica* 2.pr.1–11, *Automata* 20.1.1–7, *Dioptra* 1.1–11, *Belopoeica* 2.1–14.
[51] Hero, *Dioptra* 1.1–11.    [52] Hero, *Pneumatica* 1.pr.190–200.

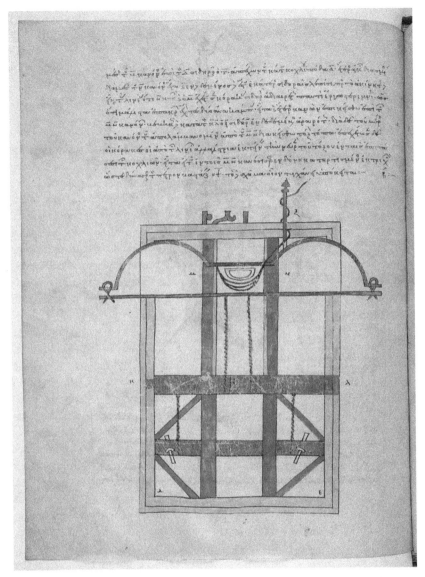

Figure 4.1 Image of a stone-throwing catapult from Biton. Paris grec 2442, fol. 63v.

Throughout his corpus, Hero thus appears not as a participant in what Berrey characterizes as "egotistic and agonistic denigration of past technical knowledge" like Eratosthenes, but rather a respectful colleague from a later cohort, conscious of how his predecessors' positive contributions outweigh their occasional missteps.[53] Hero corrects his *discipline*, not its prior practitioners. In that sense he is engaged in a different sort of work than Apollonius when he critiques Conon, or Hipparchus when he lambastes Eratosthenes' geography venomously enough to discourage Cicero from pursuing his own geographical work.[54] Whereas the exchange of ideas in Hellenistic literature often bristles with names of texts, authors, and addressees, Hero downplays the personal particulars of the authors he engages with.

Other authors are always there, to be sure; Hero is emphatic about his role as a link in a chain rather than the source of a stream. However, save the occasional praise for the disciplinary progress made by figures like Philo, Eudoxus, and Archimedes, Hero's corpus is a rather lonely landscape compared to the agonistic crowd of Hellenistic authors. He is "bookish" in the sense that he portrays himself working with texts and making disciplinary interventions through his work as an author rather than an adventurer in the world. However, he never makes a show of the specific texts he works with, seldom mentioning titles or even authors, nor does he make use of ostentatiously recherché vocabulary, so it cannot be said that we glimpse the Library through his work.

What about the experiential engagements with the world and their representations in text mentioned above? As we saw in the last chapter, Hero offers just a few indicators of the former, but invests heavily in the latter. Like the author of the Peripatetic *Mechanical Problems*, Hero frequently includes vignettes of imagined physical engagements with mechanical and other material systems in his texts. Some of these engagements would have been familiar, like packing grains of sand together at the beach or squeezing and releasing a sponge, both used as analogies for compression effects on bulk matter. Others would have been foreign to a general readership, like manipulating particular features of an automatic theater to test out the mechanism; in such unfamiliar cases the text needs to do much more work to allow the reader to envision that experience. Hero usually favors detailed descriptions of physical experiences rather than the brief analogical sketches that allow the author of the Peripatetic *Mechanical Problems* to bounce briskly from one example to the next, or Philo to quickly explain how the spring of a catapult works. In this sense, as we will see below, Hero uses strategies of experiential description that more closely resemble those characteristic of a later period in Greek technical literature. All these factors suggest that while the markers of local

---

[53] Berrey 2017: 172.    [54] Cicero, *Att.* 2.6.1.

institutions from the court to the Library did not make an impression on the Heronian corpus, it is nevertheless imprinted with the legacy of Hellenistic innovations in both mechanical and information technologies. These include individual Hellenistic "inputs" like the work of Ctesibius and Philo, as well as broader currents of influence on questions about how to negotiate between old and new knowledge.

### Alexandria to Rome

Our second possible Hero would have lived sometime during the tumultuous transitional period of the 1st century BCE to the 1st century CE, as Rome rose to new prominence as a center of scientific endeavors. The thriving culture of scientific and intellectual work at Alexandria had experienced a sharp shock when Ptolemy VIII Euergetes II expelled the scholars from the city in 145 BCE. Athenaeus lists philologists, philosophers, mathematicians, musicians, and painters among the victims, and he reports that in their exile they were forced to resort to teaching.[55] A sad fate for them, perhaps, but fortunate for Rome and the other towns across the Mediterranean where they found refuge, bringing a multidisciplinary store of knowledge with them.

Even after this mass emigration of intellectuals from Alexandria to Rome, of course Alexandria did not drop out of sight as a historical center of scholarly and scientific work. The Library of Alexandria continued to loom very large in the Roman imagination, even among technical authors, as is evident from the many Alexandrian intellectuals who star in the prefaces to Vitruvius' books on architecture.[56] As the Roman world expanded, the Alexandrian institution eventually became not merely an object to admire but something to emulate. This process might have been accelerated by its alleged destruction by Caesar's soldiers, but it is not at all clear that ancient authors ranging from Caesar himself to Plutarch and Cassius Dio in fact describe the destruction of the actual library.[57] Jacob argues that Sulla's acquisition of the remains of Aristotle's library created a precedent for books being brought back to Rome as spoils of war, thus

---

[55] Athenaeus, *Deipnosophistae* 4, 184c.
[56] On Vitruvius' appeals to Hellenistic literary figures see Callebat 1994; Fleury 1994b, 1998: 105; Jacob 2013: 65; Nichols 2017: 32–36; Novara 2005.
[57] Caesar, *Bellum Civile* 3.111; Plutarch, *Caesar* 49.6–7; Cassius Dio, *Historiae Romanae* 42.38. On the significance (or lack thereof) of the fire see Bagnall 2002: 359; Hatzimichali 2013a: 171.

opening up a niche for technical specialists who could take care of the expanding population of Greek books brought to Rome.[58]

The number of libraries at Rome where those books might find a home multiplied and expanded rapidly during this time. Pliny, Suetonius, and Plutarch recount the efforts of Julius Caesar, C. Asinius Pollio, Augustus, Octavia, Tiberius, and Vespasian to collect books and situate them in monumental libraries.[59] These libraries lent the gloss of imperial power to the older Roman tradition of great private book collections amassed by luminaries like Lucullus. Those book collections could attract negative as well as positive comment, as when Seneca complains of greedy book owners who acquire stores of books and even whole libraries too large to read through in a lifetime.[60] While part of his critique covers pointless luxury features like bookshelves of ivory and citron, the bulk of his ire is directed squarely at the waste of information: books from obscure or condemned (*inprobati*) authors piled on shelves too high to reach, owned by jaded men who know less than slaves about literature.

While there are certainly traces here of conventional Roman attacks on *luxuria*, Seneca's critique suggests as well a deepening anxiety about a world of information rapidly growing too large to handle. Hero's works, with their playful philosophical allusions to Plato on land division or the *ataraxia* borne of catapults, would fit right into a collection that already might include some philosophy. Their accessibility to a broad readership, as well as the natural divisions of several of his works into short standalone sections, could have encouraged sharing and quotation. Indeed, they are in some sense "pre-anthologized," as Hero argues that his books spare their owner the need to pore over dozens of earlier works because he has siphoned off all their best information into his own texts. His work might reflect a sensitivity to a culture of information overload like that developing at Rome at this time.

As another approach to coping with these anxieties, Hogg observes that interest in "mass organization of knowledge" had begun to develop at Rome already in the 1st century BCE. Institutional structures for collecting, storing, and propagating books united people with preexisting book collections and people with the knowledge and skill to organize them into libraries, under an intensifying Roman "organizational gaze."[61] Strabo was

---

[58] Jacob 2013: 73.

[59] Suetonius, *Jul.* 44, *Aug.* 29; Pliny, *Nat. Hist.* 7.115; Plutarch, *Marcellus* 30.11. On the competitive timing of these foundations of libraries see Bowie 2013: 239.

[60] Seneca, *Dialogi* 9.9.4–7.      [61] Hogg 2013: 139.

in many ways an embodiment of that gaze, and of the shifting balance between Greek culture and Roman political power. He advertises his *Geography* as a "colossal work (*kolossourgia*)," promising that it will treat only what is great and whole, and not the petty or partial. Strabo draws on a host of authors, mainly Greek, but including references to a few Latin sources as well, to create an expansive portrait of the *oikoumenē* that aims not to get bogged down in details, but to present each region's shape, size, nature, and relationship to the rest of the world as simply as possible.[62]

Dueck summarizes Strabo's criteria for including material in his *kolossourgia* as utility, novelty, current relevance, and fostering the glory of Rome – except for the last, all common refrains for Hero as well.[63] Strabo's treatise is intended to help with political decision-making, so it will not include much detail about the mathematical aspects of geography that are apt to be less interesting and important to his target audience.[64] As he wishes to compile a world's worth of information drawn from diverse sources into a single body of work, all while keeping his reader from losing interest, the way the individual parts are shaped to fit the whole is crucially important. Strabo indeed compares the individual components of his work to amputated limbs: Where truncation is needed, they should be surgically removed at the joints rather than hacked off randomly.[65] His geography binds together a host of constituent disciplines including astronomy, mathematics, history, poetry, and philosophy into a single complex whole.

Vitruvius advocates a similar strategy of constructing an organically complete "body of work" from a mass of individual components drawn from diverse sources and rendered into a form attractive to the general reader.[66] Like Strabo, Vitruvius ostentatiously eschews excessive technical detail in a work aimed at an elite readership. For example, he only lightly sketches out the mathematical principles that relate a catapult's payload to its size, saying that he wishes the mathematically disinclined to have the information conveniently at hand rather than being detained by calculations.[67] He spells out his principles of composition most fully at the midpoint of the work, in the preface to the fifth book, where he concedes that he is self-conscious about writing on a subject that readers will not find naturally entertaining, as they would history or poetry.

---

[62] Strabo, *Geographica* 2.5.13.    [63] Dueck 2000: 160.

[64] Strabo, *Geographica* 1.1.14, 2.5.34; see also Dueck 2000: 53–54.

[65] Strabo, *Geographica* 2.1.30; Dueck 2000: 156.

[66] On the vividness of the "body" metaphor in Vitruvius' work see McEwen 2003: 54–71; Novara 1994: 57.

[67] Vitruvius, *De architectura* 10.11.2.

Since the architect cannot count on his reader to endure repetition or cumbersome explanations of technical terms, Vitruvius will have to make his explanations brief, lucid, and memorable. He must bear in mind that his ideal reader is pressed by public and private business, leaving only brief moments of leisure for reading, so the work itself cannot be too long. At the same time, it should collect multiple bodies of knowledge into a single coherent whole, arranging the work so that the reader does not have to go searching for each subject singly, but can get them all from "a single body (*e corpore uno*)."[68] The types of knowledge that feed the discipline of architecture are as diverse as Strabo's geography: Mathematics, astronomy, philosophy, and history all fall under its rubric. The practicing architect must additionally master the legal aspects of water sources and easements, acoustics of theaters, the medical knowledge required to choose healthy building sites, as well as the craft techniques of drawing and building. Such a broad education maintains the connections between disciplines that are, as it were, the limbs that make up a single unified body.[69]

Fleury observes that while Vitruvius' aim to comprehend a whole world's worth of knowledge in a single compact package has no parallel in Hero, the two do share a concern with putting in order the knowledge they have inherited from their predecessors.[70] Yet Hero does not use the "body" metaphors that Strabo and Vitruvius employ to describe his interdisciplinary project. The way Hero constructs his system from discrete parts is exemplified particularly clearly in the *Automata*. He begins this text by claiming that "to speak summarily, every part (πᾶν μέρος) of mechanics is embraced in automaton-making, through each part one by one being perfected in it (διὰ τῶν κατὰ μέρος ἐν αὐτῇ ἐπιτελουμένων)."[71] Hero's use of the word "part" (*meros*) in this passage strongly suggests that in his systematic approach mechanics as a discipline is built up piecewise from components rather than conceived and arranged from the top down. His *Belopoeica* likewise invokes the *meros* as an epistemological unit; there the term first indicates a certain part of philosophy (that concerned with *ataraxia*) and then a certain part of mechanics (*belopoeica*).[72] Fuhrmann takes this as a sign that Hero is using a kind of systematizing approach in this work but cautions that Hero does not necessarily envision this disciplinary structure as completely cemented and static.[73] Hero's work will, in any event, turn out to be something quite different from Strabo's

[68] Vitruvius, *De architectura* 5.pr.1–5.    [69] Vitruvius, *De architectura* 1.1.1–11.
[70] Fleury 1994a: 70 n. 14.    [71] *Automata* 1.1.    [72] *Belopoeica* 1.2, 1.13, 1.21.
[73] Fuhrmann 1960: 170.

*kolossourgia* or Vitruvius' single ten-book *corpus*: not a unified whole planned to perfection from the beginning but a network of *merē* whose growth is not shaped from the start by an image of what it will look like at the end.

The Roman literary world saw a radical upswing in the propagation of texts that might be labeled "encyclopedic," including the works of Cato, Varro, Celsus, Pliny, Quintilian, and others.[74] The very diversity of these texts and authors suggests some of the possible complications of trying to group them together, to say nothing of the difficulty of leaving behind expectations for "encyclopedic" works predicated on modern exemplars of the genre.[75] Rather than attempting to capture any kind of encyclopedic orthodoxy that might have held in antiquity, it is perhaps better simply to observe that the late Republic and early Empire fostered a remarkable number of works that advertise the breadth and interconnectedness of the knowledge they draw on, as well as their own achievement of rendering that knowledge into a compact and readable form. Murphy blends the epistemic with the political, arguing that an encyclopedic work is itself an embodiment of imperial power, embodying the idea of centralized control over knowledge.[76] Indeed, König and Woolf suggest that while Hellenistic authors developed and expanded their own techniques for systematizing knowledge, Roman authors were the first to strive to deliver their readers "the world compressed into a single book."[77]

Other works did not so much aim at the "world in a book" model, but they do suggest that their subject matter is of universal interest, as in Celsus' contextualization of medicine within a larger cultural and historical picture, which Heinrich von Staden compares to the rhetoric of the "universal" historians.[78] Compared to the screeds against Greek physicians presented by Pliny (ventriloquizing Cato), Celsus offers a more measured

---

[74] On the complexities of the term see Doody 2009: 1–4.

[75] König and Woolf argue rather for seeking out various manifestations of "encyclopedic motifs and ambitions and techniques, all of them linked in some way with the idea of comprehensive and systematic knowledge-ordering": König and Woolf 2013: 23. Doody likewise argues for caution in applying the label "encyclopedia," saying that "genre is probably not a helpful model for understanding the relationship between Pliny and Varro's work": Doody 2009: 3. Pliny's work does include features familiar from modern exemplars (Doody singles it out as "a grand scale reference work with retrieval devices"), and he celebrates Greek *enkuklios paideia* as a spanning set of worthwhile subjects of study: Pliny, *Nat. Hist.* pr.14; Doody 2009: 18. Still, as Doody points out, it is far from clear that Pliny is thus making a claim that the *Natural History* itself covers all those subjects, to say nothing of the other ancient "encyclopedias" that obviously do not.

[76] Murphy 2004: 2.    [77] König and Woolf 2013: 28.    [78] von Staden 1999: 251–53.

account of the migration of Greek medicine into the Roman world.[79] He prefaces his *De medicina* with what von Staden calls a "moral" history of medicine structured along Roman concepts of value like *boni mores* and *luxuria*, with Celsus playing the role of "a non-partisan, ambitionless Roman searcher after truths that can only be approximated."[80] Celsus offers a broad history of Greco-Roman medicine, celebrating neither Greek nor Roman contributions at the expense of the other.

The distance Celsus puts between himself and any particular practice of medicine emphasizes that the *De medicina* is an account of books on medicine more than it is a medical text *per se*. His account of its fabled Asclepian origins is drawn from Homer, he catalogs how philosophical debates between the sects were waged in written form, and of course the *De medicina* itself is a self-consciously literary project, part of a larger multidisciplinary work whose other parts do not survive. As important as books are to Celsus, however, he is ambivalent about them, saying that the rise of book culture itself encouraged unhealthy bodily habits, creating the very health problems Greek medicine was designed to combat.[81] Like Strabo's synoptic geography or Vitruvius' account of the common principles that shaped the earliest home-building efforts of primitive men the world over, Celsus' work distilled comprehensible commonalities from the intimidating knowledge store of a rapidly growing and diversifying Roman world.

Hero's overtures to the universal appeal and utility of the subjects he discusses offer some parallels to Celsus' "universalizing" approach. As mentioned above, his history of catapults in the *Belopoeica* is not a history of any particular kingdom's military exploits; all geographical and historical specifics are elided as he conjures up a borderless world of pure technology. Behind his ludic opening claim that transmitting knowledge about catapults serves philosophy by providing the surest route to *ataraxia* lies a serious bid for the study of mechanics to be viewed as a source of immaterial as well as material benefits for everyone, everywhere. His universalizing history of the catapult harmonizes with similar approaches

---

[79] Pliny, *Nat. Hist.* 29.13–14. On the experiences of physicians coming from all over the Greek world to Rome see Nutton 2012.

[80] von Staden 1999: 260.

[81] Celsus, *De medicina* 1.pr.5–6: *ergo etiam post eos, de quibus rettuli, nulli clari uiri medicinam exercuerunt, donec maiore studio litterarum disciplina agitari coepit; quae ut animo praecipue omnium necessaria, sic corpori inimica est.* He redoubles this gloomy assessment of the ill effects of books on health at 1.2: *at inbecillis, quo in numero magna pars urbanorum omnesque paene cupidi litterarum sunt, obseruatio maior necessaria est, ut, quod uel corporis uel loci uel studii ratio detrahit, cura restituat.*

to other disciplines elsewhere. In the *Metrica*, for example, he contextualizes several of his mathematical results within a similarly placeless history of evolving problem-solving techniques, theorems, and approximations developed by previous mathematicians, all aiming to provide useful solutions to practical problems. Other works likewise praise other disciplines of mechanics as universally beneficial, from the dioptra's capacity to precisely map out all the land, sky, and sea to the revelations about the universal physics of materials one can glean from the pneumatic wonders. In these respects, even though his texts are dedicated to individual disciplines, Hero casts his subject matter in the same "universalizing" light as Celsus does medicine, or Vitruvius architecture.

As noted earlier, Hero frequently advertises that his goal is to make his technical subject matter accessible to everyone, echoing Strabo's and Vitruvius' anxiety that their wide-ranging works should be useful to the reader. In his commitment to didactic accessibility for a more tightly constrained range of material, his work closely resembles other Greco-Roman monographs on mechanical technologies by Athenaeus Mechanicus and Apollodorus. Athenaeus, who seems to have shared a teacher (Agesistratus of Rhodes) with Vitruvius, wrote a volume on siege machinery dedicated to a "Marcellus" who may be identified with M. Claudius Marcellus, Augustus' nephew.[82] The explicit dedication of these texts to an imperial addressee is of course quite unlike Hero, but the way that dedication shapes a text yields some striking similarities. Dedicating a technical text to the emperor incentivizes accessibility; the emperor's responsibility is not to master technical details but to demonstrate a commanding knowledge of how the technologies described fit into the strategies of the siege. Like Hero, Athenaeus emphasizes that he aims to provide an overview of technologies likely to be useful in a variety of situations rather than the details of the very latest designs.

Athenaeus begins his text with a preface (ironically rather long) largely devoted to the theme of brevity, where he also expresses fear of overly aggressive book critics.[83] Indeed, Whitehead and Blyth single out his preface as "anticipating attack in the over-heated atmosphere" of intellectuals seeking patronage at this time.[84] In this respect Athenaeus differs somewhat from Hero, who seems unconcerned with meeting the demands of any particular patron. Hero does go out of his way in the

---

[82] On the debates over Athenaeus' dates and the identities of Agesistratus and Marcellus see Athenaeus 2004: 15–20.

[83] Athenaeus Mechanicus, *Peri mēchanēmatōn* 6.2–5.     [84] Athenaeus 2004: 33.

prefaces to most of his works to spell out why a particular topic will be of interest to a nontechnical audience: Catapults deliver *ataraxia*, land-surveying divides territory up most fairly, etc. As we have seen, in the *Pneumatica*'s preface he also praises direct "perceptible proof" over the boundless bickering of natural philosophers. Still, he does not dwell on his own authorial work and its likely reception with the kind of nervous energy Athenaeus exhibits.

Athenaeus advises, citing his teacher Agesistratus, that the most important thing is to obtain "experience of *grammai*." Whitehead and Blyth take this term to refer to outline surveys rather than drawings, since Athenaeus mentions nothing about images here.[85] While Hero does not use the term in the same way, it is certainly true that at least some of his texts, the *Belopoeica* above all, are shaped to provide a comparable kind of survey. The survey format of course tends to inhibit detailed description of any single device and so makes it difficult to introduce novel technologies in the text. On this note, Athenaeus endorses another piece of advice from Agesistratus: that it is often better to use tried and tested inventions rather than feeling compelled to innovate constantly, a tactic better suited to deceiving laymen than creating reliable machinery.[86] This is not to say that the *Peri mēchanēmatōn* simply retreads old designs; Athenaeus does break into his narrative of past inventions at one point to say that while he takes pride in adding his insights to the store of useful mechanical knowledge, at the same time his "mobility of mind (εὐκινησία περὶ τὴν ψυχήν)" drives him to contribute one new invention of his own.[87] This is a device called the "little ape (*pithēkion*)," a device for keeping platforms for siege machinery stable on ships as they roll on the waves. For all his pride in contributing this new device to the annals of mechanics, however, Athenaeus gives no technical details about it, only expanding on why such a device is useful for naval forces. By contrast, even in a survey text like the *Belopoeica*, which is focused on the long history of catapult technologies rather than novel innovations, Hero still maintains a high level of technical detail.

Apollodorus likely composed his own work on siege engineering, including both machines and static structures like towers and rams, for Trajan or Hadrian. Although he lived considerably later than Athenaeus and Vitruvius, a certain conservatism in his authorial approach means he resembles them more closely than any surviving author from his own

---

[85] Athenaeus 2004: 74.      [86] Athenaeus Mechanicus, *Peri mēchanēmatōn* 7.11–8.4.
[87] Athenaeus Mechanicus, *Peri mēchanēmatōn* 32.1–33.3.

time.[88] Like Athenaeus, Apollodorus exhibits a deep concern about how his patron will receive the work. In his preface he expresses satisfaction at the patron's having chosen him to receive a "letter about machines," solicitude that his own designs should prove easy to understand and useful in the field, regret that his reply comes so late, worry that he may have included some abstruse vocabulary or references to theory that will be unclear for his patron, and hopes that the latter's talent (*megalophuia*) will allow him both to penetrate the technical mysteries and forgive Apollodorus any excursions into unpleasant technicalities.[89] These concerns evaporate in the main body of the text, but the preface sends strong signals of the work's composition for a particular patron whom Apollodorus is most eager to please, again quite unlike Hero's work.

Apollodorus shares with Hero and Athenaeus a commitment to utility and straightforward presentation, saying the devices he describes were chosen for their simple versatility and time-tested reliability, the better to meet the exigencies of war. Inadvertently, he also shares with Hero a history of postmortem textual interpolation. Despite his promise to restrain himself to simple and reliable devices, from time to time devices appear in the text that meet neither criterion: a bellows-driven flame-thrower to break brick walls, a siege ladder containing channels to pump hot oil or water up to where one's own soldiers are climbing over the walls, and so on. Lendle argued that these fanciful elaborations were the product of an aging Apollodorus revising his old work, but Blyth argued convincingly on stylistic grounds that these passages were the work of another author, and Whitehead largely agreed.[90] But as Whitehead points out, the "enlarged treatise" is an object of interest in its own right, testament to the enduring value of past knowledge in ancient warfare as well as the creative impulses that emerged from warfare's "stimulus to invention and ingenuity." Apollodorus did share with Hero an inviting accessibility, as well as a text framed as a set of discrete passages, factors that seem to invite interventions from later authors (as in the case of the more heavily interpolated Heronian works).

Other features of Hero's texts, like his lushly letter-labeled diagrams, differ from Athenaeus and Apollodorus. Their texts include no letter labels, and consequently the diagrams show only whole machines with

---

[88] On the tenuous identification of Apollodorus and his connection with Trajan or Hadrian see Apollodorus 2010: 17–24.

[89] Apollodorus, *Poliorcetica* 137.1–138.17.

[90] Apollodorus 2010: 32–34; Blyth 1992: 139; Lendle 1983: xx.

some word labels, in contrast to Hero's letter-labeled components and whole machines. While we cannot of course know what any of these diagrams looked like originally since all that survive are Byzantine copies, it is extremely unlikely that the diagrams would at any point have included letter labels with no textual referent. Hero's detailed textual references to his diagrams more closely resemble Philo's techniques, which in turn seem to be drawn from the tradition of geometrical texts. Hero thus adapts the technology of the letter-labeled diagram to a new cultural context, where it enables him to map painstakingly detailed descriptions of constructions onto a visual referent, turning the diagram into an effective tool to serve his didactic aims.

As we have seen, Hero often provides quite detailed instructions for building the mechanical devices he describes. Even in a text like the *Belopoeica*, which covers several different types of ballistic device (at least some of which were already outdated at any possible time of writing), Hero still includes details like the manual process of packing the spring cord that fires the device. There is simply nothing equivalent in the texts of Athenaeus or Apollodorus. The latter notes that he will dispatch an assistant whom he personally trained to build the structures in the text, along with a team of skilled workmen, so ensuring that the details of the machines can be transmitted while leaving the text relatively simple and accessible. Apollodorus thus offloads the deeper levels of construction detail to the domain of tacit knowledge possessed by expert craftsmen, while Athenaeus effaces them completely.

Vitruvius likewise tends to keep his immense suite of structures and devices somewhat at arm's length while moving briskly from one to the next, though there are a few cases in the *De architectura* where he goes into depth comparable to Hero on the material and structural particulars of an object. Fleury compares Vitruvius' approach to Hero's in describing two similar devices: Vitruvius on a piston-driven water pump he attributes to Ctesibius and Hero on a pump to be used fighting fires.[91] As Fleury notes, Vitruvius takes about half as long as Hero to describe his pump, a difference that cannot be attributed simply to the concision of the Latin language. Like Athenaeus and Apollodorus, Vitruvius eschews the use of letter labels for the pump's components, and there is no indication that this device enjoyed representation in one of the few images that originally accompanied the *De architectura*.[92] The next few sections of the work are

---

[91] Vitruvius, *De architectura* 10.7.1–3; Hero, *Pneumatica* 1.28; Fleury 1994a: 72–77.
[92] On the promised but missing images see Gros 1996; Stückelberger 1994: 96–99.

also devoted to devices that Hero also describes, namely the water organ and the odometer, so their relative lengths can again be compared.[93] Hero's description of the water organ is again twice as long as Vitruvius' (and Hero follows it up with a second design, this one automatically powered). The two authors' treatments of odometer designs are close to the same length, but in that space Vitruvius proposes an imaginative shipborne odometer as well as the more conventional land-based version, and so once again Hero's design is explained in considerably more detail.

The scarcity of deep accounts of manual activity in the surviving work of authors like Vitruvius, Athenaeus, and Apollodorus eliminates one potential set of strategies for turning the text into a site for exploring "experiential" engagements with physical systems. Yet this is not to say that texts from this period are devoid of any parallels to Hero's experimental narratives. Vitruvius, Seneca, and others pepper their texts with brief accounts of informal activities through which certain physical principles can be seen in action, either directly or by analogy. While these descriptions are usually short, they do sometimes approach the level of detail and familiarity that turns some of Hero's vignettes into opportunities for "virtual witnessing." Seneca makes frequent use of analogy to generate scientific understanding in the *Natural Questions*.[94] The reader is encouraged to see the principles that generate rainbows in the sky on the smaller scale of a fuller using his mouth to mist water droplets onto cloth; a spiral-shaped water heater is likened to subterranean channels where water is heated geothermally; a whirlwind's eddy is compared to a vortex of water.[95]

While Seneca's *explananda* remain firmly fixed in the natural world and an artificial device like the helical water heater is a relative rarity even as an *explanans*, Vitruvius makes more frequent use of analogies involving artifacts. A gaggle of ants circumnavigating a potter's wheel while it spins in the opposite direction serve as an analogy for the planets moving in the opposite direction from the stars; the dynamics of the winds can be appreciated from the steam exhaled by a heated bronze figurine of Aeolus; water ripples in a pond resemble the acoustic waves of the voice and thus served as guides for early theater architects to grade the rows of

---

[93] Vitruvius, *De architectura* 10.8, 10.9; Hero, *Pneumatica* 1.42, *Dioptra* 37.

[94] Armisen-Marchetti 2001. For Armisen-Marchetti's thorough catalog of Senecan analogies see Armisen-Marchetti 1989: 287–95.

[95] Seneca, *Naturales Quaestiones* 1.3.2, 3.24.2, 5.13.1–2. On Seneca's use of analogy as an explanatory technique see Williams 2012. For some complications pertaining to these analogies and further discussion of analogy in Seneca see Roby 2014b.

seats properly.[96] In this sense Vitruvius and Hero certainly seem to be engaged in a similar kind of work. While both authors may be principally concerned with describing man-made artifacts, they both take care to link their operating principles to those at work in nature and so to bring their texts into harmony with broader discourse on natural philosophy.

A version of Hero situated in this cultural context could thus be viewed as a kind of hybrid figure who adopts some of the techniques favored by Roman technical authors in this period yet overlays those techniques transparently on a background of features that more closely resemble the Hellenistic technical tradition. His work is didactically broad, and he points out links between works where they arise organically, but he does not claim an encyclopedic scope or unifying organizational principle for his corpus as a whole. He is conscious of the features that will make a book welcome reading for a nontechnical audience but not overtly concerned with pleasing a particular addressee, imperial or otherwise. He does not shy from including a large amount of technical detail about the forms, materials, and construction processes of the devices he describes, nor from requiring the reader to study the diagrams carefully with the help of the letter labels included in the text. He does not engage deeply with the power of analogy to build bridges to broader questions in natural philosophy; his mechanical and mathematical structures remain the central focus of his work.

## The Later Empire

A third possible Hero might have sprung up in the cosmopolitan Roman world of the 2nd–4th centuries CE, abutting against the *terminus ante quem* of Pappus. The latter's dates are themselves a little uncertain; a note in the *Suda* dates him to the reign of Theodosius, a note on a manuscript of Theon dates him to Diocletian, while Cuomo suggests he is best dated simply to the 4th century.[97] The three-century span this hypothetical Hero may have occupied encompassed a vast swathe of political, technological, and literary developments, and I will here only pick out a few features most relevant for imagining Hero against this backdrop.

Keyser notes a decrease in the number of known scientific and technical authors in the Roman world beginning in the 2nd century CE, correlated

---

[96] Vitruvius, *De architectura* 9.1.15, 1.6.2, 5.3.6–7. On Vitruvius' use of natural and artificial models see Roby 2013.
[97] Cuomo 2000: 6.

with a decline in trade, increased concentration of power in the person of the emperor, and the resulting shift of Roman society from a "commercial" to an authoritarian "extractive" power.[98] This shift accompanied a "turn to authority and compendia in science" that soothed readers' anxieties over the "aporia" produced by the failure to resolve certain scientific questions.[99] Compendia of differing explanations for scientific questions were, of course, nothing new; we might think of the broad spectrum of dissenting opinions on scientific questions Seneca brings to bear in his *Natural Questions* or the question-and-answer "problem" texts associated with the Peripatetic school. What Keyser identifies as novel in this period was an archaizing turn to a newly constructed canon, as well as a strong emphasis on the utility of compendia.[100] Rather than sites to restage ongoing scientific debates, compendia were viewed as one-stop shops where a reader could find a curated set of answers, packaged with an assurance that the author had done all the necessary legwork himself.

The broader Greco-Roman literary culture at this time reflects an intense interest in displays of intellectual prowess, often embodied in performances by superstar orators. The label "Second Sophistic" for this culture of education and its (often agonistic) public display was inspired by Philostratus' efforts in his *Lives of the Sophists* to connect the epideictic orators of his own day to the language and practices of their classical antecedents.[101] That term was later applied to a broader range of cultural phenomena, including the rise of high-visibility public declamation, the revival of "Attic" Greek, and the cachet of the educated (*pepaideumenos*) public figure.[102] The ideal of broad-based *paideia* practically demanded the production of books where a reader could develop at least a passing familiarity with a wide range of topics and where an author could display his erudition. Of course, books were not the only artifacts that lent themselves to such displays: Borg notes the proliferation in this period of sarcophagi depicting the full range of Muses in praise of multidisciplinary

---

[98] Keyser 2013: 28. Keyser adapts the "commercial" and "extractive" systems model from Jacobs 1992.

[99] Keyser 2018: 830.

[100] On the related topic of "big books," it may be noted that the longest of Hero's works are still only a little more than 10 percent of the length of Galen's *De usu partium* or Ptolemy's *Almagest*. They are about the same length as Nicomachus' *Arithmetica* and about half the length of Diophantus' *Arithmetica*.

[101] On Philostratus' canonical sophists see Eshleman 2008.

[102] A few key texts on these features include Anderson 1993; Swain 1996; Whitmarsh 2005. Some scholars have suggested that the term may have been overused; Brunt, for example, questions whether there was indeed a revival of oratory at Brunt 1994.

*paideia*, as well as alternative symbols of broad learning including sundials and globes.[103]

Erudite, cosmopolitan, and performative: While there were plenty of opportunities for authors to put scientific or technical knowledge on display in this environment (we might think of Aelius Aristides' globe-trotting medical adventures or Pausanias' learned geography), these epithets seem to have little in common with Hero's insistently utilitarian rhetoric and his chronologically and geographically generic work. But in other respects his writing resembles the technical literature of the 2nd and 3rd centuries quite closely. The rise of scientific compendia and the idealized breadth of *paideia* both favored the packaging of knowledge in "eisagogic" forms. Such works should begin at the beginning, as Hero often claims to do, but from that point they might either maintain a slow pace of instruction or accelerate more aggressively into more advanced material.

Nicomachus of Gerasa, who likely dates to the first half of the 2nd century CE, offers some compelling parallels to Hero in his gentle introductions to number and harmony. His *Introduction to Arithmetic* and harmonic *Enchiridion* are both explicitly addressed to readers at the beginnings of their studies rather than experts, offering scaffolding elements like definitions to help the reader on their journey and minimizing or eliminating proofs. He promises the unknown female addressee of the *Enchiridion* that his explanations of harmonics will proceed "without art or complex demonstration (χωρὶς κατασκευῆς καὶ ποικίλης ἀποδείξεως)," presenting the basic principles of harmonics in one synoptic work.[104] Keyser characterizes his approach to mathematics in both works as "discursive not demonstrative," providing necessary results without feeling compelled to reproduce others' proofs.[105]

Perhaps a century after Nicomachus, Diophantus launched a mathematical project of his own that likewise advertised itself as designed for beginners, though the contents quickly accelerate to much more difficult material. He begins his *Arithmetica* with a promise to his addressee Dionysius: Recognizing Dionysius' enthusiasm to learn about "the nature and power in numbers," he promises that he will build up a didactic system for him to approach the subject, beginning from the very foundations (*themelioi*). He acknowledges the subject may seem difficult,

ἐπειδὴ μήπω γνώριμόν ἐστιν, δυσέλπιστοι γὰρ εἰς κατόρθωσίν εἰσιν αἱ τῶν ἀρχομένων ψυχαί, ὅμως δ' εὐκατάληπτόν σοι γενήσεται, διά τε τὴν

---

[103] Borg 2008: 167.     [104] Nicomachus, *Enchiridion* 1.12–16.     [105] Keyser 2018: 833.

σὴν προθυμίαν καὶ τὴν ἐμὴν ἀπόδειξιν· ταχεῖα γὰρ εἰς μάθησιν ἐπιθυμία προσλαβοῦσα διδαχήν.

since it is not yet understood, for the minds of beginners are discouraged by correction – yet all the same it will become easy for you to grasp, through your courage and my demonstration. For enthusiasm plus teaching makes a swift path to learning.[106]

Diophantus assures Dionysius that his didactic program will carry him over this difficult terrain smoothly, but not passively: Dionysius will need to maintain his enthusiasm (*prothumia*) even in the face of correction (*katorthōsis*), and in exchange the subject will gradually come into his grasp. The closing pun on one of the technical terms Diophantus uses for arithmetic addition stamps this passage as a friendly overture from one enthusiast to another: one who has already made the didactic journey, the other just beginning.

He then proceeds to define briefly what he calls the "species (*eidē*)" of numbers, which include the unknown quantity (*arithmos*), its powers from second to sixth (*dynamis, kybos, dynamodynamis*, etc.), and the unit (*monas*). At this point, the beginner-level reader may be getting nervous about the novelty and technicality of the terminological and conceptual apparatus required, so Diophantus takes a break to explain some of his didactic tactics in more detail. It is true, he acknowledges, that there are a lot of propositions to learn, and understanding them may be a slow process; it is also true that they are therefore hard to track in the memory. To compensate, he aims to arrange the propositions, especially at the beginning, in an order that facilitates learning: "in elementary fashion (*stoicheiōdōs*)," moving from the simpler to the more complex. He promises that "in this way the path will be easy for beginners (εὐόδευτα γενήσεται τοῖς ἀρχομένοις)," and that his "guidance (*agōgē*)" will be firmly established in their memory.[107]

Diophantus iterates in this passage on the idea of a "road" to understanding, initially inviting the reader, "let us set out on the road to the propositions (ἐπὶ τὰς προτάσεις χωρήσωμεν ὁδόν)," and later promising to arrange them into an easy path (*euodeuta*). The metaphor is important here, because the reader is going to be presented with some quite difficult material indeed, couched in unfamiliar terminology and innovative notation. Diophantus' work may be intended as eisagogic, in the sense that a reader who comes in with only the knowledge of basic arithmetic he

---

[106] Diophantus, *Arithmetica* 2.9–13.    [107] Diophantus, *Arithmetica* 16.3–7.

specifies at the beginning can work their way to the end. But "eisagogic" does not necessarily mean "easy." In this sense the *Arithmetica* might find its closest Heronian match in the *Metrica*. Both texts promise to provide all the necessary material for a beginning reader to get all the way to a certain end, and to organize it with an eye on the didactic journey, but the road is a long one, and not without its challenges.

The image of the long road to knowledge was embraced most enthusiastically by Galen, who spells out in his *On My Own Books* and *On the Order of My Own Books* how a reader might best work their way toward an understanding of medicine. To be sure, he does not deliver a systematic reading list from start to finish, since the right path to learning must depend on the temperament of the student. The best starting point, he says, would be his work on *The Best Sect*, but this is only possible for those "who are by nature intelligent and friends of the truth (φύσει συνετοὶ καὶ ἀληθείας ἑταῖροι)" and well versed in logic.[108] The rest should proceed through his various works for beginners, starting with the enormous *On Anatomical Procedures*, and practice the dissections recounted there repeatedly. In order to grasp both medicine and philosophy, one must be sharp-witted, have a good memory, and really like to work. These innate features should be accompanied by all the advantages of a lifelong education in multiple foundational disciplines including mathematics, like Galen received at his father's hands. Even beginning this study looks like very hard work indeed.

Finally, after all this, one more hazard remains: language. Galen felt he was witnessing an unruly expansion of the definitions of many Attic words by medical and philosophical authors attaching new definitions to them willy-nilly. His plan to combat this problem began with a reference work he owned, a "systematic treatise (*pragmateia*)," effectively a dictionary listing alphabetically all the words used by Attic prose authors.[109] This work appears to have served as a springboard for Galen himself to compose an extravagant forty-six-book commentary on words from Attic prose authors.[110] In a further response to the growing abuse of Attic Greek in his time, he says he wrote yet another work on the correctness of those words – and this work, he says in the startling conclusion to *On the Order of My Own Books*, should in fact be the very first book of his anyone reads.

---

[108] Galen, *De ordine librorum suorum ad Eugenianum*, Kühn v. 19 p. 53.
[109] Galen, *De ordine librorum suorum ad Eugenianum*, Kühn v. 19 p. 60.
[110] At *De indolentia* 20 he mentions the loss by fire of a reference work he wrote on Attic nouns in two parts, one on prose and one on Old Comedy. He apparently had some copies made of the first, which were brought to Campania and survived.

Galen's alleged guide to launching one's study of medicine thus reads like a kind of shaggy-dog story whose real purpose is to emphasize how difficult it is to acquire the kind of broad-based knowledge necessary to become a really excellent physician like Galen himself. The picture becomes more complex still in *On My Own Books*: Even though *On the Order of My Own Books* suggests that one could begin with philosophy, in fact the contemporary philosophical scene is so weak that the student risks falling into the bad logical habits of the modern Stoics and Peripatetics Galen has encountered. Their sloppy logic often yields conflicting results, they rarely reach the proofs they aim for – and indeed, Galen says, he "might have fallen into a Pyrrhonian aporia" had he not previously been schooled in mathematics.[111] Galen's idealized model of medicine is built on firm logical foundations, themselves rooted in the demonstrative rigor associated with geometry.[112] However, the examples of foundational mathematical learning Galen provides are surprising. The glimpses of truth mathematics afforded him came in the form of eclipse predictions, the accurate time-telling of sundials and water clocks, and the principles of architecture – indeed, a rather Heronian lineup of practical applications.[113] Galen here seems to embrace a variation on the ideal of geometrical proof by portraying mathematics as embodied and accessible to the senses. This kind of mathematics, which Galen frames as "architecture" in a celebration of his father's profession, offers practical utility as well as rigor.[114]

Nor was Galen the only one celebrating the potential of the applications of mathematics at this time. Ptolemy appeals in the opening chapters of his *Tetrabiblos* to the useful benefits of astrology, promising that its predictive power is available to anyone who masters the principles of mathematical astronomy and denied only by those too ignorant to perform the calculations correctly.[115] Everyone accepts simple cyclical patterns in nature like the seasons, he says, and professionals like sailors have some specialist knowledge of additional patterns like the signs of storms. But even though these phenomena arise because of the relationships between the sun, moon, and planets, sailors do not have the knowledge to calculate their movements accurately, which creates doubt in the causal relationships that astrologers know connect heavenly and terrestrial phenomena.[116]

---

[111] Galen, *De libris propris*, Kühn v. 19 pp. 39–40.    [112] Netz 2017.
[113] Galen, *De libris propris*, Kühn v. 19 p. 40.
[114] On Galen's father's and grandfather's occupation as architects see Galen, *De indolentia* 59.
[115] He appeals to astrology as "useful and powerful" as early as *Tetrabiblos* 1.1.3.10, and he celebrates it as a "beneficial (*ōphelimos*)" art at 1.3.
[116] Ptolemy, *Tetrabiblos* 1.2.7.4–10.1.

The rewards of mastering those patterns are great, promises Ptolemy, transforming those who do into "synoptic viewers (*synoratikoi*) of things both human and divine," and granting them an understanding of what bodily goods (τὰ τοῦ σώματος) are suitable for every kind of temperament – though he acknowledges it will not make them rich.[117]

Yet acquiring these benefits, as in the case of Galen's progression toward medical knowledge, is easier said than done. The astrological knowledge of the *Tetrabiblos* is dependent on the mathematical astronomy of the *Almagest*, which is itself aimed at readers who "have already advanced to some extent" in the study of its subject matter.[118] The *Harmonics*, though its treatment of musical intervals begins from scratch, turns in its third book to the analogies between harmonic intervals and those of the celestial bodies. This discussion builds on the model of the cosmos described in the *Almagest*, where planets make their rounds about the Earth on epicyclic paths. Ptolemy also presumes some understanding of the divisions and oppositions of the zodiac, the associations of qualities with planets, and the risings of the sun, moon, and stars discussed as well in the *Tetrabiblos*. To be sure, the reader does not need most of the complicated details of Ptolemy's analysis of the planets and stars to understand the relatively simple quantitative analogies here. However, they will need some knowledge beyond the very basics to appreciate, for example, Ptolemy's mapping from the tetrachords to the timings of planetary risings relative to the sun, or his reasons for drawing connections between harmonic intervals and specific planets.[119]

Earlier authors like Vitruvius and Strabo had emphasized the importance of building up a work with a varied yet coherent "body," while "encyclopedic" authors like Pliny and Celsus (different as they are in other respects) had similarly aimed to capture a world's worth of knowledge in text. By contrast, while Nicomachus, Galen, and Ptolemy certainly continued the tradition of composing books on varied subjects, their own programmatic statements seem to suggest that the goal of broad disciplinary coverage had been supplemented by the desire to shape their corpus of texts, at least to some extent, around a reader's potential pedagogical journey. That journey might be viewed as starting from zero: Galen suggests the reader who sincerely wishes to master medicine should begin with his dictionary of Attic words, Nicomachus provides his reader with a

---

[117] Ptolemy, *Tetrabiblos* 1.3.2.5–3.7. On the philosophical context in which Ptolemy argues for the ethical value of the "mathematical way of life" see Feke 2018: 52–78.
[118] Ptolemy, *Syntaxis* 1,1.8.6–9.    [119] Ptolemy, *Harmonica* III.13.

gentle incline founded in the most elementary objects of study, while Diophantus constructs a somewhat steeper road, though still carefully shaped to support the learning process. Ptolemy, by contrast, expects the reader to have acquired the most fundamental elements elsewhere before they begin the *Almagest*, itself required reading for the *Tetrabiblos* and helpful background for the celestial analogies of the *Harmonics*. But although the precise details of the reader's trajectory may differ, these works all seem to reflect a common concern not merely for completeness of subject matter, but also a belief that the reader's journey through that material should be to some extent curated and guided by the author. These authors exhibit concern not only for the ideal of *paideia*, but also the pedagogical journey that enables it.

In this respect they have much in common with the examples of Hero's guidance for his own reader we have seen in the previous chapters. His *Definitiones* commence with a promise to outline (*hypographein, hypotypoun*) Euclid's geometrical definitions concisely (*syntomōs*) and synoptically (*eusynoptōs*) for his reader, not unlike Nicomachus' explicitly introductory texts. His *Pneumatica* is explicitly designed to be read right after his lost work on water clocks, and it builds its own treatment of the discipline from the elements on up.[120] His *Belopoeica* is designed for a readership with no prior knowledge, while the *Automata* is intended for those who have mastered the subdisciplines of mechanical knowledge it presumes. While Hero never provides a map as complete as Galen's *On the Order of My Own Books*, like Ptolemy he does provide local guidance in selected texts about how the reader may best proceed through his corpus.

Although Hero does share with these 2nd-century authors a concern for the pedagogical prerequisites of *paideia*, the resemblance breaks down somewhat when it comes to the way they perform their own learning. Ptolemy does, like Hero, promise to create a well-ordered treatise incorporating the reliable findings of his predecessors alongside his own contributions, promising that he will only briefly review his predecessors' contributions "so as not to go on too long," but he will thoroughly investigate (*epexergazesthai*) what they left unexplained.[121] In his short epilogue to the treatise, Ptolemy situates himself within a broader context of scientific progress, acknowledging the improvements in accuracy astronomers had made up to his own time as well as his own work of correction (*epanorthōsis*).[122] As for his own contributions, he here sets his seal on the

---

[120] *Pneumatica* 1.pr.9–17.   [121] Ptolemy, *Syntaxis* 1,1.8.12–16.
[122] Ptolemy, *Syntaxis* 1,2.608.

*Almagest* as a work that has gone on just long enough to be useful (*euchrēstos*) without straying into showiness (*endeixis*). Hero and Ptolemy thus appear to share some concerns about readability, as well as a self-consciousness about their place on a continuum of technical authors.

Yet Ptolemy's references to the authors whose work he is expanding and correcting are more pointed and precise than Hero's, in many ways resembling the more polemical tactics of Hellenistic Alexandrian authors engaging with their predecessors. The *Almagest* includes a large number of brief corrective engagements with specific findings from Hipparchus, Timocharis, and others. For example, in his treatment of the lunar anomaly, Ptolemy acknowledges that the reader may be wondering why Hipparchus' figures for the values of the eccentricity and epicyclic radius of the moon not only differ from his own, but even exhibit inconsistencies between two different sets of lunar eclipses Hipparchus himself used as the basis for his own calculations.[123] Without getting into the details of this problem, I simply note that Ptolemy motivates his own discussion of the problem with the apparent expectation that his reader will already have encountered Hipparchus' discussion of lunar motion, followed through the calculations, noted the discrepancies, and sought out Ptolemy's treatment to reconcile the conflict.

However, since Ptolemy performs his calculations on the same triads of lunar eclipses Hipparchus had used, he ends up repeating a considerable amount of detail from Hipparchus. He reproduces information about the locations, dates, and types of eclipses, as well as the calculations themselves, to emphasize just how far Hipparchus had missed the mark and why. Ptolemy's appeal to the reader's direct experience with Hipparchus' solution is thus something of a smokescreen. Rather than demanding the reader get access to Hipparchus' text as a necessary prerequisite, Ptolemy models the ideal work of the educated astronomer: seeking out information from all the best sources, carrying out his own calculations, and providing his own educated judgment on the right answer.[124] This model suggests the ready availability of reference material, which in this case should include not only Hipparchus' work but the eclipse records themselves.

That material might, at this time, have been owned by Ptolemy himself, held in other private hands, or have been available through some kind of public institution. As we saw earlier, Martínez and Senseney hypothesize

---

[123] Ptolemy, *Syntaxis* 1,1.337. For more detail on this problem see Neugebauer 1975: 315–19.

[124] Indeed, Neugebauer praises Toomer in similar terms for carrying out his own calculations to demonstrate that Hipparchus had used a table of chords: Neugebauer 1975: 319.

that "professional libraries" might have existed for technical professions beyond the attested collections of medical information. In Ptolemy's case, while he likely possessed his own copy of Hipparchus' work, the eclipse tables and other astronomical data he used might indeed have been available at Alexandria from such public collections, though the uncertainty over their existence is already familiar from the controversy over the eclipse records suggested by *Dioptra* 35. The skill of the *pepaideumenos* is in being able to navigate that sea of information, and Ptolemy models this behavior for his own reader.

Galen provides more anecdotal details about the mechanics of his own highly targeted engagements with scientific and technical authors past and present. Naturally, much of this investigative work was bound up with his self-assigned task of creating commentaries on the whole Hippocratic corpus.[125] Galen's deep engagement with the Hippocratic texts required access not just to those texts, but also to more recent works that had shaped his understanding (though he seldom credits them in his commentaries, preferring to give the impression that he spoke directly for Hippocrates). In *On the Order of My Own Books* he gives an overview of the materials available, suggesting that if he should happen to die before his work as a commentator was completed the interested reader could find reliable explanations of Hippocratic medicine elsewhere. The reader must know where to search, however; Galen recommends his teacher Pelops' commentaries and those of Numisianus, Sabinus, and Rufus of Ephesus, but he warns them to beware Quintus, Lycus, and Galen's previous teacher, Satyrus.[126]

Galen's commentaries typically follow the detailed "phrase-by-phrase" model that Flemming describes as "basically *de rigeur*" for medical commentary at this time.[127] Elucidating the Hippocratic texts at this level of detail required regular access to a vast number of books, and ideally several copies of each in order to investigate divergent readings. For example, in his commentary on *Epidemics* 6, he recounts that he sought out a particular textual variant Dioscorides had allegedly found in two copies of the work. Yet Galen says that "after purposefully looking at all the public libraries as well as all those of my friends," he could not find the reading

---

[125] He outlines this task at Galen, *De libris propris*, Kühn v. 19 pp. 33–37, and he further discusses his Hippocratic commentaries throughout the work. He also describes here a wide range of commentaries on other authors, like Marinus on anatomy (*Libris propris* 25–31) and works critiquing the Empiricists and Methodists (38–39).

[126] Galen, *De ordine librorum suorum ad Eugenianum*, Kühn v. 19 pp. 57–58.

[127] Flemming 2008: 336.

anywhere.[128] Galen here performs the same kind of focused consultation of past works as Ptolemy: He seeks out not only a specific volume of the *Epidemics*, but a specific textual variant he heard about from Dioscorides, just as Ptolemy is able to access specific data on lunar eclipses from Hipparchus' *On the Displacement of the Solsticial and Equinoctial Points*.[129]

In his commentary on *Epidemics* 3, Galen details another Hippocratic scavenger hunt, this time for the origins of the mysterious symbols (*charaktēres*) that follow the cases.[130] Did these symbols originate with the Hippocratic author or were they a later interpolation? To answer this question, Galen appeals to Zeuxis, an earlier commentator, who suggests that the physician Mnemon of Side might have introduced the symbols himself once the books were already in the Alexandrian Library, or he might have brought the book to Alexandria himself from Pamphylia with the symbols already written in them. Alternatively, he suggests, the forgery might have been introduced during Ptolemy's notorious process of commandeering the original versions of any books brought to Alexandria by ship and returning new copies to the former owners: The symbols might have already been present in the books when they arrived at Alexandria. The avaricious speed of the Ptolemaic copyists left little room for on-the-spot critical evaluation of authenticity; the books were left "in heaps (*sōrēdon*) in some houses" before making their way to the Library. Whatever the mechanism by which the symbols made it into the books, Mnemon alleged he was the only one who could understand them, and he interpreted them for pay.

Galen thus turns Mnemon into a grotesque parody of his own learned activities: While Galen generously exhausts himself by writing commentaries on the Hippocratic classics, Mnemon takes money to explain a pathological textual oddity that he likely created himself. At the root of his actions lies the Ptolemaic greed that created a market for such forgeries in the first place: again, a twisted version of the scholar's thirst for knowledge. Galen works the Hippocratic symbols into a tale of bibliographic malpractice but also makes himself a hero: He only needs to repeat this story in the first place, he says, since Zeuxis' commentaries are themselves unpopular and hard to find. As in the case of Ptolemy's reproduction of Hipparchus' data and calculations, part of the point of these elaborate performances of scholarly completionism is to spare the

---

[128] Galen, *In Hipp. librum vi epidemiarum comm. vi*, Kühn v. 17b pp. 194–95.
[129] Ptolemy, *Syntaxis* 1,2.12.
[130] Galen, *Comm. in Hipp. iii epidemiarum*, Kühn v. 17a pp. 606–07.

reader the need to do the same. In the case of the *Epidemics* symbols, the reader does not need to know about the symbols to understand the text, since Galen rejects the possibility of authentic Hippocratic origin. However, they represent an opportunity for him to put his bibliographic erudition on display in a localized way without bogging down the entire text with that level of detail.

When Galen and Ptolemy deploy references to other texts in this way, they give the reader confidence that they have explored the territory of available texts thoroughly and their conclusions can be trusted. In this latter respect, they have something in common with Hero's claims to spare his reader the hard work of these bibliographic expeditions by extracting the most vital information from the works of his predecessors. At the same time, they paint a much more vivid picture of their own bibliographic adventures even when they hide much of the detail of those reference texts from the reader. Names of authors and texts, references to records both formal and informal, even accounts of finding books in libraries suggest a constant flow of bibliographic resources just under the surface of their texts.

Hero, by contrast, only occasionally mentions other technical authors by name. He does make occasional references to Philo, as we have seen, usually to praise his predecessor's work while acknowledging that he has some improvements in mind. On one such occasion he does hint at access to multiple copies of a book for reference when in the *Automata* he critiques Philo's design for the mechanism by which Athena descends to strike Ajax with a lightning bolt.[131] Hero chides Philo for having mentioned this mechanism without writing down how he achieved it, saying, "I did not find this written out, though I encountered multiple *syntagmata*." The most reasonable translation of *syntagmata* here would seem to be "exemplars" or copies, as Schmidt interprets it.[132] On this one occasion, then, Hero hints at a Galenesque bibliographic hunt to resolve a textual difficulty, which does suggest that he had access to considerable bibliographic resources. In this case, Hero might be said to be playing the role Asper describes as the "good guardian" of past knowledge preserved through diligent philological research.[133]

Still, on many other occasions that might have called for a textual reference he remains mute. When he appeals to *ataraxia* in the preface to the *Belopoeica*, he does not refer the reader back to Epicurus, presumably trusting the reader to get the joke on their own, nor does he point the way back to Plato or Aristotle on the more serious matter of fair land

[131] *Automata* 20.3.    [132] Hero 1976a: 407.    [133] Asper 2019: 8.

distribution that he discusses in the preface to *Metrica* 3, and so on. Particularly telling is the pattern of references to other works in the main body of the *Metrica*. When he refers to a finding from Archimedes, he usually gives Archimedes' name and the title of the work referenced on the first occasion, and sometimes he renews the reference to Archimedes if the result recurs later on. But the *Metrica* is full of formulas and prior results that Hero does not credit to anyone in particular, though he does not claim them as his own results either. This approach is characteristic of many other texts in the metrological tradition as well, including the mathematical papyri cataloging problems in measurement, where brevity and utility take precedence over demonstrating one's scholarly legacy.[134]

Hero's relative reticence about his sources is also conducive to his eisagogic approach, where an ostentatious performance of one's own deep learning might distract or discourage a newcomer to the discipline. Here again Nicomachus offers some points for comparison. For example, when he analyzes the diatonic octave in chapter 7 of the *Enchiridion*, he launches right into his list of harmonic intervals without stopping to refer to any Pythagorean predecessors. The reader has arguably been conditioned to make a more abstract sort of connection by the preceding chapter's vivid anecdotal description of Pythagoras' experimental work, but the absence of an explicit reference is striking. In the eighth chapter, which is explicitly about Plato's treatment of the harmonics in the *Timaeus*, Plato goes almost unmentioned after the first line of the passage. The ninth chapter, on Philolaus, is an exception, since Philolaus is indeed quoted and discussed at some length in this passage, though Nicomachus does water down the direct reference by adding that "many people say similar things about this in different ways."[135] His *Arithmetica* covers territory that overlaps considerably with Euclid's *Elements*, particularly books VII–IX, but Euclid is never mentioned by name; that distinction is reserved principally for Pythagoras and followers like Archytas and Philolaus, as well as Plato (who as D'Ooge notes is treated as an honorary Pythagorean).[136] More important than the absence of name-dropping is the very different character of Euclid's work from Nicomachus'; D'Ooge characterizes the former as "defining and demonstrating" and the latter as "defining and laying down general principles with abundant illustration and explanation."[137]

---

[134] On these problems see for example Cuomo 2001: 146–48; Jones 2013; Robbins 1923; Rudhardt 1978; Shelton 1981; Taisbak and Bülow-Jacobsen 2003; Worp, Bruins, and Sijpesteijn 1977.
[135] Nicomachus, *Enchiridion* 9.12–13.   [136] Nicomachus 1972: 35.
[137] Nicomachus 1972: 34.

While Hero does of course present a great many proofs of his own in the *Metrica*, he also frequently refers the reader back to sources like Archimedes for additional results rather than replicating them in his own text, or he leaves out those references entirely. But in his most strictly introductory works, like the *Definitiones*, Hero might easily compete with Nicomachus in brevity. For example, when he introduces the concept of the "gnomon" (i.e. a figure complementary to another such that their combination makes a figure similar to the first), he simply defines first the gnomon of the parallelogram and then the more general concept of the gnomon. Even though his definition uses terms very close to Euclid's own, he does not refer the reader to Euclid's definition of the parallelogram's gnomon in book II, nor to its anticipation in a proposition of book I, nor does he mention any application of the concept.[138]

All this is par for the course for the breezy *Definitiones*, where references to Euclid are absent from the end of the preface up through definition 104, which treats the proportional relationship between the sides of the Platonic solids and their circumscribed spheres. For a work that draws so intensely on an illustrious predecessor as the *Definitiones* does on Euclid, or the *Enchiridion* on Aristoxenus, not to bog down the introductory outline with references back to the source requires real discipline and dedication to the task of creating a synoptic introductory resource. Perhaps this claim seems paradoxical given that scholars more usually ascribe "dedication" to the work of hunting down and listing every last textual connection, but brevity is hard work, too, and offers didactic advantages of its own.

Galen and Ptolemy's detailed bibliographic adventures thus suggest a very different style of engaging with past texts compared to Hero's sparse references to his sources. But they much more closely resemble Hero in the way his texts incorporate elements from the "real world" where mechanical devices of various kinds are constructed, manipulated, and deployed. By contrast to Athenaeus Mechanicus and Vitruvius, Ptolemy and Galen both provide deeply detailed descriptions of manual work that can readily be compared with Hero's vivid accounts of winding spring cord for a catapult or testing out a component in an intricate mechanical theater. Galen of course paints an extraordinarily vivid portrait of his own professional engagements with his patients and other physicians, as well as his own

---

[138] Hero, *Definitiones* 57 and 58, with Giardina's discussion at Hero 2003: 303–06. Euclid defines the gnomon in book II, def. 2, having already applied the concept in proposition I.43, where he demonstrates the construction and equality of the "complements about the diameter" of the parallelogram.

live experimental exploits.[139] The anatomical experiments themselves do not have any analogs in Hero, so I leave them aside; here I am more interested in the shared qualities of textual *representations* of exploratory work. Galen does make frequent use of analogies to natural or artificial systems to explain physiological phenomena. The closest in content to anything in the Heronian corpus is his comparison of the cardiopulmonary system first to an oil lamp and then to a cupping glass – a rapid-fire combination of devices featured in the preface to Hero's *Pneumatica*.[140] Galen lays out in some detail the correlations between the two systems: The heart acts like the wick of the lamp and the blood like the oil, while the lungs serve as an enclosure (*steganos*) for the system that acts like a perforated cupping glass while the animal is breathing and an unperforated one when it stops. Of course there is no reason to suppose that Galen had Hero in mind here; lamps and cupping glasses are simply good systems to illustrate the principles by which fluid and air can be mechanically drawn up and expelled.

Close as the subject matter of Galen's analogy is to Hero's *Pneumatica*, as we saw above it is really only in the preface to that work that Hero appeals to the kind of brisk explanatory analogy between natural and artificial systems Galen uses here. However, Galen offers a much closer match to Hero's explanatory style in his detailed textual representations of experiential engagements with objects in the material world. Like Hero, Galen frequently delves deep into the details of manual engagements with material structures. For example, in the first book of *On Anatomical Procedures* he promises to teach his reader how to avoid the missteps of his predecessors and competitors by instructing them in the correct order in which to expose the parts of the hand and the instruments best suited to each step.[141] He will continue with this approach throughout the text, pausing his descriptions of the structures often to instruct the reader what structures to manipulate and how, and with what tools. He does often emphasize that books alone are far from sufficient for anatomical study, and that his goal is to facilitate dissection work on biological specimens.[142] Even given these reservations, he nevertheless writes many vivid vignettes of the dissector's manual work into the text itself. These instructions are often couched in direct imperatives and notes to the reader on what

---

[139] On the connection between the two see Gleason 2009.
[140] Galen, *De utilitate respirationis*, Kühn v. 4 pp. 490–91.
[141] Galen, *De anatomicis administrationibus*, Kühn v. 2 p. 244.
[142] For example, see Kühn v. 2 pp. 220–21, 226–27, 278.

"you will see," a sharp contrast to Hero's impersonal directives and first-person accounts.[143]

Ptolemy, too, finds occasional opportunities to turn the text into a kind of theater where the reader can virtually observe astronomical and harmonic experiments. For example, in the *Almagest* he describes how to measure the obliquity of the ecliptic using two different instruments: the equatorial ring and the simpler quadrant.[144] In both cases he first describes the construction of the instruments themselves in some detail: The ring must be carefully lathed, the quadrant made precisely square, and so on. He then describes the experimental measurements performed on the instrument with equal attention to material details: The instruments must be positioned carefully using plumblines and shims before the user can painstakingly measure the angular height of the sun. All these efforts are described in the first person, represented as accounts of work Ptolemy himself carried out at some point, not unlike Hero's first-person descriptions of manually testing parts of the theatrical automaton. Ptolemy offers similar instructions at a few points in the *Harmonica*, as when he tells the reader how to construct a harmonic *kanōn*, whether the traditional monochord or a novel version with eight strings.[145] In that text, however, the use of first-person verbs is rarer than in the *Almagest*'s descriptions of constructing instruments, and these passages are on the whole very rare features in Ptolemy's corpus, where impersonal verbs are as much the norm as they are in Hero's.

Ptolemy also resembles Hero closely in that the apparent aim of many of these manual engagements is to explore the relationship between mathematical and material representations of a physical principle. Sometimes the two domains map onto one another closely, like the detailed geometrical models he constructs for the movement of celestial bodies or the harmonic relationships that follow arithmetical ratios with a marvelous precision. Sometimes the relationship is more complex: Celestial bodies and harmonic ratios can be precisely observed only through instruments that can be manufactured with great care but never quite perfected.[146] Like Hero, Ptolemy often seeks to assimilate his material instruments and the objects they are designed to study to geometrical objects wherever

---

[143] For example, see Kühn v. 2 pp. 254–55. On Galen's directive style see Nutton 2009; Roby 2016b: 240–42.

[144] Ptolemy, *Syntaxis* 1,1.64–67.

[145] Ptolemy, *Harmonica* 1.8.31–43, 2.2.35–43; see also Creese 2010: 70–71; Roby 2016b: 177–81, 238–40.

[146] Barker 2006: 22; Creese 2010: 100; Roby 2016b: 270–78.

possible.[147] In some cases this kind of approximation simply does not work, and Ptolemy must focus instead on more purely material parts of the construction and observation processes, like carefully shaping the rings of an armillary sphere so they will rotate smoothly or keeping one's eye carefully fixed on a particular star while measuring and recording its position on the instrument.[148]

In his self-conscious reflection on his work as gradual improvements within a long tradition of scientific investigations moderated crucially by material instruments, Ptolemy matches Hero's concerns more closely than any other surviving author. The two are not disciplinary colleagues: They operate in different areas of study, and Hero's balance is far toward the "technical" side, while Ptolemy mainly pursues "scientific" problems and discusses his instruments comparatively rarely. But in the space where they overlap, they resonate very closely, sharing techniques for elucidating experimental engagements with material objects in text as well as concerns about how to negotiate the balance between the material and mathematical aspects of those objects.

Hero's modest and impersonal texts certainly clash with the "Second Sophistic" culture of rhetorical display discerned by Philostratus and now associated with figures like Aelius Aristides, Dio Chrysostom, and indeed Galen. But of course many other intellectual currents flowed through the Greco-Roman world at this time, in particular a lively concern for how learning happens, not just the display of the finished product. Like Nicomachus and Diophantus, Hero demonstrates care for his reader's experience, promising an easy point of entry and advertising that he will provide just enough information for the reader to be able to progress without being discouraged. He offers occasional clues as to how the reader should progress from one work to another within his corpus, more like Ptolemy's offhand references than Galen's flurry of redundant instructions in *On the Order of My Own Books*. As we have seen, he remains intensely focused on techniques for negotiating the boundary between the mathematical and the material, and on shaping the reader's understanding of how to most fully apprehend material objects in all their complexity. While Ptolemy only occasionally ventures into this territory, those careful explanations of how to design, craft, and use astronomical and harmonic instruments closely match Hero's approach, as do Galen's detailed

---

[147] See for example *Harmonica* 3.2.114–32, where he models the bridges on the monochord as having circular cross-sections to normalize the lengths of string contacting each bridge.
[148] See for example *Syntaxis* 1,1.353–54.

instructions on how to explore the body through dissection. Hero's concerns for pedagogy and brevity and his abiding interest in the boundary between the mathematical and material domains all seem to follow currents of technical writing that resonate most strongly with texts from this period.

## Hero after Hero

Impossible though it is to position Hero chronologically with any certainty, nevertheless we can say that with Pappus he takes on a new function, shifting definitively from a transformer of previous texts to an author whose own works are transformed and repurposed by later authors. Pappus is a central figure in the rise of the culture often characterized, in the context of ancient mathematical texts, by "deuteronomic" texts privileging commentary on prior texts over new mathematical discoveries.[149] Some aspects of the "deuteronomic" approach might be viewed in a critical light: Netz comments for example on commentators' tendencies toward "digging too deep" into minutiae that may be irrelevant or obvious and "digging too wide" by spinning out additional cases that do not illustrate anything mathematically new.[150] Nevertheless, the product of these "deuteronomic" engagements is undeniably new in some sense, a new textual creation that transforms the reader's experience of the mathematical content. As Asper points out, "explaining" another author's text can take many forms.[151] Paraphrase and what Flemming calls "phrase-by-phrase" commentary can accompany different kinds of activity, like filling in gaps or proliferating examples, demonstrating the truth (or falsehood) of a result left unproven in the original text, and integrating comparanda from other texts entirely, yielding what Asper calls an "enriched explanation."[152]

Hero himself had already in a sense been producing "deuteronomic" texts. Besides the lost commentary on Euclid's *Elements*, works like the *Definitiones* and *Metrica* serve in some sense as implicit commentaries on the authors they draw on, predominantly Euclid and Archimedes. Although much looser than the "phrase-by-phrase" model of Galen's Hippocratic commentaries, the way Hero applies and expands on results from Euclid and Archimedes valorizes their past work while simultaneously situating it

---

[149] This term originated with a provocative article by Netz, itself inspired by Jones' earlier characterization of Pappus as the fountainhead of a "degenerate tradition" of mathematical commentary: Netz 1998; Pappus 1986: 1.

[150] Netz 1998: 263–68.      [151] Asper 2013: 44.

[152] Asper 2013: 46–47; Flemming 2008: 336, 343.

in a new context of practical utility and ready accessibility. From the very beginning of the *Definitiones*, Hero seeks to imbue the Euclidean primitives with lived experience, likening the point to an instant of time or the line to the edge of the purple border of a dyed garment. While most of the succeeding chapters dispense with those concrete comparisons, the reader has already been primed to imagine these objects as something other than pure abstractions. The *Definitiones* offers what might be seen, in Martindale's terminology, as a "rereading" of the *Elements*, constituting a new vantage point on familiar Euclidean objects like the point and line.[153] In the *Metrica*, too, Hero only sparingly refers to concrete objects, but his constant juxtaposition of numerical syntheses alongside the geometrical analyses builds a conceptual bridge to the algorithmic traditions of practical mathematics. And where he does interject objects from the real world they cement the notion of applied geometry in a memorable, even humorous way, as when a series of results from Archimedes' *Sphere and Cylinder* ends up in a washtub.[154] Even when he does not explicitly spell out the practical value of geometry, then, Hero finds ways to make those arguments implicitly.

Just as the engagements between the "historical" Hero and his pre-decessors in these texts represent an "enriched explanation" in Asper's sense, putting their concepts to work in new ways, so did the engagements with Hero's work that postdate Pappus constitute deuteronomic trans-formations of his own texts. The later metrological texts in the "Heronian" tradition amplify Hero's own emphasis on the practical aspects of geom-etry. Whereas Hero used objects like cloaks and washtubs as infrequent but highly marked reminders of the conceptual continuity between the geometrical and concrete domains, in the later metrological texts they come to dominate the scene. The problems collected in the various recensions of the *Stereometrica*, for example, augment the study of geo-metrical objects like spheres and cylinders with a wide array of analogous structures like amphitheaters, vaulted buildings, and ships.[155] In the *De mensuris*, the balance is tilted even more strongly in favor of the real-world objects. The *Definitiones* are expanded to include a considerable amount of material from Proclus and other sources, principally Neoplatonist and neo-Pythagorean. These processes of augmentation and recombination recall the practice Keyser observes in late antiquity of composing "augmented editions" of earlier authors' works, including Euclid, Galen, and Pliny.

---

[153] Martindale 1993: 13.     [154] *Metrica* 2.11–12.
[155] On the risks of trying to assert a stable textual identity for these problems see Hero 2014: 430–48.

Keyser argues that this practice was driven first by the rise of the codex (which made it easier both to produce and to use such a work) and second by the expansion of "the very ancient practice of reusing *spolia*, salvage of the past displayed in a new context, without hiding its old origin."[156] Hero's work served as *spolia* for other authors to build with, transforming not only the content of his works, but the figure of Hero himself, as they wove him into new contexts.

### Pappus and Proclus

Pappus made more explicit use of Hero than any other ancient author. The eighth book of Pappus' *Synagōgē* is devoted to mechanics, which he celebrates as the most useful of *technai* for serving life's needs. The book begins by describing mechanics as the product of a broad spectrum of practitioners, variously identified as "mechanics (*mēchanikoi*)," "device-makers (*organopoioi*)" (here specifically referring to the makers of military machinery), and "wonder-workers (*thaumasiourgoi*)."[157] Still more varied are the mechanical subdisciplines they practice, from practical applications like raising great weights, pumping water, or firing missiles, to devices aiming at wonder and discovery like pneumatic and mechanical automata, water clocks, or mechanical models of the cosmos. Pappus here brings Hero on stage alongside Archimedes as an exemplary "wonder-worker," two references to Hero (first for his pneumatic marvels, then for a now lost work on water clocks) bracketing the single reference to Archimedes (whose *Floating Bodies* seems to provide a theoretical backdrop for these applications). Elsewhere in the *Synagōgē*, Hero will remain backstage, an anonymous source for Pappus to draw on, reenacting Hero's own anonymizing transmission of his sources.

While Pappus mentions that the five simple machines are described both by Hero and Philo, he says his own explanation is based on mechanical principles he learned from Hero. To be sure, he says, he will make some adjustments, writing "more concisely (*epitomōteron*) for the recall of those who wish to learn," and adding some important information about the various kinds of cranes,

μή ποτε καὶ τῶν βιβλίων ἐν οἷς ταῦτα γέγραπται ἀπορία γένηται τῷ ζητοῦντι. καὶ γὰρ ἡμεῖς κατὰ πολλὰ μέρη διεφθαρμένοις ἐνετύχομεν ἀνάρχοις τε καὶ ἀτελέσι βιβλίοις.

---

[156] Keyser 2020: 7–8.   [157] Pappus, *Synagōgē* 8.1024.12–1026.4.

lest the difficulty of the books in which these things were written affect the
seeker. For we encountered [them] in books destroyed in many parts,
without beginnings or ends.[158]

The text of the *Mechanica* already seems to have suffered some damage by
the time Pappus encountered it, specifically yielding "books without
beginnings or ends." This description matches the codex much better than
the papyrus roll; the end of the roll is protected inside, whereas both the
beginning and the end of a codex are vulnerable to damage. Of course the
description here tells us nothing about Hero's own dates, since the codices
could have been copies of papyrus originals, but it does situate Hero's
decaying works as material participants in the book trade of late
antiquity.[159] It also shapes the reader's view of Hero, since Pappus presents
him here as a figure of some antiquity, enough that his *Mechanica* was
already starting to erode when Pappus discovered it. As Middleton argues,
readers' expectations are framed by the material matrix of the text just as
much as by its semantic content, and indeed "the book may itself produce
a competing horizon of expectations, to operate against the text's content."[160] Hero's promises of novel technological achievements and his
disciplinary histories resonate quite differently when considered from this
waypoint in their tradition, a moment when they might have been lost if
not for Pappus' reinscription of Heronian material into his own tradition.
Indeed, Middleton notes that within the sometimes troubled material
histories of ancient texts are reminders "that receptions are less sequential
than simultaneous, and that the processes of writing and reading are
coincident."[161] Even as Pappus saves Hero's mechanics from oblivion
through his diligent reading of the crumbling text, he writes it into a
new existence within his *Synagōgē*.

Pappus makes his authorial ambitions clear here: He wishes not merely
to rescue Hero's work on the five simple machines from its decaying
material matrix, but also to transform that work. First, he will slim his
findings down into a more concise format and then add new explanatory
material that will make the material easier for readers to understand than

---

[158] Pappus, *Synagōgē* 8.1116.4–7; Hero, *Mechanica* 2 fr. 1.1–9. The "one-section crane" and its
multisection variants reappear at *Synagōgē* 8.1132–34 (Hero, *Mechanica* fr. 3.2), where they are
explained in more detail.

[159] Of course, the most dramatic shift in book culture in the first few centuries CE was the rise of the
codex as the preferred form of the book. A concise introduction to the rising numbers of codices is
found at Bagnall 2009: 70–79. For more detail on the production, propagation, and consumption
of books in late antiquity see Schipke 2013.

[160] Middleton 2020: 70.     [161] Middleton 2020: 79.

the raw materials Pappus himself had to work with. The further operations Pappus performs on Hero's text are more thoroughly transformative. Cuomo describes his process as taking Hero's insistently material description of the mechanics of the simple machines and making it "operate within a mathematical frame of reference" by reducing it down to a mathematical "skeleton."[162] But Cuomo argues that Pappus' work does not stop there; he ultimately adds "flesh" of his own back as he explains the utility of those principles to real-world figures like architects. For example, in the discussion of the triangle's center of gravity, Pappus draws on a passage of Hero's *Mechanics* where (as we saw earlier) the triangle is specified as having some thickness and density, unlike Archimedes' plane figures. He then supplements the older material with additional lemmas and more discursive explanation. Finally, he concludes his discussion of centers of gravity by referring to the "mechanical utility (*chreia ... mēchanikē*)" that accompanies the mathematical *theōria* associated with problems like this.[163] Rectification, simplification, and emphasis on utility: Pappus is remediating Hero's work through strategies of transformation that often look very similar to those Hero used on his own sources.

In particular, Pappus introduces the discipline of mechanics by way of a school of thought he associates with followers of Hero (οἱ περὶ τὸν Ἥρωνα μηχανικοί).[164] They structured mechanics as a bipartite endeavor: one part "rational (*logikos*)" and one part "handwork (*cheirourgikos*)." The first part includes mathematics (geometry, arithmetic, and astronomy) plus "physical reasoning (*physikoi logoi*)," which Pappus does not describe in more detail here. The second part includes metalwork, architecture, carpentry, and painting plus manual practice in them (κατὰ χεῖρα ἄσκησις) – a very Heronian stipulation. As Cuomo observes, Pappus does not suggest that either part should take supremacy over the other, though he does point out the difficulty of mastering both in a single lifetime.[165] The emphasis on manual practice, as well as the balance between mathematical–physical and "applied" views of mechanics, suggests that Pappus identified a distinctively Heronian perspective on the old question of the classification of the sciences.

That perspective is already visible when Pappus mentions Hero in the third book of the *Synagōgē*, where he addresses the problem of finding two mean proportionals. As we saw earlier, Eutocius preserves several solutions

[162] Cuomo 2000: 116.
[163] Pappus, *Synagōgē* 8.1034.7–1040.25; Hero, *Mechanica* 2.35; Cuomo 2000: 112.
[164] Pappus, *Synagōgē* 8.1022.14–15.    [165] Cuomo 2000: 105–06.

to the problem: purely geometrical, purely mechanical (like Eratosthenes' mesolabe), and a quasi-geometrical approximation achieved by means of a ruler.[166] This last one is found in Hero's *Belopoeica* (where the problem is relevant for calculating the size of missile a catapult can fire), and Pappus and Eutocius both associate the technique with him.[167] Pappus describes the instrumentally mediated solutions he credits to Eratosthenes, Philo, and Hero as "wonderfully (*thaumasiōs*)" obtained, foreshadowing the characterization of Hero as the wonder-worker *par excellence* in the eighth book. He then goes on to celebrate Hero's solution in particular as "most fitting for manual work for those wishing to be architects." Of the four solutions Pappus provides, Hero's is the only one associated with a particular utilitarian context and with manual craft, a good match for the way he characterizes Hero's mechanical legacy in the eighth book.

When Pappus mentions Hero by name, then, he draws principally on Hero's mechanical works rather than using him for more purely geometrical results like those in the *Metrica*, though the two authors do sometimes feature the same mathematical results.[168] In Pappus we can see the beginnings of a fracture that would gradually deepen between Hero's mechanical and his mathematical works, eventually leaving the *Metrica* stranded in a single manuscript copy and the Euclid commentary lost. Pappus' catalog of solutions to the problem of the two mean proportionals remains a lone explicit tie between the mathematical focus of texts like the *Metrica* and *Definitiones* (and, presumably, the lost Euclid commentary) and the material and mechanical concerns that belong to texts like the *Mechanica*, *Pneumatica*, and the lost work on water clocks Pappus refers to.

The fracturing of the Heronian tradition into "mathematical" and "mechanical" streams highlights the reciprocal nature of the cultural shifts that occur as texts are inherited and reconfigured in new contexts. The "Transformations of Antiquity" working group at the Humboldt-Universität zu Berlin developed a capacious view of "transformation" as a dynamic operating through translations and other reconfigurations of artifacts from a "reference sphere" (e.g. classical antiquity) into a "reception

---

[166] Pappus, *Synagōgē* 3.54–68, Eutocius, *Commentarii in libros de sphaera et cylindro* 56.14–106.25.

[167] *Belopoeica* 33.54–34.42, Pappus, *Synagōgē* 3.62.14–64.18, Eutocius, *Commentarii in libros de sphaera et cylindro* 58.16–60.26.

[168] Knorr observes that while *Metrica* 1.39 explicitly cites *Sphere and Cylinder*, the terminology in the proposition differs from Archimedes' and instead matches that of Pappus, *Synagōgē* 5.382–84, and so he posits that both drew on an alternative earlier version of Archimedes' work: Knorr 1978: 240. Cuomo is skeptical, observing that at *Metrica* 2.18 Hero cites the same result but uses the wording from the normal version of *Sphere and Cylinder*. Cuomo 2000: 67 n. 39.

sphere" (e.g. early modern literature).[169] Key to the group's approach is the notion of "allelopoiesis," which proposes that the reception sphere is itself reciprocally altered in the transformative process.[170] Hero offers Pappus a model for linking the mathematical and the mechanical, and Pappus enshrines him as the root of a tradition combining "rational" and "manual" approaches whose influence on Pappus' own *Synagōgē* is unmistakable. At the same time, Pappus transforms "Hero" into something new through mechanisms that parallel the "Transformation" group's categories of "assimilation" and "focalization/obfuscation."[171] In the first case, Pappus integrates Hero's work into the context of late antique mathematics, with its thriving commentary tradition, as well as into his particular brand of Platonism, where creating space for the mathematical and material to coexist is a challenge Pappus addresses with relish.[172] In the second case, Hero's "fracturing" in Pappus into a predominant forebear in mechanics while his mathematical commonalities with Pappus are detached from his name represent respectively a "focalization" and an "obfuscation," magnifying the mechanical aspects of Hero's work at the expense of his identity as a mathematical author.

The fracture would widen with Proclus, who identifies Hero as *mēchanikos* but naturally preserves only mathematical results in his commentary to Euclid. As we saw in the previous chapter, Proclus preserves two more familiar typologies of the sciences, associated with the Pythagoreans and with Geminus. Both are specifically described as divisions of mathematics rather than mechanics, and both appear in the interpolated chapters of the *Definitiones*.[173] Proclus does go on to mention Hero briefly in his brisk classification of mechanics, which he defines as the study of "what is perceptible and material (αἰσθητὰ καὶ τὰ ἔνυλα)."[174] But he does not recount any specific features of Hero's approach to the discipline, only naming him alongside Ctesibius as having contributed to the subdiscipline of pneumatics.

Proclus' brief excursus on the structure of mechanics follows Pappus' quite closely. Both begin their typology with machines necessary for war. They then proceed to wonder-working, a subdiscipline where both highlight the pneumatic devices associated with Hero as a subject of particular

---

[169] On these concepts see Baker, Helmrath, and Kallendorf 2019; Bergemann et al. 2011.

[170] The term is introduced at Böhme 2011: 9.

[171] For a brief summary of these dynamics see Bergemann et al. 2019: 17–19.

[172] On Pappus' Platonism see Cuomo 2000: 72–73, 81–89; Mansfeld 1998: 99–121.

[173] Proclus, *In primum Euclidis elementorum librum commentarii* 35.17–41.2; *Definitiones* 138.3.

[174] Proclus, *In primum Euclidis elementorum librum commentarii* 41.10.

interest, as well as devices moved "by sinew cords and ropes" to imitate the motions of living things. Proclus inserts a third category of wonder-working having to do with weights in motion and equilibrium, exemplified not (as we might expect) by a work of Archimedes, but by the *Timaeus*. Pappus is first of the two to mention Archimedes, though he appears only briefly as the author of *On Floating Bodies* before the watery context flows onward to water clocks, where Hero takes center stage again. Pappus closes out his list of mechanical practitioners with those who know how to construct moving models of the cosmos. Proclus discusses this art too, first praising Archimedes' achievements and then using the topic to transition from mechanics to astronomy. Archimedes likewise provides the coda to Pappus' introduction, where he is credited with understanding "the cause and reason (τὴν αἰτίαν καὶ τὸν λόγον)" of every component of the discipline.

The two analyses of the discipline of mechanics cover similar territory and perhaps ultimately stem from a common source. At the same time, however, they reflect the two authors' quite different priorities, as Pappus views mechanics, through the lens of the "followers of Hero," as a fundamentally applied discipline, while Proclus downplays its material applications in favor of the theory of equilibrium and other more mathematically inflected aspects of the discipline. Proclus' principal task in the *Commentary* is to discuss Euclid, of course, and so after his brief appearance in the catalog of sciences as a notable name in pneumatics Hero is strictly a source of mathematical methods and results, sometimes named and sometimes anonymous. The two authors thus use the figure of Hero very differently. Pappus insistently associates him with results from the *Mechanica* and the *Belopoeica* and links his name with his achievements in pneumatics and other wonder-working endeavors. By contrast, even though Proclus refers to Hero as *mēchanikos*, the Heronian resources he invokes are all procedures and results drawn from the *Metrica*, which show no trace of Hero's trademark blend of the mathematical and the material.

Pappus and Proclus find more common ground on Hero elsewhere, in the context of methods for solving the astronomical problem of measuring how long the sun takes to rise from the first moment of its appearance to the time that it is fully risen over the horizon.[175] This question is part of a larger investigation into the apparent diameters of the sun and moon treated by Ptolemy, who does not mention Hero.[176] In the two

---

[175] Pappus, *Commentaria in Ptolemaei syntaxin mathematicam* 5–6 87–92; Proclus, *Hypotyposis astronomicarum positionum* 4.71–79.
[176] Ptolemy, *Syntaxis* 1,1.416.20–422.2.

commentaries, Hero is associated, through his lost work *On Water Clocks*, with a method of finding the sun's apparent diameter using a kind of clepsydra. Neither Pappus nor Proclus provides any details on his method of solution, which Ptolemy himself appears to have dismissed as inaccurate (though without mentioning Hero by name).[177] If we can judge by surviving texts like the *Belopoeica*, *Cheiroballistra*, and *Pneumatica*, it is easy to imagine that Hero's own description of the design of such a vessel would have been highly detailed and deeply engaged with the challenges of achieving uniform water flow. But Pappus and Proclus do not preserve any such details, and so Hero's appearance here remains but a tantalizing suggestion of an unrealized future in which his materially focused mechanics remained more closely bound to the continued study of the mathematical problems to which the instruments he devised could lend themselves.

### Metrology and Surveying

The text in which these approaches overlapped most obviously was the *Dioptra*, where the mechanical and material nuances of building and deploying the eponymous instrument were given the same intense attention as the geometrically framed surveying problems one could solve with it. Yet Hero's mathematical–mechanical approach to surveying seems to have turned into something of a dead end; even the *Dioptra* itself survives only in a single 11th-century manuscript and a few much later copies.[178] While the Roman *agrimensores* produced a wealth of Latin texts and commentaries in late antiquity, they were more concerned with the legal and terminological details of their work than the mathematics of land division or the mechanics of their instruments. But as Acerbi and Vitrac point out, the intense concern over the juridical and administrative aspects of surveying shown in the *Corpus Agrimensorum Romanorum* has no real analog in the *Dioptra* nor in the Heronian metrological texts.[179]

Still, a few short agrimensorial texts survive that seem to reflect a closer relationship to the Heronian corpus. The anonymous so-called *Podismus* ("measurement by feet") somewhat resembles the work of Balbus we encountered in the previous chapter, inasmuch as it is principally concerned with mathematical problems on geometrical forms rather than the legal aspects of surveying. However, Balbus still emphasizes the surveying

---

[177] Ptolemy, *Syntaxis* 1,1.416.
[178] On the manuscript tradition of the *Dioptra* see Decorps-Foulquier 2000: 41–43.
[179] Hero 2014: 532.

context of those forms, first in his prefatory praise of the practice and
second in associating at least a few of them with features of agrimensorial
interest such as lines drawn on the earth, the *cardo*, and the *decumanus*.
The *Podismus*, by contrast, is entirely separate from the context of surveying, nor do the surviving fragments seem to resemble the *Metrica* closely
since they feature algorithmic calculations rather than demonstrations.
Guillaumin points out the hint of solid geometry at the beginning of the
text, which might have originally followed a plan more like the *Metrica* –
for example, describing more classes of geometrical object than the
triangles in its surviving sections on plane geometry.[180] On the basis of
some quirky linguistic parallels and the similarities in their mathematical
content, Guillaumin describes the text as a kind of Latin translation or
adaptation of the Heronian *Geometrica*.[181] Acerbi and Vitrac, however,
argue that the *Geometrica* varies too much between manuscripts to make
such an assertion. In their own comparison between texts drawn from the
Heronian metrological corpus and the *Corpus Agrimensorum Romanorum*
they discover about a dozen close mathematical parallels, along with a few
more terminological similarities and common questions, but no Greek or
Latin texts that could really be considered "translations" of one another.[182]

The agrimensorial texts collected under the names "Epaphroditus" and
"Vitruvius Rufus" accompany the *Podismus* in several manuscripts.[183] As
in the *Podismus*, their problems are numerical and approached algorithmically rather than as geometrical demonstrations. Unlike the *Podismus*,
however, many of them are explicitly expressed as surveying problems.
For example, given a field of a certain size planted with trees regularly
spaced, the reader is asked to calculate the number of trees; given a
mountain of a certain size, to calculate its surface area in *iugera*; and so
forth. Artificial problems, to be sure, but framed in a way that seems
specifically aimed at the budding surveyor. None of these texts resembles
the *Dioptra* in combining a mathematical analysis of surveying problems
with attention to the mechanics of the instrument used in the actual
surveying. But they do more closely resemble the later Heronian metrological texts building on the practical applications of the *Metrica*'s fusion of
geometrical analysis and numerical synthesis, which was ultimately a much
more productive branch of the Heronian tree than the *Dioptra*.

[180] Balbus 1996: 95. Guillaumin here notes that one passage on solid geometry is included in
Lachmann's edition of the *Podismus* but writes it off as an interpolation.
[181] Balbus 1996: 104–05. Guillaumin provides a text, translation, and notes for the *Podismus* as well;
the text can also be found at Lachmann 1848: 295–301.
[182] Hero 2014: 524–29.      [183] Edited with translation and notes in Balbus 1996: 139–97.

Climbing further out along this branch, we find as well some resemblance between certain problems in the Heronian corpus and the surviving Greek mathematical papyri, though, again, nothing robust enough to suggest a direct relationship between any of the texts concerned. The algorithms used in the papyri are often simpler and less general than those in the *Metrica* but find closer analogs in the later collections of metrological problems. The short *P. Bagnall* 35 (P. Cornell. inv. 69), which Taisbak and Bülow-Jacobsen date to the 3rd century CE and Jones to the 2nd century CE, contains three problems on calculating quadrangular areas of land, the surveying context suggested by references to the cardinal directions and measurements using the Egyptian unit of *arourai*.[184] Taisbak and Bülow-Jacobsen note the intriguing resemblance between the diagrams in the papyrus and the first passages of the *Metrica*, including some methodological similarities between the second problem and *Metrica* I.13, as well as some numerical values common to the papyrus and Hero's numerical syntheses.[185] Jones further notes that the other two problems respectively address the same objects as *Metrica* I.12 and I.14 but, like the second problem, use different algorithms for the solutions.[186]

The closest match between a papyrus and any of the texts in the Heronian metrological corpus is found in *MPER* NS 1.1 (P. Vindobonensis gr. inv. 19996), a compilation of more than thirty problems in measuring solid figures.[187] Acerbi and Vitrac note one particular point of resemblance: The eleventh problem in this collection shows how to find the volume of a truncated pyramid using the same algorithm as *Stereometrica* I.38 in Heiberg's recension, which itself is a simplified special case of the algorithm in *Metrica* II.6.[188] The algorithm is used in the next three problems as well, and it recurs again in problems 26 and 27. But this connection remains rather tenuous; the collection of problems does not map well onto any surviving Heronian text either in organization or in the way the problems are articulated. As in the case of the Latin surveying texts, then, we should not suppose any direct exchange of problems between these corpora, but only note some commonalities in terms of the objects being investigated and the methods involved.

Tables of unit conversions, which often accompany metrological problem collections, represent an additional point of contact between the

---

[184] An image of this papyrus appeared already at Neugebauer 1969: 179 and Plate 12. The text and diagrams are analyzed in more detail at Taisbak and Bülow-Jacobsen 2003. A more recent edition with additional translation and discussion may be found at Jones 2013.
[185] Taisbak and Bülow-Jacobsen 2003: 63–64.    [186] Jones 2013: 168, 172–73.
[187] Gerstinger and Vogel 1932.    [188] Hero 2014: 558–59.

Heronian metrological texts, the mathematical papyri, the works of the Roman *agrimensores*, and the wider world of late antiquity. We have already seen that the *Stereometrica* credits the praetorian prefect Modestus with standardizing the weights and volumes of several goods, including barley and bacon, in local units. In the absence of empire-wide standards of measure, Romans developed strategies for coping with a patchwork of what Riggsby calls "hyper-local" measures.[189] He mentions inscribed tables of length measures and slabs of stone with cavities to measure certain volumes of individual products like olive oil or wheat, which would have fixed the standards for measures like the *litra* to a locality, but textual tables of conversions between those local systems could travel more freely. The later texts of the Roman *agrimensores* and Greek practical mathematical papyri often feature unit conversion tables designed to help the reader navigate the complexities of these systems.

These tables suggest a broader cultural interest in the varied systems of measurement that governed the Greco-Roman world. No one would label the *Kestoi* ("Embroideries") of Julius Africanus a technical text, and yet he seems to have found the subtle regional variations in metrological systems appealing enough to include in his work. He advertises these variations as a useful safeguard against errors in pharmaceutical dosage but immediately veers into territory far beyond the pharmacologist's minute units, like the "wood" talent from Antioch, which weighed six times more even than the talent unit for silver or gold.[190] He celebrates the differences between the Attic drachma and its Delian, Aeginetan, Rhodian, Ptolemaic, and Italian brethren, drawing on Homer and other authors for source material from the deeper past and the wider world.[191] Past and present are bridged by the common terms for units, and the present is refracted into a sparkling mosaic of local variations and a vast array of goods to be measured.

The Heronian corpus itself is not devoid of material on unit conversions that seems to serve more than a purely utilitarian purpose. The discussion of weights in the *De mensuris* begins generically enough with the talent, saying that it measures 125 *librae* and can also be divided into 6,000 *lepta* coins. But the author then connects this measurement to the story from the Gospel of Mark of the widow who contributed her two *lepta*, an unusual literary excursion for a Greek metrological text.[192] These two sections of the *De mensuris* appear to be an epitome of the late 4th-century CE work by Epiphanius, bishop of Salamis, now known as *On*

---

[189] Riggsby 2019: 105.     [190] Julius Africanus, *Kestoi* F62.18–21.
[191] Julius Africanus, *Kestoi* F62.22–35.     [192] Mark 12:41–44.

*Weights and Measures.*[193] The text survives in its entirety only in Syriac, though large parts survive in Armenian and Georgian, along with some fragments in Greek.[194] The work is a rather miscellaneous collection of information loosely centered on scriptural exegesis and scribal concerns. A discussion of scribal exegetical symbols segues into alphabetic numerology; Ptolemy's support for the translators of the Bible into Greek leads into a list of the Ptolemies and then the Roman emperors; biblical tales are conjoined to a short account of the geographical and astronomical knowledge that might have enabled Mary or Job to navigate on their travels. Weights and measures are woven into these historical and scriptural contexts throughout: Epiphanius enlivens his enumeration of monetary units with references to the money changers in the Temple, the cubit is exemplified by the dimensions of Noah's ark, and so on.

The author of the *De mensuris* has omitted some of the references to scripture found in these sections of the Syriac text; for example, the two-stater *chuza* or *zūzâ* is no longer identified with the coin Peter found in the fish.[195] Others are intact, including the widow's mite and the weight of Absalom's hair, as well as an intriguing reference to the iron obol's origins. Both texts tell the same story about the iron obol: In the war-torn days before the coming of Christ, arrows were so common that they became a kind of currency that could be exchanged for bread and other goods. These eventually became the iron obol standardized at an eighth of an ounce, distinct from the silver obol of one-tenth the weight.

What should we make of these passages of the *De mensuris*? It is of course impossible to know whether they were drawn directly from Epiphanius' text or merely shared a common source, especially given that the Greek text of Epiphanius does not preserve any of this material. However, the texts build in so much distinctive contextual material around structures that elsewhere consist more or less only of bare lists of unit conversions that direct transmission either between them or from a common source seems certain. Epiphanius demonstrates the possibility that cultural interest in the relationships between different weights and

---

[193] Though as Sprengling points out, none of the surviving manuscripts preserves a title: Epiphanius 1935: 2.

[194] Epiphanius 45–57 (67a–71d) in the Syriac edition and *De mensuris* 60; also Epiphanius 25–30 (62a–63c) and *De mensuris* 61. For the Syriac text and translation see Epiphanius 1935; the Armenian text is edited and translated in Stone 2000. The passages of interest here are found only in the Syriac version, though a short Armenian text by Anania of Širak on weights and measures seems to have been derived from passages now lost from the Armenian translation: Stone 2000: 29–31, 103–08.

[195] Matthew 17:27.

measures could go beyond the purely professional contexts with which this material is usually associated. A cosmopolitan readership that might be unused to some of the units in the biblical stories might have valued the chance to develop a more concrete sense of the widow's tiny contribution or what exactly Peter discovered in the fish. The author of the *De mensuris* might have chosen to incorporate this cosmopolitan context into his collection for similar reasons, beyond the practical utility of simply amassing a large collection of unit conversions.

The later metrological texts reflected interests in practical mathematics that seem to have had a broad appeal in late antiquity. Their emphasis on practical problem-solving, their instruction in calculation techniques, and their organization into series of discrete problems might all have been among the attractive features that led them to be recopied frequently enough to survive in several manuscripts. Those same features, particularly their discrete structure, may also help to explain why the collections vary so much from one manuscript to another. Without an overarching structure like the Euclidean organizational principles of the *Metrica* to keep the problems ordered, copyists might have aimed to create bespoke collections of the most useful applications and convenient algorithms. Of course, we cannot know for sure, but the fact remains that the *Geometrica* spans forty-three surviving manuscripts, and each of Heiberg's two books of *Stereometrica* spans more than a dozen. The vast majority of the surviving manuscripts are dated to the 15th century or later, but a dozen appear to date from between the 10th and 14th centuries, suggesting a considerable amount of Byzantine interest in the later Heronian metrological tradition.

### Hero in Byzantium

Despite the expansion of the metrological texts compiled under his name, Hero himself was recognized in Byzantine literary culture more for his pneumatic and mechanical work than any of his mathematical contributions. In Johannes Tzetzes' 12th-century *Chiliades*, Hero is positioned alongside Anthemius, Philo, and Pappus as one of the *mēchanographoi* who preserved the memory of Archimedes.[196] Tzetzes returns to Archimedes later on, saying that despite the popular claim that Archimedes wrote one book only, he himself has encountered several,

---

[196] Tzetzes, *Chiliades* 2.35.155. Hero appears in another list of *mēchanographoi* in Tzetzes' *Allegoriae in Homeri Iliadem* 5.16, this time accompanied by Philo, Apollodorus, Ctesibius, and a few others unmentioned in the *Chiliades*.

and that Hero, Anthemius, and all other engineers composed their own works on hydraulics and pneumatics based on Archimedes' work. Still, one could not say that Hero emerges from Tzetzes' work with any particular identity; he functions as a kind of sidekick to Archimedes, Tzetzes' real hero.

He remains a more central figure in the work of that other "Hero," the anonymous author of two manuals on siege warfare often identified as "Hero of Byzantium," who probably dates to the 10th century. The name "Hero" is almost certainly a fabrication; it appears in a title added to the text in *Vaticanus graecus* 1605 perhaps two or three centuries after it was first composed.[197] Still, the attribution is easy to understand, for the author resembles Hero both in his technical subject matter and in the values he ascribes to his work. He cites Hero (here given the unusual epithet *mathēmatikos*) as an influence on his *De strategematibus*, appealing to the *Belopoeica*'s introductory claim that a good understanding of catapult design and construction provides the surest route to *ataraxia*. This philosophical goal, the anonymous author says, is still very much a concern in his own time.[198]

But even before Hero makes this first named appearance, his influence can be felt in the text from its very first words, where the author cites the difficulty of understanding siege machinery and the obscurity of existing works on the topic.[199] The author's feelings about existing books on the subject are complex. He cites works by Apollodorus, Athenaeus Mechanicus, and Biton as necessary for developing a clear understanding of the topic (Hero's name is conspicuously absent from this initial list). However, they are not sufficient, since they were composed "according to the general systematic treatment prescribed by men long ago (κατὰ τὴν πάλαι συνταχθεῖσαν τῶν ἀνδρῶν καθολικὴν τεχνολογίαν)," and that system is now largely unintelligible due to shifts in terminology and the exhausting obscurity of the texts themselves. His own contribution will be to make Apollodorus' work easier to understand by collecting the essential information from his text, reframing it in simple language, elaborating the explanations where necessary, and preparing new images so that the machines can be constructed by anyone: all interventions familiar from Hero's own tradition.

The *Geodaisia*, too, begins with a claim to ease a beginner's introduction to dioptrics by selecting the simplest material from previous writers,

---

[197] "Heron" of Byzantium 2000: 2.  [198] Anon. Byz., *De strategematibus* 202–04.
[199] Anon. Byz., *De strategematibus* 197–98.

sighting by means of "simple linear methods (ψιλαῖς ἐφόδοις γραμμικαῖς)," and basing demonstrations on just a few diagrams.[200] Archaic technical vocabulary from past texts is to be translated to a more familiar idiom, potentially demoralizing geometrical proofs are to be replaced with verbal summaries, and the conceptual background is to be relocated from a lofty (*hypsēlos*) register to a low (*tapeinos*) one.[201] He promises as well to demonstrate the instrument's utility for making measurements both on land and in the sky, just like the beginning of Hero's *Dioptra*. Indeed, the influence of the *Dioptra* is clear in this text, as the author often draws on methods from Hero's work and occasionally names him as a source for certain problems. Nor is the *Dioptra* the only Heronian work the anonymous author uses; he combines his surveying problems with methods for finding areas and volumes of plane and solid figures reminiscent of the *Metrica*. The author is determined to outdo Hero in his concessions to simplicity and ease. For example, he mentions that Hero describes how to measure trapezia but declines to offer any details from the *Metrica*; he plans instead to "anthologize" a few results to pique the interest of beginners.[202]

That shift of register has something to do with simplicity, to be sure, but also with connecting potentially abstruse geometrical methods to material *realia* – with bringing surveying, literally, down to earth. The author describes how a circle's circumference and surface area can be calculated by fixing a rope representing its radius to a nail in the ground representing its center. His treatment of the problem throughout is unrelentingly material: The rope is terminated by a ring of iron that rotates around the nail, it must be kept taut throughout the measuring process, and the circle itself is "made visible (*dēlōthentos*)" through that process. The passage offers no insights into mathematics or surveying; the desired parameters are simply calculated from the (already known) radius, and the author gives no indication about how they might alternatively be measured from the circle "made visible" on the ground. The sole point of this lengthy passage, which is beautifully illustrated in the Vatican manuscript by a detailed figure of a man peering down at the circular path his rope has traced, seems to be to help the reader negotiate the mental transition from the abstraction of the circle to its concretely embodied form.[203] He enhances the picture of surveying work as concrete and localized by assimilating some of his surveying problems to points of interest around

---

[200] Anon. Byz., *Geodaisia* 1.13–17.     [201] Anon. Byz., *Geodaisia* 1.24–32.
[202] Anon. Byz., *Geodaisia* 6.38–44.     [203] Vat. gr. 1605, fol. 49v, reproduced in Sullivan's edition.

Constantinople, including the Hippodrome and the cisterns of Aetius and Aspar.[204] With the exception of the detailed references to local landmarks, in most respects the Anonymus Byzantinus constructs himself as quite a Heronian figure indeed. His drastically simplified didactic program, his aim to keep his rhetoric "low," and his emphasis on "making visible" mathematical constructs on the ground might even be seen as intensifications of some of Hero's most typical authorial traits. While of course we cannot know who appended Hero's name to his work, the author had in some sense already claimed it by his very approach.

Meanwhile, Hero the mathematician is visible at Constantinople only in the single manuscript codex that preserves the *Metrica*, the early 10th-century *Codex Seragliensis* G.I.1 or *Constantinopolitanus Palatii Veteris* 1 (S). As Lévy and Vitrac observe, the *Metrica* is mentioned only twice in late antiquity, both times by figures associated with Ammonius.[205] However, while the *Metrica* might not have enjoyed the same explosion of Byzantine interest as the later metrological works (whose volume was arguably outweighed by their variability), this codex made at least one very interesting mark on contemporary mathematics. Mordekhai Komtino was a 15th-century Jewish philosopher, mathematician, and astronomer who described himself as a "Greek of Constantinople" at a time when Constantinople hosted a vigorous industry of translations and commentaries from Greek into Hebrew.[206] Komtino's notes and commentary on Nicomachus, Euclid, and Ptolemy survive, as do his own works on astronomical instruments, biblical exegesis, and philosophy.

His works include a book entitled *Sefer ha-Ḥeshbon we-ha-Middot*, which includes mathematical sections on arithmetic as well as geometry, drawing on metrological traditions both in Greek and Hebrew.[207] Schub already identified S (the *Codex Seragliensis*) as Komtino's source for the metrological material in his treatise, which draws not only from the *Metrica* itself, but also from the later Heronian metrological works that exist in S as well as other manuscripts.[208] Lévy and Vitrac likewise conclude that S was his source, albeit on somewhat different grounds.[209] Yet Komtino attributes the material to Euclid rather than Hero, even though this requires him to accept that Euclid wrote a book on surveying that claimed that plane surfaces are defined by directions, points, lines, and

---

[204] Anon. Byz., *Geodaisia* 2–5, 9.     [205] Lévy and Vitrac 2018: 192.

[206] Lévy and Vitrac 2018: 184. On the propagation and composition of scientific works in particular see Freudenthal 2011.

[207] Silberberg 1905, 1906.     [208] Schub 1932: 57.     [209] Lévy and Vitrac 2018: 199–212.

angles.[210] Lévy and Vitrac note that the attribution to Hero is very clear in several places in the codex, and they note as well that in another work Komtino does mention Hero by name, saying that he possesses a work by him on geometry.[211] So he knew the name: Why did he substitute Euclid's here? They suggest that Komtino felt it would be more appropriate to credit the idea to a more familiar figure like Euclid for the benefit of readers whom his book was introducing to mathematics – another case of "allelopoiesis," this time combining the mechanics of "obfuscation" and "substitution."[212] Komtino, focusing on Euclid as the appropriate voice for introductory mathematics, eradicates Hero from the text and substitutes the more familiar name. At the same time, this maneuver transforms Euclid and the *Elements* in turn, transplanting the mathematical "elements" into the surveyor's terrain. Once again, Hero's general tendency to efface his own sources is reenacted on him in turn, as his name is left out of Komtino's work to avoid confusing a beginner readership with too detailed a commentary.

## The Islamic World

While the *Metrica* hung on tenuously, given new (albeit anonymous) life by Komtino, Hero's mathematical side was embodied as well in his Euclid commentary. While that text is lost in Greek, Abū al-ʿAbbās al-Faḍl ibn Ḥātim al-Nayrīzī preserved some passages in his own 9th-century Arabic commentary to the *Elements*, which was itself translated into Latin by Gerard of Cremona.[213] While Komtino effaced Hero from the record, al-Nayrīzī preserves his name alongside his contributions, as he does for Simplicius. Indeed, so enthusiastic is al-Nayrīzī about preserving names that Asper refers to his approach to deploying one's predecessors in a commentary as "names on parade."[214] Commentary in this style strings together arguments from earlier sources without embedding them in a larger argumentative structure or taking sides between them. Asper contrasts the resulting effect with that of Proclus, saying the latter produces a "group discussion" and the former an "archive." In effect, al-Nayrīzī seldom engages critically with his fellow commentators, joining his work quite seamlessly with theirs. The parts of his text that he associates with

---

[210] In fact, this text is found at the beginning of the third book of the *Geometrica* in Heiberg's edition.
[211] Lévy and Vitrac 2018: 201.      [212] Bergemann et al. 2019: 21–22.
[213] For a detailed account of Hero's contributions to the commentary see Hero 2014: 31–39. Al-Nayrīzī's text and English translation are available in al-Nayrīzī 2003, 2009.
[214] Asper 2019: 9.

Hero often explicitly list an analytic and a synthetic approach, much as Hero does in the *Metrica* (though in this case, of course, the syntheses are all geometrical rather than numerical). We might take this as an implicit celebration of Hero's method (and evidence of what the lost *Elements* commentary might have looked like), but al-Nayrīzī's uncritical attitude makes it difficult to say for certain.

There are, to be sure, some passages where al-Nayrīzī engages more actively with Hero's assertions. For example, consider the passage on *Elements* II.11, where the "golden ratio" is first introduced. Al-Nayrīzī observes that "Heron said: Lo, as for this figure, it is not possible for one to prove it without an illustration."[215] The reasons why this should be so for this proposition in particular are far from clear either from Hero's brisk assertion or al-Nayrīzī's exposition. But al-Nayrīzī does once again seem to support Hero's conclusion, saying that while he has demonstrated some previous propositions without drawings because they did not require constructions of previous results used in the proof, this one needs a construction and hence a diagram. Elsewhere he comments on Hero's remarks about authorial rather than mathematical choices, as in the preliminaries to the fourth book, where he notes Hero complained that Euclid included a definition for a figure inscribed in a rectilinear figure, even though he only inscribes figures in circles. The reason, al-Nayrīzī responds, is completeness; he goes on to add that Euclid wished to give readers the tools to carry out proofs about figures of all kinds, even when he does not construct proofs on all possible figures in the book itself. Thus al-Nayrīzī does appear to reconcile a minor scuffle between Euclid and Hero, though he carries out that resolution in a nonpolemical tone comparable to Hero's own responses to his predecessors.

Al-Nayrīzī's work was just one facet of the Heronian tradition transmitted in the Islamic world, where the fracture between Hero's "mathematical" and "mechanical" identities does not seem to have been quite so strong.[216] Abū Yūsuf Ya'qūb ibn 'Isḥāq al-Kindī names Hero as a geometer who wrote on geography, pneumatics, and made clocks and other time-telling instruments.[217] The 10th-century *Fihrist* of Abū al-Faraj Muḥammad ibn Isḥāq al-Nadīm, which catalogs the authors of Arabic and Greek texts, includes an entry for Hero that refers to works on lifting

---

[215] Translation by Lo Bello, from al-Nayrīzī 2009.

[216] For a concise discussion of the authors mentioned here see Donald Hill's introduction in Hero and Qusṭā ibn Lūqā 1988: 16–17. On the broader history of texts on mechanics in the medieval Islamic world see Wiedemann 1970: 173–228.

[217] Wiedemann 1970: 69–70.

machines, pneumatics, and the astrolabe.[218] These works from Hero's "mechanical" side are here situated next to an additional work on resolving difficulties in Euclid, which could be identified with the Euclid commentary known to al-Nayrīzī. His name appears again later in the *Fihrist* as part of an entry on books written about moving things, where a work on "things moving on their own" by Hero, likely a translation or adaptation of the *Automata*, accompanies a text on a "ball-dropping instrument" (likely a clock) attributed to Archimedes, a mechanical work by the 9th-century Banū Mūsa, and a few others.[219]

The Banū Mūsa, three brothers who composed their *Book of Ingenious Devices* in Baghdad, are of particular interest for the scattered and uncertain history of Hero's survival in the medieval Islamic world.[220] There are tantalizing indications that his *Pneumatica* and *Automata*, as well as Philo's work on pneumatics, may have served as inspiration for some of the pneumatic wonders they describe, though the Banū Mūsa do not name any sources. While the collections of devices vary slightly between the three main manuscripts, the tradition of the text and images is quite consistent overall.[221] Several of the devices in their text are found both in Hero's Greek and Philo's Arabic tradition, two are described by Philo but not found in Hero's work, and two others are found only in Hero.[222] Hill thus concludes that the Banū Mūsa had access to both authors' works in translations that he suggests likely emerged from the syncretic Sasanid Persian traditions of scientific and technical texts, though little is known for sure.[223] Beyond the similarities in the devices themselves, the images (particularly in the Topkapi manuscript) have much in common with those in the surviving Greek manuscripts of Hero's *Pneumatica*. They use many of the same basic conventions to represent three-dimensional arrangements of pipes, valves, and decorative elements like moving figures. Unlike the images in Philo's Arabic tradition, they use letter labels rather than word labels almost exclusively. It thus seems very likely that Hero's *Pneumatica* was circulating in some form in the Islamic world, though the surviving Greek manuscripts are all considerably later than the Banū Mūsa.

The *Mechanica* survives most completely in its Persian and Arabic translations. The surviving Arabic translation, as we saw earlier, was

---

[218] al-Nadīm 1970: vol. 2 p. 642; Wiedemann 1970: 174–77.      [219] al-Nadīm 1970: vol. 2 p. 672.

[220] Introduction and translation in Banu Musa Bin Shakir 1978; Truitt 2015: 20; see also Wiedemann 1970: 178–79.

[221] On the manuscript tradition of this work see Banu Musa Bin Shakir 1978: 7–16.

[222] For a list of the devices described in Philo and Hero see Banu Musa Bin Shakir 1978: 21.

[223] Banu Musa Bin Shakir 1978: 21.

produced by Qusṭā ibn Lūqā around the same time as the Banū Mūsa were transforming Hero's contributions in their own work. While, as we have seen, there is a close overlap between the surviving Greek fragments and their Arabic analogs, other features of the Arabic version of the work suggest the text underwent some transformations either before Qusṭā received it or at his hand. The first book begins with a description of a device that uses a train of differentially sized gears to move heavy objects with minimal effort. As the editors point out, this part of the text very closely resembles chapter 37 of Hero's *Dioptra*.[224] The device is quite out of context there, and it seems misplaced in Qusṭā's translation of the *Mechanica* as well, since it immediately precedes the theoretical treatment of the mechanics of tangent circles necessary to understand why such a device should work in the first place. The editors conclude that the device originally appeared in a separate work on the *baroulkos* by Hero and was taken out of that context at some point to appear in the *Dioptra* and the *Mechanica*.[225] In any event, beginning a book with a more complex device that the reader has not been given the foundations to understand is a most un-Heronian strategy, so it seems quite unlikely that this was the form that the *Mechanica* originally took.

The second book of Qusṭā's translation likewise seems to include some elements integrated into the text after Hero composed it. Section 34 takes the form of a series of question-and-answer passages, not unlike the structure of the Peripatetic *Mechanical Problems*. Indeed, many of the questions resemble particular problems from that work, like why it is easiest to break a piece of wood over the knee at its center or why a dentist uses forceps rather than his fingers to remove a tooth.[226] To be sure, there are some differences in the specifics of the responses. In the first example, the wood is broken by bringing it down over the knee in the Greek version, whereas in the Arabic text the knee is brought down onto the wood. In the dentistry example, both explain the function of the tool in terms of getting a better grip and applying leverage, but in the Arabic version the root of the tooth is identified as the fulcrum, whereas in the Greek version the tooth as a whole is positioned as the weight at one end of the lever.

While there is nothing in the content of the problems themselves that seems out of bounds for the *Mechanica*, the shift to the

---

[224] Hero and Qusṭā ibn Lūqā 2016: 311.

[225] Hero and Qusṭā ibn Lūqā 2016: 316. Of course it is tempting to consider the possibility that the *Dioptra* itself might have circulated in the Islamic world, but there is no evidence for this.

[226] Hero and Qusṭā ibn Lūqā 1988: 164–72, 2016: 124–30. Compare *Mechanical Problems* 852b21–28, 854a16–31.

question-and-answer format is extremely uncharacteristic for Hero, who never elsewhere uses this textual structure to establish a notional dialogue with the reader. The incorporation of this material into the *Mechanica* suggests that a version of the Peripatetic text, circulating either in Greek or Arabic, at some point got merged into Hero's text. Since Qusṭā's translation is so faithful to the Greek where comparisons are possible, it seems likely that these elements had already been incorporated into the text as he received it, but it is difficult to say more.

The Persian version of the text appears to vary more from Hero's. The text is extremely abbreviated, and in particular has done away with nearly all the theoretical material, leading the editors to suggest that this version of the text likely circulated as an aid for craftsmen.[227] The contents of the four surviving manuscripts differ somewhat; Ferriello, Gatto, and Gatto have reconciled them into two principal versions.[228] Both versions introduce the five simple machines along with sample problems about how to use them to lift a given weight with a given force, except for the case of the wedge, whose mechanical advantage is deemed unquantifiable. They then proceed to suggest devices made from compounds of two to four of the simple machines. One version of the text ends there; in the other, the author then moves on to material found neither in the other Persian texts nor in the Arabic version.[229] First, he briefly describes the necessary material characteristics of the simple machines, and then he explains the use of the so-called balance of wisdom, a kind of steelyard used to measure the purity of gold and silver.

Any of this material would have been quite at home in Hero's work, where the careful craftsmanship needed to ensure particular material qualities for screws and other components is a frequent concern, and detailed descriptions of the structure and measurement applications of instruments like the dioptra closely match the treatment of the "balance of wisdom." But although its practicality, focus on the material properties of the simple machines, and detailed instructions for using them certainly recall the "Heronian" approach established in the *Mechanica* and other works, nevertheless it appears to be a new addition to the Persian version. Yet Hero is not the only representative of mechanics found in the Persian text; the first version begins with a clear reference to Archimedes' famous

---

[227] Hero and Qusṭā ibn Lūqā 2016: 191.
[228] Text and English translation at Hero and Qusṭā ibn Lūqā 2016: 202–51.
[229] This version of the text is drawn from the Paris Supplément Persan 369, discovered and edited by Ferriello as her dissertation: Ferriello 1998.

claim that with a long enough lever he could move the world, though Archimedes himself is not named.[230] Moreover, the "balance of wisdom" used to detect impurities in precious metals is calibrated by means of measuring pans suspended alternately in air and in water, recalling Archimedes' famous method for determining the purity of a crown allegedly made of gold.[231] The version of the *Mechanica* in the Paris manuscript thus delivers a core of solidly Heronian mechanics bookended by references to famous Archimedean anecdotes. This seems a fitting treatment for Hero, who appears to be frequently imagined as a lesser companion to Archimedes by Pappus, Tzetzes, the Persian translator, and others.

## Conclusion

Since Hero eludes attempts to fix him as a historical figure, this chapter tries instead to locate his surviving texts within the broader environments of authorship, especially on technical topics, in each of the cultural environments onto which he has been projected. A complex task, of course, which demands some sacrifices, including oversimplifications of complicated and heterogeneous literary traditions and the imposition of bright lines between cultures where the real boundaries were of course much fuzzier. But those shortcomings granted, what portrait of Hero as an "archive" has emerged?

His works are all but devoid of any local details past or present: no catalog of prior kings and their catapults, no promises to patrons, not even clues about content that might provide hints, like Eratosthenes' Egyptian village of model mathematics problems. He does not seem to involve himself in squabbles over scholarship or to concern himself with meeting the critical demands that might please a patron, unlike the "egoistic, agonistic" environment in which Berrey portrays Apollonius of Citium jostling for position, or Athenaeus Mechanicus' nervous fears of criticism of his imperial offering. Of course this tells us nothing about whether the historical Hero actually lived and practiced in such an environment, only that he does not draw the threads of that competitive culture into his work. Instead, he more closely resembles authors like Celsus, who acknowledge technical developments without seeming to occupy a particular competitive locus within that discourse.

[230] The story of the lever is recounted at Plutarch, *Marcellus* 14.12.
[231] For the well-known (if theoretically unsatisfying) anecdote see Vitruvius, *De architectura* 9. pr.9–12.

Hero's relationship to his predecessors and contemporaries is quite clearly mediated through texts, but again he gives only a very vague impression of interactions with individual books. We might contrast the bio-bibliographical adventures that so sharply define Galen's accounts of grappling with written sources and that infuse Pliny the Elder's prefatory catalog of the peculiar Greek works (*Honeycomb, Violets, Meadow*, and so on) against which he defined his own composition and its multitude of sources.[232] Hero inscribes a few prominent sources (Euclid, Archimedes, Philo) into his work, but even known influences like Ctesibius have to be inferred. Alongside the few named sources, Hero simply assures his reader that he has knowledge of a vast number of prior works on topics from dioptrics to pneumatics, and that he has skimmed the cream from all of them, but he does not show his work. Like Nicomachus, Diophantus, and others, he suggests a pedagogical program for his reader to follow, concentrating his efforts on organically shaping the reader's journey through individual texts and the corpus as a whole rather than shaping that corpus encyclopedically to cover a predetermined scope of information in a certain order.

Not all flows of knowledge within the Heronian corpus are textual; Hero also sometimes opens up a window onto knowledge that can only be obtained by hand. Sometimes such knowledge is a last resort, like the clay-coated irregular forms of the *Metrica*; sometimes it is much to be preferred, like the "perceptible proof" of the *Pneumatica*. His appeals to experiential knowledge do not suggest a quasi-formal culture of public experimentation such as Celsus and Philo tantalizingly hint at for Hellenistic Alexandria and Galen vividly describes in imperial Rome. His experiments are instead responses to the aspects of mechanics where verbal description breaks down and a tinkering hand is required to verify a mechanism's efficacy, or small proofs of concept that draw their explanatory power from narrative amplification or analogy. In this respect he most closely resembles authors like Vitruvius and Seneca, who likewise offer analogical explanations fleshed out with vivid narrative accounts.

With Pappus, the Heronian "archive" begins to serve more as an "outward" archive in Needham's sense, an "input" to new textual currents more than an "output" from older ones. Still, the flow was not rendered entirely one-way, as the later interpolations into texts like the *Definitiones* and the metrological corpus show. Pappus characterizes the approach to mechanics associated with Hero as combining "rational" and "manual"

---

[232] Pliny, *Nat. Hist.* pr.24.

knowledge, mathematics, and handwork – a blend familiar to readers of Hero's own works. Gradually, these aspects seem to fracture somewhat, as Pappus, Proclus, and others transformed the Heronian mathematical–mechanical tradition by focalizing certain aspects while obfuscating others. The mathematical legacy Hero left in the *Metrica, Definitiones*, and the lost Euclid commentary was taken up by commentators and compilers with a singular mathematical interest. The metrological texts did take on a life of their own, drawing baskets of barley, tiled roofs, amphitheaters full of seats, and other real-world objects into the picture. Yet that picture remains resolutely mathematical; those problems are not concerned with the material properties of their objects, only with how much space they occupy or how much they weigh.

Meanwhile, Hero's more "mechanical" works like the *Mechanica* and *Pneumatica* found new life in the Islamic world, with the practical aspects of the *Mechanica* being radically expanded by descriptions not only of the devices' material properties but of the workmen who used them. The wonders of the *Pneumatica* served as fodder for the innovations of the Banū Mūsa and others, their capacity to amplify physical effects amplified by new types of pneumatic components and featured in new designs. Indeed, as we will see in the next chapter, the capacity of works like the *Pneumatica* to spark imagination and innovation never faded, and Hero's signature combination of the mathematical and material, the practical and philosophical, gained new life at the hands of the Italian humanists.

# CHAPTER 5

# Hero in the Age of Print

## Introduction

We saw in the last chapter how the Heronian tradition fragmented and flourished in the Byzantine and medieval Islamic worlds. Yet in the Latin west, Hero's trail went quite cold during this period. A few references suggest that he continued to be characterized as he was in Pappus, as a mechanical author and pneumatic wonder-worker. In the *Summa Philosophia* of the Pseudo-Grosseteste, Hero is named as an *egregius philosophus* who strove to demonstrate the void "through clepsydras and siphons and other instruments."[1] Henricus Aristippus recommends in the preface to his 1156 translation of the *Phaedo* that his pseudonymous addressee elect to stay in Sicily, where he has access to a rich library of philosophical and scientific texts, including "the *mechanica* of the philosopher Hero . . . who argues so subtly about the void."[2]

Clearly, Hero's name continued to circulate in medieval discourse on pneumatics, but the fortunes of his textual tradition in Latin are much less clear. Rose and Haskins interpret Aristippus' conflation of Hero's work on mechanics and pneumatics as indicating that he had access to a Latin translation of the *Pneumatica* rather than the *Mechanica*.[3] But as Grant points out, Aristippus immediately mentions Theoridus of Brindisi as well as a resource for Greek translation, and some of the other texts he refers to here (e.g. Euclid's *Optica*) were at the time available to Aristippus only in Greek, not in Latin, so there is no reason to assume a Latin translation of Hero's work (whichever it was) is meant here.[4] The 13th-century *Biblionomia* listing the contents of Richard de Fournival's library includes

---

[1] Grosseteste 1912: 417.
[2] "*Habes Eronis philosophi mechanica pre manibus, qui tam subtiliter de inani disputat quanta eius virtus quantaque per ipsum delacionis celeritas*": Plato 1940, vol. 2: 89. The text (originally edited by Minio-Paluello) is reprinted with additional context at Grant 1971: 656.
[3] Haskins 1960: 181–82; Rose 1866: 380–81.     [4] Grant 1971: 658.

a reference to a volume containing a copy of Palladius' book on agriculture and *"excerpta de libro Heronis de specialibus ingeniis."*[5] Birkenmajer amended *specialibus* to *spiritualibus*, suggesting that the entry referred to a Latin translation of Hero's *Pneumatica*, perhaps even the very Sicilian manuscript Aristippus had in mind.[6]

As always with Hero, questions multiply faster than answers. Still, there may indeed have been a separate Latin tradition of Hero's *Pneumatica*; a 16th-century manuscript now held by the Bibliothèque nationale de France includes a preface that differs from the text in the Greek manuscripts.[7] While it remains impossible to construct a continuous Latin tradition of the *Pneumatica* from that single 16th-century manuscript, by this time several Latin versions had already been translated from the Greek version by Cardinal Marcello Cervini, Giovanni Battista Gabio, and Francesco Burana.[8] But in 1575 Hero's fortunes would change dramatically with the publication of the first printed Latin translation of the *Pneumatica*, produced by Federico Commandino on the press at his home in Urbino. Tragically, the work only appeared after Commandino's death that year, but for Hero it was the start of a new life.

In 1592 Alessandro Giorgi's *Spiritali di Herone Alessandrino Ridotti in Lingua Volgare* was printed in Urbino by the Ragusi brothers, Bartholomeo and Simone. This Italian translation of Hero's *Pneumatica* begins with a prefatory letter to the last duke of Urbino, Francesco Maria II della Rovere, exhorting favor for a technical book that might resonate with the duke's supremely "architectonic" responsibilities as governor of his people.[9] Since Commandino's Latin version (also printed in Urbino)

[5] Delisle 1868, vol. 2: 530.

[6] Birkenmajer 1922: 30–32. Grant is again cautious about Birkenmajer's conclusion, given that no surviving Latin manuscript attributes a work with such a title to Hero, though the manuscripts in the Latin tradition of Philo's *Pneumatica* do go by this name, so he proposes the entry more likely refers to one of these (Grant 1971: 659–61). Birkenmajer argues as well that a 1274 letter composed by the arts faculty at the University of Paris upon the death of Thomas Aquinas requesting a collection of books including a *De aquarum conductibus et ingeniis erigendis* must refer to a Latin translation of Hero's *Pneumatica*, and indeed it credits the translation to William of Moerbeke (Birkenmajer 1922: 29–31). However, Heiberg finds it more likely to be one of the several copies of Philo's *Pneumatica* that were circulating, and Grant suggests that it was more likely to be the *Mechanica* than the *Pneumatica*. See Grant 1971: 667–68; Heiberg 1892: 314.

[7] Paris cod. lat. 7226b; Haskins 1960: 182–83.

[8] Cervini's translation is now lost; Gabio's is preserved in MS Barberiniano latino 310 (X, 128) and Vat. Lat. 4575; Burana's is found in BNF Fonds Latin MS 10261, Rome Biblioteca Lancisiana MS 249, and Milan Biblioteca Ambrosiana MSS J 38 inf. and G 78 inf. On these see Laird 2017: 155.

[9] Alessandro Giorgi, *Spiritali di Herone Alessandrino*, 4. The pages of Giorgi's dedicatory materials and preface are unnumbered; for convenience I have numbered them as they appear in the 1592 version. The introduction and main text are numbered by leaves, not pages, which I have thus

had already been rendered into Italian by Giovan Battista Aleotti at Ferrara in 1589, complete with four new designs of Aleotti's own devising, this new translation would have some explaining to do.[10]

Commandino's untimely death, Giorgi argues, had prevented him from putting the final touches on his translation, which was moreover based on less reliable Greek texts than those Giorgi himself had managed to secure. Giorgi also claims to have virtuously held off releasing his own translation for some time, since Daniel Barbaro claimed in his 1566 translation and commentary to Vitruvius' *De architectura* that he had already translated Hero into Italian.[11] However, when Barbaro's version failed to appear, and spurred on further by the appearance of Aleotti's translation, Giorgi evidently decided the time was right to produce his own version. In 1680 Commandino's Latin text was printed in Amsterdam in a new edition that included Aleotti's new designs, now translated from their original Italian into Latin, presumably to match the Latin *gravitas* of Commandino's text. That composite work was translated into German in 1688 by the pseudonymous "Agathus Cario"; this new version included yet more additional designs, these largely drawn from Salomon de Caus's 1624 *Les Raisons des Forces Mouvantes*.

What made Hero's *Pneumatica* the launching point of such a busy, competitive industry of translations and expansions in the 16th and 17th centuries? Interest in Hero's works flourished throughout Europe during this period, taking many forms at the hands of different authors, with varying attitudes toward knowledge of antiquity, sparking novel approaches to the creation not only of mechanical devices, but also of the books through which they propagated. Hero's shifting role in this complex of texts and technologies was shaped by new attitudes about the relationship between mathematics, physics, and mechanics, newly available components for machines and craft techniques, new social contexts for knowledge exchange and for the development and deployment of

numbered, for example, "1r" and "1v." On the history of the term "architectonic" from Vitruvius through the early modern period (including at Urbino) see McEwen 2016.

[10] Federico Commandino, *Heronis Alexandrini Spiritalium liber* (Urbino, 1575); Giovan Battista Aleotti, *Gli Artifitiosi et Curiosi Moti Spiritali Di Herrone* (Ferrara: Vittorio Baldini, 1589). Commandino himself had spent some time in Ferrara as a student; see Fiocca 2020: 352–60. Woodcroft claims that Aleotti's Italian translation came first, in 1547 (Hero 1851: xii). As Aleotti was born in 1546, it seems likely that Woodcroft simply misread the date of the 1647 Bologna edition of Aleotti's translation.

[11] Daniel Barbaro, *I Dieci libri dell'Architettura di M. Vitruvio* (Venice: Francesco de'Franceschi Senese et Giovanni Chrieger Alemano compagni, 1567), 466.

technologies, and new sites and strategies for exploration ranging from books to formal experiments.

A thorough review of the background on the myriad technical and scientific activities of this period would of course be otiose.[12] The somewhat narrower question of how Renaissance and early modern scientific authors responded to their ancient predecessors has likewise been treated quite thoroughly, particularly where Aristotle, Archimedes, and Vitruvius are concerned.[13] Even Hero's presence in the developing mechanical traditions of this period is no secret.[14] However, beyond Boas's detailed review of translations and editions of the *Pneumatica* and Drake's brief list of Heronian texts and machines that reemerged as centers of attention in the 16th century, little notice has been taken of just how central and recurrent a figure Hero was in the technological discourse of the 16th and 17th centuries. Doubtless the scanty attention paid to Hero can largely be chalked up to the rhetoric of the early modern authors themselves, who generally seem keener to highlight their connections to more illustrious figures like Aristotle, Euclid, Archimedes, and even Vitruvius than to underscore their debt to Hero.

However, their mechanical devices (both components and composites), their physical theories, and even the way they organize their knowledge convey the extent of that debt. And no wonder: The most distinctive aspects of the Heronian tradition – the rich and thoughtful interplay of practice and theory, the concern for shaping knowledge into texts that can be appreciated by a broad readership, and a way of exploring nature that aims foremost at utility – match beautifully with the epistemological and practical concerns of many Renaissance and early modern authors. My aim in what follows will be to unfold the unspoken as well as the explicit connections that cemented Hero so strongly in this new world of scientific exploration and technical practice. I will focus in particular on how the Heronian negotiations between tradition and innovation, theory and practice, and the mathematical and the material play out in this new environment, and on how the rapidly changing printing technologies

---

[12] Of the vast literature on this subject, a few works of particular relevance here include Bensaude-Vincent and Newman 2007; Daston 1998; Dear 1991; Grafton and Siraisi 1999; Peterson 2011; Roberts, Schaffer, and Dear 2007.

[13] On the reception of Aristotle and the Peripatetic *Mechanica* see especially Damerow 2004; Dijksterhuis 1959; Renn, Damerow, and McLaughlin 2003; Rose and Drake 1971. On Archimedes see especially Bertoloni Meli 1992; Laird 1991; Renn, Damerow, and McLaughlin 2003. On Vitruvius see D'Evelyn 2012; Kanerva 2006; Sanvito 2016; Torello-Hill 2015.

[14] Bedini 1964; Boas 1949; Drake and Drabkin 1969: 6, 10–11.

accelerated the broad and varied knowledge propagation Hero claimed as a particular virtue of his own works.

## Hero's Renaissance

The Italian humanist revival of classical texts began in the 14th century, and the humanists' work of editing and translating classical texts continued to flourish in Italy and beyond well into the 17th century. Witt argues that Italy was a natural wellspring for the movement, given the preponderance of secular urban communities politically organized into city-states, who naturally saw something of themselves in the classical world.[15] While most of the early humanists' efforts focused on Latin texts, increasing contact with the Byzantine world (particularly the westward migration of Byzantine scholars following the Turkish conquest of Constantinople) created a market for Greek texts as well, to be translated into Latin and vernacular languages. The collection, preservation, and translation of Greek texts was particularly vigorous at Venice, which had a long history of political and cultural bonds with Byzantium.[16] Aldus Manutius's publishing house pioneered techniques for printing in Greek, and even after his death Venice remained a central destination for scholars who wished to study Greek language and literature.[17] The rise of print culture drastically increased the potential readership for new editions and translations of classical texts, which shaped the development of new library collections throughout Europe, including works both old and new, in manuscript and print, spanning disciplines from literature to science.

Drake influentially posited two "schools" of Italian mechanics: a pragmatically minded group in northern Italy (exemplified by Tartaglia and Cardano) and a theoretically minded group in central Italy (exemplified by Commandino and Baldi).[18] In broad strokes, the members of the central Italian "school" (associated principally with Urbino) were humanistically oriented toward ancient Greek knowledge and possessed the linguistic skills needed for nuanced analysis of those texts, while the northern "school" favored medieval Latin work like that of Jordanus. At the same time, Drake emphasizes that closer analysis shows a less binary arrangement: The two "schools" were bridged by a common interest in

---

[15] Witt 1988: 52–53.     [16] Carpinato 2014: 169–89.
[17] On Manutius see Lowry 1979. On the broader book culture of Renaissance Venice see Kikuchi 2018; Piccione 2021; Pon and Kallendorf 2009.
[18] Drake and Drabkin 1969: 13.

Archimedes' multifaceted legacy of theoretical and practical works, and they sometimes adopted or rejected principles and ideas on a case-by-case basis rather than rejecting wholesale the ideas of an author like Jordanus.

Though he thus softens the boundaries between the Italian "schools," Drake maintains a more rigorous division between two alleged ancient "Alexandrian" traditions that would go on to play important roles in later mechanical work. These were the "tradition of Hero" including the *Pneumatics* and the eighth book of Pappus' *Synagōgē*, and a "technological tradition" including Hero's *Automata* and *Belopoeica* as well as Vitruvius' *De architectura* and Oribasius' *Collectiones medicae*.[19] This rather peculiar grouping of texts obviously does not reflect the ancient context very well, but it does echo ideas expressed by some early modern authors. Thus it should not be discarded entirely, but only treated with extreme caution, as the theoretical and practical aspects of mechanics clearly remained as complexly interwoven as they had been in antiquity.

The Heronian tradition flourished most extravagantly in Italy and France in this period, with smaller offshoots penetrating into England and Germany. Particularly prominent figures in Hero's resurgence included Giorgio Valla, Federico Commandino, Bernardino Baldi, Alessandro Giorgi, Giovan Battista Aleotti, and Salomon de Caus. Many of these figures were likewise conduits for other ancient revenants like Archimedes, Vitruvius, and Pappus, as well as the Aristotelian and Euclidean traditions that had remained vigorous throughout the medieval period but were now reshaped and put to new uses.

The revival of ancient mathematical and technical texts owed much to Federico Commandino, a tireless editor and translator of ancient authors including Archimedes, Euclid, Apollonius, Aristarchus, Pappus, and Ptolemy.[20] His father Battista was an architect who had been placed in charge of building fortifications at Urbino. Commandino himself, after a brief youthful career as *cameriere secreto* to Clement VII, had moved to Verona, where he served Guidobaldo della Rovere, then duke of Urbino. Upon their return to Urbino, the duke introduced him to his brother-in-law, the cardinal Ranuccio Farnese. The cardinal's patronage was

---

[19] Drake and Drabkin 1969: 6. Drake and Drabkin's notion of the "tradition of Hero" is needlessly cumbersome and not particularly helpful for analysis. When I refer to a "Heronian tradition" or "tradition of Hero" in what follows I will continue to embrace the whole, and not Drake and Drabkin's *Pneumatics*–Pappus compartment.

[20] Rose's account of Commandino's career and works is rich in detail on his editions and translations, the Greek manuscripts he used, and his own intellectual commitments (Rose 1975: 185–221). On the manuscripts circulated by Hero's humanist translators see also Laird 2017: 152–53.

instrumental to Commandino's later career; not only did the Farnese libraries provide ready access to manuscripts, but he also introduced Commandino to Marcello Cervini, a central figure in the project of producing printed editions of Greek manuscripts in the Vatican collections. Cervini had a particular interest in mathematical texts and had produced his own manuscript containing a Latin translation of the *Pneumatica*, perhaps based on the Greek manuscript now numbered 1364 in the Vatican collection.[21] His collections helped to fuel Commandino's humanistic project of editing and translating ancient mathematical works.

The Farnese family and Guidobaldo remained important patrons to Commandino for decades. He dedicated a volume of Latin translations of five works by Archimedes to Ranuccio's brother Alessandro in 1558; upon his return to Urbino, he dedicated his 1566 translation of Apollonius to Guidobaldo and the selections of Eutocius that accompanied the translation to the prince Francesco Maria of Urbino. The ducal family continued to patronize Commandino until his death, even issuing him a ducal license to install a printing press in his own home just one year before he died. The *Pneumatica* printed there was dedicated to Guidobaldo's brother, the cardinal Giulio della Rovere, and the vestigial preface written by Commandino's brother-in-law Valerio Spaccioli consists primarily of an apology to the cardinal for any faults remaining in the work after the premature death of the editor.

It is clear from the prefaces to Commandino's surviving works that he envisioned himself as unearthing the splendors of ancient mathematics, long subjected to darkness and squalor, for a modern readership that might not be prepared for their glory. In the preface to his 1558 *Archimedis Opera Nonnulla*, he compares his contemporaries to bats that cannot bear the light of the sun, and he suggests that likewise "the splendor and excellence of his divine reasoning makes the gaze of our ability squint." Indeed, Commandino himself was celebrated by his student Bernardino Baldi as bringing a "light" and "splendor" of his own to the texts he translated, thanks to the purity of his language and the precision of his thought.[22] Giorgi likewise praises him posthumously as having "roused mathematics, drawing it from the shadows, which have renounced their darkness, and

---

[21] On Cervini's possession of manuscripts in the Heronian tradition see Rose 1975: 191–93.
[22] See, for example, Baldi's *Vita di Federico Commandino*, in Ugolini 1859: 521, 525, 535.

from the ignorance of many past centuries; he illuminated it with so many famous works that the whole world knows he has gone."[23]

Baldi begins his 1589 annotated translation of Hero's *Automata* with an apologetic appeal that conjures up similar images of knowledge plunged into neglectful darkness. Though he was inspired to follow in his teacher Commandino's footsteps, after his first attempt at the work he was distracted by other events, notably Commandino's untimely death in the same year his *Pneumatica* appeared and Baldi's own elevation to the post of abbot of Guastalla in 1586. As a result, his translation of the two books of the *Automata* had to be left "sleeping," until "their sleep was on the way to becoming death." Baldi credits the count Giulio da Thiene, at the time employed as a military advisor to the duke of Ferrara, with inspiring him to "awaken" his translation and "shake off the dust" by publishing the work at last, in two nearly identical Venetian editions, the first in 1589 and the second in 1601.[24]

Humanist revivals of Greek texts are of course full of comparable images of ancient texts languishing in darkness, asleep or buried, gently decaying until an editor or translator steps in to rescue them. The tropes Commandino and Baldi invoke of ancient texts entombed in darkness, as well as philological concerns about the frailties of the manuscript tradition like those Giorgi expressed, again recall Middleton's argument that material texts frame a reader's acts of reception, and in turn create new possibilities for future realizations of the text.[25] Like Pappus' reference to the crumbling, damaged books where he discovered Hero's *Mechanica*, the "darkness" from which Commandino and others say they unearthed his works recreates Hero as a figure of fragile antiquity. In turn, their translations and commentaries will bring his work back into the light, its text refined by their philological zeal and fortified by being reproduced in print and introduced to new readerships. Every such work is the product of excavating the sediment of past versions, from the unreachable original to the variant manuscripts to the humanist edition that hopes quixotically both to illuminate the original text and to set it in a new cultural context. In the case of technical authors like Hero, the humanists' philological and cultural reconstructions of the literary past are blended with a technical past that requires readers to parse unfamiliar components and technical

[23] Giorgi, *Spiritali* 1–2.
[24] Unhappily, da Thiene himself died the year before Baldi's translation came out, and the work was dedicated instead to Jacomo Contarini, a Venetian senator who participated in and patronized a variety of mathematical and mechanical projects: Micheli 2005: 248.
[25] Middleton 2020.

terminology, setting mechanical technologies in an ancient technocultural imaginary as well as a new technical milieu still under construction.

Yet as Henninger-Voss has pointed out, the humanistic impulse to bring these ancient thinkers back to life was at least matched by the interest of men heavily invested in practical activities like mining or milling that might be streamlined or revolutionized by the revival of ancient technological systems.[26] Hero's constant emphasis on the utility of the mechanical disciplines he unfolds made him an attractive focus for translations and other receptive engagements. Baldi and Hero's other humanist translators discovered that his didactic accessibility and the elegant devices his writings describe suited their project of reviving classical texts for an elite readership. His explicit concern for the needs of his readership, and in particular his focus on making his work useful, made him an adaptable figure for later translators seeking to position his technical work (and by extension theirs) in new intellectual, philosophical, and cultural terrain.

While Urbino was of course not the only site for humanistic revivals of ancient mathematics and science, it played a unique role in Hero's renaissance. Frank notes the particular importance of mechanics and mathematics at the Urbino court since the time of the duke Federico da Montefeltro, for whom the applications of mathematics to projectile motion and fortifications were a particular concern.[27] The duke amassed as well a remarkable collection of Greek and Latin scientific and mathematical texts (including four copies of Ptolemy's *Geographia*).[28] Mathematics both ancient and recent remained an abiding interest at the Urbino court; Baldi's *Vita* recounts that Commandino was requested by the young prince Francesco Maria II della Rovere to lecture on Euclid's *Elements* and eventually to produce a new translation.[29] Commandino produced translations of Pappus as well as Archimedes, while Baldi composed an extensive collection of biographies of mathematicians from the ancient Greek and medieval Western and Islamicate worlds as well as more recent figures, biographies of the Montefeltro dukes of Urbino, Federico, and Guidobaldo, and other prose and verse both technical and courtly.[30]

Mechanics was engaged in the service of civil architecture as well as military fortifications, culminating in the mechanisms for special effects devised by Nicola Sabbattini (or Niccolò Sabbatini) for the court's theater,

[26] Henninger-Voss 2000: 239.    [27] Frank 2013: 308.    [28] Rose 1975: 54–55.
[29] Baldi, *Vita di Federico Commandino*, in Ugolini 1859: 528–29. On the translation see Gamba and Montebelli 1988: 63–64.
[30] On Baldi's life and works see Gamba 2005; Serrai 2002: 17–155.

including full-size versions of special effects such as Hero recounts (in miniature) in his *Automata*.[31] In keeping with the tradition of the Urbino elite's support for technical knowledge, some patrons of Urbinate technical authors and translators were themselves actually involved in mechanical work, particularly Guidobaldo dal Monte.[32] His 1577 *Mechanicorum liber* reflects an author steeped in the courtly culture of Urbino's ducal regime, who at the same time embraced the practical power of technical knowledge rooted in antiquity.

The interest in mathematics and mechanics at the Urbino court fostered the development of the so-called Urbino school, a vigorous culture of translation, commentary, lecture, and experimentation. Domenico Bertoloni Meli argues that the denotation of this group as a "school" should not mean they should "be seen as a monolithic group promoting the same project," but in any case Urbino was certainly the site of a remarkable efflorescence of translations of and commentaries to ancient mathematical and mechanical texts.[33] Biagioli argues that indeed for the Urbino mathematicians "Archimedes became their Cicero," offering them a classical counterpart who seemed to exemplify the elegant abstraction that could become an attribute even of mechanical work.[34]

As Jessica Wolfe observes, the culture of scientific exploration at Urbino was marked by the "impulse to mediate between the material and the immaterial, or the active and the contemplative realms."[35] Baldi says in his preface to the *De gli automati* that the mechanical arts should properly be considered in the Aristotelian sense as subaltern to mathematics, the discipline where mathematics becomes apparent to the senses.[36] Mechanics explains the multiplication of forces by means of levers, the mathematical relationship between leverage and circular motion (most famously described in the Peripatetic *Mechanical Problems*, also translated with commentary by Baldi), and the means of transforming these theoretical insights into effective fortifications and refined materials. There is no conflict, in his view, between the practical accomplishments of mechanics and the philosophical wonder it inspires as a branch of mathematics. In

---

[31] Nicola Sabbattini, *Pratica di Fabricar Scene, e Machine ne' Teatri* (Ravenna: Pietro de' Paoli e Gio. Battista Viovannelli, 1638).

[32] On the work done by Guidobaldo that is most relevant here see Bertoloni Meli 1992; Henninger-Voss 2000; van Dyck 2013. For a full-length study of Guidobaldo's mechanics see Frank 2012.

[33] Bertoloni Meli 1992: 16. For a thoughtful and detailed review of the ongoing debate over the "school" see Marr 2011: 221–24.

[34] Biagioli 1989: 60. On Archimedes' cultural status among the Urbino commentators see Gatto 2005; Micheli 2005: 258–60.

[35] Wolfe 2004: 41.    [36] Baldi, *De gli automati* 4r.

short, the intellectual attitudes toward mechanics cultivated by practitioners and patrons alike in Urbino fit perfectly with Hero's own claims for the discipline. The fluid boundary between mathematical and material ways of engaging with natural phenomena and artificial creations, the conviction that philosophical insight could be derived from hands-on exploration and experimentation, and the deep respect they held for past mechanical traditions that nonetheless might admit of further developments – these were all common ground connecting Hero to his early modern translators.

## The *Pneumatica*

Both the ancient technologies and the texts that transmitted them needed to be revived for a new reading audience. The first step of this revival was to translate Hero's works from Greek into more widely accessible languages like Latin and various vernaculars. But more than simply translating the words from one language to another, the value of the work itself had to be translated into a new cultural context. The *Pneumatica*'s renewal in the 16th century entangled Hero's devices in a new network of patronage systems, like those Commandino's work depended upon. Giorgi's dedication weaves Hero's work into the courtly culture of Urbino in its own way, picking up the Urbino tradition of the *Pneumatica* where Commandino's death had left off so abruptly. Dedicated to the duke Francesco Maria, Giorgi's version commences with elaborate praise for the fallen Commandino, who had done so much to unearth Greek learning from the shadows in which it had long rested. In Giorgi's text, a series of introductory sonnets invokes through elegant metaphors the parallel that Hero himself draws in the preface between recombinant physical elements and assemblages of textual elements.[37] The first three were written by Giovanni Battista Fazio da Urbino, whose poetic compositions appear scattered in various compilations from the late 16th century, while the fourth is a response from Giorgi to Fazio.

In the first sonnet, Fazio pleads his failure to be inspired by Apollo as the reason he cannot do Giorgi's achievement justice in poetry, wishing that a "sweeter *cantaro*" could match his merit. A *cantaro* is a drinking vessel, the name derived from a Greek vessel itself named after a pot-bellied Egyptian beetle, but the name might also gesture sonically at the etymological territory of song. Fazio thus neatly encapsulates, with one evocative

---

[37] Giorgi, *Spiritali* 5–6.

word, multiple attributes of the devices to be described in the treatise: their Greekness, their capacity as trick drinking vessels, and their burbling songs.

Apollo recurs in the second sonnet, now figuring the "courtly sun," whose light draws out Daphne's evergreen laurel leaf and most importantly permits Giorgi's and Hero's "rare ingenuity" to shine. If Giorgi's merit has not been sufficiently appreciated, if he remains solitary and self-sustaining, perhaps Fazio still has the capacity to help: In the third sonnet, he promises to raise up Giorgi's name as far as Delos, where its ruler Apollo "shines luminous and bright." Giorgi will prove his own intellectual luminosity:

> as by its illustrious and rarefied ray
> the night loses its shadowy veil,
> so at your birth, the clouds and ice
> of ignorance disperse.

Applying the sun's heat will disperse darkness, fog, and ice, an image that recalls a passage from the preface to the *Pneumatica* where Hero recounts the processes that can change one element to another.[38] He explains that the steam emanating from heated vessels is really water that has been refined into air, "destroyed by the fire" in the process as the fire dissolves and rarefies every condensed part of matter. As we saw earlier, Hero argues that the same process can be observed on the much larger scale of the Earth and the sun: When it is night, the sun is on the other side of the Earth, heating up the places closest to it, and hence the most rarefied part of the water in the Earth rises up on the other side as dew. Heated directly by the sun as it comes around, the most rarefied parts of the dew are further refined into air, while the rest is condensed together into "earthy essence" as the air rises away and sinks back down into the Earth as the sun departs. In Fazio's poem, the sun's illumination likewise brightens the Earth and summons the rarest elements upward to their deserved heights, leaving the cold condensed matter behind. Finally, Fazio brings the sonnet home to Urbino, which, thanks to Giorgi's "burning virtue," fears neither Saturnine cold nor Lethe's winter, but rather

> as on the flowers the light of Phoebus
> sprinkles a healthful humor, so you on our minds
> will breathe desire from your eternal virtue.

---

[38] *Pneumatica* 1.pr.119–83.

Giorgi's response is appropriately restrained; he acknowledges that he never hoped to reach heights equal to the "exalted swans" of Apollo – he thought not to become really famous, but at least known, "both in Urbino and in Delos." Even this modest goal, however, has been thwarted, as

> Fortune opposed her stream to my so rarefied desire,
> and broke like a fragile sail
> my beautiful thought, which has now dispersed,
> as excess of heat or cold slays the flower.

Fortune's favor is a fluid here, upon which Giorgi was able to sail all too briefly before his ambitions evaporated under her intemperate gaze. Now, "clothed in vulgar costume," he hopes only to help Fazio sail higher on the solar flood, buoyed by Apollo's genuine inspiration.

The "vulgar costume" in which Giorgi finds himself might allude to the subject of his translation as well as its language, as Hero's stance astride the borderline between theory and practice makes the devices he describes liable to be disdained as crowd-pleasing entertainment rather than serious tools for natural philosophy. Whereas Hero focuses in his own preface on the potential for his pneumatic devices to unfold the physical secrets of the tiniest particles, Giorgi at first in his introduction emphasizes the beautiful and entertaining effects pneumatic wonders can create:

> [G]roans, sputtering, gurgling, dripping, bubbling, murmuring, spraying, rumbling, music of falling water, and a thousand other delightful vagaries and strange bizarrities.[39]

But as he presents it, pneumatics can be a serious philosophical enterprise as well. "The mechanic dresses himself in the garb of the natural philosopher" when he thinks about the attributes of matter and motion, and "he does not forget he is a mathematician" when he thinks about proportion, size, and other measurables. Giorgi fits his mechanic into a broadly Aristotelian system of causes, where mechanical effects all derive originally from circular motion, are composites of mobile and immobile, and ultimately share the causes of their motion with "those of the very machine of the world."[40]

---

[39] Giorgi, *Spiritali* 3v.
[40] Berryman provides a more nuanced examination of "Aristotelian" mechanics, differentiating Aristotle's own work from the Peripatetic *Mechanica*, and he follows the reception of the "machine of the world" through late antiquity and into the early modern period at Berryman 2009: 97–104, 216–28, 236–49.

At the same time, Giorgi does not force Hero into the role of an orthodox Aristotelian. After a lengthy review of ideas about air and *pneuma* in Aristotle and elsewhere, he concludes that "our Hero has a different opinion." This was not, Giorgi argues, because he was unaware of his Peripatetic predecessor's work, but because he subscribed to another philosophical sect, or simply because he felt the explanation he gave in the *Pneumatica* was more useful and easy to understand. His own role as translator is not to adjudicate this potential philosophical battle, but to create a capacious collaborative flow where different views can coexist, not unlike Hopkins' model of literary reception as resembling a conversation where multiple mindsets can become productively entangled without needing to reach a consensus.[41]

Rather than argue about Hero's philosophical orientation, Giorgi invokes a lovely image to bridge between his own prefatory discussion of the void and the start of his translation of Hero:

> But let us see now how Hero describes his vessels, which could truly be said to be similar to the Cup of Helen, which as Homer refers to it had the power of making people forget all their woes and cares.[42]

This image closes Giorgi's introduction and is elegantly typeset in a graceful double taper that conjures up the image of the "cup" itself (Figure 5.1). In a rhetorical move that recalls Hero's prefatory remarks on *ataraxia* in the *Belopoeica* and his claim in the *Pneumatica* to transcend pure philosophical discourse with his mechanical *apodeixis*, Giorgi invites the reader to forget for the time being about philosophical controversies and to soothe their spirit through communion with the mechanical wonders to follow. Hero's eirenic blending of prior authors' ideas with his own – his nonpartisan allegiance to mechanical devices with the power to illuminate physical phenomena – is here aligned with Helen's soothing cup of wine spiked with the magical *moly* herb. Giorgi's reception of the Heronian tradition translates Hero not only between languages, but from one dialogic space to another: from the fiercely contested territory of philosophical argument to a courtly, aesthetic, sympotic context where a multitude of poetic and philosophical voices are brought together in harmony.

The work of translation itself was freighted with references to ancient culture and literature, which served both to help readers understand the

---

[41] Hopkins 2010: 13. On the applicability of Hopkins' model to engagements between ancient and modern cultural milieux see Hardwick 2020: 24–29.

[42] Giorgi, *Spiritali* 6v.

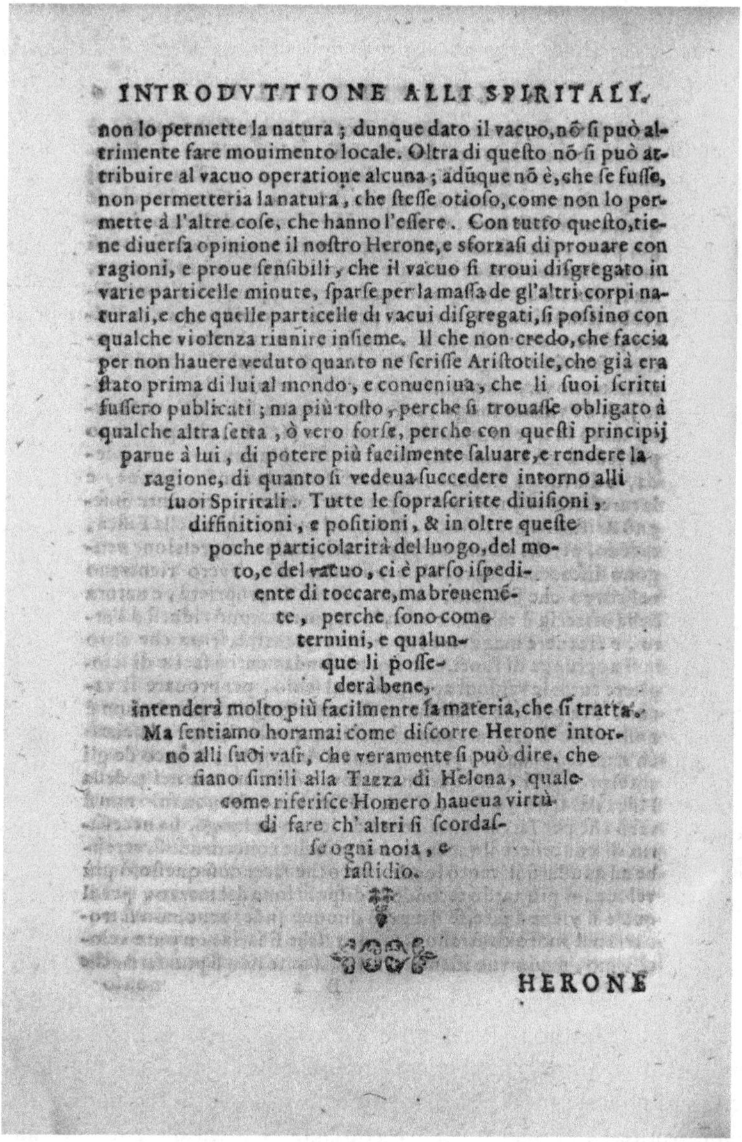

INTRODVTTIONE ALLI SPIRITALI.

non lo permette la natura ; dunque dato il vacuo, nõ si può altrimente fare mouimento locale. Oltra di questo nõ si può attribuire al vacuo operatione alcuna ; adúque nõ è, che se fusse, non permetteria la natura, che stesse otioso, come non lo permette à l'altre cose, che hanno l'essere. Con tutto questo, tiene diuersa opinione il nostro Herone, e sforzasi di prouare con ragioni, e proue sensibili, che il vacuo si troui disgregato in varie particelle minute, sparse per la massa de gl'altri corpi naturali, e che quelle particelle di vacui disgregati, si possino con qualche violenza riunire insieme. Il che non credo, che faccia per non hauere veduto quanto ne scrisse Aristotile, che già era stato prima di lui al mondo, e conueniua, che li suoi scritti fussero publicati ; ma più tosto, perche si trouasse obligato à qualche altra setta, ò vero forse, perche con questi principij parue à lui, di potere più facilmente saluare, e rendere la ragione, di quanto si vedeua succedere intorno alli suoi Spiritali. Tutte le soprascritte diuisioni, diffinitioni, e positioni, & in oltre queste poche particolarità del luogo, del moto, e del vacuo, ci è parso ispediente di toccare, ma breueméte, perche sono come termini, e qualunque li possederà bene, intenderà molto più facilmente la materia, che si tratta. Ma sentiamo horamai come discorre Herone intornò alli suoi vasi, che veramente si può dire, che siano simili alla Tazza di Helena, quale come riferisce Homero haueua virtù di fare ch'altri si scordasse ogni noia, e fastidio.

HERONE

Figure 5.1   Giorgi's "cup of Helen." Image courtesy of Bayerische Staatsbibliothek München.

terminology peculiar to pneumatic devices and to make those devices resonate with more familiar cultural touchstones.[43] Giorgi includes annotations throughout his text to help the reader through passages where either the construction of the device or the text itself presented particular difficulties. The obscurity, novelty, or technicality of certain words may create special difficulties, as when they refer to specialized instruments or locally variant measures of length, volume, or weight. For example, his notes to Hero's preface specify that the Greek *kotylē*, which he glosses *cotila*, is a measure whose Roman form equals nine ounces and its Greek form ten.[44] He invokes a host of classical authorities for his translations, ranging from canonical figures like Seneca to more technical authors like Vitruvius.

Many of Giorgi's etymological explanations might indeed be framed with the intention of building a bridge from Hero's technical devices to a more canonical zone of classical reception that might be more appealing to the broadly educated audience his prefatory material seems to suggest he aimed for in his translation. Some pneumatic devices include components named after objects that feature widely in Greek and Latin literature and hence give the translator more breadth of comparative materials. For example, a lamp designed to refill its oil supply as it burns includes a reservoir called *kalathos* in the Greek, which Commandino renders as *calathus* and Giorgi as *calice*. The Greek word's primary significance is "basket," and in particular a basket used in rituals associated with Demeter. As Giorgi notes, Ovid picks up on this significance when relating the story of Persephone in the fourth book of his *Fasti*.[45] Virgil puts the word in a bucolic context in the second *Eclogue*, where it indicates the basket of flowers the shepherd Corydon promises the nymphs would collect for Alexis. It appears again in the fifth *Eclogue*, there indicating the vessel from which Menalcas promises to pour wine from Ariusia on Chios for Daphnis. Giorgi quotes both authors, creating a poetic frame appropriate to the sympotic context of the marvelous self-sustaining lamp. He supplements the *Pneumatica*'s anthology of mechanical wonders with his own anthology of poetic connections, recontextualizing the cultural significance of Hero's devices by weaving them into a web of literary references, whereas Hero had positioned himself against a backdrop of philosophical rather than literary discourse.

---

[43] On the challenges faced by Urbino translators of ancient scientific texts more broadly see Gamba and Montebelli 1988: 60–69.

[44] Giorgi, *Spiritali* 12v n. 8.    [45] Ovid, *Fasti* 4.420–620.

Sometimes Giorgi's annotations serve as a site for polemical engagement with his fellow translators. *Pneumatica* 1.37 describes a little figure of a satyr holding a wineskin, from which he continually pours liquid into a nearby basin. What is the basin properly called? Giorgi translates the Greek *louthridion* as *pilo*, explaining his reasoning as follows:

> "Pilo": the Greek text says "*loutēridion*," the Latin "*labellum*," diminutive of "*labium*," used by Vitruvius in the tenth chapter of his fifth book for a bath-vessel. I have translated it "pilo," which is properly the vessel where the water of artificial fountains is collected. Aleotti in his translation has called it "avello"; this seems to me improper, since (if I am correct) this word is not found used by any author, except for a sepulcher, or for the vessel where in ancient times the ashes of dead bodies were kept after being burnt according to the custom of those times.[46]

Aleotti's *avello* is clearly cognate with the Latin *labellum*, but Giorgi argues that the very different associations of the Italian cognate overwhelm the etymological resemblance. In drawing his reader's attention to the twists and turns of this etymological maze, Giorgi highlights what Katz calls "etymological alterity," reminding the reader of the chronological depth that separates him from Hero's age.[47] Other words baffle even Giorgi, like the mysterious "*merismatio*" of chapter 5; Giorgi says he has found one text with the Greek spelled *smerismation* and another spelled *merismation*, and he cannot in any case find a parallel from another author.[48] Hence, he says, the reader will be better able to glean its meaning from the image, "which allows one to see what it means, than by going in search of another etymology." The image depicts the "*merismatio*" as a slender pipe that fits into a dedicated sleeve (Woodcroft translates the word as "double tube"), its male and female components letter-labeled separately.

Though Aleotti, as a direct competitor to Giorgi's project, is a more obvious target for critical textual correction, Giorgi occasionally makes explicit his improvements to Commandino's text as well. He faults neither Hero nor Commandino for the problems he promises to address as he "excavate[s] the rich treasure of knowledge" the texts of antiquity can provide.[49] In Aleotti's view, Hero is not to be blamed for the havoc time has wrought upon his text, while Commandino did not have access to the best manuscripts and was furthermore prevented by his untimely death from making a final editorial sweep through the text. Ultimately, however, Giorgi concedes that some corrections are beyond his power. Notably, he

---

[46] Giorgi, *Spiritali* 44r.    [47] Katz 2016.    [48] Giorgi, *Spiritali* 18v.    [49] Giorgi, *Spiritali* 4.

remarks on a Greek text he had encountered in circulation, which included some further designs (*theoremi*),

> no less lovely and ingenious than anything contained in this book, but at the moment they have been so badly treated that beyond the text being extremely disordered, the images as well are missing, to the extent that it is not possible to restore them to a state such that they could be allowed to make their way into the light.[50]

The remaining *theoremi* were unknown to Commandino, and hence not available from Aleotti either. But Giorgi optimistically looks forward to the day when another copy of the missing designs will appear in better shape, so that they can join their erstwhile companions in the sun, perhaps accompanied by some novel pneumatic inventions. Giorgi thus offers a guarded assessment about what anyone stepping onto the field of translations of the *Pneumatica* after him could offer. His own text is built on a foundation of the best texts, and in composing it he weighed the worst as well. Therefore, the majority of the text will not allow of much further improvement, and a later version including the missing theorems would need to incorporate some novelties in order to justify itself. Giorgi's assurance to his reader that he has done the best anyone could with the previous texts available to him is reminiscent of Hero's series of claims that he has salvaged the best from the earlier works that have come down to him, obviating the need for the reader to seek them out for himself. Giorgi's frank account of the bad state in which he found many of his key sources is itself reminiscent of Pappus' lament for the "*aporia*" that might be experienced by a reader trying to learn more of Hero's treatment of the simple machines, which he himself had encountered "largely destroyed, in books without beginnings or ends."[51]

The device numbered 71 in the translations of Commandino, Aleotti, and Giorgi shines a spotlight on the textual problems they had to wrestle with.[52] The device (mentioned in the introduction as the device Hero likens to the so-called steam engine) features an altar upon which a fire is lit, mounted atop a transparent enclosure with miniature figures inside. The air heated by the fire is conveyed into a central channel and then into smaller tubes arranged so that their outlets run along the exterior of the enclosure; pressure from the heated air makes them spin around, carrying the figures around with them. The two branches of the manuscript

---

[50] Giorgi, *Spiritali* 80r.      [51] Pappus, *Synagōgē* 8.1116.4–7; Hero, *Mechanica* 2 fr. 1.1–9.
[52] *Pneumatica* 2.3.

tradition distinguished by Schmidt as the "a" and "b" recensions contain different text for this device and are located at different places within the book as a whole.[53] The manuscripts of the "b" branch are identified by Schmidt as a later version compiled by a "pseudo-Hero."[54] Their verbal and visual descriptions of the device are letter-labeled, and the Greek text gives a detailed account of the arrangement of pipes running through the device, how they are mounted on a pivot, and how the rotation works. By contrast, the "a" branch manuscripts do not include letter labels either in the text or the diagram, and the account is briefer, giving a sketchier description of the device's inner workings that focuses more on structure than function.

Giorgi observes in the "annotation" that follows this section that Commandino's text leaves much to the imagination because the manuscript he was able to access at Rome was missing this device entirely, so that he had to consult another. Giorgi was evidently able to find a more satisfying manuscript, so whereas Commandino's text has the sketchier account of the "a" tradition, Giorgi's has the more detailed, letter-labeled account of the "b" tradition. Giorgi also suggests in his annotation that he was able to draw on the more highly developed understanding of devices like this in his own time compared to antiquity. In Giorgi's view, even the humanist philological project of restoring the text to its most pristine condition may profit from technological developments that make the subject matter more widely accessible.

The work of correction Giorgi, Baldi, and others applied to Hero's text recalls Hero's own corrective engagements with his predecessors. As we saw earlier, Hero presents himself as having profited from their authorial and mechanical work, even as he promises to reorganize it to make it more useful and accessible, correcting errors where he finds them in the process. Of course, he also adds his own novel contributions as he goes, and Aleotti follows his lead. The changing technological environment provided opportunities for new pneumatic designs, and indeed Aleotti follows up his translation of Hero's *Pneumatica* with four new "spectacles (*theoremi*)" of his own. The first of these is in fact a reworking of Hero's piece where

[53] The "a" branch includes Marcianus gr. Z 516 (13th century), Gudianus 13 (16th century), and Taurinensis B, V, 20 (from 1541); the "b" branch includes Vat. Barberinianus I 162 (from 1499), Constantinopolitanus 19 (15th century), and Parisinus 2515 (16th century). The versions of this passage of the text may be compared in Schmidt's edition (Hero 1976d: 214–16).

[54] On the possibility that a preliminary version of the *Pneumatica* was composed by Hero and posthumously refined by a "pseudo-Heron" see Drachmann 1948: 79–80, 161–67.

Hercules fires arrows at the dragon guarding the golden apples.[55] In Aleotti's version, Hercules instead strikes the hissing dragon with a club (which it must be said is much closer to Hercules' usual style), at which point the dragon retaliates by spitting water at him.

The mechanism makes use of a conical valve, a device introduced into the pneumatic tradition established by Philo and Hero only after its transmission to the medieval Islamic world; these valves are an innovation characteristic of the Banū Mūsa.[56] Even though Hero's humanist translators privilege the Greek tradition and ignore the medieval Arabic and Latin traditions that came between, the novel technologies developed within those traditions had already percolated into the technical tradition, and they make themselves felt in new devices like Aleotti's updated Hercules tableau. Aleotti's other new *theoremi* blaze a new trail: A figure of Triton rises from the depths of a basin of water to blow a trumpet and then sink down again (in a device that shares some mechanical components with Hero's owl-and-birds tableau); four blacksmiths gather around an anvil to hammer a piece of metal as water droplets fly up to imitate the sparks hurled from a smithy; and finally, a full-sized room is constructed with pipes running below its floors, driving water and compressed air so that those in the room may be refreshed by misty breezes flowing from figures of the winds mounted around the walls. Aleotti's refreshing air-cooled room takes the technology from the miniature to the human scale, becoming a way for pneumatic devices to delight not only the eyes and ears of elites, but their whole bodies.

These devices in particular exploit the sense of haptic possibilities Herder's *Plastik* celebrates as the appropriate sensory modality through which to experience sculpture.[57] As Slaney points out, a viewer need not literally touch a sculpture to invoke a haptic imaginary built on past tactile experiences.[58] Aleotti's detailed descriptions and images of his designs may trigger that same kind of imagination on the reader's part, while a viewer encountering their concrete forms would have a rich multisensory experience offering surprise as well as delight. A viewer who dared to reach over the "smithy" would discover that the jumping "sparks" were cool water droplets rather than burning flakes of metal, while wandering into the "spritz" room would create a frisson of surprise thanks to the near invisibility of the cooling vapor. Aleotti capitalizes on the impression that

[55] *Pneumatica* 1.41.
[56] Hill discusses the distinctive association of the Banū Mūsa with the cone valve at al-Jazarī 1974: 9.
[57] Herder 1889: 282–84.    [58] Slaney 2016: 87–91.

mechanical devices like these have a life of their own – that they are not merely waiting politely to be experienced by a viewer but can actively interfere with their experience, however pleasurably.

Aleotti's playful new devices for elite entertainment reflect the context in which he sought patronage for his work. His translation of the *Pneumatica* is dedicated to the duke Alfonso II d'Este, whom he already served as director of fortifications for the city. The work's preface locates it definitively within an environment controlled by the patron; all the efforts of workmen (*operarii*), he says, must be directed toward serving the patron, since he employs them for their daily wages. Even though Aleotti's post places him in a different milieu from the day laborer, he is still compelled to explain away the time he spent on this less obviously practical project by saying that in 1586 he had fallen ill for several months. The real service his translation performs, he says, is to shape Hero's work into a form suitable for all – accessible even to the "mediocre *ingegno*," but elegant enough to appeal to the duke, the "new Maecenas of the *virtuosi*."[59]

This brief dedicatory text, similarly to Giorgi's translation, is followed by a series of sonnets exchanged between Aleotti and Luigi Zenobi "Anconitano," himself a fixture of the court of Ferrara. Zenobi was an illustrious cornet player and favorite of the Ferrara court, where he arrived in the year Aleotti's translation was printed; indeed, he was the best-paid musician in the court's whole history.[60] Zenobi seems to have set himself the task of using "*spirito*" and its cognates in as many ways as possible in his sonnets (sixteen times in fifteen lines in his first poem, fifteen times in fourteen lines in his second, whereas Aleotti's response to the first includes only three cases). Indeed, his own virtuosity with the cornet must be part of the "*spirito*" joke.

Even if their aesthetic merits are not immediately apparent, however, the sonnets are clearly located in an atmosphere of courtly play and friendly, sophisticated rivalry between courtiers. Each offers elaborate praise of Hero's work to illuminate his artificial *spiritali*, measured mourning for the lost *spirito* of the dead, and a promise to apply their own *spirito* to the work at hand. The three poems narrate a drama over the work itself: First Zenobi applauds Aleotti for making the spirit of the "ancient sage" Hero speak again; then Aleotti demurs, concerned that his talents are an "infertile river" insufficient to the task; finally, Zenobi promises that he is more than equal to the task – that he has not just a river's worth of resources to draw on, but an ocean or a mother lode. The language of

---

[59] Aleotti, *Artifitiosi* 2.     [60] Blackburn and Lowinsky 1993: 63–65.

elements (air especially, but also water, fire in the form of light, and earth in the form of stone) recurs throughout the poems, a reminder of Hero's own motivations in the *Pneumatica* to explore the physics of the elements. Images of artifice using *spirito* to bring the nonliving to life are also threaded throughout the poems.

The poems that introduce Giorgi's and Aleotti's translations of Hero reflect a growing familiarity with pneumatic wonders and automata in elite society. Indeed, Rabelais lists tabletop pneumatic experiments as one of the activities that structured Gargantua's leisurely days with Ponocrates.[61] After some recitation of Virgil and other poetry, they would dine while enjoying a trick (allegedly learned from Cato) whereby wine would be mixed into a basin of water and then recovered again with a funnel. Meanwhile, the water was made to move from glass to glass, and Gargantua and Ponocrates devised "a thousand automata, that is engines moving by themselves." The easy slippage between different subdisciplines of ancient mechanics and the citation of Cato (perhaps the least likely of all Romans to have had an interest in contriving delightful dinnertime entertainments) as their progenitor reshape Hero to fit into the ludic context of pneumatic experimentation in this era.

## Baldi's *Automata* and *Belopoeica*

Bernardino Baldi translated Hero's *Automata* and his *Belopoeica* into Italian and Latin respectively. Authorship and disciplinary history were both strong concerns for the humanistically minded Baldi, who included a *Vita Heronis* in his *Belopoeica* and copious information on the *longue durée* of each discipline in its respective work. To be sure, it was a common practice to preface translations with historical and bibliographic context that establishes both the value of the work itself and the translator's familiarity with the subject matter. But Baldi's prefatory material is extraordinarily detailed and complex, reflecting his deep knowledge of the technical, historical, and bibliographic information pertaining to Hero himself as well as related authors and practitioners both ancient and contemporary. For example, in the bibliographic essay on Hero that follows his translation of the *Belopoeica*, he provides considerable detail on the journey from manuscript to book:

---

[61] Rabelais, *La vie très horrifique du grand Gargantua, père de Pantagruel* 1.24.

> Emmanuel Margounios of Crete, a learned and sober man, while I spent time at Padua for the sake of my studies, handed me the remarkable book on Belopoeica, which I copied in Greek in my own hand (though it was swarming with innumerable errors), and then I rendered it into Latin, which was never attempted by anyone before.[62]

Emmanuel (Maximos) Margounios, who would go on to be appointed bishop of Cythera, was teaching Greek at Padua when Baldi arrived there as a twenty-year-old student.[63] He already possessed the beginnings of what would become a vast collection of books in Greek, many of which he collaborated on having copied and translated. While most of their work together seems to have focused on more canonical texts, it was fortunate that a manuscript of the *Belopoeica* also fell into Baldi's hands. His frank account of the struggle he experienced in copying it out and the pride he takes in being its very first translator into Latin lend color to his lifelong relationship with Hero – from the moment when the *Belopoeica* first came to him as a young man, to the eventual printing of his translation just a year before his death.

In the preface to his *De gli automati*, Baldi emphasizes the disciplinary proximity of automaton-making to mathematics. All kinds of mechanical activities, he argues, involve some blend of mind and hand, which tends more toward the intellect in the case of the stationary automata than it does for pneumatic devices, and more still for the mobile automata. Baldi has some special pleading to do here, since apparently the once well-regarded art of automaton-making has been tainted by vulgar associations. Mercenary hustlers, he says, appropriated the art when they saw the money-making potential of mechanical wonders that crowds so craved to look on they would spare no expense to see them. Automaton-making has since been tinged with their *bruttura* and the title of "mechanic" applied indiscriminately to the untutored man who sets the device in motion as well as to its designer, as "architect" is sometimes vulgarly used to refer to a builder.[64] Baldi aims to correct all this, and Hero will provide an ideal vehicle for doing so.

Baldi picks up the thread of architecture again in the preface to his 1616 translation of Hero's *Belopoeica*:

> The fields of architecture are very rich with an abundance of the most beautiful things. Hence it is much to be mourned that in this unlucky age

---

[62] Baldi, *Belopoeica* 73.
[63] On Margounios and his contributions to reviving Greek literature see Ciccolella 2020.
[64] Baldi, *De gli automati*, 1589 edition, pp. 10–11.

of ours, they are very few who entirely devote the useful (indeed necessary) work to their cultivation. Whether this is on account of some failing of the age, or because of some other reason, I could not judge. Certainly I am not unaware of this: the useful arts are nurtured and propagated with honors and rewards, while many of the greatest intellects everywhere perish through the great avarice or neglect of men.[65]

Here, too, architecture appears as a technical discipline that has lost some of its luster. Baldi cites his youthful "fierce love" for the arts that others risk neglecting, still burning even now that his worldly responsibilities have grown. In the course of his lucubrations, he says, he returned to Hero's *Belopoeica*. The reasons for neglecting the design of catapults in Baldi's time were obvious: Cannon warfare had already become common enough that new principles of fortification had to be devised against artillery.[66] Baldi uses the classical term *tormenta* for these devices, but he asks rhetorically whether they might better be called "monsters (*monstra*)" or "thunderbolts (*fulmina*)." Rendered obsolete by the proliferation of these new weapons, ancient works on catapults were not merely neglected, but "forbidden from fire and water," in the traditional Roman formula for exile Baldi resurrects. Baldi sets himself the task of recovering them from their exile, since "no one in their right mind would deny that these ancient things are incitements to great ideas for modern minds (*neotericis ingeniis*) – or at least they could be."[67] He entreats his addressee, the bishop of Bagnorea Laelio Ruino, to devote any free time he finds to reading the *Belopoeica*: He may not find utility through it, but "certainly a noble pleasure, and one not unworthy of a free man."[68]

Hero's *Automata* turns out to be an even stronger flashpoint for questions about how nobility, utility, and wonder play out in the discipline of mechanics. Like their ancient predecessors, automata in the 16th and 17th centuries were sometimes featured as elaborate entertainments at dinners and other courtly occasions calling for a ludic sense of wonder. Baldi's translation of Hero's *Automata* is prefaced by a brief history of recently devised mechanical marvels: His contemporaries and recent predecessors have produced animal automata, singing birds, geared clocks, and pressurized fountains, all to inspire wonder in their spectators. Baldi openly admires many of the automata of his own time, from moving figurines

[65] Baldi, *Belopoeica* i.     [66] On these developments see Biagioli 1989: 44–46.
[67] Baldi, *Belopoeica* ii.     [68] For a different reading of this passage see Laird 2017: 163.

to playful fountains to models of the cosmos, which "cede nothing to the ancients."[69]

Some of the animal automata Baldi cites were majestically large, like an eagle designed by artisans at Nuremberg so that when the Emperor arrived at the city, the eagle first flew to him and then turned around to accompany him as he entered the gates. Others were comically small, like a mechanical fly designed to be released from the hand at a dinner party, to fly around among the guests, and then (like the eagle) to return "as though weary" to its point of release. Later he cites an animal automaton perhaps more welcome at the dinner table than the artificial fly: the silver tortoise designed by Bartolomeo Campi da Pesaro. This tortoise, with mobile legs, tail, and head, was made to walk along the table until it reached the center, at which point it would open up its shell to reveal toothpicks to which the guests might help themselves.[70]

From here Baldi goes on to cite machines made for more practical uses, such as the attempt to dredge up the shipwrecked "Venice galleon" from the bottom of the sea. While evidently unsuccessful in its aims, this salvage effort is at least credited with demonstrating its inventor's understanding of how to raise great weights through mechanical means. For the classically minded Baldi, any mention of heroic efforts to drag ships around by machines must summon up the memory of Archimedes, who famously served his own ruler by creating a mechanical device to move a fantastically heavy ship nearly effortlessly.[71] Indeed, Baldi immediately brings up Archimedes' creation of defensive siege engines to defend his city as it was besieged by Rome. This resonates with Baldi's invocation of Archimedes as the creator of astronomical automata at the beginning of his preface, where he even offers a translation of Claudian's 4th-century poem on Archimedes' achievement.[72]

Baldi extends the Archimedean thread by reminding readers that devices like the *sphaera* most famously attributed in antiquity to Archimedes are still in production:

> And as to spheres similar to that of Archimedes, Peter Ramus writes of having seen two in Paris, one in the house of [Giovanni] Ruellio the

---

[69] Baldi, *De gli automati* 8r. For further consideration of Baldi's engagement with the classical past of these machines see Roby 2021: 116–21.

[70] For the tortoise and other celebrated automata at the Urbino court see Marr 2011: 32–34. On the links Baldi forges between ancient and contemporary automata see Gamba 2005: 343–44.

[71] Athenaeus, *Deipnosophistai* 5.40.1–38 (206d–207b); Jaeger 2008: 102–05.

[72] Baldi, *De gli automati* 7r–7v. On Claudian's poem (*Minora* 51) see Jaeger 2008: 123–27; Roby 2016a: 14, 21.

physician, brought from the sack of Sicily, the other of Orontius the royal mathematician, won in the German wars.[73]

The paired *sphaerae* here deliberately echo the pair that Cicero mentions in his *De re publica*, one of which was made by Archimedes and looted from Sicily when it was sacked by the Roman army under the general Marcellus.[74] Archimedes' name here marks the Syracusan's perennial significance as a bridge between contemplation and action, the mathematically abstract and the mechanically concrete. While others might echo Plutarch's characterization of Archimedes as a kind of Platonist, a mathematician who dabbled in mechanics only out of civic duty, Baldi here keeps the focus squarely on the mechanics of his wondrous celestial model.[75] The other *sphaera* in Cicero's example, however, was a solid celestial map like the so-called sphere of Eudoxus, not a mechanical marvel at all.

Baldi locates himself in a world where mechanical orreries are more plentiful than in antiquity, where discoveries by the likes of Archimedes are the foundation for later elaborations. The more recent *sphaerae* mentioned here are associated with figures who, like Baldi himself, combine polymathic scholarship with high social status. Giovanni Ruellio was a physician known for his Latin translations of Dioscorides' *De materia medica* (1550) and the Greek *Hippiatrica* (1530), and Oronce Finé enjoyed the position of Chair of Mathematics at the Collège Royal. Urbino would furnish *sphaerae* of its own in later years, notably the silver armillary sphere commissioned by the Urbinate Mutio Oddi for Cardinal Federico Borromeo in the 1620s, which Borromeo intended to serve as a model for a room-sized wooden sphere he wished to have built next to the Biblioteca Ambrosiana.[76]

Baldi then moves on from astronomical models to clocks, another means of tracking the movements of celestial bodies.[77] Clocks that depended upon interlocking toothed gears rather than the systems of floats attached to rack-and-pinion systems that drove ancient water clocks represented a significant improvement in the convenience and compactness of clocks in Baldi's time, and far enough before him that he says he cannot find any written record of when these were devised. He cites as a possible

---

[73] Baldi, *De gli automati* 8r.

[74] Cicero, *De re publica* 1.21–22. On this passage and the *sphaera* in Archimedes' afterlife see Jaeger 2008: 48–72.

[75] On Archimedes' positioning at Urbino astride the boundary between mathematics and mechanics see Frank 2016; Henninger-Voss 2000; Wolfe 2004: 50–54.

[76] Marr 2011: 160–66.          [77] On Baldi's own interest in horology see Gamba 2005: 344–46.

starting point a clock "ordered by Charlemagne from the king of Persia, made with miraculous art; this one distinguished the hours with a pointer, and signaled them with a song."[78]

The book on water clocks that Hero alludes to in the preface of the *Pneumatica* is lost, but Baldi is certainly correct that time-telling technologies in particular had advanced considerably since antiquity. It is true that Vitruvius describes some sophisticated water clocks, attributed originally to Ctesibius, which added moving figures, sounding trumpets, and other features to their time-tracking effects.[79] Noble and Price have suggested that comparable mechanisms might have been put on display on a monumental scale in the Tower of the Winds at Athens, on the basis of surviving structures that could have served as the basins whose steady drainage powers a water clock.[80] But great progress would be made in water clocks over the next few centuries, owing much to the development of the conical valve mentioned above as a key component in one of Aleotti's additional *theoremi*. This mechanism appears in a crude form in a treatise on water clocks attributed to Archimedes that survives in Arabic and is refined in later Arabic works like the Banū Mūsa's *Book of Ingenious Devices*, finally being perfected into the true conical valve (whose components are made to fit snugly together by being ground together with emery) in Ismāʿīl ibn al-Razzāz al-Jazarī's 12th-century *Book of Knowledge of Ingenious Mechanical Devices*.[81] Mechanical clocks of great precision were in turn developed thanks to crucial technologies like the verge-and-foliot escapement, making it possible to build clocks that combined precise time-telling with other features like moving figures and noisemakers in a very compact space.[82]

But despite the technical achievements in automata since antiquity, something has gone wrong with their cultural position:

> Nevertheless it appears that among the people they have lost in part their natural splendor, after they began to be mishandled by impostors, jugglers, hustlers, and other vile and mercenary people. The result is that the word "mechanic," which to Greek ears resonated with the honored title of "inventor and fabricator of machines," to people of this time (especially Italians) signifies nothing other than a vile, low, vulgar, and sordid mercenary. . . . So calling those who work mechanical devices "mechanics" has propagated the name of the brutishness which it carries today.[83]

---

[78] Baldi, *De gli automati* 8r. On this clock, given by Harun al-Rashid to Charlemagne, and its mechanical context see Truitt 2015: 20–21.

[79] Vitruvius, *De architectura* 9.8.     [80] Noble and Price 1968.     [81] al-Jazarī 1974: 10.

[82] On these mechanisms see Truitt 2015: 141–47.     [83] Baldi, *De gli automati* 11r.

Micheli observes that Baldi's description of the nobility of machines in antiquity seems to presuppose a conceptual continuity between the design and operation of ancient automata that has been lost in his own time.[84] While Baldi veils the nature of the automata of which he disapproves in silence, he might be thinking of the animal automata that had enjoyed popularity in Europe for several centuries at this point. While as we have seen he does not disparage representations of animals in principle, some emphasized hilarity over nobility in a way he may have disapproved. These ranged from the 14th-century mechanical monkeys (covered in badger skin for authenticity and requiring annual repairs) that delighted the court at the French castle of Hesdin to a rabbit designed by Giovanni Fontana in the 15th century to be propelled forward by a jet of flames emitted from its rear end.[85] Baldi might alternatively have been thinking of installations designed to spray visitors with water from below or puff flour into their faces, somewhat less dignified variants of Aleotti's "spritz" room. Whatever his particular objections, Baldi believes that automata can do better.[86]

Baldi's disparaging reference to jugglers may represent a glimpse of the courtly reality underlying his disapproval, as Castiglione's *Book of the Courtier* specifically discourages the would-be courtier from engaging in acrobatics like a juggler to make an impression, though other athletic activities like swimming, jumping, and hurling stones are suitable, since they correspond to skills useful in war.[87] Like Baldi, Castiglione identifies a right and a wrong way to supply the court with the novel spectacles it craves; like the courtiers' physical contests, automata demand a delicate balance between the novel and the canonical, the practical and the spectacular. Indeed, Wolfe observes that the complex courtly rules for appropriate human physical activity made both automata and trained animals appealing spectacles at court.[88] Baldi's judgment also echoes some aspects of the discourse on mechanics of his fellow Urbinate Guidobaldo dal Monte (himself part of a newly noble family): As Henninger-Voss puts it, "Aristotle had projected an intellectual hierarchy onto a social one, and so did the intellectual nobleman Guidobaldo."[89] But still, Guidobaldo himself worked closely with laborers and craftsmen, and the preface to

---

[84] Micheli 2005: 262–64.
[85] On the automata of Hesdin see Truitt 2015: 122–37. On Giovanni Fontana's creations see Grafton 2007.
[86] For an assessment of the success Baldi had in exciting a new tradition of automata based in classical antiquity in the short and the long term see Prou 1884: 121–23.
[87] Castiglione, *Il libro del cortegiano* 36.      [88] Wolfe 2004: 32–33.
[89] Henninger-Voss 2000: 245.

Filippo Pigafetta's 1581 Italian translation of Guidobaldo's *Liber mechanicorum* emphasizes both the nobility of mechanics and its utility.[90]

The balance between the courtly and the vulgar, the practical and the provocative, is related to the balance between the material and the mathematical. Baldi never denies or disparages the materiality of automata, whether ancient or modern. Even his initial definition of automata focuses on their materiality, emphasizing function over form:

> Automata are composed of counterweights, cords, wheels, spindles, pulleys, drums, reels, and other such things. Their material can draw on pneumatics and use the stuff of which vessels tend to be made, such as clay, glass, tin, copper, steel, and other similar materials. As for the mobile ones: wood, iron, lead, and flax, and other useful and available materials.[91]

While some automata may be made from high-status materials, like the silver fly and tortoise, Baldi celebrates the humbler materials at the very core of what constitutes an automaton.

Baldi's further discourse on what automata should and should not do likewise suggests something more complex than an exclusionary, elitist attitude toward automata as the proper possession of courtly society. The *bruttura* that now afflicts the reputation of automata may emerge from their popularity with ignorant crowds, but that very abuse of automata is a symptom of a larger cultural problem: This did not happen, says Baldi, "when their designers were treated as great philosophers." If automata were treated properly as the products of *ingegno*, he argues, the viewer would be impelled to contemplate the mathematical, physical, and ultimately philosophical principles behind their operation, rather than merely gawking at an entertaining spectacle. Baldi dreams, indeed, that performances by automata and texts like his own could reshape their audiences, reconnecting them to an imagined classical past in which the sight of an automaton sparked philosophical wonder and a more purely intellectual response than he posits most contemporary viewers have been trained in.

Baldi's sentiment is echoed a few years later in his fellow Urbinate Alessandro Giorgi's translation of Hero's *Pneumatica*. Giorgi argues that "the mechanic dresses himself as in the garb of the natural [philosopher]" when he contemplates the qualities of matter in motion and at rest, and that "at the same time he does not forget he is a mathematician" when he considers proportion, size, distance, and the causes of mechanical effects.[92] The "hustlers" Baldi attacks wear garb quite unlike the natural

---

[90] Henninger-Voss 2000: 246.      [91] Baldi, *De gli automati* 9r.      [92] Giorgi, *Spiritali* 3v–4r.

philosopher's, and they have certainly forgotten the roots of their discipline in mathematics. But mechanics is presented here as a liminal space between nature and artifice, philosophy and profit, and it can be shifted over to what Baldi sees as the proper side of the threshold by practitioners who approach the discipline in the correct frame of mind.

Baldi's reflections on the relationship between the mathematical and the material recur in the *Vita Heronis* appended to his translation of the *Belopoeica*. He praises Hero for his mechanical inventiveness, saying that indeed his acumen should come as no surprise, since he did not neglect his mathematical studies on the way to mechanics, "as indeed many today do, who though their fundamentals are lacking nevertheless arrogantly approach this edifice."[93] He cites Pappus (in Commandino's translation) on the bifurcation of mechanics, according to the "mechanicians associated with Hero," into logic and craftwork, as seen in the previous chapter. Baldi uses Pappus' thoughts on the dual nature of mechanics as a springboard to praise Hero's more mathematical works like the *Definitiones*, as well as his work in theoretical mechanics. The latter he praises particularly for the elegant simplicity with which Hero, "with Archimedean subtlety and skill," reduces the actions of all the simple machines down to a single common principle.[94]

Marr claims that the association Baldi draws between mathematics and mechanics in his translation of the *Automata* is a novel "encroach[ment] on territory traditionally separate from mathematics" and a result "of the increasing application of mathematics to natural philosophy in the early modern period."[95] It would be fairer to say that Baldi is part of a tradition extending back at least to Archimedes of bringing mathematical principles to bear on those aspects of mechanics that lend themselves to such treatment. Neither Hero nor Baldi tries to force the whole automaton into a mathematical mold in order to secure the high status of mathematics for their discipline. Instead, they draw out certain aspects of these complicated devices that can best be analyzed mathematically, productively juxtaposing them with other attributes better suited to a materials-oriented analysis. The parts of the artifact that lend themselves to mathematical analysis may be privileged, as the rigor and precision of mathematical reasoning has been privileged since antiquity, but they are not presented in isolation from their richly material substrate.

The disciplinary jockeying in Baldi's time between mechanics, mathematics, and philosophy tested the values associated with theory and utility,

---

[93] Baldi, *Belopoeica* 67.    [94] Baldi, *Belopoeica* 70.    [95] Marr 2006: 156.

materiality and abstraction, rarefaction and popular appeal. Baldi quotes Girolamo Cardano as saying of Hero's pneumatic works that they are undeniably "ingenious and pleasurable, but they are short on convenience and utility to offer to human uses."[96] Baldi critiques Cardano's view of what constitutes utility as unnecessarily restrictive:

> Whoever says and believes these are useless is both incorrect and perverse, for they serve a noble pleasure, and have the power to refresh and elevate a spirit wearied with the weight of cares with a sweet and innocuous delight. Who denies, except out of arrogance and obstinacy, that the "gourds," lamps, siphons, clocks, and the six hundred other instruments of this kind everywhere bring a great utility and convenience to human needs for everyday use?[97]

The revisions Baldi hopes to make to the cultural role of pneumatic wonders and automata would elevate them beyond being thought of as mere toys and efface the simplistic opposition between "useful" and "wondrous" to focus on the real benefits of experiencing wonder. Hero's pneumatic delights elaborate on more workaday solutions to practical needs like producing light or moving fluids from one place to another; beyond this, they inspire a kind of philosophical contemplation and delight that is a useful end in itself. In order to experience the psychological work they can do, one must simply approach them with a properly honed understanding of their full cultural context.

Even more than the devices in the *Pneumatica*, the theatrical automaton's primary purpose is to create a spectacle that will carry some cultural significance for its audience. Hero positions his choice of the *Nauplius* as part of the development of automata from their primitive past as a mere mask with blinking eyes to a present day where engineers have enhanced both the elegance and the variety of their creations.[98] For Baldi, too, the *Nauplius* engages questions about the automaton's cultural role.[99] He argues that his translation is meant not only to be enjoyed by readers already familiar with antiquity, but also for craftsmen who may not know ancient literature well. Hence he will provide some additional details on the stories the automata refer to, "since he who has first been well informed

---

[96] Baldi, *Belopoeica* 73. On Cardano's use of Valla and Hero see Laird 2017: 156–57.
[97] Baldi, *Belopoeica* 73.
[98] *Automata* 22.2–3. On the relationship between Sophocles' lost *Nauplius* and the play described by Hero see Marshall 2003.
[99] These questions, and Baldi's response, are considered further at Roby 2021: 127–30.

about the nature of the story will much better understand the power of the arrangement."[100]

Baldi's concern for the comprehensibility of his own work elicits questions about how automata like Hero's were understood more broadly, both through the lens of texts like Baldi's and directly in performance. Different groups of readers or spectators could of course perceive the automaton, as a compound of technical and cultural elements, in very different ways. Foster critiques the tendency of scholars in classical reception to conceive of "single, stable and unitary readers or viewers," when even a single audience member might experience a performance from different perspectives as they "try out different selves."[101] To be sure, theatrical performances (even by automata) involve an element of spectacle that may be appreciated in a general sense even by an audience that does not recognize all the nuances of their story. At the same time, though an "in-group" and an "out-group" may both enjoy the show, Foster observes that their experiences will differ depending on their expectations and "cognitive context."[102] Yet the experience of the performance itself will change that cognitive context, a "circularity" Foster praises as having the potential to draw in new enthusiasts and gradually turn them into experts.[103]

Davies identifies the anxieties felt by 19th-century British spectators of plays and burlesques featuring classical themes, which could be amplified by newspaper reviews that scoffed at the ignorance of the audience or departures from the classical tradition in the performance itself.[104] Spectacles like the 1854 *Siege of Troy, or, the Giant Horse and the Miss-Judgment of Paris* might not have demanded a classical education to be enjoyed, but some background knowledge would have been necessary to understand the story – and, more importantly, to get the jokes. Davies notes that spectators could draw that knowledge not only from reading the classics themselves, but from summaries in penny magazines and other popular written sources. While Baldi's hefty text, expensively illustrated with engravings, would not have been nearly so broadly available, he does seem to subscribe to the idea that a text can play the role of cultural

---

[100] Baldi, *De gli automati*, 14v.     [101] Foster 2020: 43.     [102] Foster 2020: 41.
[103] Foster 2020: 51. Foster here cites Benjamin Jowett and others as seeing performances of classical drama in its rigor and difficulty "as a way to signal that theater could be respectable, and education should be for all." On the other hand, Martindale critiques the "banality" of current classical reception scholarship based on films that are not "important works of art nor complexly interesting," a category to which it seems Hero's automaton theater might likely be relegated: Martindale 2013: 176.
[104] Davies 2018: 170–94.

translator to make a performance more accessible. To this end, he includes summaries of the stories behind both of Hero's recommended automaton narratives.

The mobile automaton is perhaps still comprehensible to modern audiences, as Baldi optimistically hopes that "there is just about no one so vulgar that he does not know" the basic facts about Bacchus, his symbols, and the stories about his worshippers. Even so, Baldi proceeds to fill in the necessary background, in service of his goal of making the automaton's appeal clear to a broad readership including craftsmen. In particular, he needs to explain the presence of a figure of Victory on the shrine in which the god is housed, which he believes might confuse some viewers. Baldi thus introduces the reader to stories that cast Dionysus as a conqueror in Egypt and India rather than the instigator of wine-soaked reveries. Baldi chooses to focus on the god's exploits in India, drawing on Diodorus Siculus, who says that wise men among the Indians tell the story that Dionysus marched through India with an army but concluded his conquest by sharing his knowledge of wine-making with them. The Victory celebrated by Baldi, then, maintains the celebratory sympotic associations of the automaton even while it alludes to Dionysus' military career.[105]

The stationary automaton, by contrast, features the rather recherché tale of Nauplius, which might be unknown even to an educated audience. As we saw earlier, Hero's narration of the automaton's performance is primarily devoted to its mechanical details, and he provides only a brief description of each scene of the play.[106] Baldi, by contrast, makes special mention of the obscurity of the story and chooses to supplement Hero's brief explanation of the action with the deeper background of the tale, drawn largely from Pausanias.[107] Nauplius, the son of Neptune and Amymone and king of Euboea, fathered Palamedes, who, as Baldi notes, became an enemy of Ulysses when he uncovered the latter's pretense of madness and when he succeeded in supplying the army with grain after Ulysses had failed to do so. This background context, while interesting, is not really necessary to understand the simple story enacted by the automaton as Hero tells it. But Baldi elegantly brings Ulysses into closer contact with Hero's automaton, presenting him as "machinating" against Palamedes by forging letters from Priam to make him appear a traitor, as a result of which Palamedes was put to death.[108]

---

[105] Diodorus Siculus, *Bibliotheca historica* 2.38.3–5.    [106] *Automata* 22.3–6.
[107] Baldi, *De gli automati* 15r–16v.    [108] Baldi, *De gli automati* 15v.

Baldi then accelerates his story, quickly approaching the part of it told by the automaton: Nauplius, angry about the trick Ulysses had carried out, went home after the war with the rest of the fleet, and in his vengeful fury led them to shipwreck. Near a rocky island called Caphareus, Nauplius raised some lights that the sailors interpreted as lighthouses, and upon steering for them they were wrecked on the rocks, a scene that features prominently in the automaton's version of the story. Baldi then moves on to the final, climactic scene mentioned by Hero, where Ajax appears swimming in the water and Athena strikes him with lightning. Unlike Hero, Baldi pauses to remind his reader why this scene is important, backtracking once again to tell the story of the two Ajaxes: The lesser Ajax assaulted Cassandra while she sought refuge in Athena's temple (though Baldi identifies her as a priestess of Athena rather than Apollo) and Athena struck him down in vengeance.

Baldi closes his narration of the play, and the preface as a whole, by quoting Virgil's version of the story. His decision to end with this most elevated of Latin authors provokes some questions about what "reception" means for less canonical authors like Hero. In his relative obscurity (itself amplified by decisions like Komtino's to efface Hero from the inherited written record) and his technical focus, Hero might seem an uneasy fit for the humanist project of reviving the canonical works of Greece and Rome. In a sense, Baldi uses Virgil as a kind of Trojan horse to smuggle Hero's work into the esteem of a readership accustomed to a particular image of classical literature. This strategy harmonizes with contemporary approaches like Commandino's placement of Hero alongside Euclid, Pappus, and Archimedes as a part of a mathematical–mechanical canon and the poetic prefaces into which Giorgi and Aleotti weave the themes of his *Pneumatica*. It capitalizes as well on the growing enthusiasm at Urbino for the kind of theatrical design that would be popularized by the theatrical engineer Nicola Sabbattini. His designs for the Urbino court's theater and the Teatro del Sole in nearby Pesaro reflect the combined interest in both mathematical perspective and spectacular special effects he explores in his *Pratica di Fabricar Scene, e Machine ne' Teatri.*

In Baldi's formulation, Hero's automaton serves not merely to amuse crowds with a puppet play, but to embody the figures of classical literature using a medium that is itself intellectually stimulating. Baldi emphasizes that while the pleasure of watching the automaton may derive from the senses, it is nonetheless noble:

> In sum, it is not itself directed at gain, but only at a pleasure that among those of the senses, is pure and honorable, like that of music, and

contributes no less to the recreation of the intellect. A sign of this is that we see that while the figurines are moving, the men who watch them sit as though immobilized, as the figurines of the spectacle should by nature stand. In my opinion, it is no small indication of the application of the soul to see a man immobile, and as it were hanging upon the thing to which he has applied himself. Such is the nature of these machines.[109]

The alchemy of the automaton exchanges the bodily regimes of spectator and spectacle – figurines made of inanimate matter move freely, while the living viewer is frozen still with wonder, spirit completely invested in the machine's work. The bodily stillness enabled by the automaton plays with the rhetoric of bodily control emphasized in Castiglione's *Book of the Courtier*. Wolfe observes the emergence in that work of "anxieties about the instrumental nature of those courtly practices which demand the regulation of natural impulses by artificial means," which manifest aporetically in the dialogue.[110] The immobility derived from the automaton, by contrast, comes not by princely fiat but from the spectator's own wonder.

Moreover, the power of performance is such that the experience of being transfixed by the automaton is available not only to elite viewers who would be more familiar with that milieu of courtly control, but also to the broader audience including craftsmen that Baldi aims to welcome into appreciation of ancient automata. Even if some details of the (lost) classical text were lost on such a viewer, they can still be gripped by the automaton's transformative power. Baldi thus transforms Hero's automata for a new readership, not only by translating the work into Italian and making its stories comprehensible for his contemporaries, but by giving the automaton itself a new social purpose.

The "circularity" Foster sees in the capacity performances of classical drama have to gradually transform the expectations and "cognitive context" of the audience is another reminder that "reception" is a two-way street, perhaps better viewed through the lenses of "transformation" and "allelopoiesis" discussed earlier. Each viewing of an ancient drama transforms the viewer's notion of what "ancient drama" could be, and an elaborate mechanical performance of a lesser-known story from antiquity would bring about a radically transformative expansion of an audience's expectations about ancient literature and technology alike. Even as Baldi transforms Hero by linking him to more canonical areas of classical literature, those very links reconfigure the notion of the "classical" available to Baldi's reader. References to Virgil and other canonical classical authors

---

[109] Baldi, *De gli automati* 11v–12r.    [110] Wolfe 2004: 33–34.

might lend the material more immediate appeal to a humanistic reader, but at the same time Baldi's impassioned defense of the power of material artifacts to refine the intellect could dramatically shift that reader's expectations of classicized nobility. For a reader imbued with *sententia* from classical authors like Plato, Xenophon, or Seneca critiquing manual work and other engagements with the material, Baldi's notion that those very engagements could elevate the intellect and spirit would represent a radically transformative view.

## Visual Traditions

New contexts for designing and deploying artifacts inspired by Hero's work were accompanied in this period by radical changes in the technologies of book production and systems for their distribution. By the late 15th century, manuscripts began to be widely supplanted by printed works, a technological shift that ultimately made reproducing books cheaper and more highly scalable.[111] Not only the verbal text of a work but also its images became readily reproducible, as woodcut blocks made the transition from printing designs on textiles to printing on paper. The rise of paper mills in Europe in the 13th and 14th centuries gradually made printing on paper an affordable business, and while the earliest generations of printed books were usually without images, by the 1490s printed books with woodcut images began to appear, notably the magnificent Nuremberg *Weltchronik* in 1493. The 16th and 17th centuries saw the rise of intaglio printing techniques like engraving and etching, which were more difficult to make and integrate into books than woodcuts but could incorporate more detail into the images.[112]

The advent of the printed book did not itself effect any immediate radical change in the Heronian tradition, particularly given that the first few generations of printed works in the late 15th and early 16th centuries drew deliberately on the design and ornament of manuscripts. The Venetian humanist Giorgio Valla collected a variety of Greek mathematical and scientific manuscripts, including copies of Hero's *Pneumatica* and the Heronian *De mensuris*.[113] His 1501 *De expetendis et fugiendis rebus*

---

[111] The *locus classicus* for the reproducibility of early printed media is Eisenstein 1979. But Johns 1998 offers some important correctives, showing that in fact printed media admitted of a great deal of potential variation, particularly before the rise of modern copyright.

[112] On the historical practices relating to the production of printed images in woodcut, engraving, and etching see Griffiths 1996.

[113] Laird 2017: 153–54; Rose 1975: 32–35, 47.

covered a dazzling array of topics in its forty-nine books; while Rose observes that "mathematics holds pride of place" in the work, Valla collects material on subjects that range well beyond the mathematical.[114] He proceeds from arithmetic, harmonics, and geometry to astronomy and astrology, and then to medical matters including medical applications of astrology, mineral medicines, the substances of human and animal bodies, and the symptoms of and therapies for various ailments. From there he shifts briefly to rhetoric and moral philosophy before returning to the sphere of medicine to discuss the medicinal properties of foods and wines, which provide a natural segue to agricultural practices, and from there to military practices. In the last few books he discusses the soul and medical diagnostic techniques including examination of the pulse and of urine, and finally he closes with a book covering fate, fortune, and friendship.

Hero thus plays a quite localized role within Valla's sprawling work, as Valla draws Hero into his ambit in a very different way from the translators. Valla's material on pneumatics is confined to a single book, which also includes material on catoptrics and optics.[115] But within this book, Hero's influence is unmissable: Valla proceeds through familiar devices like siphons, following Hero's explanations in detail, to some of the most prominent devices of the *Pneumatica*. The water organ is here, as is the aeolipile, the "spring" that models the hydrological cycle, and the singing thyrsus that comes between them in Hero's text.

Hero's influence is obvious not only in the text itself, but also in the illustrations, which closely match the diagrams featured in the earliest manuscripts of Hero's *Pneumatica*. Valla's images readily adopt the iconography familiar from the manuscript tradition: Pneumatic vessels are shown in cutaway view from the side, vessel walls and pipes alike rendered with parallel lines, cords linking to counterweights as sinusoidal lines, and the counterweights themselves as trapezoids. Compare, for example, Valla's image of the design for a mechanism to make temple doors open when an altar fire is lit and shut again when it is extinguished (Figure 5.2) to the earliest surviving manuscript of the *Pneumatica*, dating to the late 13th or early 14th century (Figure 5.3).[116]

The woodcut illustrations for Valla's text do lose the informational dimension of color used in many manuscript images to demarcate different subsystems of a device or different liquids (usually rendered as stacked rows

---

[114] Rose 1975: 49.     [115] Valla, *De expetendis et fugiendis rebus* 15.
[116] On the manuscripts of ancient mathematical and scientific texts to which Valla had access see Rose 1975: 35, 46–49.

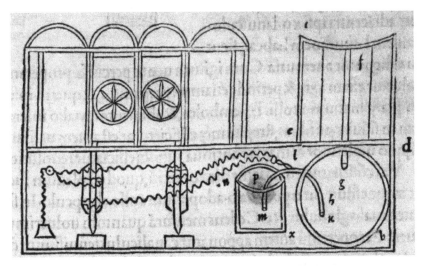

Figure 5.2 Device to open temple doors illustrated in Giorgio Valla, *De rebus expetendis et fugiendis*, 15.1. Image courtesy of Bayerische Staatsbibliothek München.

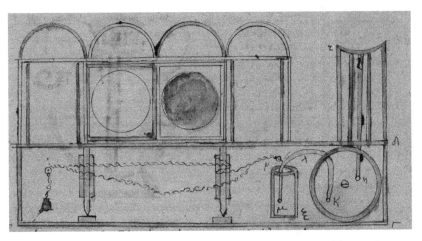

Figure 5.3 Temple-door device illustrated in Marcianus Gr. Z 516, fol. 181v. Image courtesy of Biblioteca Nazionale Marciana.

of small circles); perhaps it is for this reason that Valla's vessels are shown empty of liquids. Overall, however, the images in this book maintain a strong continuity with the manuscript tradition, from their visual style to their positioning inset with the text. Nor should this come as a surprise;

particularly in this early era, printed books adopted many attributes from the manuscript codices that were not merely their ancestors but continued to be produced alongside them for centuries.

Maintaining continuity with the visual tradition transmitted in the manuscripts was not the result of technological stagnation. Indeed, many visual forms that were readily transmitted by hand turned out to present challenges to designers of woodcuts. The Latin translation of Euclid printed in Venice by Erhard Ratdolt in 1482, for example, included diagrams printed using a novel relief technique that Ratdolt tantalizingly alludes to but declines to explain. Baldasso argues that he likely used bent strips of metal inset in a block to render the delicate forms of the geometrical objects.[117] Novel though his scheme for integrating the printing block with the metal strips may have been, however, the resulting diagrams are marred by gaps and interruptions in the lines and arcs. By the 16th century, diagrams of geometrical, mechanical, and architectural constructions were being rendered precisely and accurately in woodcuts and engravings. The ability to transmit these technical images in bulk, with negligible variation, profoundly altered the possibilities for propagating and circulating technical knowledge.

Commandino's 1575 translation of the *Pneumatica* reflects developments in visual style that still remain entrenched in the most recent Teubner edition. In its woodcut images, water is more often represented by fine wavy lines than by stacked circles, three-dimensional objects are shown from a single point of perspective enhanced by crosshatched shadows, and the "physics demonstration" pneumatic vessels as well as the "performance" pieces include some decorative touches. Dotted lines are not used here to represent an object obscured by another; the task of understanding the relative depths of objects is left up to the viewer, as it had been in the cutaway views of the manuscript images.

Aleotti's translation of Commandino's Latin into Italian was first printed at Ferrara in 1589, its images translated into a new idiom along with the text. Though the images in Commandino's version bear some decorative notes, they maintain a stylistic simplicity that allows the viewer to focus on their pneumatic and hydraulic components. The devices as represented in Aleotti's images are much more elaborate: The decorative elements of the vessels and performance pieces have flourished, producing

---

[117] Baldasso 2009: 67. On special copies of Ratdolt's edition of the *Elements* featuring gold lettering on blue paper, as well as blue paper copies of Commandino's commentary on Euclid, see Anderson 2020.

dragons and convoluted scrollwork where once there were simple handles, encrusting formerly plain vessel walls with fantastical beasts, and so on. The shift is not radical – clearly the images in Aleotti's version draw their basic structure from Commandino's – but it is pervasive.

The most consequential difference between the two is that Aleotti's images leave little "white space" in the image compared to Commandino's, particularly in the sections representing the interiors of vessels. Both versions of the "dancing figures" device, for example, use a shaded area to communicate depth and perspective. In Commandino's 1575 version, that shaded area is outside the vessel, leaving the figures inside it surrounded by plenty of white space (Figure 5.4).

In Aleotti's 1589 edition, the shadowed area has been moved inside the vessel, where it suggests the depth and curvature of the vessel more strongly than in Commandino's version, but it crowds the interior scene, demanding more attention from the reader to parse the figures within and the mechanisms of their rotating stage (Figure 5.5).

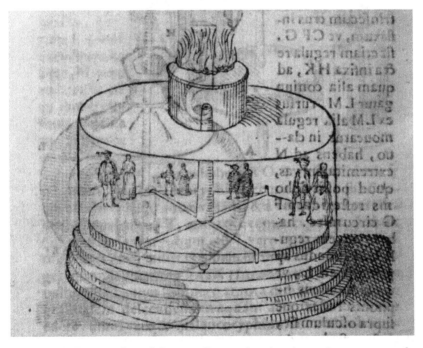

Figure 5.4   "Dancing figures" device in Commandino (1575), 71v. Image courtesy of Bayerische Staatsbibliothek München.

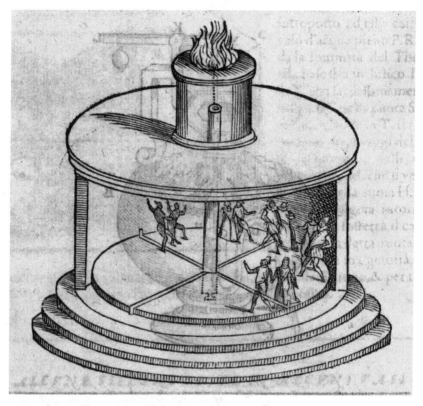

Figure 5.5   "Dancing figures" device in Aleotti, p. 76. Image courtesy of Bayerische
Staatsbibliothek München.

In the 1680 edition including Commandino and the Latinized Aleotti, the images have reverted to Commandino's style. The woodcuts have been most faithfully reproduced except for the obvious difference that they are reversed left to right, suggesting their printing blocks were copied from a printed exemplar. Only in the smallest of details, such as the specific pattern of water waves within a vessel, are the differences readily detectable.

As the reversion to Commandino's images in the 1680 edition suggests, it would be a mistake to think that the shift in style between Commandino's and Aleotti's images marked a monotonic transition from simple hand-drawn manuscript images to increasingly elaborate presentations in printed books. Alessandro Giorgi's Italian translation, which followed so closely on the heels of Aleotti's, uses Commandino's images; the woodblocks were either reused or very skillfully copied. Like

Commandino's, Giorgi's work was published in Urbino. While it might be tempting to argue that the woodblocks were simply conveniently available to the printers in Urbino, there is a larger question of visual rhetoric at stake. The abundant white space of Commandino's images is not localized to the *Pneumatica*; his *Archimedis Opera Nonnulla*, for example, allows its delicate woodcut diagrams to occupy vast amounts of space on the page, as does his *Elements* commentary.[118] The "light" and "splendor" associated with Commandino's translations and editions of mathematical and scientific works come to the fore in these images, which ostentatiously free the diagram from the cramped confines of manuscript pages' margins. Giorgi's choice to use Commandino's spacious, simple images thus looks like a conscious adoption of the mathematical and textual rigor associated with his fellow citizen of Urbino against Aleotti's elaborate novelties.

Whereas Commandino did not survive to give a rationale for the design of his images, Baldi explicitly notes his intentions for the diagrams of the *Automata* as well as the *Belopoeica*. In the prefatory letter that precedes his translation of the *Automata*, he remarks that "as for the figures, which through their antiquity and the ignorance of copyists had been degraded, as you know, and as the Greek exemplars are destroyed, I have modernized them."[119] In the *Vita Heronis* he appends to his translation of the *Belopoeica*, after noting his first encounter with a manuscript of the work thanks to his teacher Emmanuel Margounios, he claims he has "adorned it with figures conceived after the mind of the author, and then made it clearer and more illuminating with some little annotations."[120] Here, too, he looks back on his translation of the *Automata*, which "on my own initiative I illustrated with images modeled after the mind of the author, and gave them to the light printed in Venetian type, with nobility suited to the text." This note is a reminder that the visual experience of the book is not only about the images themselves, but also the thoughtful *mise en page* that juxtaposes them with well-set type.

Baldi's search to recreate Hero's own intentions for his images emerges from his sadness over the state in which he found the manuscripts. In reviewing the brisk prose of the *Cheiroballistra*, which moreover only survives partially, he regrets that the images he has access to cannot supplement the text as he supposes Hero meant them to:

> It is fair to believe that the author tempered the brevity and obscurity of these words with most precise figures, which is inferred from his words. But

---

[118] Anderson 2020: 552.    [119] Baldi, *De gli automati* ii–iii.    [120] Baldi, *Belopoeica* 73.

in fact the diagrams now extant in the manuscript codices (for they are not circulated in print) are so bad and barbarous that I would call them sketches, so they really get in the way of offering any aid to those who read carefully. Just about all books on mechanics from the Greeks which were copied from ancient exemplars and survived until our time labor under this shortcoming.[121]

While he leaves the text of the *Cheiroballistra* that accompanies his translation of the *Belopoeica* both untranslated and unillustrated, Baldi certainly seeks to remedy the problems he finds with the manuscript images for the *Automata* and *Belopoeica*. He includes numerous images in each text, often corresponding to images in the manuscript but more detailed and numerous, frequently including several views where the manuscripts have only one.

For example, the "belly-bow (*gastraphetēs*)" is illustrated in the earliest surviving manuscript of the *Belopoeica* with a single complex image (Figure 5.6). In Baldi's version, the elements of that single manuscript image are spread over several pages (Figure 5.7). The dovetailed rod that is one of the first components described is illustrated separately, from a perspective that makes it easy to see how the dovetail works, whereas the manuscript image of the bow shows the whole thing from a top-down perspective that obscures how the dovetail fits together. The trigger assembly gets its own detailed illustration on a separate page of Baldi's book, contrasting with the rather simple image that is nested into a hollow of the bow itself in the manuscript. The ratchets that engage the "slider" to hold the tension in the bow are shown in yet another image, as part of the assembled bow, whereas in the manuscript version they are wedged into yet another hollow of the bow, shown from a sideways perspective that makes it easy to see how the teeth fit together, but not how the assembly fits into the bow as a whole.

The same is true for the rest of the text. Along with his expanded visualizations of single images from the manuscripts, Baldi includes some images of structures and processes merely described in Hero's text without being associated with any illustration, such as the multiple schemes for pulling back the arms of a torsion catapult or the way the arm of the torsion device is inserted in the skein of spring cord.[122] Cuomo has argued that diagrams may have been a way for Vitruvius to address the "limits of the text" adumbrated by the territory of tacit knowledge, and the same might be said of Hero.[123] Yet Baldi's approach to the images does a better

---

[121] Baldi, *Belopoeica* 71–72.     [122] Baldi, *Belopoeica* 10–15.     [123] Cuomo 2016: 142.

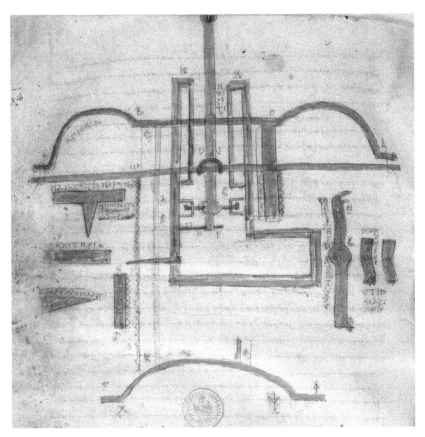

Figure 5.6   Belly-bow (*gastraphetēs*) in Cod. Parisinus suppl. gr. 607, fol. 47v. Image
courtesy of Bibliothèque nationale de France.

job of conveying the tacit knowledge that is difficult to convey either in
image or in words. The text of the *Belopoeica* in particular does often give a
rather sketchy picture of the catapults it describes in the interest of creating
a readable account for beginners. Just how a dovetail fits together, or how
the arm of a torsion catapult fits into the coil of spring cord – these are
things an experienced builder of catapults would know, having learned
them on the job, but a beginner might not. Even though the *Belopoeica*
emphasizes that it is not written for experts, Baldi's evolution of its images
creates a version of the text that accomplishes the text's aim to be friendly
to beginners better than the manuscript images. Perhaps this is, in part,
what Baldi means when he says his images are what Hero would have had
in mind.

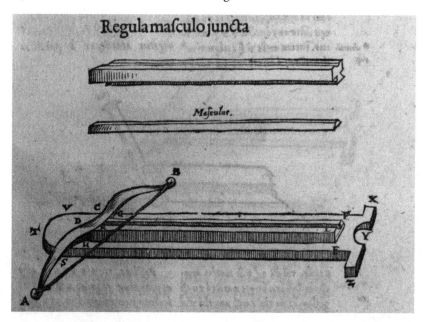

Figure 5.7   *Gastraphetēs* in Baldi's *Belopoeica*, pp. 5–7. Image courtesy of Bayerische Staatsbibliothek München.

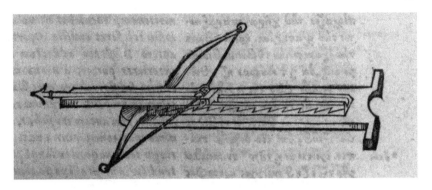

Figure 5.7 *(cont.)*

Baldi's translation of Hero's *Automata* takes the improvement in the detail of the images still further than the *Belopoeica* would, including not only precise woodcuts, but also a large number of elaborate engravings. Some of these serve the aim of illustrating complex subassemblies of the automaton in greater detail than woodcuts might have permitted, like the series of diagrams in different perspectives of the assembly for raising and lowering sets of wheels to allow the moving automaton to move at right angles or swerve along a serpentine path (Figure 5.8). The detailed rendering in these images of the differential axles that control the speed with which the wheels turn, the mechanism for connecting the axles to the turning screws, and the way each component is connected back to the main cord is an effective visual argument for the efficacy of the mechanisms Hero recommends.

Other images seem to be a pure celebration of the medium itself, like the beautifully detailed image of the counterweight assembly, where numerous individual millet grains occupy much of the full-page engraving (Figure 5.9).Engravings were more difficult and expensive to integrate into a book than woodcuts as they require a separate intaglio printing stage. This full-page image of a subassembly described thoroughly in the text but never pictured in any detail in the manuscripts makes a strong statement of Baldi's desire to reclaim Hero's work – and the study of automata more broadly – for an elite readership. As we saw above, part of his plan for doing so involves highlighting the associations of that work with a widely admired classical culture, embodied in his classicizing image of the moving automaton with its figures of Dionysus, the Maenads, and Nike (Figure 5.10). Baldi's visual rhetoric in the *Automata* is at once a celebration of classical literary and technical culture and of contemporary developments both in precision machinery and in book production itself.

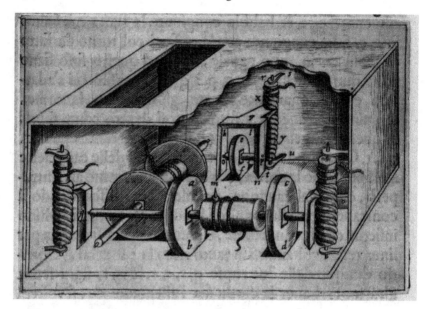

Figure 5.8    Engraving of the wheel mechanism in Baldi's *De gli automati*, fol. 24r. Image courtesy of Bayerische Staatsbibliothek München.

Images are essential for communicating the content of technical texts like Hero's, and they are inextricably linked to the text by their defining letter labels. As we saw in the case of Giorgi's *merismatio* and Baldi's regretful attitude toward the quality of the "barbarous" manuscript images that have been transmitted to him, translators of those technical texts were acutely aware of how important images were for clarifying particularly tricky elements of the verbal translation. The varied *visual* translations of the images in the Heronian tradition serve as a reminder that the cultural repositioning of these texts' visual components was every bit as entangled in questions of tradition, innovation, and readers' responses as their verbal translations.

## Heronian Science in the Age of Print

As Hero's works were updated by his many translators for an early modern readership, the physical premises that underlay his mechanical devices sometimes ran afoul of contemporary theories, particularly as Peripatetic thought (which denies the existence of extended void) came to dominate. Hero's translators and commentators sometimes chose to attempt a

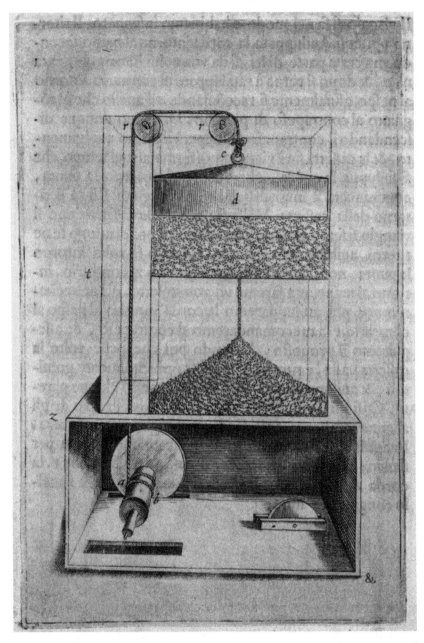

Figure 5.9 Counterweight assembly from Baldi's *De gli automati*, 21v. Image courtesy of Bayerische Staatsbibliothek München.

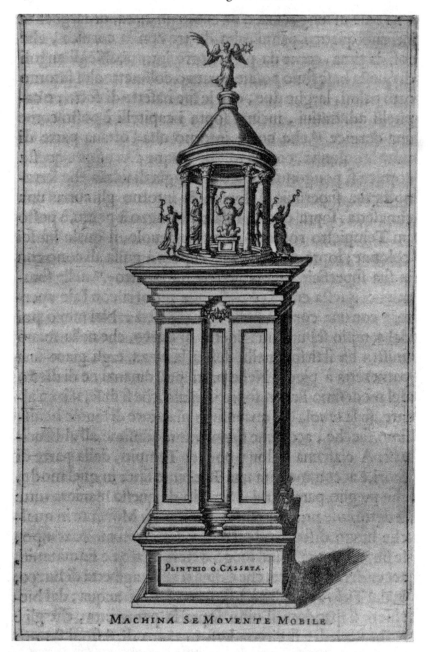

Figure 5.10    Baldi's design for the moving Dionysus tableau, *De gli automati*, 19r. Image
courtesy of Bayerische Staatsbibliothek München.

reconciliation between the two conflicting theories, sometimes to mini-mize the differences and sometimes to insist on throwing Hero's theory out entirely. The first strategy appealed to Oreste Vannocci in his 1582 manuscript translation of the *Pneumatica* into Italian. Vannocci takes Hero as a kind of Peripatetic *manqué*, suggesting that he would have hewed more precisely to Aristotle's views had the Peripatetic school come into its own by his time.[124] As such, he does not differentiate between the Heronian concepts of contraction and expansion on the one hand and the Peripatetic concepts of condensation and rarefaction on the other. But as Valleriani observes, Vannocci has to expand the definition of condensation to explain the effects seen in pneumatic vessels, where air condenses without altering its form in the Aristotelian sense. He refers these effects to "excessive condensation, which is also hated by nature, and tolerated only because of a temporarily short violence."[125] The resulting theory yields a somewhat unsatisfying explanation of exactly what happens to air in vessels under continuous heating.

In an afterword to Hero's preface to the *Pneumatica*, Aleotti seems to advertise the third, more combative approach in the updated examples he provides, but he ends up taking something more like the second. Aleotti adapts Hero's strategy of using familiar objects to make the principles of pneumatics come alive for his own readership, who of course occupy a world populated by somewhat different everyday objects than Hero did. Some of the objects Hero mentions are no longer familiar, while new technologies have appeared that illustrate pneumatic physics in new ways. For example, he begins with some observations on the effects of compres-sion and evacuation on a musket.[126] If a ramrod that exactly fits the dimensions of the barrel is pushed in and the vent (*fogone*) is covered up, a vacuum will be created that makes it difficult to remove the ramrod; if the vent is first covered and then the ramrod inserted, it will be difficult because the air inside has to be compressed.

He then abruptly shifts from artillery to maternity, picking up the connection Hero draws between the physical principles in the *Pneumatica* and their applications in medical devices like cupping glasses and the syringe whose design he describes in the *Pneumatica*.[127] While cupping glasses were no longer in vogue by Aleotti's time, a sort of breast pump had been invented whereby mothers could siphon off milk in excess

---

[124] Vannocci, *Libro de gli artifizii* fol. 2r.    [125] Vannocci, *Libro de gli artifizii* fol. 3v.
[126] Aleotti, *Artifitiosi* 8.
[127] Aleotti, *Artifitiosi* 8; *Pneumatica* 2.18. On the syringe see Bliquez and Oleson 1994.

of that consumed by their infants. Aleotti describes two variants of this device, both made of glass. The first is made with a body designed to fit over the nipple and a neck long enough for the woman to reach it with her mouth, "from which they suck the air which is in the vessel, and the milk follows suddenly in its place, escaping out of the breast." The second is a small ampoule (*ampolla*) of glass that is heated before being placed over the nipple. In Aleotti's account, the heated, rarefied vapor within the vessel escapes upwards through the tiny pores in the glass; as the pores are too small to admit air from outside, this leaves a void behind that is filled by drawing milk from the breast. The functional principle of this second type, says Aleotti, is the same as in kilns, where the fire creates a vacuum toward which the fire and the heated vapor it produces are both drawn. If the fire is situated at the mouth of the furnace, he argues, the heavier, colder outside air cannot enter the furnace by moving over the lighter, warmer vapor within, so the fire continues to create vapor until it has fully evaporated, leaving a vacuum so that the fire is then drawn up and inside the furnace.

Initially, Aleotti seems to promise a very different physical argument from Hero's as to what physical phenomena his examples demonstrate. Unlike Hero, Aleotti never acknowledges air as being made up of particles and interstitial voids (nor does he provide an alternative explanation). Indeed, he argues for the incompressibility of elemental air and against the possibility of extended void, even though he introduces this discussion as "conforming with what Hero said above."[128] As Keller points out, however, Aleotti's examples do not in fact call the existence of interstitial voids into question and so do not refute Hero's views.[129] Keller suggests that Aleotti's about-face on the existence of void reflects his practical rather than theoretical orientation, while "his very confusion shows how new ideas could slip in, almost unawares."[130] More charitably, Aleotti might have been attempting the same kind of fusion of variant explanations of the compression and expansion of matter as Hero himself does in the preface to the *Pneumatica*, where including diverse ways of thinking took precedence over strict allegiance to any one philosophical school.

Valleriani suggests that Aleotti might have indeed developed a novel theory (albeit murkily expressed) in tracing the relationships in technical texts at this time between the Peripatetic ideas of condensation and rarefaction and their Heronian analogs of contraction and expansion.[131]

---

[128] Aleotti, *Artifitiosi* 8.   [129] Keller 1967: 343.   [130] Keller 1967: 342–43.
[131] Valleriani 2007: 345–46.

The former are predicated on a theory of matter and form whereby condensation or rarefaction is accompanied not by a change in matter, but a change in form such as water changing into vapor. The latter, by contrast, are conceived of precisely as changes in matter. Valleriani describes Hero's account of air being heated as its becoming "a sort of corrupted body," as the action of fire on the air causes the air particles to attenuate, while "the interstitial vacua are supposed to become larger because they 'compensate' the volume that is reduced due to the loss of particles."[132] Upon removal of the heat source, the voids shrink back to their normal state, "and thus 'pull' the matter around and towards themselves." While Hero's treatment of the subject is slightly murkier than Valleriani's lucid account, this does indeed seem to be what Hero is getting at with his lengthy treatment of the *taxis* of sponges and horn shavings, as well as being a kind of inverted view of Berryman's conjecture that Hero imagines the particles of air themselves being compressible.

The action of the breast pump Aleotti describes is thus predicated neither on Heronian expansion nor Aristotelian rarefaction, but on a new conjecture for what happens when air is heated. Rather than air particles being attenuated so they can escape the vessel, Aleotti seems to regard the heat itself as "a thin vapor that penetrates the vase and pushes away the air."[133] The "slippage" Keller detects in Aleotti's account thus does indeed admit of a new concept of air's behavior when subjected to heating. Aleotti's explanation has problems of its own, notably that it does not really explain what air is. But it is still possible, as Valleriani suggests, that Aleotti's view influenced later scientific explanations of the relationship between temperature and pressure. In any case, it is clear that the translations of Hero's works in this period served as vehicles not only for new technological innovations, but also for new ways of thinking about the science behind them as well.

Laird argues that Hero's physical theory of matter and void would not be taken seriously until Bernardino Baldi discussed it in the *Vita Heronis* appended to his translation of the *Belopoeica* in 1616. Previous translators had instead "[dismissed] it out of hand with arguments taken from Aristotle," so Aleotti may have felt compelled to walk the line as well.[134] Whatever Aleotti's motivations, Keller argues that the particular confusion here might have been over what precisely was meant by his saying that a vacuum could not exist except "by force and outside Nature," the phrase

---

[132] Valleriani 2007: 344.    [133] Valleriani 2007: 350.    [134] Laird 2017: 161.

that closes his addition. Rather than indicating an "absolute impossibility," says Keller, the term "here appears only to mean 'unnatural'."[135]

Keller's argument about the ambiguity of phrases like "*fuori di Natura*" is expanded considerably by Berryman, who develops a nuanced argument about ancient and early modern responses to the idea that mechanics works "contrary to nature" in the sense of breaking the laws of nature. Galileo's rejection of the idea might be taken as a blow against Peripatetic mechanical thinking, since the author of the *Mechanical Problems* categorizes mechanical force as working *para phusin*. However, Berryman traces translations of the Greek term into the Latin *extra naturam*, rather than the more radical *contra naturam*, in the *translatio vetus* of Aristotle's *Physics* and Thomas Aquinas's commentary.[136] The mechanical forces described in the Peripatetic corpus seem in antiquity and well beyond to have been taken not to break the laws of nature (in the Galilean formulation), but simply to put matter to work in ways that are only possible under artificial amplification. Aleotti's plugged musket, breast pump, and kiln do not violate natural law. Like Hero's own devices, they merely offer the opportunity to see it in action thanks to their ability to amplify compression and rarefaction effects more strongly than naturally occurring systems do.

Full translations of Hero's work were part of a more complex landscape of textual transmission and transformation that included partial translations and paraphrases. In 1601 Giambattista della Porta published his three-book *Pneumatica* at Naples, to be translated into Italian just five years later. Della Porta approaches Hero as an antagonist, criticizing various claims about particular machines as well as his basic physical principles. He was committed to the view that the cosmos must be composed of contiguous matter, an unbroken flow of influence from superior to inferior bodies, which would be catastrophically interrupted were a void to intercede.[137] Hero's claims that a void could be produced through artificial means presented an obvious affront to della Porta's views, and he pulls no punches in responding to Hero's work. Della Porta begins his preface with an appeal to the long history of ancient pneumatic work, saying that he read about Ctesibius in Vitruvius. Hero is next to be mentioned, but a cloud immediately appears over his name, as della Porta scoffs, "as I see it, he was a mechanician and not a philosopher or a mathematician," since della Porta's tests of Hero's devices apparently often failed to deliver the desired results.[138]

---

[135] Aleotti, *Artifitiosi* 8; Keller 1967: 343–44.    [136] Berryman 2009: 44–48.
[137] della Porta, *Pneumatica* 11.    [138] della Porta, *Pneumatica* 1.

Della Porta dedicates his first book to reviewing the opinions on the void held by various ancient figures, offering counterarguments where their views do not correspond to his own. Hero receives two chapters of his own in this book. The first recounts some highlights from Hero's preface, concluding with a sudden transition from the analysis of wine mixing with water from Hero's preface to a related passage from the Peripatetic *Problemata*.[139] As we saw earlier, Hero offers the familiar tendency of wine to mix easily with water as a ready proof that liquids have some small voids between their particles, so the wine falls smoothly and mixes readily with the water.[140] The passage from the *Problemata*, on the other hand, proposes that wine and water both contain air, and hence that an unlimited amount of ash can be mixed into a vessel of water, as the water enters the empty spaces in the ash.

The following chapter is dedicated to refuting Hero's arguments. Such is the claim, at any rate, though the arguments attacked there do not always resemble Hero's, and those that do have often been modified into straw men. He begins by attacking Hero's claim that wine mixes easily into water as "empty and puerile, and inconsonant with experience."[141] But he turns Hero's argument that the wine passes temporarily through the voids between the particles of water into a caricature, suggesting that it could only occur in a manner like the water and ash from the Peripatetic *Problemata*, resulting in no increase in volume in the mixture. He correctly notes that the mixture of water and wine does in fact increase in volume (offering as a helpful example that combining equal parts of the two liquids yields twice as much of the mixture). But his refutation does not address any argument actually made by Hero, who neither in the preface nor the main body of the work suggests that a liquid into which another is poured fuses with it so that the mixture occupies the same space as the original. Indeed, many of Hero's liquid-mixing devices rely precisely on that increase in volume, like the *miliarion* or water boiler that dispenses hot water when cold water is poured in and forces the already heated water through its spigot.[142]

Della Porta's assault on Hero continues with an assertion that the incompressibility of liquids can be seen by tossing a solid object into a vessel full of water and observing that a volume of liquid spills out equal to the volume of the object. As we have seen from the "bathtub" volume measurement in the *Metrica*, Hero was well aware of this principle, and

[139] *Problemata* 15.8.    [140] *Pneumatica* 1.pr.316–21.    [141] della Porta, *Pneumatica* 8.
[142] *Pneumatica* 2.34.

nowhere does he argue that liquids can be observed being compressed. He does say in the experiment with the inverted vessel from the *Pneumatica* preface that "the water does not admit of much compression (οὐ πάνυ λαμβάνει πίλησιν)," for the somewhat obscure reason that water does not by its nature have much "squeeze (*ekthlipsis*)" to it.[143] That Hero does not rule out the possibility that water might be slightly compressible (which indeed it is) correlates to the novel theory of matter Berryman proposes for the *Pneumatica*, which admits of temporary compressions of particles themselves, as well as the more widespread view of particles compressing into voids.[144] It is clear from the additional discussion in the preface and from the numerous devices in the main text that rely quite explicitly on the effective incompressibility of water that Hero did not somehow believe that the voids in liquids left them highly compressible.

In his final attack on Hero in this chapter, della Porta says Hero "devolves into ineptitude" in his arguments about air compression, offering for his part the example of a gun (*tormentum* in Latin, from a term for a catapult, clarified in the Italian translation *archibuggio*).[145] This example, indeed, follows Aleotti's example of the musket and ramrod very closely, only suggesting that the ramrod should be greased to maintain an airtight seal. Though he claims to be offering a refutation of Hero's theory of the nature of air, he expresses no competing explanatory theory of his own, not even mentioning the nascent theory Aleotti suggests. He ends the chapter by affirming that "there is no void in nature, though it is found in rarefied and compressed air," a somewhat surprising acknowledgment.

The remaining two books of della Porta's *Pneumatica* consist of explanations for the behavior of air and water, often bolstered by experiments that one might perform. The second book begins with a promise to move on from rational discourse about physics, which "appealed more to mind than to sense" (a phrase itself taken from Giorgio Valla's preface to the pneumatic section of *De expetendis, et fugiendis rebus*, and reminiscent of Hero's αἰσθητικὴ ἀπόδειξις, to experiment. Those experiments are in turn accompanied by physical explanations discovered by a series of ingenious thinkers, each of whom "lighted upon the principles and causes, by which he could find and follow up new things."[146] In particular, della Porta promises to bring Hero's errors into the light, "lest anyone be deceived in

---

[143] *Pneumatica* 1.pr.267–71.    [144] Berryman 2011: 287–88.

[145] della Porta, *Pneumatica* 9; *Spiritali* 17. Baldi uses this term as well for artillery in the preface to his translation of Hero's *Belopoeica* (ii).

[146] della Porta, *Pneumatica* 21.

operating these devices." In the third book, he promises to introduce some new devices of his own, "so that an ingenious craftsman could seize the opportunity for making others."[147]

Many of these devices are adapted (or simply adopted) from Hero, and della Porta includes copious notes on experiments and explanatory concepts from Hero that he believes to be incorrect. For example, he criticizes a device proposed by Hero that can hold two types of liquid and dispense one at a time or a mixture of both.[148] The vessel has a partition in the interior perforated with small holes on one side and a pipe leading from the lower part through the hollow handle, opening on the handle so that the mouth of the pipe can be covered or uncovered at will. When the hole is covered, the liquid in the upper part cannot pass into the lower part, just as liquid cannot exit a small hole at the bottom of a can unless there is an aperture for air to enter. But della Porta's physics do not admit of this principle, so he proposes a different device for mixing wine and water, which he claims can even unmix them afterward. His device consists of a cup and a perforated glass ball that can sit atop it. The cup is filled with wine and the ball with water, and the ball is placed on the cup. At this point, says della Porta,

> we will see the water run down into the vessel below, as its weight compels the wine (which is everywhere surrounded by water) to climb into the ball through the same hole, all the way up to its top F, going through the water without mixing with the water, so that it produces a delightful spectacle, and does this until all the water has descended and the wine ascended, and nor does the least part of wine remain in the water, which you will recognize by smell and color, and if you have carried it out well, you will fulfill your promise.

If a little water is still mixed with the wine, he says, a paintbrush will remove it. In fact, given that wine consists mostly of water and that the alcohol in wine is chemically miscible with water, della Porta's device is doomed to failure. But statements like "you will see" and "you will fulfill your promise" carry a weight of conviction stronger than Hero's less dramatic accounts of the action of his own vessels outside his preface.

It is not my purpose here to determine whether della Porta really experienced all – or any – of the experimental successes he claims. His intense antagonism toward Hero derived simply from Hero's status as the sole surviving ancient mouthpiece of a pneumatic theory that conflicted

---

[147] della Porta, *Pneumatica* 48.     [148] Hero, *Pneumatica* 1.9; della Porta, *Pneumatica* 48–50.

strongly with della Porta's own Aristotelian principles. In their authorial commitments to drawing material from past sources to combine it with their own new ideas, to their detailed descriptions of devices that turned pneumatic principles into spectacles, and to proof through experiment, the two had more in common than della Porta would probably have liked to admit. Laird dismisses the importance of Hero's *Automata* and *Pneumatica* in this period as "merely amusing and entertaining because they concerned largely frivolous though ingenious toys."[149] But the very vitriol with which della Porta meets Hero's physical arguments signals the importance of Hero's work as a blueprint for thinking through questions of matter and void and their physical demonstrations.

Over the course of the 16th and 17th centuries, the application of pneumatic technology not just to miniature devices and automata but to immersive environments like Aleotti's refreshing "spritz" room became increasingly popular in the gardens and grottoes of wealthy patrons in Italy, France, and elsewhere. Notable among these was the sprawling garden of Pratolino, just north of Florence and originally commissioned by the Grand Duke Francesco I, whose interests in engineering, metallurgy, and alchemy perennially attracted him more than the work of governing the duchy. Much of the design of the garden was delegated to the gifted Bernardo Buontalenti, whose similarities to Hero have themselves been discussed by Valleriani.[150]

The garden once featured a wide variety of pneumatic devices to enliven the experience of visitors, from relatively staid elements like fountains and automata to features that would surprise guests by spraying them playfully with water. While the remains of these devices do not survive today, Valleriani has reconstructed much of the content of the garden from documentary evidence.[151] Most important here, he shows that indeed Buontalenti used Hero's *Pneumatica* as a model for the design of the garden, drawing not only on the basic technologies Hero describes, but also on their principles of aesthetics and composition. Several of his designs recall specific devices from the *Pneumatica*; Pratolino even featured its own version of the "owl and birds" tableau. Moreover, some of the adaptations of Hero that Aleotti had conceived of a few years earlier seem to have made it into the garden as well. The so-called Forge of Vulcan recalls Aleotti's "smithy" design, while Giovanni Guerra's designs for the garden include a grotto featuring a Hercules tableau that closely resembles Aleotti's first new

---

[149] Laird 2017: 163.     [150] Valleriani 2014: 138. On Pratolino see Zangheri 1987.
[151] Valleriani 2014: 142–47.

design, where Hero's arrow-firing Hercules is rearmed with his more traditional club.[152]

The English tourist Richard Lassels commented on his experience of several of these Heronian features at Pratolino in his 1670 travelogue *The Voyage of Italy*.[153] The water organ "plays to you while you dine there in Fresco at that Table, if you have meat," while "in the mean time you see Smiths thumping, Birds chirping in trees, Mills grinding." Another tableau, "where the Country Clown offers a Dish of Water to a Serpent, who drinks it, and lifteth up his head when he hath drunk," strongly recalls the drinking animals in Hero's *Pneumatica*, while Pratolino's representations of more practical devices like an automated model olive press hint at other works like the *Mechanica*. Hunt comments on the Ovidian referents of some of the features of Pratolino, like a figure of the sea nymph Galatea emerging from a grotto in a dolphin-drawn chariot.[154] Yet Lassels' experience highlights the juxtaposition of those lofty literary notes with tableaux where mechanics and craftwork are not merely an invisible part of the background, but celebrated in mechanical representations of mechanical work.

Slaney describes the "temporal density" of a viewer's encounter with antique sculpture or architecture, or a landscape of ruins, freighted with awareness of "an interiority predicated on occluded experience: a form of depth."[155] The obscurity of that depth can only be plumbed by developing a "sympathetic intuition" or "aesthetic imagination" to supplement the direct visual and haptic experience, and effort is needed to develop a conscious awareness of the temporal layering that separates the "now" from the "ancient." Even an environment that is not literally ancient but is filled with references to antiquity can spark this kind of cognitive process. Slaney cites the Villa Borghese Gardens in Rome, a neoclassical reworking of a baroque garden landscape featuring classical subjects. Despite the conceptual "slippage" that this ersatz antiquity might trigger, Slaney argues that "a skillful reproduction may indeed resonate as powerfully as the genuine article."[156] Pratolino's combination of classicizing sculptural tropes like Galatea in her chariot with mechanical marvels (many of which, like Guerra's Hercules, themselves take their forms from antiquity) creates a complex layering of ancient imagery with mechanical novelty. For a viewership familiar with Hero's work, through Aleotti's

---

[152] Valleriani 2014: 163–64.
[153] Richard Lassels, *The Voyage of Italy, or a Compleat Journey through Italy* (part 1), 206–08.
[154] Hunt 2016: 54–55. [155] Slaney 2016: 87. [156] Slaney 2016: 97.

translation or otherwise, the layering is more complicated still: an ancient text rooted in its own disciplinary tradition yet promising novel mechanical innovations, newly popularized in translation, and now materially embodied in a garden blending old and new.

The balance between elegance and practicality maintained both in the *Pneumatica* itself and its echoes at Pratolino is reflected as well in the work of the French landscape architect Salomon de Caus, perhaps the most prominent early modern designer of pneumatic wonders as points of interest for gardens and grottoes.[157] Like Aleotti, and Hero himself, he was clearly inspired by earlier efforts at creating elaborately engineered landscapes. His 1615 *Raisons des Forces Mouvantes* builds up a toolbox of pneumatic devices, starting from Hero and working toward a large array of creations both useful and entertaining, some of which would later appear in his gardens. Its frontispiece features a portrait of Hero working on a siphon alongside Archimedes with a balance, both surrounded by the products of their labor and ingenuity (Figure 5.11). Archimedes has his water screw, the multiple-pulley system called the *polyspaston*, a burning mirror, and the crown whose alloy composition he is meant to have discovered in the bath.[158] Hero, on his side of the room, is flanked by a pneumatic piston, a device from the *Pneumatica* that makes a little ball dance on a jet of water, and the pipes of a water organ.

De Caus begins his *Raisons des Forces Mouvantes* with a reference to Vitruvius' threefold distinction between various types of machines: machines for heavy lifting, scaffolding and siege ladders, and pneumatic wonders.[159] In fact, de Caus already begins adapting the ancient tradition here, transforming Vitruvius' *genus acrobaticon* (which he denotes with Vitruvius' Latin translation *scansorium*) into the type of machine "that serves to lift all kinds of burdens up high, which carpenters and masons use, as well as merchants, to draw all kinds of merchandise from ships." Vitruvius' *genus tractorium* category, which would have included these lifting devices, is adjusted in de Caus's formulation to *banauson*, the category of machines that not only lift and carry weights, but also "serve as a force to do many things difficult for us without this help, like windmills and water mills, pumps, presses, clocks, balances, and smiths' bellows." De Caus does not signal where Vitruvius' categorization ended

[157] A detailed study of de Caus's garden designs and his debt to classical culture can be found in Morgan 2007.

[158] The stories of these devices and their afterlives in Roman culture are explored in Jaeger 2008.

[159] Vitruvius, *De architectura* 10.1.1–2. On his classification scheme see Roby 2016b: 47–48.

Figure 5.11 Frontispiece from Salomon de Caus, *Raisons des Forces Mouvantes*, featuring Hero and Archimedes. Image courtesy of Bayerische Staatsbibliothek München.

and his own began, which turns out to be characteristic of how he handles the material he draws from ancient authors.

His prefatory material is full of classical and biblical references, from Juba's invention of musical instruments to Pliny's description of waters of different densities and mineral compositions. Hero himself is mentioned a few times at the beginning of the work as the author of the *Pneumatica* and *Automata*, but de Caus rejects his argument that matter incorporates interstitial voids. Like many of his contemporaries he adopts an Aristotelian view of matter and void, and indeed he explicitly denies that matter is composed of atoms and void early in the work, saying that if there is a void it is beyond human experience.[160] De Caus does chalk up his differences of opinion on the operational principle of the siphon to bad translations of Hero's explanation rather than errors on Hero's part, and he commends one of Hero's water-lifting devices as "a most elegant and subtle invention."[161] At least at the beginning of the work, Hero's status as an important progenitor of the science de Caus will develop is clear.

In the main part of the work, de Caus deploys references to ancient predecessors much more sparsely, though they do not vanish completely. Vitruvius, for example, receives due credit for his description of a crane with pulleys and windlasses, and Hero is mentioned as the originator of the owl-and-birds tableau that de Caus updates with new mechanisms and a greater variety of birdsong.[162] But other devices with a distinctly Heronian character do not refer back to their ancient antecedent, like a device that uses a mixture of pressurized air and water to simulate birdsong or a figure of an animal that drinks water when offered.[163] De Caus also includes updated versions of devices from Hero's *Pneumatica* without mentioning their origins, like the fire engine and the water organ.[164]

There is, to be sure, a vast amount of new material in de Caus's work; his new versions of the owl-and-birds piece and water organ feature clockwork components and other new technologies that set them apart from Hero's designs – there is even a kind of player-piano variant of the water organ, with included musical score.[165] In addition to these, the work

---

[160] de Caus, *Les Raisons des Forces Mouvantes* fol. 3r.

[161] de Caus, *Les Raisons des Forces Mouvantes* fols. 3v–4v; Hero, *Pneumatica* 2.14.

[162] de Caus, *Les Raisons des Forces Mouvantes* fol. 7r, book 1 problem 23; compare Hero, *Pneumatica* 1.16.

[163] de Caus, *Les Raisons des Forces Mouvantes* book 1 problems 10, 11; compare Hero, *Pneumatica* 1.15, 1.29.

[164] de Caus, *Les Raisons des Forces Mouvantes* book 1 problem 20, book 2 problem 28; compare Hero, *Pneumatica* 1.28, 1.42.

[165] de Caus, *Les Raisons des Forces Mouvantes* book 2 problems 28, 30.

includes a large number of new inventions. Some of these are classicizing showpieces for garden grottoes, like a figure of Galatea who glides along the surface of a lake accompanied by dolphins.[166] The work also includes a host of devices for pumping out water, sawing and drilling wood, and other practical tasks; de Caus arguably does a better job than Hero of showing how both pleasure and utility can be served by pneumatic devices. But it is difficult to explain why Hero all but vanishes from the text after a few early references when his work clearly influenced de Caus so strongly.

In 1688 a book authored by a pseudonymous "Agathus Cario" was published at Frankfurt, blending together devices from Hero, Aleotti, and de Caus, largely without credit. Given de Caus's somewhat cavalier attitude toward acknowledging Hero's influence on his own work, Cario's casual amalgamation may provoke somewhat less outrage on de Caus's behalf than it otherwise might. The author, whom Maclean identifies as Tobias Nislen of Württemberg, undertook a German translation of Kircher's *Phonurgia Nova* in 1684 under the same pseudonym.[167] The book itself is a remarkable pastiche, combining a German translation of the *Pneumatica* based on Commandino's Latin, a German translation of Aleotti's additional *theoremi*, and a selection of water mills and garden grotto installations drawn largely from de Caus. The Aleotti section is most likely based on the 1680 Amsterdam edition combining Commandino's Latin with a Latin translation of Aleotti, while the final section of more modern devices is drawn from the expanded 1624 edition of *Les Raisons des Forces Mouvantes*.

The images chosen for the book are a fascinating combination of new and old. The translation of Hero is illustrated with woodcuts that very closely resemble those of the 1680 Commandino–Aleotti, which are slightly cruder and less detailed than those in the 1575 Commandino. The translation of Aleotti is likewise illustrated with woodcuts, unlike Aleotti's original edition and the 1680 translation, which feature engravings. All the images in the final section are engravings, based on those in de Caus but not copied directly from them. This work may seem like a jumble of hydraulic devices drawn from diverse sources, but in fact Nislen seems to have seen the through line from Hero to contemporary developments in hydraulic technologies (both useful and beautiful) more clearly than most. His vision of Hero's lasting influence is charmingly illustrated in the frontispiece, where Hero is portrayed working on his pneumatic devices – both in written form and with the devices scattered beside him – inside a garden grotto (Figure 5.12).

---

[166] de Caus, *Les Raisons des Forces Mouvantes* book 1 problem 24.  [167] Maclean 1905: 199.

Figure 5.12    Frontispiece of "Agathus Cario's" edition of Hero, Aleotti, and de Caus.
Image courtesy of Bayerische Staatsbibliothek München.

## Conclusion

Nislen's 1688 version of the *Pneumatica* pulls together many of the threads
of Hero's shifting influence in the early modern period. In this one
volume, we find translations into and between vernacular languages (not

only Latin into German, but also Italian into Latin into German and French into German) and transformations of the visual component of the work and its successors between different styles and media. Through de Caus's influence on the book we also glimpse a changing role for both Hero's technology and his science in an environment where Peripatetic theories of the void dominated and pneumatic technologies had been drafted into a host of new applications. Hero's texts were enfolded with new bodies of knowledge, from the vast scope of Valla's work to Baldi's classicizing approach to reviving automata as privileged objects.

We might think of this as one final "bookworld" to accompany those explored in the last chapter, one final version of Hero viewed not as a singular historical figure but as a capacious author who drew liberally on his progenitors in order to create works that could be used and processed just as freely by his successors. Hero lived again at the hands of his translators in the 16th and 17th centuries. Distant as they may have felt themselves from the culture in which Hero himself lived and worked and inadequate as they may sometimes have felt the chain of manuscripts that offered them a tenuous connection with antiquity, they managed to remake him. More than that, they managed to build new conceptual and technological structures onto the material they had inherited, just as had happened through the interpolations in works like the *Definitiones*, and just as Hero had done with the material he himself inherited. These new structures reflected the aspects of Hero's work that resonated most strongly with their own cultural and technological priorities, from resurrecting an approach to mechanics that embraced both its mathematical and craftsmanlike aspects to concentrating effort on the practical prospects of hydraulic technologies.

They also reflected the changing informational affordances of a world where printing technologies made texts, including their images, far easier to reproduce and circulate than they had been. As Henninger-Voss observes, libraries in this era increasingly included practical technical handbooks as well as more theoretically oriented treatises.[168] This allowed Hero's translators opportunities to encounter, at least in textual form, the kind of craft knowledge that remains tantalizingly remote in ancient technical texts. Practical and theoretical knowledge could be propagated in verbal and visual printed forms that in turn could be readily excerpted, adapted, and outright copied. This process could yield not only new editions of the same work, but also entirely new books. The critical

---

[168] Henninger-Voss 2007: 11.

reclamation and reshaping of information Hero performed on his sources –
and later interpolators and commentators performed on Hero – could now
be amplified, accelerated, and propagated further and faster than Hero
ever dreamt.

Hero's particular success among the humanists of Urbino stemmed
from the remarkable overlap between his aims (both as an author and a
technologist) and the Urbinate culture of humanistically learned, mathematically inflected mechanical inquiry. Hero's carefully curated ties to his
predecessors, his accessible guides to the disciplines of mechanics, lightly
inflected with philosophical concerns but never dogmatic, and his creative
storehouse of delightful and thought-provoking machines – all these made
him a magnet for translators. He resembles in many respects an ancient
analog of Mutio Oddi, a mathematical polymath who made his name in
Urbino in this period with a brand of mathematics that, as Marr observes,
combined utility with a classicizing "august pedigree."[169] Hero's popularity among the humanists likewise owed much to the balance he struck
between the utility and accessibility of the methods and mechanisms he
unfolded in his texts on the one hand and their Greek "pedigree" and
mathematical rigor on the other.

Once translated into an array of languages other than Greek, Hero's
works became fair game not only for humanists who wished to recover the
ancient texts as precisely as possible, but also for technologists with their
eyes on the new. Authors like Giambattista della Porta may have loudly
rejected the philosophical foundations of his work, and those like Salomon
de Caus may have merged his designs with their own without drawing a
bright line between them. But in replicating Hero's mechanical designs
and his textual structures, they carry on his original line of work in a deeply
meaningful sense. Though they may not always have credited him by
name, under Hero's influence these early modern mechanical authors
renewed the commitments to the critical collection of past material, to
collaboration between theoretical and practical disciplines, and to the
development of new techniques for explaining and exploring the world
that had shaped his own work.

Hero's humanistic revival makes a fitting end to a story about the
inheritance and transformation of technical traditions. We began with
two images of Hero: Lichius' fantastical wonder-worker and the practical
herald of steam-driven meat extract manufacture. Now we can add two
more: the frontispiece images from Salomon de Caus's and Nislen's

[169] Marr 2011: 62.

pneumatic–mechanical works. In de Caus's image he sits peaceably on the floor alongside Archimedes, surrounded by his instruments. While as we have seen Hero is often represented as a kind of sidekick to Archimedes, that portrait rather conveys that each occupies his own territory in the workspace: Hero is simply doing a different kind of work from Archimedes. His approach is practical and accessible, and claims to individual achievement take a back seat to establishing a tradition of problem-solving techniques. In Nislen's image Hero dresses in antiquated garb but sits in a fashionably ornate garden grotto – itself a structure whose artificial excrescences of rock and shell hint at geological "deep time."[170] The floor around him is crowded with instruments, emphasizing his practical approach, and yet his attention is seized completely by the book in front of him: His most visible efforts go into his authorial projects rather than his mechanical innovations. Hero's placement in the grotto even as he creates novel instruments and texts lends an additional sense of the chronological depth of the reception of Hero's name and works, which is particularly resonant in such a densely sedimentary work as Cario's.

Over time, Hero himself becomes a tool that later authors put to use, his corpus an artifact instrumentalized for Pappus' mathematical mechanics, Aleotti's new *theoremi*, and de Caus's practical pumps and delicate clock-work birds. The philological zeal of humanists like Commandino to restore the ancient texts to an imagined pristine perfection was a challenge answered by later authors like Aleotti and Salomon de Caus, for whom Hero's pneumatic designs were part of a living tradition, his texts a kind of raw material for their own new work. In a sense, just as Hero recruited macroscopic structures like siphons as "elements" of his more complex creations, so did the Banū Mūsa, Aleotti, de Caus, and others take his designs as inputs for their own recombinant technologies.

Indeed, the Heronian corpus overall resists the kind of crystallized philological purification Commandino aimed at, harmonizing more with the idea of living, changing technical and textual traditions embodied by those other translators and authors. The easy accessibility Hero lauds in his own work is not just a matter of rendering a static mass of past material easier to read, but of opening a door onto those living traditions. When Hero describes his own interventions and manipulations of the traditions he inherited, he implicitly trains the reader to do the same with his own work. When he remarks on the mathematical problems that seemed

---

[170] On "deep time" and the inspiration it provided to the "Deep Classics" project see Butler 2016: 3–8.

inconceivable before Eudoxus or Archimedes came along or comments on developments like improved approximations for pi, he primes the reader to seek out new techniques that might still be emerging. When he fades out the figures of patrons, past authors, and even himself from his work, he creates an empty space that invites the reader in, to imagine themselves as part of that tradition.

And his readers did indeed take up that invitation, spinning off new styles of metrological problems, turning the *Definitiones'* hints at the duality of mathematical and material objects into a framework for Neoplatonic philosophical discourse, hybridizing Hero's mechanics with the question-and-answer format of the Peripatetic *Mechanical Problems*, and so on. The interventions of Aleotti, de Caus, and other early modern technical authors were just the latest stage in a long history of readers feeling empowered to step through the doors Hero opened and engage with those traditions in their own right. The resulting corpus is indeed a philological nightmare – as much emphasis as Hero places on *taxis* in his individual works, the corpus as a whole is decidedly *ataktos*. Just like the cord in the automaton or the "rootlike or rocklike (ῥιζῶδη ἢ πετρῶδη)" solids that cannot be measured mathematically, Hero defies attempts to fully capture him in a neatly ordered corpus. As his artifacts burst from the page into the world, his corpus bursts messily out of its boundaries, sparking (to borrow Cerquiglini's words once more) a "joyful excess" of contributions to the living mechanical tradition he established.

# Bibliography

"Heron" of Byzantium (2000) *Siegecraft: Two tenth-century instructional manuals.* Edited by D. Sullivan. Washington, DC: Dumbarton Oaks Research Library and Collection.

Acerbi, F. (2011) "The language of the 'Givens': Its forms and its use as a deductive tool in Greek mathematics," *Archive for History of Exact Sciences,* 65(2), pp. 119–53.

Adler, A. (1971) *Suidae lexicon.* Stuttgart: Teubner (Sammlung wissenschaftlicher Commentare).

al-Jazarī, Ismā'īl ibn al-Razzāz (1974) *The book of knowledge of ingenious mechanical devices.* Dordrecht: Reidel.

al-Nadīm, Abū al-Faraj Muḥammad Ibn Isḥāq (1970) *The Fihrist of al-Nadīm: A tenth-century survey of Muslim culture.* New York: Columbia University Press.

al-Nayrīzī, Abū al-'Abbās al-Faḍl ibn Ḥātim (2003) *The commentary of Al-Nayrizi on Book I of Euclid's elements of geometry, with an introduction on the transmission of Euclid's Elements in the Middle Ages.* Translated by A. Lo Bello. Boston: Brill Academic Publishers.

(2009) *The Commentary of al-Nayrizi on Books II–IV of Euclid's elements of Geometry: With a translation of that portion of Book I missing from MS Leiden Or. 399.1 but present in the newly discovered Qom Manuscript.* Translated by A. Lo Bello. Boston: Brill Academic Publishers.

Anderson, E. R. (2020) "Printing the bespoke book: Euclid's *Elements* in early modern visual culture," *Nuncius: Journal of the History of Science,* 35(3), pp. 536–60.

Anderson, G. (1993) *The second sophistic: A cultural phenomenon in the Roman Empire.* London: Routledge.

Apollodorus (2010) *Apollodorus Mechanicus, siege-matters = Poliorketika.* Edited by D. Whitehead. Stuttgart: Steiner.

Archimedes and Eutocius (2004) *The works of Archimedes: Translated into English, together with Eutocius' commentaries, with commentary, and critical edition of the diagrams.* Edited by R. Netz. Cambridge: Cambridge University Press.

Argoud, G. (ed.) (1994a) *Science et vie intellectuelle à Alexandrie (Ier–IIIe siècle après J.-C.).* Saint-Étienne: Publications de l'Université de Saint-Étienne.

Argoud, G. (1994b) "Héron d'Alexandrie, mathématicien et inventeur," in *Science et vie intellectuelle à Alexandrie (Ier–IIIe siècle après J.-C.)*. Saint-Étienne: Publications de l'Université de Saint-Étienne, pp. 53–65.

(1998) "Héron d'Alexandrie et les Pneumatiques," in Guillaumin, J.-Y. and Argoud, G. (eds.), *Sciences exactes et sciences appliquées à Alexandrie*. Saint-Étienne: Publications de l'Université de Saint-Étienne, pp. 127–45.

(2000) "Utilisation de la dioptre en hydraulique," in Argoud, G. and Guillaumin, J.-Y. (eds.), *Autour de "La Dioptre" d'Héron d'Alexandrie*. Saint-Étienne: Publications de l'Université de Saint-Étienne, pp. 233–56.

Argoud, G. and Guillaumin, J.-Y. (eds.) (1998) *Sciences exactes et sciences appliquées à Alexandrie*. Saint-Étienne: Publications de l'Université de Saint-Étienne.

Ariño Gil, E. and Gurt, J. M. (2001) "La inscripción catastral de Ilici. Ensayo de interpretación," *Pyrenae: Revista de Prehistòria i Antiguitat de la Mediterrània Occidental*, 31–32, pp. 223–26.

Aristotle (2000) *Problemi meccanici*. Edited by M. E. Bottecchia Dehò. Soveria Mannelli: Rubbettino.

Armisen-Marchetti, M. (1989) *Sapientiae facies: Étude sur les images de Sénèque*. Paris: Les Belles Lettres.

(2001) "L'imaginaire analogique et la construction du savoir dans les Questions Naturelles de Sénèque," in Courrént, M. and Thomas, J. (eds.), *Imaginaire et modes de construction du savoir antique dans les textes scientifiques et techniques*. Perpignan: Presses Universitaires de Perpignan, pp. 155–74.

Asper, M. (2001a) "Dionysios (Heron, Def. 14. 3) und die Datierung Herons von Alexandria," *Hermes*, 129(1), pp. 135–37.

(2001b) "Stoicheia und Gesetze: Spekulationen zur Entstehung mathematischer Textformen in Griechenland," in *Antike Naturwissenschaft und ihre Rezeption*. Trier: Wissenschaftlicher Verl. Trier, pp. 73–106.

(2007) *Griechische Wissenschaftstexte: Formen, Funktionen, Differenzierungsgeschichten*. Stuttgart: Steiner.

(2013) "Explanation between nature and text: Ancient Greek commentators on science," *Studies in History and Philosophy of Science Part A*, 44(1), pp. 43–50.

(2019) "Personae at play. 'Men of Mathematics' in commentary," *Historia Mathematica*, 47, pp. 4–15.

Athenaeus (2004) *On machines = Peri mēchanēmatōn*. Translated by D. Whitehead and P. H. Blyth. Stuttgart: Steiner.

Bagnall, R. S. (2002) "Alexandria: Library of dreams," *Proceedings of the American Philosophical Society*, 146(4), pp. 348–62.

(2009) *Early Christian books in Egypt*. Princeton, NJ: Princeton University Press.

Baird, D. (2004) *Thing knowledge: A philosophy of scientific instruments*. Berkeley: University of California Press.

Baker, P., Helmrath, J., and Kallendorf, C. (eds.) (2019) *Beyond reception: Renaissance humanism and the transformation of classical antiquity*. Berlin: De Gruyter.

Balbus (1996) *Présentation systematique de toutes les figures*. Translated by J.-Y. Guillaumin. Naples: Jovene.

Baldasso, R. (2009) "La stampa dell'*editio princeps* degli *Elementi* di Euclide (Venezia, Erhard Ratdolt, 1482)," in Pon, L. and Kallendorf, C. (eds.), *Il libro Veneziano – The books of Venice*. Venice: La Musa Talìa, pp. 61–100.

Banu Musa Bin Shakir (1978) *The book of ingenious devices*. Translated by D. R. Hill. New York: Springer.

Barker, A. (2006) *Scientific method in Ptolemy's Harmonics*. Cambridge: Cambridge University Press.

Bedini, S. A. (1964) "The role of automata in the history of technology," *Technology and Culture*, 5(1), pp. 24–42.

Bensaude-Vincent, B. and Newman, W. R. (2007) *The artificial and the natural: An evolving polarity*. Cambridge, MA: MIT Press.

Bergemann, L. et al. (2011) "Transformation: Ein Konzept zur Erforschung kulturellen Wandels," in Böhme, H. et al. (eds.), *Transformation: Ein Konzept zur Erforschung kulturellen Wandels*. Paderborn: Fink, pp. 39–56.

(2019) "Transformation: A concept for the study of cultural change," in Baker, P., Helmrath, J., and Kallendorf, C. (eds.), *Beyond reception: Renaissance humanism and the transformation of classical antiquity*. Berlin: De Gruyter, pp. 9–25.

Berrey, M. (2017) *Hellenistic science at court*. Berlin: De Gruyter.

Berryman, S. (2009) *The mechanical hypothesis in ancient Greek natural philosophy*. Cambridge: Cambridge University Press.

(2011) "The evidence for Strato in Hero of Alexandria's *Pneumatics*," in Desclos, M.-L. and Fortenbaugh, W. W. (eds.), *Strato of Lampsacus: Text, translation, and discussion*. New Brunswick, NJ: Transaction Publishers, pp. 277–91.

Bertoloni Meli, D. (1992) "Guidobaldo dal Monte and the Archimedean revival," *Nuncius: Journal of the History of Science*, 7(1), pp. 3–34.

Biagioli, M. (1989) "The social status of Italian mathematicians, 1450–1600," *History of Science*, 27(1), pp. 41–95.

Birkenmajer, A. (1922) *Vermischte Untersuchungen zur Geschichte der mittelalterlichen Philosophie*. Münster: Aschendorff.

Blackburn, B. and Lowinsky, E. E. (1993) "Luigi Zenobi and his letter on the perfect musician," *Studi Musicali*, 22, pp. 61–114.

Bliquez, L. and Oleson, J. P. (1994) "The origins, early history, and applications of the *pyoulkos* (syringe)," in Argoud, G. (ed.), *Science et vie intellectuelle à Alexandrie: (Ier–IIIe siècle après J.-C.)*. Saint-Étienne: Publications de l'Université de Saint-Étienne, pp. 83–119.

Blum, R. (1991) *Kallimachos: The Alexandrian Library and the origins of bibliography*. Madison: University of Wisconsin Press (Wisconsin Studies in Classics).

Blyth, P. H. (1992) "Apollodorus of Damascus and the *Poliorcetica*," *Greek, Roman, and Byzantine Studies*, 33(2), pp. 127–58.

Boas, M. (1949) "Hero's *Pneumatica*: A study of its transmission and influence," *Isis*, 40(1), pp. 38–48.

Böhme, H. et al. (eds.) (2011) *Transformation: ein Konzept zur Erforschung kulturellen Wandels*. Paderborn: Fink.

Borg, B. E. (2008) "Glamorous intellectuals: Portraits of pepaideumenoi in the second and third centuries AD," in *Paideia: The world of the Second Sophistic*. Berlin/Boston: De Gruyter, pp. 157–78.

Boutot, A. (2012) "Modernité de la catoptrique de Héron d'Alexandrie," *Philosophie Antique*, 12, pp. 157–96.

Bowie, E. (2013) "Libraries for the Caesars," in König, J., Oikonomopoulou, A., and Woolf, G. (eds.), *Ancient libraries*. Cambridge/New York: Cambridge University Press, pp. 237–60.

Brunt P. A. (1994) "The Bubble of the Second Sophistic," *Bulletin of the Institute of Classical Studies*, 39, pp. 25–52.

Bur, T. C. D. (2016) *Mechanical miracles: Automata in ancient Greek religion*. Thesis. Available at: https://ses.library.usyd.edu.au/handle/2123/15398 (accessed June 27, 2022).

Butler, S. (2016) *Deep classics: Rethinking classical reception*. London: Bloomsbury Academic.

Callebat, L. (1994) "Rhétorique et architecture dans le 'De Architectura' de Vitruve," in Gros, P. (ed.), *Le projet de Vitruve: objet, destinataires et réception du De architectura*. Rome: Ecole française de Rome, pp. 31–46.

Cameron, A. (2005) "Isidore of Miletus and Hypatia: On the editing of mathematical texts," *Greek, Roman, and Byzantine Studies*, 31(1), pp. 103–27.

Cancik, H. and Schneider, H. (eds.) (1996) *Der Neue Pauly: Enzyklopädie Der Antike*. Stuttgart: J.B. Metzler.

Canfora, L. (1990) *The vanished library*. Berkeley: University of California Press.

Carpinato, C. (2014) "Studiare la lingua greca (antica e moderna) in Italia. Retrospettiva e prospettive future," in Carpinato, C. and Tribulato, O. (eds.), *Storia e storie della lingua greca*, 1st edition. Venezia: Edizioni Ca' Foscari (Antichistica. Filologia e letteratura, 1).

Cavalieri-Manasse, G. (2000) "Un document cadastral du complexe capitolin de Vérone," *Dialogues d'histoire ancienne*, 26(1), pp. 198–200.

Cerquiglini, B. (1989) *Eloge de la variante: histoire critique de la philologie*. Paris: Editions du Seuil.

Chouquer, G. (2010) *La terre dans le monde romain: anthropologie, droit, géographie*. Paris: France.

Chouquer, G. and Favory, F. (2001) *L'arpentage romain: histoire des textes, droit, techniques*. Paris: France.

Ciccolella, F. (2020) "Maximos Margounios (c.1549–1602), his Anacreontic Hymns, and the Byzantine revival in early modern Germany," *Brill's Studies in Intellectual History*, 303, pp. 215–32.

Clayman, D. L. (2014) *Berenice II and the golden age of Ptolemaic Egypt*. Oxford: Oxford University Press.

Collins, H. M. (2010) *Tacit and explicit knowledge*. Chicago/London: University of Chicago Press.

Coqueugniot, G. (2013) "Where was the royal library of Pergamum? An institution found and lost again," in König, J., Oikonomopoulou, A., and Woolf, G. (eds.), *Ancient libraries*. Cambridge/New York: Cambridge University Press, pp. 109–23.

Corcoran, S. (1995) "The Praetorian Prefect Modestus and Hero of Alexandria's 'Stereometrica,'" *Latomus*, 54(2), pp. 377–84.

Creese, D. E. (2010) *The monochord in ancient Greek harmonic science*. Cambridge/New York: Cambridge University Press.

Crowley, T. J. (2005) "On the use of 'stoicheion' in the sense of 'element'," *Oxford Studies in Ancient Philosophy*, 29, pp. 367–94.

Cuomo, S. (1998) "Collecting authorities, constructing authority in Pappus of Alexandria's *Synagōgē*," in Kullmann, W., Althoff, J., and Asper, M. (eds.), *Gattungen wissenschaftlicher Literatur in der Antike*. Tübingen: G. Narr, pp. 219–38.

  (2000) *Pappus of Alexandria and the mathematics of late antiquity*. Cambridge/New York: Cambridge University Press.

  (2001) *Ancient mathematics*. London: Routledge.

  (2002) "The machine and the city: Hero of Alexandria's *Belopoeica*," in Tuplin, C. and Rihll, T. E. (eds.), *Science and mathematics in ancient Greek culture*. Oxford/New York: Oxford University Press, pp. 165–77.

  (2007) *Technology and culture in Greek and Roman antiquity*. Cambridge/New York: Cambridge University Press.

  (2016) "Tacit knowledge in Vitruvius," *Arethusa*, 49(2), pp. 125–43.

Damerow, P. (2004) *Exploring the limits of preclassical mechanics: A study of conceptual development in early modern science: Free fall and compounded motion in the work of Descartes, Galileo, and Beeckman*. New York: Springer.

Daston, L. (1998) "The nature of nature in early modern Europe," *Configurations*, 6(2), p. 149.

Davies, R. B. (2018) *Troy, Carthage and the Victorians: The drama of classical ruins in the nineteenth-century imagination*. Cambridge/New York: Cambridge University Press.

De Groot, J. (2014) *Aristotle's empiricism: Experience and mechanics in the fourth century bc*. Las Vegas: Parmenides Press.

Dear, P. (ed.) (1991) *The literary structure of scientific argument: Historical studies*. Philadelphia: University of Pennsylvania Press.

Decorps-Foulquier, M. (2000) "Remarques liminaires sur le texte de la 'Dioptre' de Héron d'Alexandrie et ses sources," in Argoud, G. and Guillaumin, J.-Y. (eds.), *Autour de "La Dioptre" d'Héron d'Alexandrie*. Saint-Étienne: Publications de l'Université de Saint-Étienne, pp. 37–43.

Delisle, L. (1868) *Le cabinet des manuscrits de la Bibliothèque impériale: étude sur la formation de ce dépôt comprenant les éléments d'une histoire de la calligraphie de la miniature, de la reliure, et du commerce des livres à Paris avant l'invention de l'imprimerie*. Paris: Imprimerie impériale.

Desclos, M.-L. and Fortenbaugh, W. W. (eds.) (2011) *Strato of Lampsacus: Text, translation, and discussion*. New Brunswick: Transaction Publishers.

Diels, H. (1893) "Über das physikalische System des Straton," in *Sitzungsberichte der Preussischen Akademie der Wissenschaften*. Berlin: Preussische Akademie der Wissenschaften, pp. 101–27.

Dijksterhuis, E. J. (1959) "The origins of classical mechanics from Aristotle to Newton," in Institute for the History of Science and Clagett, M. (eds.), *Critical problems in the history of science*. Madison: University of Wisconsin Press, pp. 163–96.

Dilke, O. A. W. (1961) "Maps in the treatises of Roman land surveyors," *Geographical Journal*, 127(4), pp. 417–26.

(1971) *The Roman land surveyors: An introduction to the agrimensores*. Newton Abbot: David and Charles.

Doody, A. (2009) "Pliny's *Natural History*: Enkuklios Paideia and the ancient encyclopedia," *Journal of the History of Ideas*, 70, pp. 1–21.

Drachmann, A. G. (1932) *Ancient oil mills and presses*. Kobenhavn: Levin & Munksgaard.

(1948) *Ktesibios, Philon and Heron; a study in ancient pneumatics*. Copenhagen: Munksgaard.

(1950) "Heron and Ptolemaios," *Centaurus*, 1(2), pp. 117–31.

Drake, S. and Drabkin, I. E. (trans.) (1969) *Mechanics in sixteenth-century Italy: Selections from Tartaglia, Benedetti, Guido Ubaldo, & Galileo*. Madison: University of Wisconsin Press.

Dueck, D. (2000) *Strabo of Amasia: A Greek man of letters in Augustan Rome*. London/New York: Routledge.

Eisenstein, E. L. (1979) *The printing press as an agent of change: Communications and cultural transformations in early modern Europe*. Cambridge: Cambridge University Press.

El-Abbadi, M. (2004) "The Alexandria Library in history," in Hirst, A. and Silk, M. S. (eds.), *Alexandria, real and imagined*. Aldershot/Burlington: Ashgate (Centre for Hellenic Studies, King's College, London: publications, 5), pp. 167–83.

Epiphanius (1935) *Epiphanius' Treatise on weights and measures: The Syriac version*. Edited by J. E. Dean. Chicago: University of Chicago Press.

Eshleman, K. (2008) "Defining the Circle of Sophists: Philostratus and the construction of the Second Sophistic," *Classical Philology*, 103(4), pp. 395–413.

D'Evelyn, M. M. (2012) *Venice & Vitruvius: Reading Venice with Daniele Barbaro and Andrea Palladio*. New Haven: Yale University Press.

Feke, J. (2014) "Meta-mathematical rhetoric: Hero and Ptolemy against the philosophers," *Historia Mathematica*, 41(3), pp. 261–76.

(2018) *Ptolemy's philosophy: Mathematics as a way of life*. Princeton: Princeton University Press.

Feyel, M. (2000) "Comment restituer la dioptra d'Héron d'Alexandrie?" in Argoud, G. and Guillaumin, J.-Y. (eds.), *Autour de "La Dioptre" d'Héron d'Alexandrie*. Saint-Étienne: Publications de l'Université de Saint-Étienne, pp. 191–225.

Ferriello, G. (1998) *Il sapere tecnico-scientifico fra Iran e Occidente, una ricerca nelle fonti*. Naples: Università degli Studi di Napoli "L'Orientale."

Fiocca, A. (2020) "Le facoltà delle arti e le accademie a Padova e Ferrara al tempo di Federico Commandino," *Bollettino di Storia delle Scienze Matematiche*, 40(2), pp. 333–65.

Flemming, R. (2007) "Empires of knowledge: Medicine and health in the Hellenistic world," in A *Companion to the Hellenistic world*. Hoboken: Wiley-Blackwell, pp. 449–63.

(2008) "Commentary," in Hankinson, R. J. (ed.), *The Cambridge companion to Galen*. Cambridge/New York: Cambridge University Press, pp. 323–54.

Fleury, P. (1993) *La mécanique de Vitruve*. Caen: Université de Caen, Centre d'études et de recherche sur l'antiquité.

(1994a) "Héron d'Alexandrie et Vitruve : à propos des techniques dites 'pneumatiques'," in *Science et vie intellectuelle à Alexandrie (Ier–IIIe siècle après J.-C.)*. Saint-Étienne: Publications de l'Université de Saint-Étienne, pp. 67–81.

(1994b) "Le *De Architectura* et les traités de mécanique ancienne," in Gros, P. (ed.), *Le projet de Vitruve: objet, destinataires et réception du De architectura*. Rome: Ecole française de Rome, pp. 187–212.

(1998) "Les sources alexandrines d'un ingénieur romain au début de l'Empire," in Argoud, G. and Guillaumin, J.-Y. (eds.), *Sciences exactes et sciences appliquées à Alexandrie*. Saint-Étienne: Publications de l'Université de Saint-Étienne, pp. 103–14.

Foster, C. L. E. (2020) "Familiarity and recognition: Towards a new vocabulary for classical reception studies," in de Pourcq, M., de Haan, N., and Rijser, D. (eds.), *Framing classical reception studies: Different perspectives on a developing field*. Leiden: Brill (Metaforms: Studies in the reception of classical antiquity, volume 19), pp. 33–69.

Frank, M. (2012) *Guidobaldo dal Monte's mechanics in context*. Pisa: Pisa University. Available at: http://etd.adm.unipi.it/theses/available/etd-04012012-122156/ (accessed August 25, 2021).

(2013) "Mathematics, technics, and courtly life in late Renaissance Urbino," *Archive for History of Exact Sciences*, 67(3), p. 305.

(2016) "The curious case of QP.6: The reception of Archimedes' mechanics by Federico Commandino and Guidobaldo dal Monte," *Revue d'histoire des sciences*, 68(2), pp. 419–46.

Fraser, P. M. (1972) *Ptolemaic Alexandria*. Oxford: Clarendon Press.

Freudenthal, G. (ed.) (2011) *Science in medieval Jewish cultures*. Cambridge/New York: Cambridge University Press.

Fuhrmann, M. (1960) *Das systematische Lehrbuch; ein Beitrag zur Geschichte der Wissenschaften in der Antike*. Göttingen: Vandenhoeck & Ruprecht.

Gamba, E. (2005) "Bernardino Baldi e l'ambiente tecnico-scientifico del Ducato di Urbino," in Nenci, E. (ed.), *Bernardino Baldi (1553–1617) studioso rinascimentale: poesia, storia, linguistica, meccanica, architettura: atti del convegno di studi di Milano, 19–21 novembre 2003*. Milan: FrancoAngeli, pp. 339–51.

Gamba, E. and Montebelli, V. (1988) *Le scienze a Urbino nel tardo Rinascimento.* Urbino: QuattroVenti (Biblioteca del Rinascimento).

Gandz, S. (1940) "Heron's date. A new terminus ante quem (+150)," *Isis*, 32(2), pp. 263–66.

Gatto, R. (2005) "Bilance e leve nel trattato *In mechanica Aristotelis problemata exercitationes* di Bernardino Baldi," in Nenci, E. (ed.), *Bernardino Baldi (1553–1617) studioso rinascimentale: poesia, storia, linguistica, meccanica, architettura: atti del convegno di studi di Milano, 19–21 novembre 2003.* Milan: FrancoAngeli, pp. 269–301.

Gendler, T. S. (2004) "Thought experiments rethought – and reperceived," *Philosophy of Science*, 71(5), pp. 1152–63.

Gerstinger, H. and Vogel, K. (1932) *Eine stereometrische Aufgabensammlung im Papyrus Graecus Vindobonensis 19996.* Vienna: Österreichische Staatsdruckerei (Mitteilung aus der Nationalbibliothek in Wien, Papyrus Erzherzog Reiner, Neue Serie 1).

Gibson, R. K. (1998) "Didactic poetry as 'popular' form: A study of imperatival expressions in Latin didactic verse and prose," in Atherton, C. (ed.), *Form and content in didactic poetry.* Bari: Levante, pp. 67–98.

Gille, B. (1978) *Histoire des techniques: technique et civilisations, technique et sciences.* Paris: Gallimard.

Gleason, M. (2009) "Shock and awe: The performance dimension of Galen's anatomy demonstrations," in Gill, C., Whitmarsh, T., and Wilkins, J. (eds.), *Galen and the world of knowledge.* Cambridge/New York: Cambridge University Press, pp. 85–114.

Gorges, J.-G. (1993) "Nouvelle lecture du fragment de Forma d'un territoire voisin de Lacimurga," *Mélanges de la Casa de Velázquez*, 29(1), pp. 7–23.

Grafton, A. (2007) "The devil as automaton: Giovanni Fontana and the meanings of a fifteenth-century machine," in Riskin, J. (ed.), *Genesis redux: Essays in the history and philosophy of artificial life.* Chicago: University of Chicago Press, pp. 46–62.

Grafton, A. and Siraisi, N. (eds.) (1999) *Natural particulars: Nature and the disciplines in Renaissance Europe.* Cambridge: MIT Press.

Grant, E. (1971) "Henricus Aristippus, William of Moerbeke and two alleged mediaeval translations of Hero's *Pneumatica*," *Speculum*, 46(4), pp. 656–69.

Griffiths, A. (1996) *Prints and printmaking: An introduction to the history and techniques*, 2nd edition. Berkeley: University of California Press.

Grillo, F. (2019) *Hero of Alexandria's Automata: A critical edition and translation, including a commentary on Book One.* Glasgow: University of Glasgow. Available at: http://theses.gla.ac.uk/76774/ (accessed November 2, 2021).

Gros, P. (1996) "Les illustrations du *De Architectura* de Vitruve: histoire d'un malentendu," in Nicolet, C. and Gros, P. (eds.), *Les littératures techniques dans l'Antiquité romaine.* Geneva: Fondation Hardt, pp. 19–44.

Grosseteste, R. (1912) *Die Philosophischen Werke des Robert Grosseteste, Bischofs von Lincoln.* Edited by L. Baur. Münster: Aschendorff.

Guillaumin, J.-Y. (1992) "La signification des termes *contemplatio* et *observatio* chez Balbus et l'influence héronienne sur le traité," in Guillaumin, J.-Y. (ed.), *Mathématiques dans l'Antiquité*. Saint-Étienne: Université de Saint-Étienne, pp. 205–14.

(1997) "L'éloge de la géométrie dans la préface du livre 3 des 'Metrica' d'Héron d'Alexandrie," *Revue des études anciennes*, 99(1), pp. 91–99.

Gurd, S. (2007) "Cicero and editorial revision," *Classical Antiquity*, 26(1), pp. 49–80.

Gurd, S. A. (2012) *Work in progress: Literary revision as social performance in ancient Rome*. Oxford: Oxford University Press.

Hairie, A. (2000) "Aspects pratiques de la 'Dioptre' d'Héron d'Alexandrie: étude théorique et expérimentale de la précision de mesures réalisables," in Argoud, G. and Guillaumin, J.-Y. (eds.), *Autour de "La Dioptre" d'Héron d'Alexandrie*. Saint-Étienne: Publications de l'Université de Saint-Étienne, pp. 257–71.

Hammer-Jensen, I. (1913) "Ptolemaios und Heron," *Hermes*, 48(2), pp. 224–35.

Handis, M. W. (2013) "Myth and history: Galen and the Alexandrian Library," in König, J., Oikonomopoulou, A., and Woolf, G. (eds.), *Ancient libraries*. Cambridge/New York: Cambridge University Press, pp. 364–376.

Hannah, R. (2009) *Time in antiquity*. London: Routledge.

Harder, A. (2013) "From text to text: The impact of the Alexandrian Library on the work of Hellenistic poets," in König, J., Oikonomopoulou, A., and Woolf, G. (eds.), *Ancient libraries*. Cambridge/New York: Cambridge University Press, pp. 96–108.

Hardiman, C. I. (2013) "'Alexandrianism' again: Regionalism, Alexandria, and aesthetics," in Ager, S. L. and Faber, R. (eds.), *Belonging and isolation in the Hellenistic world*. Toronto: University of Toronto Press (Phoenix. Supplementary volume, 51), pp. 199–222.

Hardwick, L. (2020) "Aspirations and mantras in classical reception research: Can there really be dialogue between ancient and modern?" in de Pourcq, M., de Haan, N., and Rijser, D. (eds.), *Framing classical reception studies: Different perspectives on a developing field*. Leiden: Brill (Metaforms: Studies in the reception of classical antiquity, volume 19), pp. 15–32.

Haskins, C. H. (1960) *Studies in the history of mediaeval science*. New York: Ungar Publishing Company.

Hatzimichali, M. (2013a) "Ashes to ashes? The Library of Alexandria after 48 BC," in König, J., Oikonomopoulou, A., and Woolf, G. (eds.), *Ancient libraries*. Cambridge/New York: Cambridge University Press, pp. 167–82.

(2013b) "Encyclopaedism in the Alexandrian Library," in König, J. and Woolf, G. (eds.), *Encyclopaedism from antiquity to the Renaissance*, pp. 64–83.

Heath, T. L. (1921) *A history of Greek mathematics*. Oxford: Clarendon Press.

Heiberg, J. L. (1892) *Les premiers manuscrits grecs de la bibliothèque papale* (1 online resource (16 pages) volume). Copenhagen: Bianco Luno (CIC NEH Dittenberger-Vahlen Microfilming Project, v. 21, no. 4).

Henninger-Voss, M. (2000) "Working machines and noble mechanics: Guidobaldo del Monte and the translation of knowledge," *Isis*, 91(2), pp. 233–59.

(2007) "Comets and cannonballs: Reading technology in a sixteenth-century library," in Roberts, L., Schaffer, S., and Dear, P. (eds.), *The mindful hand: Inquiry and invention from the late Renaissance to early industrialisation*. Amsterdam/Bristol: Koninkliijke Nederlandse Akademie van Wetenschappen, pp. 10–31.

Herder, J. G. (1889) *Herders Werke*. Stuttgart: Union deutsche verlagsgesellschaft.

(2002) *Sculpture: Some observations on shape and form from Pygmalion's creative dream*. Translated by J. Gaiger. Chicago: University of Chicago Press.

Hero (1851) *The pneumatics of Hero of Alexandria, from the original Greek*. Translated by B. Woodcroft. London: Taylor, Walton and Maberly.

(1864) *Heronis Alexandrini Geometricorum et Stereometricorum reliquiae: accedunt Didymi Alexandrini Mensurae marmorum et anonymi variae collectiones ex Herone, Euclide, Gemino, Proclo, Anatolio aliisque*. Edited by F. Hultsch. Berlin: apud Weidmannos.

(1976a) *Heronis Alexandrini opera quae supersunt omnia* (vol. 1). Edited by W. Schmidt. Stuttgart: Teubner.

(1976b) *Heronis Alexandrini opera quae supersunt omnia* (vol. 2). Edited by W. Schmidt and L. L. M. Nix. Stuttgart: Teubner.

(1976c) *Heronis Alexandrini opera quae supersunt omnia* (vol. 3). Edited by H. Schöne. Stuttgart: Teubner.

(1976d) *Heronis Alexandrini opera quae supersunt omnia* (vol. 4). Edited by J. L. Heiberg. Stuttgart: Teubner.

(1976e) *Heronis Alexandrini opera quae supersunt omnia* (vol. 5). Edited by J. L. Heiberg. Stuttgart: Teubner.

(1976f) "Pneumatica," in Schmidt, W. (ed.), *Heronis Alexandrini opera quae supersunt omnia*. Stuttgart: Teubner, pp. 2–332.

(1976g) "Automata," in Schmidt, W. (ed.) *Heronis Alexandrini opera quae supersunt omnia*. Stuttgart: Teubner, pp. 338–452.

(1997) *Les Pneumatiques d'Héron d'Alexandrie*. Edited by G. Argoud and J.-Y. Guillaumin. Saint-Étienne: Publications de l'Université de Saint-Étienne.

(2003) *Erone di Alessandria: le radici filosofico-matematiche della tecnologia applicata: Definitiones: testo, traduzione e commento*. Edited by G. R. Giardina. Catania: CUECM.

(2014) *Metrica*. Edited by F. Acerbi and B. Vitrac. Pisa: Fabrizio Serra Editore (Mathematica graeca antiqua, 4).

Hero and Qusṭā ibn Lūqā (1988) *Les mécaniques, ou l'élévateur des corps lourds*. Translated by B. Carra de Vaux. Paris: Les Belles Lettres.

(2016) *The Baroulkos and the Mechanics of Heron*. Edited by G. Ferriello, M. Gatto, and R. Gatto. Firenze: L.S. Olschki (Biblioteca di Nuncius, 76).

Hirschfeld, O. (1901) *Die Rangtitel der römischen Kaiserzeit* (Sitzungsberichte der Königlich Preussischen Akademie der Wissenschaften zu Berlin, 25). Berlin: Verlag der Königlich Akademie der Wissenschaften.

Hogg, D. (2013) "Libraries in a Greek working life: Dionysius of Halicarnassus, a case study in Rome," in König, J., Oikonomopoulou, A., and Woolf, G. (eds.), *Ancient libraries*. Cambridge/New York: Cambridge University Press, pp. 137–51.

Hopkins, D. (2010) *Conversing with antiquity: English poets and the classics, from Shakespeare to Pope*. Oxford: Oxford University Press.

Hunt, J. D. (2016) *Garden and grove: The Italian Renaissance garden in the English imagination, 1600–1750*. Philadelphia: University of Pennsylvania Press.

Iulius Africanus (2012) *Cesti: The extant fragments*. Edited by M. Wallraff et al. Translated by W. Adler. Berlin/Boston: De Gruyter (Die Griechischen Christlichen Schriftsteller der Ersten Jahrhunderte Ser., N.F. 18).

Jacob, C. (1998) "La bibliothèque, la carte et le traité: Les orms de l'accumulation du savoir à Alexandrie," in Argoud, G. and Guillaumin, J.-Y. (eds.), *Sciences exactes et sciences appliquées à Alexandrie*. Saint-Étienne: Publications de l'Université de Saint-Étienne, pp. 19–37.

(2013) "Fragments of a history of ancient libraries," in König, J., Oikonomopoulou, A., and Woolf, G. (eds.), *Ancient libraries*. Cambridge/New York: Cambridge University Press, pp. 57–84.

Jacobs, J. (1992) *Systems of survival: A dialogue on the moral foundations of commerce and politics*. New York: Random House.

Jaeger, M. (2002) "Cicero and Archimedes' tomb," *The Journal of Roman Studies*, 92, pp. 49–61.

(2008) *Archimedes and the Roman imagination*. Ann Arbor: University of Michigan Press.

Johns, A. (1998) *The nature of the book: Print and knowledge in the making*. Chicago: University of Chicago Press.

Jones, A. (2013) "P. Cornell. inv. 69 revisited: A collection of geometrical problems," in Ast, R. et al. (eds.), *Papyrological texts in honor of Roger S. Bagnall*. Durham, North Carolina: The American Society of Papyrologists, pp. 159–175.

Kanerva, L. (2006) *Between science and drawings: Renaissance architects on Vitruvius's educational ideas*. Helsinki: Finnish Academy of Science and Letters.

Katz, J. T. (2016) "Etymological 'alterity': Depths and heights," in Butler, S. (ed.), *Deep classics: Rethinking classical reception*. London: Bloomsbury Academic, pp. 107–26.

Keller, A. G. (1967) "Pneumatics, automata and the vacuum in the work of Giambattista Aleotti," *The British Journal for the History of Science*, 3(4), pp. 338–47.

Keyser, P. (1988) "Suetonius *Nero* 41.2 and the date of Heron Mechanicus of Alexandria," *Classical Philology*, 83, pp. 218–20.

(1992) "A new look at Heron's 'steam engine'," *Archive for History of Exact Sciences*, 44(2), pp. 107–24.

Keyser, P. T. (2013) "The name and nature of science: Authorship in social and evolutionary context," in Asper, M. and Kanthak, A.-M. (eds.), *Writing science: Medical and mathematical authorship in ancient Greece.* Berlin: De Gruyter, pp. 17–61.

(2018) "Science in the 2nd and 3rd centuries CE: An aporetic age," in Keyser, P. T. and Scarborough, J. (eds.), *Oxford handbook of science and medicine in the classical world.* Oxford: Oxford University Press, pp. 829–46.

(2020) *Recovering a late-antique edition of Pliny's Natural History* (Online-Ressource, XII, 282 Seiten 13 Illustrationen vol). New York: Peter Lang. Available at: https://doi.org/10.3726/b15521 (accessed April 23, 2021).

Keyser, P. T. and Irby-Massie, G. L. (2008) *The encyclopedia of ancient natural scientists: The Greek tradition and its many heirs.* London/New York: Routledge.

Kikuchi, C. (ed.) (2018) *La Venise des livres: 1469–1530.* Ceyzérieu: Champ Vallon (Époques, 0298-4792).

Knorr, W. R. (1978) "Archimedes and the elements: Proposal for a revised chronological ordering of the Archimedean corpus," *Archive for History of Exact Sciences,* 19(3), pp. 211–90.

(1989) *Textual studies in ancient and medieval geometry.* Boston: Birkhäuser.

König, J. and Woolf, G. (2013) "Encyclopaedism in the Roman Empire," in König, J. and Woolf, G. (eds.), *Encyclopaedism from antiquity to the Renaissance.* Cambridge/New York: Cambridge University Press, pp. 23–63.

Krafft, F. (1970) *Dynamische und statische Betrachtungsweise in der antiken Mechanik.* Wiesbaden: Steiner.

(1973) "Kunst und Natur: Die Heronische Frage und die Technik in der klassischen Antike," *Antike und Abendland; Beiträge zum Verständnis der Griechen und Römer und ihres Nachlebens,* 19, pp. 1–19.

Lachmann, K. (ed.) (1848) *Die Schriften der römischen Feldmesser.* Berlin: G. Reimer.

Laird, W. R. (1991) "Archimedes among the humanists," *Isis,* 82(4), pp. 628–38.

(2017) "Hero of Alexandria and Renaissance mechanics," in *Mathematical practitioners and the transformation of natural knowledge in early modern Europe.* Cham: Springer (Studies in History and Philosophy of Science), pp. 149–165.

Landels, J. G. (2000) *Engineering in the ancient world,* revised edition. Berkeley: University of California Press.

Lang, P. (2011) "Medical and ethnic identities in Hellenistic Egypt," *Apeiron,* 37 (4), pp. 107–32.

Latour, B. (1986) "Visualisation and cognition: Drawing things together," *Knowledge and Society: Studies in the Sociology of Culture Past and Present,* 6, pp. 1–40.

Lendle, O. (1983) *Texte und Untersuchungen zum technischen Bereich der antiken Poliorketik.* Wiesbaden: Steiner.

Leventhal, M. (2017) "Eratosthenes' letter to Ptolemy: The literary mechanics of empire," *American Journal of Philology,* 138(1), pp. 43–84.

Lévy, T. and Vitrac, B. (2018) "Hero of Alexandria and Mordekhai Komtino: The encounter between mathematics in Hebrew and the Greek metrological corpus in fifteenth-century Constantinople," *Aleph: Historical Studies in Science & Judaism*, 18(2), pp. 181–262.

Lewis, M. J. T. (2001) *Surveying instruments of Greece and Rome*. Cambridge/New York: Cambridge University Press.

(2012) "Greek and Roman surveying and surveying instruments," in Talbert, R. J. A. (ed.), *Ancient perspectives: Maps and their place in Mesopotamia, Egypt, Greece, and Rome*. Chicago/London: University of Chicago Press, pp. 129–62.

Lichius, B. and Ali, R. (2013) *Hero of Alexandria #1*. San Diego: Ape Entertainment.

Lloyd, G. E. R. (1971) *Early Greek science: Thales to Aristotle*. New York: Norton.

(1975) "A note on Erasistratus of Ceos," *The Journal of Hellenic Studies*, 95, pp. 172–75.

Lowry, M. (1979) *The world of Aldus Manutius: Business and scholarship in Renaissance Venice*. Ithaca: Cornell University Press.

Maclean, C. (1905) "The principle of the hydraulic organ," *Sammelbände der Internationalen Musikgesellschaft*, 6(2), pp. 183–236.

Mansfeld, J. (1998) *Prolegomena mathematica: From Apollonius of Perga to late Neoplatonism: With an appendix on Pappus and the history of Platonism*. Leiden: Brill.

Marasco, G. (1998) "Cléopâtre et les sciences de son temps," in Argoud, G. and Guillaumin, J.-Y. (eds.), *Sciences exactes et sciences appliquées à Alexandrie*. Saint-Étienne: Publications de l'Université de Saint-Étienne, pp. 39–53.

Marr, A. (2006) "'*Gentille curiosité*': Wonder-working and the culture of automata in the late Renaissance," in Marr, A. and Evans, R. J. W. (eds.), *Curiosity and wonder from the Renaissance to the Enlightenment*. Aldershot: Ashgate, pp. 149–70.

(2011) *Between Raphael and Galileo: Mutio Oddi and the mathematical culture of late Renaissance Italy*. Chicago: University of Chicago Press.

Marsden, E. W. (1969) *Greek and Roman artillery: Historical development*. Oxford: Clarendon Press.

(1971) *Greek and Roman artillery: Technical treatises*. Oxford: Clarendon Press.

Marshall, C. W. (2003) "Sophocles' *Nauplius* and Heron of Alexandria's mechanical theater," in Sommerstein, A. H. (ed.), *Shards from Kolonos: Studies in Sophoclean fragments*. Bari: Levante, pp. 261–79.

Martin, T. H. (1854) *Recherches sur la vie et les ouvrages d'Héron d'Alexandrie, disciple de Ctésibius, et sur tous les ouvrages mathématiques grecs, conservés ou perdus, publiés ou inédits, qui ont été attribués à un auteur nommé Héron*. Paris: Imprimerie impérial.

Martindale, C. (1993) *Redeeming the text: Latin poetry and the hermeneutics of reception*. Cambridge: Cambridge University Press.

(2013) "Reception – A new humanism? Receptivity, pedagogy, the transhistorical," *Classical Receptions Journal*, 5(2), pp. 169–83.

Martínez, V. M. and Senseney, M. F. (2013) "The professional and his books: Special libraries in the ancient world," in König, J., Oikonomopoulou, A., and Woolf, G. (eds.), *Ancient libraries*. Cambridge/New York: Cambridge University Press, pp. 401–16.

Masià, J. (2015) "On dating Hero of Alexandria," *Archive for History of Exact Sciences*, 69(3), pp. 231–55.

Mayer, M. and Olesti Vila, O. (2001) "La sortitio de Ilici. Del documento epigráfico al paisaje histórico," *Dialogues d'histoire ancienne*, 27(1), pp. 109–30.

McEwen, I. K. (2003) *Vitruvius: Writing the body of architecture*. Cambridge: MIT Press.

(2016) "The architectonic book," in Sanvito, P. (ed.), *Vitruvianism: Origins and transformations*. Berlin: De Gruyter, pp. 101–11.

Méasson, A. (1994) "Alexandrea ad Aegyptum," in Argoud, G. (ed.), *Science et vie intellectuelle à Alexandrie (Ier–IIIe siècle après J.-C.)*. Saint-Étienne: Publications de l'Université de Saint-Étienne, pp. 9–52.

Meißner, B. (1999) *Die technologische Fachliteratur der Antike: Struktur, Uberlieferung und Wirkung technischen Wissens in der Antike (ca. 400 v. Chr.–ca. 500 n. Chr.)*. Berlin: Akademie Verlag.

Micheli, G. (2005) "La traduzione de gli *Automata* di Erone," in Nenci, E. (ed.), *Bernardino Baldi (1553–1617) studioso rinascimentale: poesia, storia, linguistica, meccanica, architettura: atti del convegno di studi di Milano, 19–21 novembre 2003*. Milan: FrancoAngeli, pp. 247–68.

Middleton, F. (2020) "Of mice and manuscripts: Literary reception and the material text," in de Pourcq, M., de Haan, N., and Rijser, D. (eds.), *Framing classical reception studies: Different perspectives on a developing field*. Leiden: Brill (Metaforms: Studies in the reception of classical antiquity, volume 19), pp. 72–80.

Moatti, C. (1993) *Archives et partage de la terre dans le monde romain (IIe siècle avant–Ier siècle après J.-C.)*. Rome: École française de Rome.

Morgan, L. (2007) *Nature as model: Salomon de Caus and early seventeenth-century landscape design*. Philadelphia: University of Pennsylvania Press.

Murphy, T. M. (2004) *Pliny the Elder's Natural history: The empire in the encyclopedia*. Oxford/New York: Oxford University Press.

Needham, P. (2000) "Concepts of paper study," in Mosser, D. W., Saffle, M., and Sullivan, E. W. (eds.), *Puzzles in paper: Concepts in historical watermarks: Essays from the International Conference on the History, Function and Study of Watermarks, Roanoke, Virginia*, 1st edition. New Castle/London: Oak Knoll Press/British Library, pp. 1–36.

Netz, R. (1998) "Deuteronomic texts: Late antiquity and the history of mathematics," *Revue d'histoire des mathématiques*, 4(2), pp. 261–88.

(2009) *Ludic proof: Greek mathematics and the Alexandrian aesthetic*. New York: Cambridge University Press.

(2011) "The bibliosphere of ancient science (outside of Alexandria)," *NTM International Journal of History and Ethics of Natural Sciences, Technology and Medicine*, 19(3), pp. 239–69.

(2017) "Mathematical expertise and ancient writing *more geometrico*," in König, J. and Woolf, G. (eds.), *Authority and expertise in ancient scientific culture.* Cambridge: Cambridge University Press, pp. 374–408.

Neugebauer, O. (1938) *Über eine Methode zur Distanzbestimmung Alexandria-Rom bei Heron.* Copenhagen: Levin and Munksgaard (Historisk-filologiske meddelelser, 26).

(1969) *The exact sciences in antiquity.* New York: Dover Publications.

(1975) *A history of ancient mathematical astronomy.* Berlin/New York: Springer-Verlag (Studies in the history of mathematics and physical sciences, v. 1).

Nichols, M. F. (2017) *Author and audience in Vitruvius' De architectura.* Cambridge: Cambridge University Press.

Nicolet, C. (1991) *Space, geography, and politics in the early Roman Empire.* Ann Arbor: University of Michigan Press.

Nicomachus (1972) *Introduction to arithmetic.* New York: Johnson Reprint Corp.

Nightingale, P. (2009) "Tacit knowledge and engineering design," in Meijers, A. (ed.), *Philosophy of technology and engineering sciences.* Amsterdam/London/Boston: Elsevier/North Holland, pp. 351–74.

Noble, J. V. and Price, D. J. de S. (1968) "The water clock in the Tower of the Winds," *American Journal of Archaeology*, 72(4), pp. 345–55.

Novara, A. (1994) "Faire œuvre utile: la mesure de l'ambition chez Vitruve," in Gros, P. (ed.), *Le projet de Vitruve: objet, destinataires et réception du De architectura.* Rome: Ecole française de Rome, pp. 47–61.

(2005) *Auctor in bibliotheca: essai sur les textes préfaciels de Vitruve et une philosophie latine du livre.* Louvain/Dudley: Peeters (Bibliothèque d'études classiques, 46).

Nutton, V. (2009) "Galen's authorial voice: A preliminary enquiry," in Taub, L. C. and Doody, A. (eds.), *Authorial voices in Greco-Roman technical writing.* Trier: Wissenschaftlicher Verlag Trier, pp. 53–62.

(2012) "Galen and Roman medicine: Or can a Greek become a Latin?" *European Review; Cambridge*, 20(4), pp. 534–42.

Pappus (1986) *Book 7 of the collection.* Edited by A. Jones. New York: Springer-Verlag.

Peachin, M. (2004) *Frontinus and the curae of the curator aquarum.* Stuttgart: Steiner.

Pedersen, O. (1974) *A survey of the Almagest.* Odense: Odense Universitetsforlag.

Perilli, L. (2006) "'Il dio ha evidentemente studiato medicina.' Libri di medicina nelle biblioteche antiche: il caso dei santuari di Asclepio," in Naso, A. (ed.), *Stranieri e non cittadini nei santuari greci: atti del convegno internazionale.* Grassina (Firenze): Le Monnier Università, pp. 472–510.

Peterson, M. A. (2011) *Galileo's muse: Renaissance mathematics and the arts.* Cambridge: Harvard University Press.

Pfeiffer, R. (1968) *History of classical scholarship from the beginnings to the end of the Hellenistic age.* Oxford: Clarendon Press.

Philo (1902) *Le Livre des appareils pneumatiques et des machines hydrauliques, par Philon de Byzance, édité d'après les versions arabes d'Oxford et de*

*Constantinople, et traduit en français par le Baron Carra de Vaux*. Translated by B. Carra de Vaux. Paris: C. Klincksieck.

(1974) *Pneumatica: the first treatise on experimental physics, western version and eastern version. Facsimile and transcript of the Latin manuscript, CLM 534, Bayer. Staatsbibliothek, Munich. Translation and illustrations of the Arabic manuscript, A.S. 3713, Aya-Sofya, Istanbul*. Translated by F. D. Prager. Wiesbaden: Reichert.

(2001) "Les Pneumatiques de Philon de Byzance," in Sezgin, F. (ed.), Carra de Vaux, B. (trans.), *Archimedes and Philon in the Arabic tradition: Texts and studies*. Frankfurt am Main: Institute for the History of Arabic-Islamic Science at the Johann Wolfgang Goethe University.

Piccione, R. M. (2021) *Greeks, books and libraries in Renaissance Venice*. Berlin: De Gruyter (Transmissisons, 1).

Piganiol, A. (1962) *Les documents cadastraux de la colonie romaine d'Orange*. Paris: Centre national de la recherche scientifique.

Plato (1940) *Plato latinus*. Edited by R. Klibansky et al. Translated by Henricus Aristippus. London: Warburg Institute.

Polanyi, M. (2009) *The tacit dimension*. Chicago/London: University of Chicago Press.

Pon, L. and Kallendorf, C. (eds.) (2009) *Il libro Veneziano – The books of Venice*. Venice: La Musa Talìa.

Prou, V. (1884) "Les théâtres d'automates en Grèce au IIe siècle avant l'ère chrétienne d'après les Αὐτοματοποιῖκά d'Héron d'Alexandrie," *Mémoires présentés par divers savants étrangers à l'Académie*, 9(2), pp. 117–274.

Ptolemy (2000) *Ptolemy's Geography: An annotated translation of the theoretical chapters*. Edited by J. L. Berggren and A. Jones. Princeton: Princeton University Press.

Renn, J., Damerow, P., and McLaughlin, P. (2003) "Aristotle, Archimedes, Euclid, and the origin of mechanics: The perspective of historical epistemology," in Montesinos Sirera, J. L. (ed.), *Symposium Arquímedes Fundacion Canaria Orotava de Historia de la Ciencia*. Berlin: Max-Planck-Inst. für Wissenschaftsgeschichte, pp. 43–59.

Riggsby, A. (2019) *Mosaics of knowledge: Representing information in the Roman world*. Oxford: Oxford University Press.

Rihll, T. E. (2007) *The catapult: A history*. Yardley: Westholme Publishing.

Risselada, R. (1993) *Imperatives and other directive expressions in Latin: A study in the pragmatics of a dead language*. Amsterdam: J.C. Gieben.

Robbins, F. E. (1923) "A Greco-Egyptian mathematical papyrus," *Classical Philology*, 18(4), pp. 328–33.

Roberts, L., Schaffer, S., and Dear, P. (eds.) (2007) *The mindful hand: Inquiry and invention from the late Renaissance to early industrialisation*. Amsterdam/Bristol: Koninkliijke Nederlandse Akademie van Wetenschappen.

Roby, C. (2013) "Natura machinata: Artifacts and nature as reciprocal models in Vitruvius," *Apeiron*, 46(4), pp. 419–45.

(2014a) "Experiencing geometry in Roman surveyors' texts," *Nuncius: Journal of the History of Science*, 29(1), pp. 9–52.

(2014b) "Seneca's scientific fictions: Models as fictions in the *Natural Questions*," *The Journal of Roman Studies*, 104, pp. 155–80.

(2016a) *Technical ekphrasis in Greek and Roman science and literature: The written machine between Alexandria and Rome*. Cambridge/New York: Cambridge University Press.

(2016b) "Embodiment in Latin technical texts," in Short, W. M. (ed.), *Embodiment in Latin semantics*. Amsterdam: John Benjamins (Studies in language companion series, 374), pp. 211–38.

(2017) "Framing technologies in Hero and Ptolemy," in Platt, V. J. and Squire, M. (eds.), *The frame in classical art: A cultural history*. Cambridge: Cambridge University Press, pp. 514–43.

(2018) "Geometer, in a landscape: Embodied mathematics in Hero's *Dioptra*," in Sialaros, M. (ed.), *Revolutions and continuity in Greek mathematics*. Berlin/Boston: De Gruyter, pp. 67–88.

(2020) "Popular mechanics: Hero of Alexandria from antiquity to the Renaissance," in Muñoz Morcillo, J. and Robertson-von Trotha, C. Y. (eds.), *Genealogy of popular science: From ancient ecphrasis to virtual reality*. Bielefeld: Transcript (History of science and technology, 1), pp. 221–43.

(2021) "Moving wood, man immobile: Hero's *Automata* at the Urbino court," in Hedreen, G. M. (ed.), *Material world: The intersection of art, science, and nature in ancient literature and its Renaissance reception*. Leiden: Brill (NIKI studies in Netherlandish–Italian art history), pp. 108–32.

Rome, A. (1938) "Review of *Über eine Methode zur Distanzbestimmung Alexandria-Rom bei Heron*. (K. Danske Videnskabernes Selskab. Hist.-filologisk Meddelelser. XXVI (1938), fasc. 2)," *L'Antiquité Classique*, 7(2), pp. 460–62.

Rose, P. L. (1975) *The Italian Renaissance of mathematics: Studies on humanists and mathematicians from Petrarch to Galileo*. Geneva: Librairie Droz.

Rose, P. L. and Drake, S. (1971) "The Pseudo-Aristotelian questions of mechanics in Renaissance culture," *Studies in the Renaissance*, 18, pp. 65–104.

Rose, V. (1866) "Die Lücke im Diogenes Laërtius und der alte Übersetzer," *Hermes: Zeitschrift für klassische Philologie*, 1, pp. 367–97.

Roux, S. (1992) "Le premier livre des Equilibres plans: Réflexions sur la mécanique archimédienne," in Guillaumin, J.-Y. (ed.), *Mathématiques dans l'Antiquité*. Saint-Étienne: Université de Saint-Étienne, pp. 95–160.

Rudhardt, J. (1978) "Trois Problèmes de Géométrie, Conservés Par Un Papyrus Genevois," *Museum Helveticum*, 35(4), pp. 233–40.

Sáez Fernández, P. (1990) "Estudio sobre una inscripción catastral colindante con Lacimurga," *Habis*, 21, pp. 205–28.

Saito, K. and Sidoli, N. (2010) "The function of diorism in ancient Greek analysis," *Historia Mathematica*, 37(4), pp. 579–614.

Sanvito, P. (ed.) (2016) *Vitruvianism: Origins and transformations*. Berlin: De Gruyter.

Schiefsky, M. (2008) "Theory and practice in Heron's mechanics," in Laird, W. R. and Roux, S. (eds.), *Mechanics and natural philosophy before the scientific revolution*. Dordrecht/London: Springer, pp. 15–49.

(2015) "*Technē* and method in ancient artillery construction: The *Belopoeica* of Philo of Byzantium," in Holmes, B. and Fischer, K.-D. (eds.), *The Frontiers of ancient science: Essays in honor of Heinrich von Staden*. Berlin: De Gruyter, pp. 613–51.

Schipke, R. (2013) *Das Buch in der Spätantike: Herstellung, Form, Ausstattung und Verbreitung in der westlichen Reichshälfte des Imperium Romanum*. Wiesbaden: Reichert.

Schub, P. (1932) "A mathematical text by Mordecai Comtino (Constantinople, XV century)," *Isis*, 17(1), pp. 54–70.

Schumacher, L. (2018) "Hausgesinde – Hofgesinde: Terminologische Überlegungen zur Funktion der Familia Caesaris im 1. Jh. n. Chr.," in *Historischer Realismus: kleine Schriften zur alten Geschichte*. Göttingen: Vandenhoeck & Ruprecht, pp. 179–202.

Schürmann, A. (1991) *Griechische Mechanik und antike Gesellschaft: Studien zur staatlichen Förderung einer technischen Wissenschaft*. Stuttgart: Steiner.

(2002) "Pneumatics on stage in Pompeii: Ancient automatic devices and their social context," in Castagnetti, G. (ed.), *Homo faber: Studies on nature, technology, and science at the time of Pompeii*. Rome: "L'Erma" di Bretschneider, pp. 35–56.

Serrai, A. (2002) *Bernardino Baldi: la vita, le opere, la biblioteca*. Milan: S. Bonnard.

Shapin, S. and Schaffer, S. (1985) *Leviathan and the air-pump: Hobbes, Boyle, and the experimental life: Including a translation of Thomas Hobbes, Dialogus physicus de natura aeris by Simon Schaffer*. Princeton: Princeton University Press.

Shelton, J. (1981) "Mathematical problems on a papyrus from the Gent Collection (SB III 6951 Verso)," *Zeitschrift Für Papyrologie Und Epigraphik*, 42, pp. 91–94.

Sidoli, N. (2011) "Heron of Alexandria's date," *Centaurus*, 53(1), pp. 55–61.

(2018) "The concept of given in Greek mathematics," *Archive for History of Exact Sciences*, 72(4), pp. 353–402.

Silberberg, M. (1905) "Ein handschriftliches hebräisch-mathematisches Werk des Mordechai Comtino (15. Jahrhundert)," *Jahrbuch der Jüdisch-Literarischen Gesellschaft*, 3, pp. 277–292.

(1906) "Ein handschriftliches hebräisch-mathematisches Werk des Mordechai Comtino (15. Jahrhundert)," *Jahrbuch der Jüdisch-Literarischen Gesellschaft*, 4, pp. 214–37.

Slaney, H. (2016) "Perceiving (in) depth: Landscape, sculpture, ruin," in Butler, S. (ed.), *Deep classics: Rethinking classical reception*. London: Bloomsbury Academic, pp. 87–105.

Souffrin, P. (2000) "Remarques sur la datation de la 'Dioptre' d'Héron par l'éclipse de lune de 62," in Argoud, G. and Guillaumin, J.-Y. (eds.),

*Autour de "La Dioptre" d'Héron d'Alexandrie.* Saint-Étienne: Publications de l'Université de Saint-Étienne, pp. 13–17.

von Staden, H. (1989) *Herophilus: The art of medicine in early Alexandria: Edition, translation and essays.* Cambridge: Cambridge University Press.

(1996) "Body and machine: Interactions between medicine, mechanics, and philosophy in early Alexandria," in J. Paul Getty Center for the History of Art and the Humanities (ed.), *Alexandria and Alexandrianism.* Malibu: J. Paul Getty Museum, pp. 85–106.

(1999) "Celsus as historian?" in van der Eijk, P. J. (ed.), *Ancient histories of medicine,* Leiden: Brill (Studies in Ancient Medicine, volume 20), pp. 251–94.

Stein, A. (1912) *Griechische Rangtitel in der römischen Kaiserzeit.* Vienna: Gerold.

Stone, M. E. (2000) *The Armenian texts of Epiphanius of Salamis De mensuris et ponderibus.* Leuven: Peeters.

Straton (1944) "Fragmenta," in Wehrli, F. (ed.), *Die Schule des Aristoteles, Texte und Kommentare.* Basel: B. Schwabe, pp. 12–42.

Stückelberger, A. (1994) *Bild und Wort: das illustrierte Fachbuch in der antiken Naturwissenschaft, Medizin und Technik.* Mainz am Rhein: P. von Zabern.

Swain, S. (1996) *Hellenism and empire: Language, classicism, and power in the Greek world, ad 50–250.* Oxford: Clarendon Press.

Taisbak, C. M. and Bülow-Jacobsen, A. (2003) "P. Cornell inv. 69: Fragment of a handbook in geometry," in Piltz, A. (ed.), *For particular reasons: Studies in honour of Jerker Blomqvist.* Lund: Nordic Academic Press, pp. 54–70.

Takács, S. A. (1995) "Alexandria in Rome," *Harvard Studies in Classical Philology,* 97, pp. 263–76.

Tannery, P. (1883) *Sciences exactes dans l'antiquité.* Toulouse: Edouard Privat.

Taub, L. C. (2008) "Eratosthenes sends greetings to King Ptolemy," in Dauben, J. W. (ed.), *Mathematics celestial and terrestrial: Festschrift für Menso Folkerts zum 65. Geburtstag.* Stuttgart: Deutsche Akademie der Naturforscher Leopoldina; Wissenschaftliche Verlagsgesellschaft, pp. 285–302.

Tittel, K. (1901) "Heron und seine Fachgenossen," *Rheinisches Museum für Philologie,* 56(3), pp. 404–15.

Toneatto, L. (1994) *Codices artis mensoriae: i manoscritti degli antichi opuscoli latini d'agrimensura (V–XIX sec.).* Spoleto: Centro italiano di studi sull'alto Medioevo.

Too, Y. L. (2010) *The idea of the library in the ancient world.* Oxford: Oxford University Press.

Torello-Hill, G. (2015) "The exegesis of Vitruvius and the creation of theatrical spaces in Renaissance Ferrara," *Renaissance Studies,* 29(2), pp. 227–46.

Truitt, E. R. (2015) *Medieval robots: Mechanism, magic, nature, and art.* Philadelphia: University of Pennsylvania Press.

Tybjerg, K. (2003) "Wonder-making and philosophical wonder in Hero of Alexandria," *Studies in the History and Philosophy of Science,* 34, pp. 443–66.

(2004) "Hero of Alexandria's mechanical geometry," *Apeiron,* 37, pp. 29–56.

Ugolini, F. (1859) *Versi e prose scelte de Bernardino Baldi: Ordinate e annotate.* Firenze: Felice Le Monnier.

Vallance, J. (2000) "Doctors in the library: The strange tale of Apollonius the Bookworm and other stories," in MacLeod, R. M. (ed.), *The Library of Alexandria: centre of learning in the ancient world.* London: I.B. Tauris, pp. 95–115.

Valleriani, M. (2007) "From 'condensation' to 'compression': How Renaissance Italian engineers approached Hero's *Pneumatics*," in Böhme, H., Rapp, C., and Rösler, W. (eds.), *Übersetzung und Transformation.* Berlin/New York: De Gruyter, pp. 333–53.

(2014) "Ancient pneumatics transformed during the early modern period," *Nuncius: Journal of the History of Science*, 29, pp. 127–73.

van Dyck, M. (2013) "'*Argumentandi modus huius scientiae maxime proprius.*' Guidobaldo's mechanics and the question of mathematical principles," in Becchi, A., Meli, D. B., and Gamba, E. (eds.), *Guidobaldo del Monte (1545–1607): Theory and practice of the mathematical disciplines from Urbino to Europe.* Berlin: Max-Planck-Gesellschaft zur Förderung der Wissenschaften, pp. 9–34.

van Leeuwen, J. (2013) "The text of the Aristotelian *Mechanics*," *The Classical Quarterly (New Series)*, 63(1), pp. 183–98.

(2014) "Thinking and learning from diagrams in the Aristotelian *Mechanics*," *Nuncius: Journal of the History of Science*, 29(1), pp. 53–87.

Vincent, A. J. H. (1858) "Extraits des Manuscrits Relatifs à La Géométrie Pratique des Grecs: Traité de La Dioptre," in *Notices et extraits des banuscrits de la Bibliothèque Impériale et autres bibliothèques*, vol. 19. Paris: Imprimerie impériale, pp. 157–337.

Vitrac, B. (2003) "Mécanique et Mathématiques à Alexandrie : Le Cas de Héron." Available at: https://hal.archives-ouvertes.fr/hal-00175171 (accessed June 15, 2013).

(2005) "Les classifications des sciences mathématiques en Grèce ancienne," *Archives de Philosophie*, 68(2), pp. 269–301.

(2008a) "Faut-il réhabiliter Héron d'Alexandrie?" in *Faut-il réhabiliter Héron d'Alexandrie?* Montpellier: Les Belles Lettres, pp. 281–96.

(2008b) "Promenade dans les préfaces des textes mathématiques grecs anciens," in Radelet-de Grave, P. and Brichard, C. (eds.), *Liber amicorum Jean Dhombres.* Louvain-la-Neuve/Turnhout: Brepols (Réminiscences, 8), pp. 518–56.

(2009) "Mécanique et mathématiques à Alexandrie: le cas de Héron," in *Sciences, mathématiques et philosophie de l'Antiquité à l'Age classique.* Paris: Université Paris Diderot – Paris 7 (Oriens-occidens, 7), pp. 155–99.

(2010) "Héron d'Alexandrie et le corpus métrologique: état des lieux," in *Géométrie(s), pratiques d'arpentage et enseignement : quels liens et dans quel contexte?* Available at: https://hal.archives-ouvertes.fr/hal-00473981/document (accessed January 26, 2019).

Whitmarsh, T. (2005) *The Second Sophistic.* Oxford: Oxford University Press.

Wiedemann, E. E. G. (1970) *Aufsätze zur arabischen Wissenschaftsgeschichte.* Hildesheim: G. Olms.

Williams, G. (2012) *The cosmic viewpoint: A study of Seneca's Natural Questions.* New York: Oxford University Press.

Witt, R. G. (1988) "Medieval Italian culture and the origins of humanism as a stylistic ideal," in Rabil, A. (ed.), *Renaissance humanism: Foundations, forms, and legacy.* Philadelphia: University of Pennsylvania Press, pp. 29–70.

Wolfe, J. (2004) *Humanism, machinery, and Renaissance literature.* Cambridge: Cambridge University Press.

Worp, K. A., Bruins, E. M., and Sijpesteijn, P. J. (1977) "Fragments of mathematics on papyrus," *Chronique d'Égypte,* 52, pp. 105–11.

Zangheri, L. (1987) *Pratolino, il giardino delle meraviglie.* 2a ed. con aggiunta di documenti e tavole. Firenze: Gonnelli.

# Index

CPSIA information can be obtained
at www.ICGtesting.com
Printed in the USA
LVHW081822160723
752578LVOO001B/4